AF540993

ABSENT IN POLITICS AND POWER

ABSENT IN POLITICS AND POWER

Political Exclusion of Indian Muslims

ABDUR RAHMAN

MANOHAR
2024

First published 2024

ISBN 978-81-19139-48-4 (Hb)
ISBN 978-81-19139-49-1 (Pb)

Published by
Ajay Kumar Jain *for*
Manohar Publishers & Distributors
4753/23 Ansari Road, Daryaganj
New Delhi 110 002

Typeset by
Kohli Print
Delhi 110 051

Printed and bound in India

Contents

List of Tables 7

Preface 9

1. Introduction 13
2. Historical Context of Muslim Representation 24
3. Representation in the Lok Sabha 49
4. Representation in State Assemblies 101
5. Policy Issues Related to Political Representation 174
6. Ground Level Factors Affecting Muslim Representation 195
7. Other Issues Concerning Muslim Representation 233
8. Conclusions and Way Forward 264

Appendices

1. Analysis of Assembly Constituencies of Andhra Pradesh 319
2. Analysis of Assembly Constituencies of Bihar 321
3. Analysis of Assembly Constituencies of Gujarat 325
4. Analysis of Assembly Constituencies of Karnataka 327
5. Analysis of Assembly Constituencies of Rajasthan 330
6. Analysis of Assembly Constituencies of Telangana 332
7. Analysis of Assembly Constituencies of Uttar Pradesh 334
8. Analysis of Assembly Constituencies of West Bengal 339

Some Important Works Referred 343

Index 345

List of Tables

3.1: Muslim Representation and Deprivation in Lok Sabha (1952-2019) 52
3.2: Party Affiliations of Muslim MPs and their Nomination in 14th Lok Sabha (2004) 57
3.3: Muslim Representation in Lok Sabha from Assam 63
3.4: Muslim Representation in Lok Sabha from Bihar 64
3.5: Muslim Representation in Lok Sabha from Jammu & Kashmir 65
3.6: Muslim Representation in Lok Sabha from Kerala 66
3.7: Muslim Representation in Lok Sabha from Maharashtra 66
3.8: Muslim Representation in Lok Sabha from Uttar Pradesh 67
3.9: Muslim Representation in Lok Sabha from West Bengal 68
3.10: Analysis of PCs as per Presence of Muslim Voters 69
3.11: PCs and their Contribution to Muslim Representation in Past Five Elections 70
3.12: Sizeable Muslim Constituencies 73
3.13: Near Majority Muslim Constituencies 74
3.14: Performance of Near-majority PCs Since 1967 Election 75
3.15: Muslim-majority Constituencies 76
3.16: Performance of Muslim-majority Constituencies Since 1967 Election 78
3.17: Performance of Rampur in Returning Muslim Candidates from 1952 to 2019 80
3.18: Nomination of Muslims in General Elections by INC (INCI), BJP(BJS), CPI and CPI(M) 85
3.19: Nomination of Muslims in General Elections by PSP, JP Formations and JD 86
3.20: Nomination of Muslims in General Elections by JD Formations 88

3.21: Nomination of Muslims in General Elections by BSP and SP 89
3.22(A): Nomination of Muslims in General Elections by Regional Parties: 2009, 2014 and 2019 Elections 90
3.22(B): Nomination of Muslims in General Elections by Regional Parties: 2009, 2014 and 2019 Elections 91
3.23: Nomination of Muslims in General Elections by Muslim Base Parties: 2009, 2014 and 2019 Elections 93
4.1: Representation of Muslims in State Assemblies and State Cabinets 103
4.2: Representation of Muslims in Andhra Pradesh Assembly 106
4.3: Representation of Muslims in Assam Assembly 110
4.4: Representation of Muslims in Bihar Assembly 112
4.5: Representation of Muslims in Chhattisgarh Assembly 115
4.6: Representation of Muslims in Delhi Assembly 116
4.7: Representation of Muslims in Gujarat Assembly 118
4.8: Representation of Muslims in Haryana Assembly 122
4.9: Representation of Muslims in Jharkhand Assembly 124
4.10: Representation of Muslims in Karnataka Assembly 125
4.10(A): Muslim-dominated Constituencies in Karnataka 128
4.11: Representation of Muslims in Kerala Assembly 130
4.12: Representation of Muslims in Madhya Pradesh Assembly 134
4.12(A): Nomination of Muslims by National Parties 135
4.13: Representation of Muslims in Maharashtra Assembly 138
4.14: Representation of Muslims in Rajasthan Assembly 142
4.15: Representation of Muslims in Tamil Nadu Assembly 145
4.16: Representation of Muslims in Telangana Assembly 148
4.17: Representation of Muslims in Uttar Pradesh Assembly 151
4.18: Representation of Muslims in Uttarakhand Assembly 158
4.19: Representation of Muslims in West Bengal Assembly 161
5.1: Adverse Gerrymandering in Cases of some Parliamentary Constituencies 187

Preface

Along with being voiceless, Indian Muslims today face a tremendous hostility, discrimination, mob violence, dehumanization, and planned communal hate campaigns. While writing my previous book, *Denial and Deprivation: Indian Muslims after the Sachar Committee and Ranganath Mishra Commission Reports*, I came across the huge socio-economic backwardness and educational deficits that Indian Muslims face. On most socio-economic indicators, they perform poorly, and on many their condition is worse than that of the most marginalized. Despite consistent demands from the community, its leaders and elected representatives, the government has not enacted a single legislation to ensure safety and security, and correct the backwardness. I believe that this sorry state of affairs will persist until Muslims get a proper political share. My purpose in writing this book is to bring into the public domain the huge political underrepresentation of Muslims, the possible causes, factors affecting it and to suggest measures to become a political force. Only then will their voice be heard and their demands addressed. After all, political empowerment is the key to all empowerment.

Chapter 1 observes that in India, it is the governed, especially the deprived and marginalized who want democracy primarily for equality, dignity and equal share in the governance. On the contrary, the elite and high caste sections use democracy as a tool to govern the masses, deprive them of even essential needs and block the path of social justice. Muslims have greater faith in democracy as is shown by their voting percentage; they have greater faith in institutions of democracy and in efficacy of the government. Also, there are several constitutional and international obligations which say that all racial and religious minorities must get opportunities to have a fair representation in elective bodies. In spite of all these positive factors, they are absent in politics and power.

Chapter 2 briefly discusses the historical context of minority political representation. When our Constitution was being framed, the issue of political representation of the Muslim community was discussed at several forums: social, political, community, constitutional, etc. The Congress had also committed to all minorities that there would be fair representation in politics and governance. The Advisory Committee on this subject had duly recommended the reservation of seats in accordance with the population share of minorities, and this was duly noted in the Draft Constitution. Unfortunately, the proposal of reservation of seats was scrapped. While doing this, all minorities were assured that the electoral system would be reviewed after ten years from the point of view of minority representation. Sadly, this never happened.

Chapter 3 discusses the representation of Muslims in Lok Sabha. In 17 General Elections, Muslim Members of Parliament (MPs) constituted only 5.78 per cent of total MPs. Only 520 Muslims got elected, although the community expected 1,070 members, thus suffered a 51.40 per cent deprivation. Muslim MPs generally hail from J&K, UP, Bihar, Assam, West Bengal, Kerala, and Telangana. There are other states which have significant share of Muslim population, but do not send a single Muslim MP. Under-nomination and mainstream parties not fielding Muslims even in Muslim-dominated seats seem to be the main reasons. Today, as per their share in the population, Muslims deserve at least 77 MPs. There are numerous parliamentary seats spread across many states where Muslims account for more than 30 per cent of voters. If political parties nominate them in these seats, ensure that other voters support them, and Muslims adopt few pragmatic political approaches, they will gain their proportional share.

Chapter 4 discusses representation in state assemblies of major states. At present, they constitute about 7 per cent of all Members of Legislative Assembly (MLAs), and thus suffer a almost 50 per cent deprivation. Except for J&K, they are not duly represented anywhere else. The deprivation is lower in Bihar, Assam, West Bengal, UP, Kerala and Telangana, while it is acute in the assemblies of Rajasthan, Delhi, Haryana, MP, Gujarat, AP, Maharashtra, Karnataka and Tamil Nadu. Low nomination, division of Muslim votes among many secular party candidates, and fielding of non-Muslim candidates in Muslim-dominated seats seem to be the major reasons. In all states, there are several Muslim-dominated seats from where only Muslims can get elected if they are given tickets.

Chapter 5 discusses the non-inclusive nature of Indian democracy which deprives Muslims, Other Backward Classes (OBCs) and the poor from their genuine share of politics and power and provides huge benefits to the rich, elite, and Upper-Caste Hindus (UCH). Less important and cosmetic issues of electoral reforms have been given undue importance, but important issues like deprivation of Muslims, OBCs, women, and the poor alike, etc., have not caught the attention of the media, academics, government or the Election Commission of India. Various reports on electoral reforms, reports on condition of Muslims, such as the Sachar Committee and Ranganath Mishra Commission, including the ones published in states, have not dared to touch the acute political marginalization. This chapter also throws more light on under-nomination, denial of Scheduled Caste (SC) status to Dalit Muslims, reservation of Muslim-dominated seats for SCs, adverse gerrymandering of Muslim areas and no provision of reservation for women belonging to Muslims and OBCs in the proposed Women Reservation Bill.

In Chapter 6, I have enumerated the factors affecting Muslim representation, how to deal with these and how the Muslim community must endeavour hard to build a genuine leadership from within its own ranks. The community must also seek out ways to devise unity with Dalits with whom they share a lot of similarities.

Chapter 7 examines how the Muslim community, which is so sociologically diverse is treated as a monolithic entity by all parties. This perception has also created the myth of the 'Muslim vote bank', which assumes that all Muslims regardless of differences vote in the same manner. Herein, I also look at the state of a very significant campaign, the Pasmanda Muslims' movement.

In the conclusion part, i.e. the Chapter 8, I have delved closely into what strategies Muslims must adopt to have at least proportional share and introspection within the community on how to create an effective political space. I have also suggested the various ways in which this can be done.

My analysis of issues that I have delved into in depth in this book has convinced me that there has to be a forceful change of attitudes, thinking and actions on the part of all factors involved: government, political parties, media, academic circles and the community alike. The government must take cognizance of the community's political marginalization. The political parties, especially the mainstream ones must desist from mere lip-service and engage publicly with the issues that Muslims face, nominate them in fair numbers and strategize their victory as they do with other candidates. The academic and media circles must focus attention on acute political deprivation of Muslims as its urgent correction is required for social cohesion and nation building. Last, but most important, the Muslim community itself must learn to prepare good leaders from within their fold, learn the dynamics of politics and support political leaders who raise secular essential issues that truly matter for the empowerment and make alliances with Dalits, Tribals, and OBCs. Only when these conditions are fulfilled will they find proper political representation and improved social and developmental status.

I have dared to hope that my book will contribute to a healthy and fruitful debates on this crucial subject.

I extend sincere thanks to my family members who encouraged and supported me and contributed a lot in writing the book. In the process, they made many sacrifices. This book would not have been possible without invaluable help of Vinod Patil, who typed the manuscript and arranged the tables, Lina Mathias, who thoroughly edited it before sending for publication, and Sanjar Alam who provided with many required information. I owe a lot to them. I am also grateful to Sanjay Kumar of Lokniti (CSDS) for giving me data on Muslim-dominated parliamentary and assembly constituencies.

I extend my sincere gratitude to Mr Ajay Jain and Mr Ananya Jain of Manohar Publishers & Distributors, New Delhi, and also to Subin Sabu (Editor), and Sanjay Kala (Production in-charge) at Manohar, who saw the volume through the press. Although a great care has been taken, responsibility of any error lies with the author.
I dedicate this book to my *abbu*, late Aas Mohammad Mian.

ABDUR RAHMAN

CHAPTER 1

Introduction

There has been a gradual, but steady change in the contours of democratic institutions in India over the past two decades. In the manner that it has actually functioned democracy in India has not lived up to the expectations of modern India's founding architects. However, I believe that it is the people of this country who have primarily kept democracy alive (even with the various kind of threats that it continues to face). If one considers the voter turnout across India, both urban and rural, one realizes that it is the poor and the marginalized, who constitute the bulk of those queuing up to vote. They continue to believe that their vote is their power. And it is they who are the biggest source of strength for democracy in India. They want democracy as they believe that it has empowered them on many fronts. On the other hand, influential sections, the elites and the upper castes have consistently manipulated democratic institutions in their favour by depriving the poor, the weak and religious minorities, especially the Muslim community. The overwhelming presence in politics of these powerful players shows that they are not ready to loosen their grip on the polity, society and economy. Usage of violence, manipulation of elections, disproportionate share in party nominations and division of the society on communal lines are some of the prime methods used to retain political power. Down the decades, several steps of empowerment and poverty alleviation schemes of the government and the resultant social and economic benefits have not reached to the poor and marginalized. One has to only look at the social and economic disparity in India to know the actual reality of this situation.

And yet, this state of affairs is not due to lack of intention or efforts. We began our journey as an independent nation on a daringly hopeful note. Among the countries that are former British colonies, India can rightfully claim the premier position in terms of its democratic institutions. In fact, the very choice of democracy as the form of government for a free India, by the people who led us to independence, gained India an enviable reputation. However, the very sections of Indian society who have believed in democracy and contributed to its upkeep the most—the poor, the marginalized and religious minorities especially the Muslims—find themselves very often left out from power structures and electoral representation.

An independent India first chose democracy because the great leaders like Mahatma Gandhi, Jawaharlal Nehru, Dr. Babasaheb Ambedkar, Sardar Vallabhbhai Patel, Maulana Abul Kalam Azad and several others saw great potential in this form of governance and envisaged that the hopes and dreams of millions of Indians would find fulfilment. Gandhi said, 'I understand democracy as something that gives the weak the same chance as the strong'.[1] Ambedkar pointed out 'Democracy is not merely a form of government. It is primarily a mode of associated living, of conjoint communicated experience. Democracy is essentially an attitude of respect and reverence towards our fellow men.'[2] It was India's first Prime Minister Jawaharlal Nehru who was explicit about what he meant by a democratic India. Nehru wanted a political democracy to be merged with economic democracy in order for India to really progress. At a seminar on parliamentary democracy in 1956, he said,

> Democracy has been spoken of chiefly in the past as political democracy, roughly represented by every person having a vote. But a vote by itself does not represent very much to a person who is down and out, to a person, let us say, who is starving or hungry. Political democracy by itself is not enough except that it may be used to obtain a gradually increasing measure of economic democracy, equality and the spread of good things of life to others and removal of gross inequalities.[3]

DEMOCRACY AND THE PEOPLE

During the 75 years of its functioning, Indian democracy, argued by socio-political observers, has taken a deep root in the society and expanded its base among all the sections of society. Universal adult franchise, which is operational in India, gives one vote each of equal value to every citizen and is a remarkable instrument of empowerment. The common masses look to democracy as a source of emancipation, equality, justice and progress. The governed in India—vulnerable, lacking in basic means of life, looked down upon, with no support, deprived in many senses—are the source of strength for democracy. It must be acknowledged that in many ways, the democratic process has made huge attempts and succeeded in bringing about a shift in political power from the middle and higher castes and classes of urban society to the backward classes and the rural poor.

However, the people who govern, the elite class and the high castes look upon democracy as a tool to acquire power and maintain status quo in the society. The leadership, often in collusion with the most conservative lot, use democracy for limited reformation rather than for emancipatory transformation.

The institutions of democracy, such as checks and balances, universal adult suffrage, public education, free press, the Election Commission of India (ECI), Comptroller and Auditor General (CAG), Supreme Court (SC) and the legislative wings have also helped democracy survive. But in reality, in terms of the vulnerable sections, how effective has been the implementation of the power wielded by these institutions, is a question worth asking.

Through constitutional provisions, a certain number of seats in the Parliament and state assemblies are reserved for the Scheduled Castes (SC) and Scheduled Tribes (ST). However, we find that upper-caste Hindus (henceforth, UCH) like Brahmins, Rajputs, Baniyas, Bhumihars, etc., are over represented in politics in terms of their presence in the population. These castes use various methods to ensure a huge representation in politics and power. On the other hand, other minorities like Christians, Sikhs, Buddhists, Jains, etc, due to regional concentration and other reasons, are more or less adequately represented in politics. However, I believe the biggest losers in the game of politics in India are Muslims and the Hindu Other Backward Classes (OBC).

In his book, *Who Wants Democracy?* the social activist and thinker Javeed Alam writes:

In India the life of democracy has come to depend on the politics of the governed. Those who wield power, present the people and govern the country are not the guardians of democracy. The system works despite their failures, despite their broken promises.[4]

Using the surveys, Alam concludes that the governed want democracy in India, and wanted to protect and preserve it despite the flaws and internal contradictions. He finds that democracy with its struggles, agitations, mobilizations, electoral participation broke the rigidity of the social structure.[5]

MUSLIMS AS A VULNERABLE POPULATION AND DEMOCRACY

The vulnerable sections comprize those who are exploited, socially oppressed and communally targeted. Along with Dalits and tribals, Muslims constitute the most vulnerable population, as they face humiliation, discrimination and are communally targeted almost on a daily basis. Alam has shown in his book that the Muslims and other vulnerable sections consider democracy to be a tool of empowerment and their faith in it, and its institutions has increased considerably over the years. Muslim community have shown a tendency towards growing acceptance of democracy as it has provided space for them to fight for dignity and rights.

Further, Alam observes that the voting percentage within the community in 1971 was 7 per cent below the national average. In 1996, it was exactly 1 per cent below the national average approximately 58 per cent. While the voting figure for Muslims remained below average in both years, it should be noted that the increase in electoral participation was huge and the difference had narrowed down to an insignificant degree way back in 1996. As regards the effectiveness of votes in democracy, 59 per cent of the people in 1996 as against the 49 per cent in 1971 felt that their vote had an effect on the way the country is governed. In 1996, a little over 60 per cent of Muslims believed that their vote had an effect on the nature of democracy. On the question of the acceptance of democracy as the preferred model of governance, nearly 69 per cent of Indians found democracy desirable in 1996. Muslims were well above the average by 3 per cent (72 per cent) in finding democracy desirable. On the question of the efficacy of the vote, Muslims in both the years, 1971 and 1996, had been above the national average by approximately 1.5 per cent. On the overall acceptance of the democratic system of governance, Muslims were below the average by 4 per cent in 1971, and above the average by more than 3 per cent in 1996.[6]

Muslims are an integral part of the Indian population and they identify themselves with other vulnerable sections like the Dalits, Adivasis, OBCs, the poor, etc. Alam argues on the basis of cross-polity surveys and other types of similar aggregate data from different parts of the world, that the survival of democracy is negatively related to the persistence of illiteracy, poverty, oppression and related features.

In my view, the related features also include communal targeting, discrimination, injustice, etc., due to religious identity of minorities. All vulnerable sections, as Alam has described, have contributed immensely to the survival of democracy in India, which include Muslims as well. Due to the repercussions of 1947 Partition, their participation in democratic processes got off to a slow start, but increased considerably thereafter and on all parameters whether be it electoral participation, faith in the functioning of democratic institutions, etc., has been above the national average. In spite of this, Indian Muslims have remained a politically marginalized community. At all three levels, i.e. parliament, state assemblies and local bodies, their representation has been poor. Despite this low share in the Parliament and state assemblies and the resultant disadvantage, Muslims often outnumber Hindus in participation in the electoral process. This political engagement is crucial for the survival and strengthening of Indian democracy.

POLITICAL REPRESENTATION OF MUSLIMS

Since Independence, Muslims have faced gross political under-representation at all levels due to various reasons. During the past 75 years of vibrant parliamentary democracy in the country, they have not got their due share in the Parliament and state legislatures. The situation is worse in the local bodies—the gram panchayats, nagarpalikas, city corporations, etc.

As of July 2023, out of 776 MPs, only 39 of them are Muslims (13 in the Rajya Sabha, and 26 in the Lok Sabha). They constitute around 5.58 per cent of the 233-member Rajya Sabha and 4.79 per cent of the 543-member Lok Sabha. There are Muslim MPs elected to Rajya Sabha from only 8 states out of the total 28 states, and from two Union Territories (UT). Muslim MPs are elected to the Lok Sabha from only 10 states and one UT out of the 36 states and UTs. In other words, not a single Muslim is in the Rajya Sabha on behalf of 20 states and two UTs. In the same way, not a single Muslim Lok Sabha member has been elected from as many as 18 states and six UTs. Assam, West Bengal, Kerala, Bihar, UP and Maharashtra have sizeable proportions of Muslim population but these states do not send Muslim MPs commensurate with their share in the population. There are states that have a sizeable Muslim population but do not send a single Muslim MP. These include Madhya Pradesh, Chhattisgarh, Jharkhand, Rajasthan, Punjab, Uttarakhand, Haryana, Delhi, etc. A similar situation prevails in state assemblies. Out of a total of 4,123 MLAs in all states (including two UTs) only 296 hail from the Muslim community. Thus, on the national level Muslims constitute 7.18 per cent of the total MLAs. There are many states with sizeable Muslim populations that do not send a single Muslim MLA to their respective legislatures.[7] Similarly, in the municipal corporations of Delhi, Mumbai, Kolkata, Chennai, Hyderabad, Ahmedabad, Patna, Bengaluru, etc., Muslims are not represented in proportion to their percentage in the population. Their issues are not raised at the national, state and local levels, as a result of this situation.

There are many other contributory conditions such as the reluctance of political parties to field them as candidates, communalization of the political space, reservation of Muslim-dominated constituencies for SCs, lack of support from non-Muslim voters and so on. In 2006, Sachar Committee Report (SCR) documented how the underrepresentation of Muslims in India's governance structure had harmed the entire community on the social, economic and educational fronts. This massive marginalization is the key factor for their backwardness. Moreover, they do not get reservation in accordance to what they are entitled. Their pitifully inadequate representation is insufficient to influence the working of the power structure.

UNITED NATION'S CONCERN FOR MINORITY POLITICAL REPRESENTATION

The fair representation of minorities and their proper participation in the political life of a country, contribute to socio-economic progress and political stability of that country, is a well accepted principle. The United Nations (UN) has repeatedly stressed that 'promotion and protection of the rights of minorities contribute to the political and social stability of the states in which they live'. This commitment is reinforced in subsequent UN legal frameworks and preamble of regional associations. The Framework Convention for Protection of National Minorities (FCNM) states that 'the protection of national minorities is essential to stability, democratic security and peace in a nation'. It also mentions that a pluralistic and genuinely democratic society should not only respect the ethnic, cultural, linguistic and religious identity(ies) of each person belonging to a national minority, but, also create appropriate conditions by enabling them to express, preserve and develop this identity. Through her findings on the study on minorities, the South African academic and lawyer Claire Palley establishes that in those countries where there are fair arrangements for equitable share of power and resources by minorities, the system enjoys peace and stability, and those that do not ensure such an arrangement are ridden with strife.[8]

The UN charter, subsequent declarations and legal instruments have sufficient provisions to ensure a proper political participation of minorities in the political affairs of States. The International Covenant on Civil and Political Rights (ICCPR) which was adopted in they 1966 deals with the right to political participation. Article 25 of the Covenant says that:

'Every citizen shall have the right and the opportunity, without any of the distinctions mentioned in Article 2 and without unreasonable restrictions:

(a) To take part in the conduct of public affairs, directly or through freely chosen representatives;
(b) To vote and to be elected at genuine periodic elections which shall by universal and equal suffrage and shall be held by secret ballot guaranteeing the free expression of the will of the electors;
(c) To have access, on general terms of equality, to public service in his country.'

Similarly, the UN Declaration on the Right of Persons Belonging to National or Ethnic, Religious and Linguistic Minorities (1992) also has the provisions for political participation of minorities. Article 2.2 says, 'Persons belonging to minorities have the right to participate effectively in cultural, religious, social, economic and public life.' Article 2.3 advocates that political participation enables the voices of minorities to be heard.

The concern for provision of mechanism for effective participation of minorities derives from the experience that even the limited rights of minorities to enjoy their own culture, to profess and practice their own religion, and to use their own language guaranteed in the Article 27 of the ICCPR cannot be realized without their effective participation in the political process as enunciated in Articles 2.2, 2.3 and 2.4 of the UN Declaration on the Rights of Persons Belonging to National or Ethnic, Religious and Linguistic Minorities. Prof. Asbjorn Eide, the Chairperson of the UN Working Group on Minorities (2001), made the following observations:

> Effective participation requires representation in legislative, administrative and advisory bodies and more generally in public life. Persons belonging to minorities, like all others, are entitled to assemble and to form their associations, and thereby to aggregate their interest and values to make the greatest possible impact on national and regional decision-making. They are entitled not only to set up and make use of ethnic, cultural and religious associations and societies, but also to establish political parties, should they so wish.[9]

The European concern for providing an effective participation to their national minorities, besides guaranteed educational and cultural rights derives from their realization that it is the neglect and inadequate attention to the issues related to minorities that has caused periodic havoc in the twentieth century. The Council of Europe's study of November 2000, observes that 'with a view to prevention or solution of conflicts pertaining to the situation of minorities, it is clear that a fair participation of minorities in the political process is a key issue and should be accorded great attention'.[10]

In this regard, the recommendations of an international expert seminar organized by the European Centre for minorities issues, held at Flensburg, Germany from 30 April to 2 May 1999 included these mechanisms of effective participation: Proportional Representation (PR), guaranteed minority seats, reduced voting thresholds, minority legislative veto, administrative, advisory, and consultative bodies for minorities.[11]

In another expert study titled 'The Participation of Minorities in Decision Making' for the Council of Europe organized in November 2000, the authors note that 'the majority of states provide for special measures designed with the specific purpose to facilitate the reflection of minority interests in the political process'. The study explains how the electoral system in various European countries facilitates minority representation by:

1. Lowered thresholds for entering parliament,
2. Reserved seats,
3. Favourable delimitation of the constituencies in particular, in the case of majority voting, and
4. Privileged funding for minority parties.[12]

The study concludes that such special measures may be treated as a common standard for ensuring an effective political participation of minorities. The Liberal Declaration on the Rights of Minorities (2000) also advocates the political participation of minorities along with the common domain of preservation of identity(ies) and protection of existence. For effective participation of minorities in the politics of the country, it recommends adoption of electoral system of Proportional Representation with a waver of the minimum requirement electoral support for the minorities. When PR is not in operation, the Declaration recommends (i) avoidance of gerrymandering in constituency formation, and (ii) an adequate number of special additional designated constituencies reserved for minority electorate. Similarly attention should be paid to the recruitment of minorities into positions in central administration (particularly in military, police, judiciary and intelligence service).[13] In another study on Public Participation and Minorities, Yash Ghai, a Kenya based academic in constitutional law, notes:

> In the last two decades there has been a marked shift from the limited protection against discrimination that characterised the original efforts of the United Nations (UN) regarding minorities towards a more active engagement of the state in facilitating the development of minority cultures and promoting a political role for minorities.
>
> In order to ensure effective participation, it is necessary that special procedures, institutions and arrangements be established through which members of minorities are able to make decisions, exercise legislative and administrative powers, and develop their culture.[14]

All these advocacies and recommendations conclude that the UN's legal frameworks, its associate bodies and its regional associations, along with the common domain of protection of existence, preservation of identity and non-discrimination in several matters, also advocate fairer political participation of minorities. For this, they have recommended various measures such as the PR system, reservation of seats in legislatures, favoured delimitation, etc. They also conclude that the just and adequate political participation of minorities contribute towards peace, progress and stability of the nation they live in.

In this book, I have attempted to show how the single largest religious minority, the Indian Muslims, have fared in terms of political representation and what factors (both internal and external) have influenced it. The community has always aspired and tried to contribute to the peace and progress of the country it lives in, and fair political representation will effectively help in fulfilling those aspirations fully.

NOTES

1. https://www.mkgandhi.org/articles/democracy.html
2. https://inc.in/our-values/democracy
3. https://www.mainstreamweekly.net/article6814.html
4. Javeed Alam, *Who Wants Democracy?*, Delhi: Orient Black, 2006, p. ix.
5. Ibid., pp. 18-23.
6. Ibid., pp. 26-40.
7. https://byjus.com/govt-exams/members-rajya-sabha/and https://eci.gov.in/
8. Claire Palley, *Constitutional Law and Minorities*, Minority Rights Group (MRG), London, 1978.
9. Asbjorn Eide, *Commentary to the Declaration on the Rights of Persons belonging to National or Ethnic, Religious and Linguistic Minorities* (Adopted by the UN General Assembly; Resolution 47/135, 18 December 1992), E/CN, 4/Sub/2/AC.5/2001/2.
10. *Towards Effective Participation of Minorities*, E/CN.4Sub.2/AC.5/1999/ WP.4.
11. Ibid.
12. J.A. Frowein and Roland Bank, *The Participation of Minorities in Decision Making*, E/CN.4/Sub.2/AC.5/2001/CRP.6.
13. https://www.india-seminar.com/2001/506/506%20%20iqbal%20a.%20ansari.htm
14. Yash Ghai, *Public Participation and Minorities*, London: MRG International, 2001, pp. 4-5.

CHAPTER 2

Historical Context of Muslim Representation

Genesis of Denial of Political Rights

Political representation is one of the primary means of not only strengthening the democratic values, but also helping the participation of the marginalized, weak and minorities. In this chapter, I will attempt to trace the trajectory of the political deprivation of the Muslim community through examination of the debates in the Constituent Assembly of India, and also in the different forums of the Indian National Congress (henceforth, Congress) during the 1920s and 1930s. The ensuing deprivation of Muslims in the legislatures, both Parliament and local governing bodies has continued to this day and even grown in the last decade. The Constituent Assembly Debates (henceforth, known as CAD) show that, while certain groups got the collective representation they demanded, others did not. Nor, is it that it is only the community that has suffered immensely; Indian democracy has been affected negatively in many ways.

The 1947 Partition had many unfortunate effect, but one of the obviously adverse ones was the summary treatment given to all suggestions for adoption of corrective electoral devices and alternate electoral systems for due representation of both the political spectrum and the social diversity prevailing in the country.

The position of Indian Muslims on this issue was especially sensitive. As Granville Austin noted, Partition had made Muslims a smaller group and hence, less powerful and a highly suspect group. In fact, so emotively charged was the issue of political representation since it was being discussed immediately after the Partition that some members, who genuinely cared for minority rights, suggested postponing the debate till the impact of the Partition had subsided.

In undivided India, Muslims had contributed a significant share to the country's population. The persecution following the 1857 Revolt convinced the Muslims of their subjugation under the British rule, and they began participating in all forms of the freedom struggle movements. They had an overwhelming presence in the Congress and other organizations formed to educate the public about the ill effects of British imperialism and contributed through these bodies in the pre-Independence days. Although the British sowed the seeds of communalism, the Muslim masses largely remained unaffected and participated in every movement initiated by Mahatma Gandhi.

When it became plausible that the British would be leaving India, Indian Muslims as a religious minority (similar to trends seen in other parts of the world), became apprehensive about their social, economic and political rights. During this period, one issue however took on urgent importance: that of political representation. The debates and discussions ranged far and wide, but mainly between the idea of a separate electorate (as proposed by the Muslim League) and reservation of seats in joint electorates with application of the PR system (as advocated by the Congress).

The overall impression that gained ground was that the provision of reservation of seats for minorities in the legislature had been abolished as a result of the unanimous demand from the minorities themselves, especially Muslims. Various facts and circumstances, however, do not support this view. But it is also true that the opinion of the Muslim members of the CAD on the resolution pertaining to this provision on 25 and 26 May 1949, was also divided, and not unanimous.

Sardar Hukum Singh, in the CAD, whilst supporting the PR system pointed out that every section of the population, whether a numerical or political minority, had the right to proper representation. And, he observed very pertinently, it was the majority's responsibility to ensure that the minorities felt secure. Unfortunately, his recommendation, as also that of Z.H. Lari, Muhammad Saadullah, Shibban Lal Saksena, Maulana Hasrat Mohani, D.H. Chandrasekharaiya and several others, to ensure proper representation to religious and political minorities through the PR system, was not considered sincerely. The expert committees chose to dismiss them without any serious critical scrutiny. Sardar Vallabhbhai Patel decided to ignore the proposal of PR on the ground that it was complicated and, therefore, completely unsuited to the prevalent conditions in India. Patel also argued that lakhs of the newly enfranchised voters were ignorant and illiterate and therefore, would find the PR system difficult to comprehend. In the absence of Mahatma Gandhi and the changed attitude of Nehru, Patel got the proposal for reservation of seats for minorities in the draft Constitution abolished.

ASSURANCES AND PROMISES BEFORE INDEPENDENCE

One interesting aspect that emerged in the political discussions of the 1920s and 1930s was the Congress' attempt to balance the national with segmental interests. During its 42nd session held in Madras on 28 December 1927, the Congress resolution on minority representation included this paragraph:

> That, with a view to give full assurance to the two great communities that their legitimate interests will be safeguarded in the Legislatures such representation of the communities should be secured for the present, and if required, by the reservation of seats in joint elections on the basis of population in every province and in the Central Legislature.[1]

In the same session, it took two major decisions in response to the setting up of the Simon Commission. First, it decided not to cooperate with the Commission and second, it set up an All Parties Conference to draft a Constitution for India. This conference, on 19 May 1928, constituted a committee headed by Motilal Nehru to draft the constitution. Jawaharlal Nehru, the son of Motilal Nehru, was appointed secretary of the committee. The committee was given the brief 'to consider and determine the principles of the Constitution of India along with the issue of communal representation and issue of dominion status'.[2]

The Nehru Committee Report of 10 August 1928 made the recommendation for 'reservation of seats, when demanded, for

Muslim minorities both in Central and Provincial legislatures, in strict proportion to their population, with the right to contest additional seats for a fixed period of ten years'. It also examined the solution to the problem of communal representation in an alternative electoral system of PR. It observed:

> We feel strongly attracted to this method and are of opinion that it offers the only rational and just way of meeting the fears and claims of various communities. There is a place in it for every minority and authentic adjustment takes place of rival interests. We have no doubt that proportional representation will in future be the solution of our problem.[3]

The report observed that, although the PR system was complicated to be workable in Indian conditions, it was possible to overcome the difficulties and the system should be tried out. However, it did not make a positive recommendation for PR system in the report due to lack of unanimity among some of the Committee members.

As the Nehru Committee did not suggest 'separate electorates', its recommendations were rejected by the Sikhs and Muslims altogether. However, the Congress remained committed to minority rights and the session held at Lahore in 1929 assured the minorities that 'no solution thereof i.e. of communal question in any future constitution will be acceptable to the Congress that does not give full satisfaction to the parties concerned'. However, it must be noted that the same resolution underlined that 'in Independent India communal question can only be solved on strictly national lines.' Thus, we could see that while the Congress was interested in protecting the rights of the minorities, it was also mindful of the 'national' line of thinking. This ambivalent attitude was symptomatic of how it was trying to grapple with the problem of harmonizing the 'national' with 'segmental' interests.

Jawaharlal Nehru wrote in *Young India* on 15 May 1930, that:

> the history of India and of many of the countries of Europe has demonstrated that there can be no stable equilibrium in any country so long as an attempt is made to crush a minority or force it to conform to the ways of the majority. . . .[5]

In the same note Nehru forcefully affirmed that on economic matters 'it will be the business of the state to give favoured treatment to minority and backward communities'. However, on the issue of political representation he found himself gripped in the same confusion of the 'national' and 'communal' making him state that 'in free India, political representation can only be on the national lines'. Nehru had visualized that there would be no division of minds on economic issues. He assumed that having ensured the freedom to diverse religious and cultural identities to minority groups, through legal provisions, major issues in legislatures would be economic ones, all which division could not be drawn on the communal lines. He also assured that the method of representation that would be adopted in future should carry the 'goodwill of minorities'. He realized that mere assurance and magnanimity was not enough. He also cautioned that it was through creation of 'public opinion, strong enough to prevent an aggressive and evil-intentioned majority from going astray', that the majorities' bona-fides could get established in eyes of the minorities. He concluded with the note by reminding the Congress that, 'it will prove to the minority communities that in Independent India, for which we strive, theirs will be an honoured and favoured place'.[6]

Between 1930 and 1932, three Round Table Conferences were organized in Britain to discuss the constitutional reforms in India along with the issue of minority representation. Mahatma Gandhi, led the Congress delegation and presented the Congress scheme for communal settlement during the second Round Table Conference of October 1931. It included the following formula:

3. (a) Joint electorates shall form the basis of representation in the future Constitution of India. *(Note B. Wherever possible the electoral circles shall be so determined has to enable every community, if it so desires, to secure its proportionate share in the Legislature.)
3. (b) That for Hindus in Sind, the Muslims in Assam and the Sikhs in the Punjab and the North-West Frontier Province and for Hindus and Muslims in any Province, where they are less than 25 per cent of the population, seats shall be reserved in the Federal and Provincial Legislatures on the basis of population with the right to contest additional seats.
5. In the formation of Federal and Provincial cabinets interests of minority communities should be recognised by convention.

6. The future Constitution of the country shall be Federal. The residuary powers shall vest in the Federating Units, unless, on further examination, it is found to be against the best interest of India.[7]

Note B was not part of the original scheme, but was included by Gandhi as not being inconsistent with the scheme. From the wording of the scheme, it is clear that the Congress had adopted, from its inception, 'pure nationalism as its ideal' which precluded it from 'setting forth any communal solution of the communal problem'. The party also claimed that the scheme presented by it was 'as nearly national as possible and generally acceptable to the communities concerned'. In the concluding observations, it also said that the scheme had been a compromise between 'undiluted communalism' and 'undiluted nationalism'.

Even after the failure of the Round Table Conferences and the subsequent passage of the Government of India Act, 1935, the Congress' stand did not change; it tried to accommodate minorities and opposed separate electorates. The Working Committee of the Congress adopted the following resolution on Minority Rights in 1937:

The Congress has solemnly and repeatedly declared its policy in regard to the rights of the minorities in India and has stated that it considers its duty to protect these rights and ensure the widest possible scope for the development of these minorities and their participation in the fullest measure in the political, economic and cultural life of the nation. The objective of the Congress is an independent and united India where no class or group or majority or minority may exploit another to its own advantage, and where all the elements in the nation may co-operate together for the common good and the advancement of the people of India. This objective of unity and mutual co-operation in a common freedom does not mean the suppression in any way of the rich variety and cultural diversity of Indian life, which have to be preserved in order to give freedom and opportunity to the individual as well as to each group to develop unhindered according to its capacity and inclination.[8]

The resolution basically assured the minorities that in independent India measures would be taken to ensure the participation of minorities in the political, economic and cultural life of the nation. The late author and professor of Aligarh Muslim University Iqbal A. Ansari reviewed the above resolution in the following words:

It was aimed at reassuring minorities, especially Muslims, that in an independent united India governed under the principle of one person one vote, the interest of minorities including their right to due representation and participation in the political life of the country would not suffer any deprivation and that their right to distinct cultural identity would not be subjected to any process of assimilation, leading to suppression of country's rich diversity.[9]

MAKING OF THE CONSTITUTION AND MINORITY REPRESENTATION

With the above assurances and commitment to safeguard the interest of minorities and to ensure their adequate political participation, the Congress entered the 1940s, a decade which witnessed Independence, Partition and making of the Constitution of India. The discussion on minority representation gained momentum during the making of the Constitution. After the publication of the Cabinet Mission Plan on 16 May 1946, the Congress and other parties formed the Constituent Assembly to devise a new Constitution. In view of the specific mandate to the Constituent Assembly regarding minorities, the Objectives Resolution moved by Jawaharlal Nehru on 13 December 1946 included the promise of 'adequate safeguards for minorities' in the Constitution, which led to the formation of the Advisory Committee on Fundamental Rights and Minorities, etc.

G.B. Pant moved the resolution in the Constituent Assembly for setting up of the Advisory Committee on 29 January 1947, and made the following observations:

> A satisfactory solution of the question pertaining to minorities will ensure the health, vitality and strength of the free State of India. . . . So far, the minorities have been incited and have been influenced in a manner which has hampered the growth of cohesion and unity. But now it is necessary that a new chapter should start and we should all realize our responsibility. Unless the minorities are fully satisfied, we cannot make progress; we cannot even make peace in an undisturbed manner.[10]

Sardar Patel was made the Chairman of the Advisory Committee that had 61 members. Under Patel's chairmanship the committee held its first meeting on 27 February 1947, and decided to set up four sub-committees, including one on Fundamental Rights and the other on Minorities. The Sub-committee on Minorities had 28 members (including four Muslim members), apart from the chairman. Several members of the sub-committee were not members of the Constituent Assembly; they were co-opted by other committee members. While Maulana Abul Kalam Azad was a member of the Constituent Assembly, Ibrahim Ismail Chundrigar, Muhammad Saadullah and Chaudhari Khaliquzzaman were appointed to the sub-committee by the then President Rajendra Prasad in June 1947. Care was taken to ensure that the sub-committee was representative of all communities and classes. H.C. Mookerjee (1877-1956), a Christian member from Bengal, was made the chairman of the sub-committee. He was first and foremost an educator, and had been associated with various Christian and teachers' associations. He was later appointed the Governor of Bengal. He was rather a pliant member and ready to toe the government's line. And that he was ever ready to play a subservient role became very clear during the debate on the report on Minority Rights, when he went to the extent of declaring that there was no place for the concept of minorities in a secular state. This was an indication that he was not interested in preserving minorities' rights and giving an honourable share to minorities in politics. The sub-committee had begun its work early in the spring of 1947, but it was concerned primarily with the negative rights of minority groups. It turned its attention to the state's positive obligation towards minorities in the mid-July. From 21 to 27 July, the sub-committee members, under Mookerjee's chairmanship, considered the question of minorities' representation in the legislatures, executive bodies, and public services. Most minority groups and their representatives in the Constituent Assembly sought reservations for themselves. The Sikh leaders, including the Akali Sikh leader and Union Defence minister, Baldev Singh demanded reservation for the Sikh community. Homi Modi, supported reservation for Parsi community until Sardar Patel dissuaded him. The leader of the Congress Untouchables, Jagjivan Ram and H.J. Khandekar, as well as Dr. Ambedkar demanded reservation for the Scheduled Castes. Although Mookerjee himself wanted to forego reservation, he feared that his community would not agree.[11] Yet, under pressure from Patel, exercized through K.M. Munshi, he ultimately decided to deny reservation, solemnly and strongly, and become a leader of the movement against it. The Anglo-Indians, under Frank Anthony, demanded a special treatment. And among Muslims, including 'nationalist' Congress Muslims leaders, as well as the Muslim League representatives, there was a strong support for reservation. Several voices were even raised in favour of separate electorates.[12] After considering these views and holding prolonged discussions among themselves, the members of the Minorities sub-committee rejected separate electorates by 26 votes to three and by the same margin accepted the principle of reserved seats for certain minorities for a ten year period, after which the question would be considered again.[13]

The minority communities had hoped that they would get a fair share in the ministries when earlier it had been proposed that ministers should be elected by PR system. However, the Constituent Assembly rejected this proposal and thus closed a major route through which minority groups could enter the government. This could not but generated fear among the minority communities and rightly so. As Dr. Ambedkar had said, in a country so communal minded as India it could not be expected that the authorities would give equal treatment to those not belonging to their own community. The Constituent Assembly members however, realized that the minorities must be assured of representation in the Executive in order to feel that their interests were protected. B.N. Rau had asked in his questionnaire, 'should provision be made to secure representation of different communities on the Executive? If so, how?' Some answers pointed out that in appointing ministers, the President should have due regard for the interests of the minorities and geographical considerations. The members of the Union Constitution Committee, however, voted against minority representation in the Executive.[14]

The decision disappointed and annoyed several minority representatives who brought the matter before the Minorities sub-committee in July. Both Jagjivan Ram and Khandekar had recommended that seats be reserved for minorities in cabinets.

After prolonged discussion, however the sub-committee, by a narrow margin of eight votes to seven, rejected a resolution that advocated reservation of seats for minorities in cabinets. It was, then, decided that the national interest would be better served by including an Instrument of Instructions in a Schedule to the Constitution, enjoining Governors and the President as far as practicable to appoint members of important minority communities to the ministries.[15] Having decided the issues of reservation of seats in legislatures and in executive, the sub-committee made the following recommendations in its Report of 27 July 1947.[16]

1. Reservation of seats for recognized minorities under any of the several methods of joint electorates that could be devised.
2. No statutory provision for reservation of seats for minorities in cabinets, yet providing for such representation through a convention under a Schedule to the Constitution.

The Advisory Committee took up the sub-committee's decision at a meeting held on 28 July on both the issues: representation in politics and nomination of minorities in ministries. Voting on the sub-committee's recommendation that separate electorates be abolished, only three of the 58 members that were present opposed abolition.[17] Chaudhari Khaliquzzaman and Muhammad Saadullah later supported separate electorates for Muslims on the floor of the Constituent Assembly. However, the Committee recommended that seats were to be reserved for minorities on the basis of their percentage in the general population to prevent apprehensions among them. The representatives of the micro-minorities like Parsis and the Christians on the Advisory Committee had turned down reservation for their communities, and a decision on Sikh representation was postponed, because it was impossible until details of the Partition were settled. The Anglo-Indians on the Committee led by the doyen of the community, Frank Anthony at first called for a form of special representation in legislature that amounted to weightage, but ultimately gave up their demand in favour of a provision allowing the President and provincial governors to nominate Anglo-Indians to legislatures if they were inadequately represented through elections.[18] On the issue of nomination of minorities in the Executive, the Committee concurred with the sub-committee's recommendations and suggested in its report on minority rights that an Instrument of Instructions like that issued under the 1935 Act be included in the Constitution. After due deliberations, the Advisory Committee made the following recommendations in its report of 8 August 1947:

1. *Electorates*: All elections to the Central and Provincial Legislatures will be held on the basis of joint electorates. Provided that as a general rule, there shall be reservation of seats for the minorities shown in the schedule in the various legislatures on the basis of their population. Provided further that such reservation shall be for 10 years; the position to be reconsidered at the end of the period.
2. *Additional Rights to Minorities*: The members of a minority community who have reserved seats shall have the right to contest unreserved seats as well.
3. *No Condition for a Minimum Number of Votes of One's own Community*: There shall be no stipulation that a minority candidate standing for election for a reserved seat shall poll a minimum number of votes of his own community before he is declared elected.
4. *Method of Voting*: There may be plural member constituencies but cumulative voting shall not be permissible.
5. *No Reservation for Minorities in Ministries*: There shall be no statutory reservation of seats for the minorities in Cabinets, but a convention on the lines of Paragraph VII of the Instrument of Instructions issued to Governors under the Government of India Act, 1935 shall be provided in Schedule to the Constitution.[19]

The Report on Minority Rights was discussed in the Constituent Assembly on 27 and 28 August 1947. The elaborate discussion resulted in the adoption of all the clauses of the Report as presented above. [20]

In February 1948, these clauses were duly retained in the Draft Constitution in Part XIV as Articles 292 and 294 under the title 'Special Provisions relating to Minorities'. Articles 293 and 295 had provisions for nomination of members of the Anglo-Indian community in case, they were inadequately represented in central or state legislatures. This special provision of representation in legislatures for a distinct ethno-religious community, whose numbers and territorial dispersal made it well-nigh impossible to secure due representation on its own, was indicative of the recognition and preservation of the collective right of all minority groups to representation.

CONSTITUENT ASSEMBLY DEBATES (CAD)

The debate on the Report on Minority Rights on 27 and 28 August 1947 reflected an extensive range of views. Extreme majoritarian views, which fully rejected the concept and distinct existence of minorities and historical as well as UN conventions to preserve their rights, were aired. The moderate views supported the distinct rights of minorities, while extreme views among the minorities even supported the system of separate electorates. The extreme majoritarian view, for example, was expressed by Mahavir Tyagi, a Congress member who termed representation of religious minorities as 'ridiculous'. Tyagi offered the minorities the choice of loyalty to the majority or becoming extinct. He said, 'Minorities will in the long run be reduced to one entity and that entity would be one unadulterated unity of people of democracy. . . .' He expressed his resolve 'to dissolve minorities into the majority with justice'.[21] G.B. Pant, though apparently more accommodating came very close to majoritarian views when he advised minorities that 'your safety lies in making yourselves an integral part of the organic whole which forms the real genuine state'. However, even while using the term 'organic' for the State, Pant did not envisage extinction or dissolution of minorities, as he visualised for them 'an effective decisive voice in the affairs and in the deliberations of the Legislatures and the Parliament of this free country'.[22] Sardar Patel, who put a great deal of pressure on members of minority communities in private, during his major intervention in the debate made it clear that the provision of population based quota of seats under joint electorate for minorities was adopted as a compromise between 'pure nationalism' and 'pure communalism' to prevent partition.[23]

It must be noted that the majoritarian views reflected by Tyagi, Patel and Pant came out in the open due to the immediate provocation provided by two Muslim League members, B. Pocker Sahib Bahadur and Khaliquzzaman who had moved amendments for adoption of separate electorates for minorities along with reservation of seats. While presenting the justification for his demand of separate electorate, Pocker made persuasive reference to the fact that all the ills of the country including the partition did not owe themselves to separate electorate, as was illustrated by Hindu-Muslim fraternal relations of the non-cooperation days of 1920, in spite of the separate electorate in exercise. Khaliquzzaman tried to make out his case for separate electorate in cautious and conciliatory terms. Arguing that separate electorates would help in returning true representatives of minorities, who would put their grievances and claims before the national government, he begged the House to discard suspicions about Muslims and consider the issue afresh. He said that Muslim loyalty to India was sincere.

The grounds for separate electorates presented by Pocker and Khaliquzzaman provoked Sardar Patel who held out what amounted to a threat:

> If the process that was adopted, which resulted in the separation of the country, is to be repeated, then I say: Those who want that kind of thing have a place in Pakistan not here (Applause). Here, we are building a nation and we are laying the foundations of 'One Nation', and those who chose to divide again and sow the seeds of disruption will have no place, no quarter, here, and I must say that plainly enough (Hear, Hear).[24]

The idea of One Nation—undiluted and pure—was again expressed in the concluding speech of Dr. S. Radhakrishnan, wherein he advised that the Special Provision for Minorities adopted by the House should have a preamble stating that:

> 'it is not our desire in this House to have these minorities perpetuated. We must put an end to the disruptive elements in the state. What is our ideal? . . . It is our desire to develop a homogeneous democratic secular state' and that 'the devices hitherto employed to keep minorities as separate entities within the state be dropped and loyalty to a single National State developed'.

As we have noted above the issue was being discussed immediately after the Partition in a highly charged atmosphere. It was suggested by some members that discussion on this issue be postponed. One Muslim member, K.T.M. Ahmed Ibrahim Sahib Bahadur expressed his desire that 'left to myself I would have wished that this Report on the Rights of Minorities was considered at a time when this country was free from all passion and the heat of the moment has subsided and died down, but unfortunately it has been taken up now'.[25]

One obvious adverse effect of the heat and passion aroused by Partition was the superficial treatment given to all suggestions for adoption of corrective electoral devices and alternate electoral systems for due representation of both the political spectrum and the social diversity prevailing in the country. There were several members who had different perspectives on the issue of minority representation—other than the Pocker-Patel polarized perspective. These members made proposals and suggested amendments in the electoral system during the debate in the Assembly. Jerome D'Souza, while welcoming the provision of reserved seats under joint electorate as reassuring to minorities wanted it to be viewed not as an evil to be temporarily tolerated, but to be treated as one of the ways of securing a satisfactory working of the electoral principle. He made a reference to the evil effects of majoritarian democracy, and suggested that 'this bold experiment (of reserved seats) might save democracy from one of its obvious dangers and might perhaps set an example for a solution of minority problems which may be accepted elsewhere'.[26]

K.T.M. Ahmed Ibrahim suggested that it should be binding on the candidates of reserved minority seats to secure at least 30 per cent of votes polled of their own community to get elected. It was to ensure that the members thus elected command the confidence of that community. Kazi Syed Karimuddin strongly supported the proposal. The proposal was, however, not only dismissed, but an amendment moved by K. Santhanam was adopted to strengthen the intent of Clause 7 which prohibited cumulative voting in any plural member constituency. It was made explicit that 'voting shall be distributive, that is, each voter will have as many votes as there are members and he should give only one vote to a candidate'. This was done to 'disinfect' the process of joint electorate from any communal pollution.

In that polarised climate, a thorough analytical presentation was made by D.H. Chandrasekharaiya about a variant of the PR system with Single Transferable Vote (STV) or Non-Transferable Vote (SNTV) to ensure the representation of all political, social, communal and territorial groups in the country according to their strength. This was also summarily dismissed. Pointing out that a representative democracy should properly and fully reflect the diversity of public opinion of the country, he suggested the PR 'which is fair and just to all' and 'which gives representation to all majorities and minorities in proportion to their respective voting strength' should be adopted, instead of the one prevailing in the country which favoured the majority, causing exclusion of minorities. He repeatedly said that he was more concerned with political minorities and not merely religious minorities. Having realized the criticism that PR with STV might be too complicated to implement and operate, he suggested the system of multimember constituencies with voters having SNTV which 'was simple and well-suited to the circumstance of our country'.[27]

Ajit Prasad Jain, the member of the Constituent Assembly, who served as the president of the UP Congress Committee, found fault with the SNTV, as it was divisive and diluted the desired effect of a joint electorate. He feared that the system contained the possibility of spreading factional and communal sentiments. Sardar Patel refused to consider the proposal of PR, because he felt that it was too complicated for the Indian situation and that the lakhs of newly enfranchised voters would not be at ease with it. An opportunity to discuss the issue of political representation of minorities was again provided, when discussion on the Draft Constitution began on 8 November 1948. Z.H. Lari raised the issue of right to representation of smaller political groups as well as of permanent minorities in a democracy governed by the majority, which single-member constituency under FPTP denied, almost disenfranchizing 49 per cent of the electorates. Lari advocated the adoption of PR system by STV or cumulative voting by citing the example of Ireland, Switzerland, and France.[28] Hussain

Imam observed that there could not be an effective opposition with single seat constituencies. He pointed out how large percentage of voters would be unrepresented under the system, whereas there was a need to provide representation to every shade of opinion. In his opinion, PR with 10 to 12 member constituencies and the list system would better serve the interests of smaller parties, as well as of minorities than would religion-wise reservation of seats as was then proposed.[29]

Participating in the debate on the composition of Parliament on 4 January 1949, Syed Kazi Karimuddin opposed the FPTP system, as it favoured the tyranny of the majority over the minority. He proposed adoption of the PR system with multi-member constituencies by means of cumulative vote.[30] He opposed reservation for religious minorities, pointing out how PR took care of minority interests without communalism. K.T. Shah favoured PR with STV to provide due representation to all shades of political opinion.[31] Mahboob Ali Baig also favoured PR with STV to provide for both the principle of political representation, as well as for effective protection of minority rights.[32] Hukum Singh also opposed the reservation of seats for religious minorities. He cogently expressed their unfortunate condition:

> If separate electorates are detestable and if reservation of seats is objectionable, then some method has to be devised by which the rights of minorities can be safeguarded and that is the only method suggested in the amendment (i.e. PR) that can be considered.[33]

Dr. Ambedkar, who was a member of the Minorities sub-committee of the Advisory Committee, and had demanded reservation for the SCs, opposed the system of PR which in his opinion was not suitable for the Parliamentary system. According to him the PR system required literacy. Moreover, he put forward the usual objection to PR—that it encouraged fragmentation of polity and instability of government. He visualized one single party forming the government of the day. His other argument was that the minorities should have the right to a guaranteed quota, which had been provided by reservation. He wanted the choice between enjoying a fixed quota of seats that had already been provided and having more effective voice in the election of their representatives to be left to the concerned minorities.[34] Unfortunately, no such choice was offered to minorities when the provision for quota reservation was abruptly removed in May 1949.

CHEATING WITH THE MINORITIES

The debate on the legislative provisions of the Draft Constitution began on 3 January 1949, when the Constituent Assembly, in its clause-by-clause consideration of the Draft, reached Article 67 which related to composition of the Parliament. A few days earlier, the Advisory Committee had met to consider minority representation in legislatures. In a meeting convened on 30 December 1948, several members had suggested that due to 'vast changes since August 1947' reservation of seats for minorities 'should be abolished'. Three members of the committee had actually given notice to this effect, and it was apparent that sentiment had begun slowly to flow in this direction.[35] These members were H.C. Mookerjee, a Christian; Tajamul Hussain, a Shia Muslim from Bihar, and L.K. Maitra, a Hindu. Hussain's membership in the Shia community was of some importance. Shia Muslims who basically belong to the *ashraf* category (upper castes), had not been advocates of reservation during the British rule, unlike the Sunni Muslims. Patel, however, was too considerate of minority fears—and too much the strategist—to force the issue, preferring to wait until time and other persons had achieved this end for him. The giving up of reservation should not be forced on any minority, he said. 'For example, if the Muslims, by general agreement among themselves felt they did not want any reservation, their view should be accepted, but the proposal should come from them and not from member of any other community.'[36] Although a final decision was not taken, reservation had been threatened, and it must have been clear to the Constituent Assembly members that amid the sentiments that was building up against the reservation, it might soon be done away with.

On 3 January 1949, in an apparent response to the mood of the Advisory Committee meeting, four Muslims and one Sikh member demanded in the Constituent Assembly that both, the Council of States and the House of the People, should be elected by PR. They apparently believed that the presence of minority groups in Parliament would be endangered by the end of reservation, and sought to secure the representation of their community in another way.

Through a letter that Sardar Patel wrote to the President of the Constituent Assembly, reported that during its meeting of 30 December 1948 some members of the Advisory Committee,

> [F]elt that, conditions having vastly changed since the Advisory Committee made their recommendations in 1947, it was no longer appropriate in the context of free India, and of present conditions that there should be reservation of seats for Muslims, Christians, Sikhs or any other religious minority. Although the abolition of separate electorates had removed much of the poison from the body politic, the reservation of seats for religious communities, it was felt, did lead to a certain degree of separation and was to that extent contrary to the conception of a secular democratic state.[37]

Patel further reported that the Advisory Committee adjourned till it met again on 11 May 1949, during which period he wanted members from minority communities to ascertain the views of their respective communities so that 'a change, if effected, would be one voluntarily sought by the minorities themselves and not imposed on them by the majority community'.[38]

On 11 May 1949, the Advisory Committee met to take up H.C. Mookerjee's resolution that reservation be abolished and for which support had been solicited during the previous months. While moving the resolution, Mookerjee said all that religious groups needed for their protection were the negative rights already in the Constitution and not safeguards in the legislatures. He also said, 'There should be no more thinking in terms of sub-national, minority groups, I have all along held. India is one nation.' Nearly everyone present agreed with this. R.K. Sidhwa, a Parsi member, said he had opposed reservation for Parsis. The Sikhs agreed, after a lengthy discussion, to drop their claims for reservation and weightage, if certain conditions were met in relation to the Sikh Scheduled Castes—a matter that had been considered at an earlier meeting between the Sikhs in the Constituent Assembly, and those of the East Punjab Legislative Assembly. Naziruddin Ahmad, a Muslim League representative in the Assembly, was reported to have written to the President Prasad that the Muslims of West Bengal did not want reservation. Begum Aizaz Rasul, a League representative of the Assembly from the United Provinces, posed herself as spokesman for the Muslim community. The Muslims, she said, now realize that it was in their own best interest no less than in the country's that reservation be abolished.

Nehru thought that with the end of separate electorates, most of the 'poison' had gone; had the minorities demanded it, he would have accepted some scheme of reservation, he said. Nevertheless, he believed that it was 'manifestly absurd to carry on with this reservation business'. The dissenters were the members of the Scheduled Castes. Speaking for them, Muniswami Pillai said that he was surprised that Mookerjee's resolution had not provided for reservation for the SCs and tribes, particularly since at the time of the Committee's report of August 1947, Gandhi had personally 'set his seal on it'. The meeting accepted Pillai's amendment to Mookerjee's resolution. Finally, the meeting adopted the resolution, 'that the system of reservation for minorities other than scheduled castes in Legislatures be abolished'.[40]

According to Patel, of the about 40 members present at the meeting, only one voted against the resolution. While moving the Committee Report in the Constituent Assembly on 25 May 1949, he observed that 'time has come when the vast majority of the minority communities have themselves realized after great reflection the evil effects in the past of such reservation on the minorities themselves, and the reservation should be dropped'.[41]

Thus, we see that the impression given was that the provision of reservation of seats for minorities in legislature had been abolished as a result of the unanimous demand from the minorities themselves, especially the Muslims. However, this impression is not supported by the facts. It is said that of the four Muslim members present in the said meeting of 11 May 1949, Maulana Azad being the member of the Cabinet, remained neutral, so did Maulana Hifzur Rahman. Out of the remaining two, one supported and the other opposed the resolution.[42] The opinion of the Muslim members of the Constituent Assembly during the debate on the particular resolution on 25 and 26 May 1949 was also divided and not unanimous.

The Constituent Assembly took up the Advisory Committee's report during its two day debate on 25 and 26 May 1949, during which, members expressed almost complete support for the Committee's decision. Two Muslim members, Mohammed Ismail and Saadullah, supported reservation, but were opposed by other Muslim members. Tajamul Hussain blindly supported Sardar Patel, and even opposed the insertion of word 'minority' in the Constitution. He vehemently intervened in the debate opposing reservation of seats for minorities. He declared 'the term minority is a British creation. The British created the minorities. The British have gone and minorities have gone with them. Remove the term "minority" from your dictionary (hear hear). There is no minority in India. . . .'[43]

When it was absolutely clear that sentiments were against reservation of seats and the Constituent Assembly would abolish it, some members tried to ensure minority representation through universally acceptable electoral methods. During the debate Lari, opposing the provision of reserved seats, again made a forceful plea for giving all minorities due representation through PR system with multi-member constituencies. In his support, he referred to the resolution of the Socialist Party, and an article published in the Communist Party's organ *People's Age* on the PR system. The paper advocated that the best, most democratic and non-communal way of ensuring minority representation through PR. It also expressed confidence that it would not breed separatism. Lari also referred to successful experiments of the system in Ireland and Switzerland. Though Saadullah, as pointed out above, was in favour of retaining reservation of seats, but prepared to dispense with it, if some alternative scheme like the one suggested by Lari was adopted.[44]

Saksena agreed that PR was a great system to ensure fair representation of each group, but opposed its introduction not only on grounds of the illiteracy of a large number of voters, but also for its communally divisive potential. He expressed the pious hope that the majority community would honour its commitment to return large member of Indian Muslims.[45] Mohani, the member of the Constituent Assembly, expressed agreement with the proposal of PR to enable the country to have political coalition.[46] Hukum Singh reiterated that 'it was the birth-right of every section of the population, numerical or political minority, to have proper representation. The dispute is about the method of securing such representation'. He was ready to support the abolition of reservation of seats, on a trial basis, for ten years, after which he felt it would be reviewed. He made the majority realize that 'by agreeing to this (i.e. abolition of reservation) minorities are placing the majority to a severe test. A heavy responsibility would be cast on the majority to see that in fact the minorities feel secure'.[47] Unfortunately, recommendations of Lari, Saadullah, Saksena, Mohani, Singh, etc., to ensure proper representation of religious and political minorities through PR system was not considered sincerely and dismissed without any serious critical scrutiny through some expert committees. Finally, Patel said, 'Let God give us the wisdom and the courage to do the right thing to all manner of people'.[48] And with this benediction and resolve, the Assembly abolished the statutory basis of reservation of seats for minorities in politics.

Experts believe it was the concern of majoritarian nationhood that explains why the provision of reserved seats which was considered a temporary compromise with communalism was scrapped when after the Partition of India, the need for appeasement of nationalist Muslims did not exist. After abolition of reservation, Nehru expressed exultation calling it 'a historic turn in our destiny'. He expressed his opinion, contrary to the one he had expressed in his note on minorities of 1930, that any demand of safeguards by minorities betrayed a lack of trust in the majority. He was, however, graceful enough to call it 'an act of faith above all for the majority community because they will have to show after this that they can behave to others in a generous, fair and just way. Let us live up to that faith'.[49]

Those who opposed reservation for minorities declared that their objective was to set up a homogeneous, democratic, and a secular state in India. During the same debate, Patel bluntly expressed the opinion that even the provision of population based quota of seats under joint electorate for minorities was adopted as a compromise between 'pure nationalism' and 'pure communalism' to prevent Partition. He also said that the formula undermined their endeavour towards building 'One Nation'. It is largely due to the vision of a homogeneous, secular, democratic India combined with majoritarianism that the already adopted resolution of reservation of seats was abolished. The Constituent Assembly also dismissed, without any serious critical scrutiny, all proposals regarding electoral systems during the debates at various stages from August 1947 to May 1949, for PR, multimember constituencies and for cumulative voting with a view to ensuring the representation of minorities without reservation of seats.

Sardar Patel dissuaded Hormasji Pherozeshah Mody, also known as Homi Mody, from demanding reservation for the Parsi community. The Anglo-Indians under Frank Anthony demanded special treatment meaning nomination of his community members in legislatures in case they were not properly represented. The Sikhs agreed, after a lengthy discussion, to drop their claims for reservation and weightage if certain conditions were met in relation to Mazhabi Sikhs (Sikh Scheduled Castes). They were interested in gaining SC status for the Dalits belonging to the Sikh community. The Christians were more interested in their right to propagate their religion. That it was a part of a deal between the majority community and the Christians was betrayed by K.M. Munshi during the debate on the right to propagate religion as an essential part of right to freedom of religion under Draft Article 19 (now Article 25), which Christians considered essential part of their religion for which they were willing to forgo the reservation of seats in legislatures.[50] In this way, Patel dealt with every minority groups separately and persuaded them, by using all political means, to forgo the demand of reservation of seats in legislatures.

Granville Austin, an American historian of the Indian Constitution, writes:

> There can be little doubt that Patel, despite his belief that the minorities must make their own decisions on such issues and not be simply outvoted by caste Hindus, quietly and privately put a great deal of pressure on the minorities to relinquish special privileges. On the other hand, it is quite possible that the

minorities themselves realized that the nation's best interest would be served by their self-denial and the creation of an at least politically homogeneous society. The Indian Muslim's position on this issue was especially delicate. Partition had made them a smaller—and hence less powerful—and a highly suspect group. Should they, therefore, give up all special protection and throw themselves on the mercy of the Congress? Or did they need the protection of separate electorates and reservation even more than previously? The community was deeply split by the issue. Ultimately it would decide, along with the other minorities—excepting the Anglo-Indians and the Untouchables—to forgo even reservation in the Legislature, hoping by its sacrifice to ensure fair treatment from the Hindu majority.[51]

Patel played a major role in abolishing the reservation of seats for minorities, and to a great extent he must be held responsible for the pitiable representation of minorities in politics today. He manipulated each minority group separately with different tactics and even wrote to the Constituent Assembly not to consider the clauses in the Constitution draft. It was abolished two years after Partition when much of the heat had died down. In the absence of Mahatma Gandhi and the changed attitude of Nehru, Patel got the proposal abolished. This can be termed the biggest legislative cheating of the minorities. Minorities, particularly Muslims, are paying the price even today.

Muslims sacrificed their claim of reserved seats in the hope that the majority would understand their sentiment and extend fair treatment to them. This has not ocurred so far as the majority has not acknowledged the huge political deprivation of Muslims. Besides, Hukum Singh's proposal that the electoral system would be reviewed after ten years from the point of view of minority representation has not materialized so far.

NOTES

1. The INC Resolution (All India Congress Committee), Madras, 1928.
2. The Nehru Committee Report, 1928.
3. *The Nehru Report*, Michiko Panjathan, New Delhi (rpt.), 1975.
4. Resolution No. VIII, Congress Session, 1929, Lahore.

5. Aftab Alam, 'Protecting Rights of Minorities is Essential', *The Tribune*, 19 December 2018.
6. Jawaharlal Nehru, 'Note on Minorities', *Young India*, 15 May 1930.
7. The Indian Round Table Conference (Second Session), Proceedings of the Minorities Committee, 1931.
8. Resolution No. XVII, Congress Working Committee, 26 October to 1 November, 1937, Calcutta.
9. Iqbal A. Ansari, *Political Representation of Muslims in India: 1952-2004*, New Delhi: Manak Publications, p. 3.
10. Constituent Assembly Debates (CAD), Lok Sabha Secretariat, New Delhi (2nd rpt.), 1989, vol. II, pp. 310-11.
11. Letter from Mookerjee to Prasad, 22 March 1947; *Law Ministry Archives*, File CA/24/Com/47-I.
12. Austin Granville, *The Constitution: Cornerstone of a Nation*, New Delhi: Oxford University Press, 2016, pp. 186-7.
13. Report of the Minorities Sub Committee, dated 28 August 1947; *Law Ministry Archives*, File CA/24/Com/47-II.
14. Minutes of Meeting, 9 June 1947; *Prasad Papers*, File 3-C/47.
15. See Report of the Minorities Sub Committee to the parent Advisory Committee, dated 28 July 1947; *Law Ministry Archives*.
16. B. Shiva Rao, *The Framing of India's Constitution: Select Documents*, vol. II (New Delhi: Indian Institute of Public Administration, 1968), pp. 396-401.
17. Minutes of the meeting, 28 July 1947; *Prasad Papers*, File 4-C/47.
18. *Reports of the Advisory Committee on the Subject Minority Rights*, dated 8 August 1947, para 2; *Reports, Second Series*, p.30.
19. B. Shiva Rao, *The Framing of India's Constitution: Select Documents*, vol. II (New Delhi: Indian Institute of Public Administration, 1968), pp. 411-22.
20. *CAD*, vol. V, pp. 198-285.
21. Ibid., pp. 218-19.
22. Ibid., vol. V.
23. Ibid., vol. V, p. 271.
24. Ibid.
25. Ibid.
26. Ibid.
27. Ibid., pp. 273-5.
28. Ibid., vol. VII, p. 299.
29. Ibid., p. 303.
30. Ibid., p. 1233.

31. Ibid., pp. 1236-8.
32. Ibid., pp. 1244-5.
33. Ibid., p. 1250.
34. Ibid., pp. 1261-3.
35. Minutes of the Advisory Committee meeting, 30 December 1948; *Prasad Papers*, File 4-C/47.
36. Ibid.
37. *CAD*, vol. VIII, p. 311.
38. Ibid.
39. Proceedings of the Advisory Committee meeting, 11 May 1949; *Law Ministry Archives*, File CA/19 (11)/CDns/49.
40. Ibid.
41. *CAD*, vol. VIII, p. 270.
42. *Reports of the Advisory Committee*, 11 May 1949; *Reports*, Third Series, pp. 240-5.
43. *CAD*, vol. VIII, p. 333.
44. Ibid., pp. 303-5.
45. Ibid., pp. 319-21.
46. Ibid.
47. Ibid., pp. 321-2.
48. Ibid., p. 354.
49. Ibid., p. 332.
50. Ibid., vol. VII, p. 837.
51. Austin, op cit., pp. 188-9.

CHAPTER 3

Representation in the Lok Sabha

Insignificant Voice in the Parliament to Influence Policy Making

The average Muslim representation in the Lok Sabha at 5.78 per cent has been significantly less than the community's share in the total population. Except for rare interludes, this representation has been on a gradual decline reaching the lowest level of 4.42 per cent in the year 2014. The under-nomination of Muslim candidates in the elections by national and regional parties is the main reason for this, though there are many other factors that also contribute. And yet, there is hardly or negligible debate and discussion on this disturbing aspect in the public sphere and mainstream media. According to the *Pace of Socio-Economic Change and Development* report issued by the National Commission to Review the Working of the Constitution (NCRWC):

> At present, the political representation of minority communities in legislatures especially Muslims, has fallen below their proportion of population. The proportion of Backward Classes (BC) among them is next to nil. This can lead to a sense of alienation. It is recommended that in situation of this kind, it is incumbent for political parties to build up leadership potential in the minority communities, including BCs, SCs and STs among them, for participation in political life. The role of the state for strengthening the pluralism of Indian polity has to be emphasized.[1]

Muslims constitute 14.2 per cent of the total national population making them the second largest majority and the largest minority group in India. However, since the 1st election held in 1952 till the 17th election of 2019, they have never been proportionately represented in the lower house of the Parliament i.e. Lok Sabha. They, thus, face huge representational deficits and are almost marginalized politically even in states that have a sizeable Muslim population. As we shall see in the analysis of the results of elections, this picture can change if the political atmosphere is not deliberately vitiated and the major political parties nominate Muslim candidates in proportion to their population.

In the first General Elections (1952) 21 Muslims got elected out of 489 directly elected members. As per 1951 Census, the share of Muslims in the population was 9.91 per cent, and therefore, 49 Muslims should have been elected. But they suffered 57 per cent deprivation in the very first Lok Sabha. In the second General Elections (1957) 24 Muslims were elected out of a total of 494 Members of Parliament (MP). Again, they faced 51 per cent deprivation. Their representation peaked at 49 in 1980, which was 9.26 per cent and was very close to their 11.21 per cent share in the population (1971 Census). They continued to face deprivation in successive elections, and this state of affairs continues even today. In the 16th parliamentary elections (2014), 23 Muslim MPs were elected translating to 4.24 per cent of the total MPs, indicating a huge deprivation. These 23 MPs came from seven states and one Union Territory (UT), out of the total 28 states and eight UTs. In other words, not a single Muslim MP was elected, from the other 21 states and seven UTs. In the 17th General Elections (2019), 26 Muslim MPs got elected which is 4.79 per cent of the total MPs. As per 14.2 per cent population share, the community deserved to have 77 MPs representing it. Thus, herein they suffered 67.5 per cent deprivation. These 26 MPs come from nine states and one UT. The other 19 states and seven UTs did not send a single MP to Parliament. The states thus unrepresented by even a single Muslim member in the Lok Sabha, include major states like Rajasthan, Gujarat, Madhya Pradesh (MP), Chhattisgarh, Odisha, Jharkhand, Karnataka, Punjab, and Haryana. What is noteworthy is that these states have a sizeable Muslim population. Maharashtra too falls into this category. However, it sent a Muslim member after 2004. Some states like Andhra Pradesh (AP), Telangana, Assam, Bihar, Kerala, Uttar Pradesh (UP) and West

Bengal (WB) have a high proportion of Muslims in their respective populations and yet, Muslims face a huge deprivation in Lok Sabha from these states.

LOK SABHA ELECTIONS

In the 17 general elections held since 1952, a total of 8,992 MPs were elected, of whom 520 were Muslims. This translates to 5.78 per cent of the total. As per their share in the total population Muslims deserved 1,070 members. Thus, 550 less Muslim MPs got elected which indicates Muslims have suffered almost 52 per cent deprivation (see Table 3.1).

However, in 2004, a substantial number of 36 Muslim MPs were sent to Parliament with the deprivation amounting to 45.45 per cent. The current Parliament has 26 Muslim MPs taking the deprivation to 66.23 per cent. The highest deprivation of 68.83 per cent suffered by Muslims in India was in 2014 when only 23 MPs were elected. This was the year when Narendra Modi came to power with a clear majority of 282 seats. This supports the observed trend that whenever right wing-parties rise politically, Muslims tend to decline in politics.

In the first General Election, besides Janab Amjad Ali of the Socialist Party from Goalpara Garo Hills (Assam), and B. Pocker of the Muslim League from Malappuram Constitency (erstwhile Madras Presidency), the other 19 MPs belonged to the Congress. The regional variations show that a majority of the members were elected from Bihar (3), Madhya Pradesh (2), Uttar Pradesh (7), West Bengal (2) and erstwhile Hyderabad state (3). The Congress Muslim candidates were elected even from Banaskantha of the then Bombay state and Hoshangabad and Chanda in Madhya Pradesh.

It is noteworthy that these constituencies had less than 10 per cent Muslim voters indicating that voter behaviour was not uniformly communalized then, and Muslim candidates could get elected even from areas which had less Muslim voters. The Congress nominated only 21 Muslims out of its 479 candidates for as many seats which means that only 4.38 per cent Muslim candidates

TABLE 3.1: MUSLIM REPRESENTATION AND DEPRIVATION IN LOK SABHA (1952-2019)

L.S. No.	*Election Year*	*Total MPs Elected*	*Muslim MPs Elected*	*Muslim MPs % to Total*	*Muslim MPs Expected on basis of Population*	*Deprivation (%)*
I	1952	489	21	4.29	49	57.14
II	1957	494	24	4.86	49	51.02
III	1962	494	23	4.66	53	56.60
IV	1967	520	29	5.58	56	48.21
V	1971	518	30	5.79	58	48.28
VI	1977	542	34*	6.27	61	44.26
VII	1980	529[1]	49*	9.26	59	16.95
VIII	1984	542	46*	8.48	62	25.81
IX	1989	529[2]	33	6.24	60	44.00
X	1991	534[3]	28	5.24	65	56.92
XI	1996	543	28	5.16	66	57.56
XII	1998	543	29	5.34	66	56.06
XIII	1999	543	32	5.89	66	51.52
XIV	2004	543	36	6.63	73	50.68
XV	2009	543	28	5.17	73	61.64
XVI	2014	543	24*	4.42	77	68.83
XVII	2019	543	26	4.79	77	66.23
TOTAL		8,992	520	5.78	1,070	51.40

Notes: [1] Elections were not held in Assam (12) and Meghalaya (1).

[2] Elections were not held in Assam (14).

[3] Elections were not held in J&K (6) and countermanded in two seats of Bihar, and one of UP.

* Includes Muslims elected in bye-elections.

were nominated by the Congress resulting in their huge under-representation. Did such under-nomination constitute a serious breach of faith on the part of the Congress to honour the solemn pledge given to the minorities just three years before? It is reported that Nehru realized this, and was eager to increase the representation of Muslims in the Lok Sabha. Out of these concerns, he wrote to the party managers reminding them of the promises given to minorities about a fair share in politics, when the proposal of reservation of seats for minorities was not passed in the Constituent Assembly.

Among the non-Congress parties, the Socialist Party nominated eight Muslims out of its total 254 candidates, which amounted to 3.15 per cent, while Communist Party of India (CPI) nominated only one out of its 49 candidates, which was about 2 per cent.

In the 1957 General Elections, a total of 24 Muslim MPs were elected, which amounted to 4.86 per cent of the total 494 members. As per share in population, they deserved 49 seats and thus, their deprivation was 51.02 per cent, 6.12 percentage points lower than the first Lok Sabha. That year too, 19 Muslim members were elected on Congress tickets. The Praja Socialist Party (PSP) sent two members, while the CPI and Chhota Nagpur and Santhal Parganas Janta Party sent one member each. K. Pocker was elected as an independent from Manjeri (Kerala). The regional distributions showed that UP sent six MPs who all belonged to the Congress, Bihar and Andhra Pradesh sent three each, while West Bengal, Bombay, Assam, and Madras each sent two members. Punjab, Mysore, Kerala and MP each sent one member. However, constituencies with low Muslim population percentage like Dindigul and Tiruchirapalli (Madras), Banaskantha (Bombay) and Warangal (Andhra Pradesh) returned Muslim members, all on Congress tickets. Similarly, a PSP Muslim candidate from Chitradurga (erstwhile Mysore state) and a CPI Muslim candidate from Howrah, also won. Those constituencies had a low percentage of Muslim voters. The Congress gave tickets to 27 Muslims out of a total of the 490 seats it contested, the percentage going up to 5.51 per cent. The PSP nominated seven Muslims out of 189 seats that it contested (3.70 per cent), while the CPI nominated seven out of total 110 members which was 6.63 per cent. Rajasthan with 6.21 per cent Muslim population remained absent in the Lok Sabha. The constituencies which returned Muslim candidates in the first and second Lok Sabha indicate three features that have persisted till the 15th Lok Sabha (2009). These are: (i) constituencies with sizeable Muslim voters, say, from 25 to over 50 per cent were especially selected for nomination of Muslim candidates; (ii) even constituencies with marginal Muslim presence returned Muslim candidates; and (iii) some regions/states with significant Muslim presence such as Gujarat, Rajasthan, Delhi, Madhya Pradesh, Maharashtra, Karnataka, etc., remained grossly under-represented.

The seventh General Elections (1980) saw the reversal of fortunes of the Congress, which returned to power after its defeat in 1977 by the Janata Party. In what is the highest number ever in the history of the Lok Sabha, 48 Muslim MPs were elected. In Dhubri (Assam) a Muslim candidate was elected in a by-election in 1983 on a Congress ticket thus, raising the total number to 49. This brought the Muslim presence in the seventh Lok Sabha to 9.26 per cent. As per their share in population according to the 1971 Census (11.21 per cent), they deserved 59 seats and suffered 16.95 per cent deprivation which is the least so far recorded. Thirty-one Muslims got elected on Congress tickets, out of which 11 were from UP. The Janata Party (Secular) (JNPS) sent seven members, while the CPI(M) with five, National Conference (NC) with two, Muslim League with two and Congress (U) with one member were other parties which sent Muslim members. Vellore in Tamil Nadu with just about 8 per cent Muslim voters returned AKA Abdul Samad as an independent MP. If we see the regional variation, UP sent 18 MPs while 13 seats had been expected on the basis of the population. This showed a kind of wave in favour of Muslim candidates in UP. West Bengal contributed seven, while Bihar with five, Kerala, Karnataka and Jammu & Kashmir with three each and Maharashtra with two MPs were the major states contributing to the Muslim count in the Parliament. Gujarat sent Ahmed Patel from Broach constituency and Haryana sent T. Hussain from Faridabad, both on Congress tickets. Rajasthan, however, remained absent. The Congress gave tickets to 41 Muslims out of a total of 492, which was 8.33 per cent. The JNPS nominated 21 candidates out of its total of 432, i.e. 4.86 per cent. The CPI(M) gave tickets to six out of its total 63 candidates, which was 9.52 per cent, of which five got elected, all from West Bengal. Political scientists have propounded numerous reasons for the electoral success story of Muslims in 1980, which was also repeated on a slightly lower scale in 1984 (45 MPs). Some of the main reasons are: (i) The Congress gave 8.33 per cent tickets to Muslims which was more than its average of 6.7 per cent which had direct bearing on the better representation; (ii) Five Muslim candidates of the CPI(M) got elected from West Bengal which was more than its usual win of one or two; and (iii) Five MPs from Bihar and 18 from UP (11 on Congress tickets) indicated that there was a wave of support for the Congress as voters ignored the religious affiliation of the candidates.

The eighth General Elections (1984) was held in the wake of Indira Gandhi's assassination. The subsequent pro-Congress wave which sent 45 Muslim MPs was the second highest mark. A Congress Muslim candidate from Udhampur (Jammu & Kashmir) won the bye-election held in 1988 raising the total number to 46. Thus, the share of Muslims in the 8th Lok Sabha was 8.49 per cent. Muslims constituted 11.35 per cent share in the population (1981 Census), and deserved 62 seats. They faced 25.81 per cent deprivation, which is the second lowest so far. As far as party affiliations were concerned, 31 were elected on Congress tickets while the CPI(M) with four, NC with three, Indian Union Muslim League with two, Asom Gana Parishad (AGP) with two, United Minorities Front with one and Lok Dal with one MP, were the other parties which returned Muslims. Sultan Salahuddin Owaisi of All Inida Majlis-e-Ittehadul Muslimeen (AIMIM) won from Hyderabad as an independent candidate. In terms of regional distribution, UP reached its second highest level of 12 members—11 on Congress tickets, and one on Lok Dal which had fielded 19 Muslim candidates in UP. Assam recorded an improvement reaching the highest mark of three members, while Bihar reached its highest level of six MPs. West Bengal returned six MPs. It was in this election that Rajasthan sent the only Muslim MP ever. Mohammad Ayub Khan won from the Rajasthan's Jhunjhunu seat (which had only 11 per cent Muslims) on a Congress ticket. Maharashtra sent two MPs from Ratnagiri and Washim which had respectively 10 and 9 per cent Muslim voters. It is worth noting here that a Muslim Lok Dal nominee lost the election from Saharanpur in UP, which had 38 per cent Muslim voters. Madhya Pradesh in 1980 returned two MPs, one from Satna with 13 per cent Muslim voters, and the other from Betul with just 3 per cent Muslims. In Bihar, Godda with 15 per cent, and Giridih with 14 per cent voters returned Muslim nominees of the Congress, while the Muslim candidate of the Lok Dal failed to win from Darbhanga, which had 22 per cent voters. As far as nomination of candidates is concerned, the Congress fielded 41 candidates out of its total 517, which was 7.93 per cent. The CPI(M) nominated six candidates out of its total of 64 (9.38 per cent) with four being elected from West Bengal.

The results of the 1980 and 1984 General Elections demonstrate that given the right political atmosphere and willingness of political parties to give tickets to minorities, the latter can hope to improve their political representation within the existing majoritarian system. These elections returned Muslim nominees even from constituencies having very low share of Muslim voters (less than 10 or 15 per cent). This is possible only when there is a wave of support in favour of a political party that nominates a fair number of Muslims and the political space is not polarized against minorities. Party affiliation is more important than the candidate's popularity.

The 14th Lok Sabha (2004) had 36 Muslim MPs which is the third highest so far (6.62 per cent). As per share in the population (13.43 per cent: 2001 Census) Muslims deserved 73 seats, facing 50.68 per cent deprivation. Those MPs got elected on tickets of 11 different parties. Their party affiliations, nominations by different parties and percentage win is presented in Table 3.2. The Congress, CPI(M), Samajwadi Party (SP), Bahujan Samaj Party (BSP) and Rashtriya Janata Dal (RJD) were the parties which contributed a good number of Muslims MPs. The Bhartiya Janata

TABLE 3.2: PARTY AFFILIATIONS OF MUSLIM MPs AND THEIR NOMINATION IN 14TH LOK SABHA (2004)

S. No.	*Party*	*Total Nominated*	*Muslim Nominated*	*% Muslim Nomination*	*Muslims Elected*	*Ratio of Muslims (Elected: Nominated)*
1.	INC	417	30	7.19	10	1:3
2.	CPI(M)	69	11	15.94	5	1:2 (App.)
3.	SP	237	38	16.03	7	1:9 (App)
4.	BSP	435	52	11.95	4	1:13
5.	RJD	41	5	12.19	3	3:5
6.	MLKSC	1	1	100	1	1:1
7.	JD(U)	73	6	8.22	1	1:6
8.	AIMIM	2	2	100	1	1:2
9.	DMK	16	1	6.25	1	1:1
10.	JKNC	5	5	100	2	2:5
11.	PDP	3	3	100	1	1:3

Source: Iqbal A. Ansari, *Political Representation of Muslims in India: 1952-2004*, New Delhi: Manak Publications.

Party (BJP) under Atal Behari Vajpayee wanted to project itself as Muslim-friendly party and nominated nine Muslims out of its total 364 candidates (2.47 per cent), which is the highest nomination of Muslims ever by the BJP though none of them won. Even so, the nomination of Muslims by the BJP was very low compared to nomination by other parties. Moreover, these tickets were given in constituencies where the chances of victory were very low. In terms of regional distribution, 11 MPs came from UP, and five and four from WB and Bihar respectively. Jammu & Kashmir and Kerala each contributed three MPs. The DMK made its first contribution from Madras (South), while the Congress Muslim nominee won from Periyakulam, which had 5 per cent Muslim voters. In 2004, Gujarat, Rajasthan, MP, Haryana, and Delhi, however, continued to have no Muslim representation. After the gap of years 1998 and 1999, Maharashtra sent Abdul Rahman Antulay from Kolaba constituency on a Congress ticket. Of those 36 MPs, 13 were returned from marginal and medium (3 to 18 per cent) Muslim constituencies; 14 members from sizeable Muslims constituencies (20 to 50 per cent) and nine from Muslim-majority constituencies. The Muslim-majority constituency of Jangipur in West Bengal could not return the Muslim nominee of the CPI(M), who had earlier won the seat in 1998 and 1999.

The first full term National Democratic Alliance (NDA) government (1999-2004) headed by the BJP set off apprehensions and fear among many minority communities and deprived groups. Although the BJP did not have an absolute majority, it did try to implement many agendas of the Rashtriya Swayamsevak Sangh (RSS), such as saffronization of textbooks, communalization of social space, etc. The NDA government also witnessed the massacre of Muslims in Gujarat in 2002. Consequently, in the 2004 elections, Muslims had to tactically balance their true concern of defeating the BJP that was primarily responsible for communal riots in Gujarat with electing a fair number of their candidates. The result indicated that they were successful in defeating the BJP. In UP, they faced a serious dilemma in choosing secular candidates that could defeat the BJP. They had to make a difficult choice in certain Parliamentary Constituencies (PC), where there were triangular fights between the BJP, the SP and the BSP. Their tactical voting succeeded in securing 11 seats out of 80, which is the third highest level reached in UP after the peak of 18 in 1980, and 12 in 1984. Their voting behaviour, as reported by the Centre for the Study of Developing Societies (CSDS), seems to have succeeded in inflicting heavy losses on the BJP and its allies. The communal carnage in Gujarat in 2002 did cast a shadow on the fate of the BJP in UP as well as in several other crucial states. Perhaps, for the first time, it was truly appreciated that Muslim participation in the electoral process is capable of becoming a force to be reckoned with especially in situations where elections become a referendum. In a bid to defeat the BJP, Muslim voters even preferred non-Muslim secular candidates over the candidates of their own community, and in the process they could not maintain their fair representation.

The 15th General Elections of 2009 sent a meagre 28 Muslim MPs (5.17 per cent), while as per their proportionate share they deserved 73 MPs, thus, suffering a huge deprivation of 61.64 per cent. Of these, 10 MPs belonged to the Congress, while the BSP contributed four, the NC three and AITC (henceforth, Trinamool

Congress or TMC) and Indian Union Muslim League (IUML) each contributed two MPs. The BJP, AIMIM, All India United Democratic Front (AIUDF), CPM, and Dravida Munnetra Kazhagam (DMK) each contributed one MP. An independent candidate, Hasan Khan won the Ladakh seat in J&K. The BJP's only Muslim candidate Shahnawaz Hussain won from Bhagalpur in Bihar. The DMK's only Muslim candidate won from Vellore, which had between 10 and 20 per cent of Muslim voters. In Assam, the AIUDF president Badruddin Ajmal won from Dhubri, a Muslim-majority constituency becoming the first MP of his party. As regards regional distribution, the highest, i.e. seven MPs came from UP followed by West Bengal which sent six MPs. All four BSP MPs came from UP. The SP failed to do so perhaps, because Mulayam Singh Yadav lost sections of the Muslim vote due to the BSP, and because of the entry of Kalyan Singh into his party. Jammu & Kashmir four MPs, Bihar sent three, while Kerala, Assam and TN sent two MPs each. AP and Lakshadweep sent one MP each. Maharashtra, Karnataka, Gujarat, MP, Rajasthan, Odisha, Delhi, Jharkhand and Haryana were the major states that despite having a sizeable Muslim population failed to elect even a single Muslim MP. In Maharashtra, though the community leaders had been asking the Congress and Nationalist Congress Party (NCP) to nominate at least five Muslim candidates from parliamentary constituencies that had a sizeable number of Muslim voters, only Antulay (Congress) and Azam Pansare (NCP) were nominated, both failed to win. Likewise in Gujarat, which had not sent a single Muslim MP for the last 25 years, Muslims including Ahmed Patel worked hard to ensure the victory of the Congress candidate Aziz Tankarvi from Broach that had been won by Ahmed Patel in 1980 and 1984. Tankarvi also failed to win. Karnataka that had a few regular Muslim faces like C.K. Jaffer Sharief in its list of MPs, too could not send a single Muslim to Parliament.

In 2009, a total of 780 Muslim candidates contested the election, most of them being independents. This figure reflected their will to take part in the political process of the world's largest democracy. But in most of the states, including Muslim-majority Jammu & Kashmir the percentage of Muslim candidate was far below the percentage of Muslims in the population. In Assam, where Muslims constituted 30 per cent of the population, 19 per cent candidates were Muslims; in UP, where Muslims were 18.5 per cent, they were 11 per cent of candidates; and a similar proportion noticed in Bihar where Muslims were 16.5 per cent. More importantly, in most of the states, majority of Muslim candidates were independent. In Maharashtra, 52 per cent, in Gujarat and MP 54 each, in Haryana 66, and in Rajasthan, 80 per cent contested as independents. These figures reflected the reluctance of the national parties to nominate Muslim candidates. Excluding Jammu & Kashmir, less than 30 Muslims had been given tickets by the Congress while BJP nominated only five Muslims. A total of 52 Muslim candidates came at second positions of which 14 were defeated by Muslim candidates, and 38 by non-Muslims belonging to national and regional parties.

It is a commonly observed trend that the rise of the BJP almost always leads to shrinking of political space for Muslims and the 16th General Elections (2014) is a striking example. The BJP won this election with a full majority of 282 MPs, but none was a Muslim. With only 23 MPs, Muslims had one of the lowest share in the Parliament. In 2018, in the Kairana by-election, Tabassum Hassan won on a RLD ticket, and the number of Muslim MPs rose to 24 taking their share in the Parliament to a mere 4.42 per cent. As per share in the population they deserved 77 seats, which means they suffered a deprivation of 53 MPs (68.83 per cent), the highest ever. Among these 23 MPs, the Congress and Trinamool Congress contributed four each, Jammu & Kashmir People's Democratic Party (PDP) with three, and AIUDF, NCP, IUML and CPI(M) with two MPs each were other major contributors. The AIMIM, RJD, Lok Janshakti Party (LJP), and All India Dravida Munnetra Kazhagam (AIADMK) each contributed one MP. As far as regional distributions are concerned, West Bengal contributed eight MPs. Bihar contributed four, Jammu & Kashmir and Kerala three each, and Assam two MPs. Both the MPs of Assam—Sirajuddin Ajmal from Barpeta and Badruddin Ajmal from Dhubri—belonged to the AIUDF. AP, Lakshadweep and Tamil Nadu each sent one MP.

The anti-Muslim rhetoric and communal polarization wreaked by the Muzaffarnagar riots of 2013 were so strong that UP failed to send even a single Muslim though they constituted 20 per cent share in the state population deserving 16 MPs. The effect of this polarization was felt in other states too. As usual, Maharashtra, MP, Gujarat, Chhattisgarh, Rajasthan, Delhi, Haryana, Karnataka and Jharkhand could not send even a single MP. A surprising feature of the 2014 elections was that 54 Muslim candidates finished as runners-up, 11 of these were defeated by Muslim, and 43 by non-Muslim candidates. Out of the latter 43 candidates six were defeated by a margin of less than 10,000 votes. In Ladakh, Ghulam Raza, an independent was defeated by Thupstan Chhewang, a BJP nominee by a margin of just 36 votes. In UP, the most important state from the point of view of Muslim representation, 19 Muslim candidates came at second positions. Of these 10 belonged to the SP, eight to the BSP and one to the Congress. In Bihar, six candidates finished as runners-up—five belonged to the RJD and one, Shahnawaz Hussain, to the BJP.[2] The BJP contested 428 seats out of which seven had Muslim candidates. However, only Hussain, the three-time MP was expected to win. The Congress and other regional parties like the SP, BSP, RJD and TMC had fielded less number of Muslim candidates.

In the 17th General Elections (2019), Muslim representation increased slightly. There are 26 Muslim MPs out of 543 making 4.79 per cent of the total. As per share in the population (14.2 per cent: 2011 Census), Muslims deserved 77 seats. As they had only 26 MPs, they suffered a deprivation of 51 MPs (66.23 per cent). This is the second highest deprivation Muslims suffered in the Lok Sabha. The TMC sent five Muslim MPs, all from West Bengal. Its Muslim candidates won Arambagh, Basirhat, Jangipur, Murshidabad and Uluberia. The Congress, SP, BSP, and IUML contributed three MPs each. While the Congress' Muslim nominee won from Barpeta in Assam, Kishanganj in Bihar, and Malda Dakshin in West Bengal, the NC won Anantnag, Baramulla and Srinagar, and SP won Moradabad, Rampur and Sambhal. The AIUDF won Dhubri in Assam. The CPI(M) Muslim nominee won Alappuzha in Kerala, and NCP won its traditional seat of Lakshadweep. The AIMIM contributed two seats. As far as geographical variations are concerned, West Bengal and UP contributed with six MPs each, Kerala and Jammu & Kashmir three each, Bihar and Assam two each and Tamil Nadu, Telangana, Lakshadweep and Maharashtra one member each. Maharashtra sent its first Muslim MP after 2004. Syed Imtiyaz Jalil of AIMIM defeated Chandrakant Khaire of the Shiv Sena by a thin margin of 4,492 votes in Aurangabad in Marathwada region. As usual, MP, Chhattisgarh, Gujarat, Rajasthan, Delhi, Haryana, Odisha, Karnataka, AP, and Jharkhand failed to send a single Muslim MP.

The detailed listing above helps us to see that in a polarized environment created by the BJP, the mainstream national and regional parties hesitate to give tickets to Muslims in proportion to their share in the population. The BJP gave tickets to six Muslim candidates, all from Muslim-majority areas; two Muslim candidates in West Bengal, where the community accounts for about 27 per cent of the state's population, one in Lakshadweep which has over 95 per cent Muslims, and three in Muslim-majority Kashmir valley. None of the six candidates won or were in the lead.[3] In 2019, 23 Muslim candidates stood at second positions, nine of them were defeated by Muslim and 16 by non-Muslim candidates, some of them losing by thin margins. Dr. Mumtaz Sanghmita of the TMC was defeated by the BJP's S.S. Ahluwalia by a margin of 2,439 votes in Bardhaman-Durgapur constiuency. In Meerut in UP, Haji Mohammad Yaqoob of the BSP was defeated by the BJP's Rajendra Agarwal by a margin of 4,729 votes. Influential Muslim leaders like Nasimuddin Siddiqui, Salman Khurshid, and Begum Tabassum Hassan also lost in this election.

STATE-WISE REPRESENTATION

The analysis of Muslim representation in Lok Sabha according to states shows us a definite pattern across the country. Muslim representation mainly comes from UP, WB, Bihar, Assam and J&K. There are certain pockets which also contribute such as Telangana (crstwhile AP), North Kerala, parts of TN and Karnataka and Lakshadweep. Sometimes, Jharkhand, Gujarat, Maharashtra and Puducherry also contribute with one or two members. Hyderabad (present-day Telangana State) had been represented earlier by Sultan Salahuddin Owaisi and currently by Asaduddin Owaisi of AIMIM. Tamil Nadu's Vellore, Periyakulam and Ramanathapuram have returned Muslim candidates. Lakshadweep which has 95 per cent Muslims has always returned a Muslim MP. Puducherry with a 6.54 per cent Muslim population returned a Muslim MP in 1991, 1996 and 1999. Gulbarga, Bangalore (North) and Dharwad (South) in Karnataka have returned Muslim MPs. Godda in Jharkhand with some gaps has also returned Muslim MPs.

Now, let us turn our attention to Muslim representation in Parliament from states like Assam, Bihar, UP, West Bengal, Kerala, Maharashtra and Jammu & Kashmir over the years.

Goalpara Garo Hills, Jorhat, Dhubri, Barpeta, Silchar, Mangaldoi, Nowgong and Cachar are PCs, which have returned Muslims. For the last two decades, Barpeta and Dhubri have been sending Muslim MPs, earlier on Congress and now on Congress/AIUDF tickets (Table 3.3).

TABLE 3.3: MUSLIM REPRESENTATION IN LOK SABHA FROM ASSAM

Election	*Year*	*Total Seats*	*Muslim in State (%)*	*Expected MPs*	*Muslims Nominated*	*Muslims Elected*
1.	1952	12	22.6	3	1	1
2.	1957	12	22.6	3	4	2
3.	1962	12	24.7	3	5	2
4.	1967	14	24.7	3	3	2
5.	1971	14	24.03	3	7	3*
6.	1977	14	24.03	3	5	3
7.	1980		Elections not held			
8.	1984	14	26.17**	3	12	3
9.	1989		Elections not held			
10.	1991	14	28.3	4	13	1
11.	1996	14	28.3	4	10	2
12.	1998	14	28.3	4	7	2
13.	1999	14	28.3	4	12	2
14.	2004	14	30.92	4	14	2
15.	2009	14	30.92	4	16	2
16.	2014	14	34.22	5	24	2
17.	2019	14	34.22	5	23	2
TOTAL		204	27.49	55	156	31

Total elected in 15 elections: 31; Deprivation suffered: 43.64 per cent.

Notes: * Elected in the by-election of 1974 in Cachar constituency.

** Share of Muslims in 1984 is taken as average of 1971 & 1991 Census figures.

Bettiah, East Champaran, Siwan, Gopalganj, Madhubani, Katihar, Darbhanga, Kishanganj, Purnea, Sheohar, Bhagalpur, Begusarai, Araria and Khagaria have returned Muslim MPs; a maximum of six MPs were returned in 1991 and 1998. Earlier, those MPs were elected on Congress tickets and later on Janata Dal and now on RJD, Congress and JD(U) tickets (Table 3.4).

TABLE 3.4: MUSLIM REPRESENTATION IN LOK SABHA FROM BIHAR

Election	*Year*	*Total Seats*	*Muslim in State (%)*	*Expected MPs*	*Muslims Nominated*	*Muslims Elected*
1.	1952	55	11.28	6	4	3
2.	1957	53	11.28	6	9	3
3.	1962	53	12.45	7	17	2
4.	1967	53	12.45	7	10	2
5.	1971	53	13.48	7	12	3
6.	1977	54	13.48	7	13	2
7.	1980	54	13.48	7	17	5
8.	1984	54	14.13	8	17	6
9.	1989	54	14.13	8	11	3
10.	1991	54	14.81	8	19	6
11.	1996	54	14.81	8	26	4
12.	1998	54	14.81	8	25	6
13.	1999	54	14.81	8	27	3
14.	2004	40	16.53	7	22	4
15.	2009	40	16.53	7	53	3
16.	2014	40	16.87	7	59	4
17.	2019	40	16.87	7	38	2
TOTAL		859	14.25	123	379	61

Total elected in 17 elections: 61; Deprivation suffered: 50.4 per cent.

There are only six Parliamentary constituencies in Jammu & Kashmir of which Baramulla, Srinagar and Anantnag have been regularly returning Muslim members on PDP and NC tickets, alternately. On some occasions, Ladakh has also returned Muslims, and on most occasions Udhampur and Jammu have returned non-Muslim MPs (Table 3.5).

In Kerala, erstwhile constituencies like Manjeri, Cannanore, Chirayinkil and Calicut have returned Muslim nominees. Recently,

TABLE 3.5: MUSLIM REPRESENTATION IN LOK SABHA FROM JAMMU & KASHMIR

Election	*Year*	*Total Seats*	*Muslim in State (%)*	*Expected MPs*	*Muslims Elected*
IV	1967	6	68.30	4	3
V	1971	6	65.85	4	3
VI	1977	6	65.85	4	3
VII	1980	6	65.85	4	3
VIII	1984	6	64.19	4	3
IX	1989	6	64.19	4	3
X	1991		No election held		
XI	1996	6	64.18	4	3
XII	1998	6	64.18	4	4
XIII	1999	6	64.18	4	4
XIV	2004	6	66.97	4	3
XV	2009	6	66.97	4	4
XVI	2014	6	68.31	4	3
XVII	2019	6	68.31	4	3
TOTAL		78	65.95	52	42

Total elected in 13 elections: 42; Deprivation suffered: 19.23%.

Ponnani, Malappuram, Kozhikode, Wayanad and Alappuzha have returned Muslims. The IUML, CPI(M), and Congress have regularly been sending Muslim MPs from the state (Table 3.6).

In 1952, Abdus Sattar Chavda was elected on a Congress ticket from Banaskantha (now in Gujarat). In 1957, Banaskantha and Jalna returned Muslim MPs. Kolaba (now Raigad), Akola and Aurangabad have been retuning Muslims on irregular basis. In 2004, Antulay was elected from Raigad, but no member was elected in 2009 and 2014. In 2019, Syed Imtiyaz Jaleel was elected from Aurangabad on AIMIM ticket. In Maharashtra, Muslims constitute almost 12 per cent of the state population and thus deserve at least 5 to 6 MPs. However, they have suffered huge political deprivation in the Parliament (Table 3.7).

UP has a sizeable Muslim population of 19.26 per cent (2011 Census). It has contributed almost 25 per cent of the Muslim MPs elected in 17 elections. The PCs of Moradabad, Rampur, Badaun, Bareily, Unnav, Bahraich, Dumraiganj, Ghazipur,

TABLE 3.6: MUSLIM REPRESENTATION IN LOK SABHA FROM KERALA

Election	Year	Total Seats	Muslim in State (%)	Expected MPs	Muslims Nominated	Muslims Elected
II	1957	18	17.57	3	4	0
III	1962	18	17.91	3	4	2
IV	1967	19	17.91	3	5	2
V	1971	19	17.50	3	2	2
VI	1977	20	17.50	4	5	4
VII	1980	20	17.50	4	4	3
VIII	1984	20	21.25	4	3	3
IX	1989	20	21.25	4	6	3
X	1991	20	23.33	5	4	2
XI	1996	20	23.33	5	8	2
XII	1998	20	23.33	5	6	2
XIII	1999	20	23.33	5	8	3
XIV	2004	20	24.70	5	6	3
XV	2009	20	24.70	5	14	2
XVI	2014	20	26.56	5	34	3
XVII	2019	20	26.56	5	19	3
TOTAL		314	21.51	68	132	39

Total elected in 16 elections: 40 (one indepenent in 1957); Deprivation suffered: 41.18 per cent.

TABLE 3.7: MUSLIM REPRESENTATION IN LOK SABHA FROM MAHARASHTRA

Election	Year	Total Seats	Muslim in State (%)	Expected MPs	Muslims Nominated	Muslims Elected
I	1952*	45	7.61	3	1	1
II	1957*	66	7.61	5	3	2
III	1962	44	7.67	3	2	1
IV	1967	45	7.67	3	3	2
V	1971	45	8.4	4	4	3
VI	1977	48	8.4	4	1	0
VII	1980	48	8.4	4	9	2
VIII	1984	48	9.25	4	6	2
IX	1989	48	9.25	4	5	1
X	1991	48	9.67	5	5	1
XI	1996	48	9.67	5	15	1

Contd.

TABLE 3.7: *Contd.*

Election	*Year*	*Total Seats*	*Muslim in State (%)*	*Expected MPs*	*Muslims Nominated*	*Muslims Elected*
XII	1998	48	9.67	5	9	0
XIII	1999	48	9.67	5	9	0
XIV	2004	48	10.60	5	26	1
XV	2009	48	10.60	5	58	0
XVI	2014	48	11.54	6	65	0
XVII	2019	48	11.54	6	51	1
TOTAL		821	9.25	76	272	18

Total elected in 17 elections: 18; Deprivation suffered: 76.32 per cent.
Note: *In 1952 and 1957 Maharashtra was part of Bombay state.

Farrukhabad, Etah, Meerut, Muzaffarnagar, Saharanpur, Amroha, Kairana, Azamgarh, etc., have been regularly sending Muslim MPs (Table 3.8).

In West Bengal, Malda, Jangipur, Murshidabad, Uluberia, Serampore, Katwa, Arambagh, Bashirhat, Malda Dakshin, Malda Uttar, Barrackpore, Calcutta (North), etc., have returned Muslim MPs earlier on Congress, CPI(M) and now on TMC tickets (Table 3.9).

TABLE 3.8: MUSLIM REPRESENTATION IN LOK SABHA FROM UTTAR PRADESH

Election	*Year*	*Total Seats*	*Muslim in State (%)*	*Expected MPs*	*Muslims Nominated*	*Muslims Elected*
I	1952	86	14.28	12	11	7
II	1957	86	14.28	12	12	6
III	1962	86	14.63	13	21	5
IV	1967	85	14.63	12	23	5
V	1971	85	15.48	13	15	6
VI	1977	85	15.48	13	24	10
VII	1980	85	15.48	13	46	18
VIII	1984	85	15.93	14	34	12
IX	1989	85	15.93	14	48	8
X	1991	85	17.33	15	55	3
XI	1996	85	17.33	15	59	6

Contd.

TABLE 3.8: *Contd.*

Election	*Year*	*Total Seats*	*Muslim in State (%)*	*Expected MPs*	*Muslims Nominated*	*Muslims Elected*
XII	1998	85	17.33	15	65	6
XIII	1999	85	17.33	15	68	8
XIV	2004	80	18.50	15	85	11
XV	2009	80	18.50	15	101	7
XVI	2014	80	19.26	15	124	0
XVII	2019	80	19.26	15	72	6
TOTAL		1,428	16.53	236	863	124

Total elected in 17 elections: 125 (one independent in 1989); Deprivation suffered: 47.46 per cent.

TABLE 3.9: MUSLIM REPRESENTATION IN LOK SABHA FROM WEST BENGAL

Election	*Year*	*Total Seats*	*Muslim in State (%)*	*Expected MPs*	*Muslims Nominated*	*Muslims Elected*
I	1952	34	19.46	7	2	2
II	1957	36	19.46	7	3	2
III	1962	36	20.00	7	8	3
IV	1967	40	20.00	8	10	3
V	1971	40	20.46	8	13	4
VI	1977	42	20.46	9	11	3
VII	1980	42	20.46	9	23	7
VIII	1984	42	20.51	9	23	6
IX	1989	42	20.51	9	22	6
X	1991	42	23.61	10	18	5
XI	1996	42	23.61	10	21	5
XII	1998	42	23.61	10	17	6
XIII	1999	42	23.61	10	30	6
XIV	2004	42	25.25	11	31	5
XV	2009	42	25.25	11	40	6
XVI	2014	42	27.01	11	82	8
XVII	2019	42	27.01	11	59	6
TOTAL		690	22.37	157	413	83

Total elected in 17 elections: 85 (indepenents: 1962 & 1967); Deprivation suffered: 45.86 per cent.

CONSTITUENCY-WISE REPRESENTATION

Muslims are not uniformly distributed all over India. In a majority of the PCs the presence of Muslim voters is extremely low whereas in a few others they are in an absolute majority or dominant position (Table 3.10).

TABLE 3.10: ANALYSIS OF PCs AS PER PRESENCE OF MUSLIM VOTERS

S.No.	*Type of Constituencies*	*% of Muslim Voters*	*No. of Seats*
1.	Marginal	Up to 10	291
2.	Medium	From 10 to 20	165
3.	Sizeable	From 20 to 30	42
4.	Near Majority	From 30 to 40	21
5.	Majority	40 and above	24
TOTAL	All		543

Source: CSDS.

For the purpose of my analysis, I have categorized PCs into marginal, medium, sizeable, near-majority and majority Muslim constituencies. A majority of PCs in India (291) can be categorized as marginal, wherein the Muslim voter percentage is upto 10 per cent. The 165 medium constituencies have a voter percentage between 10 to 20 per cent, while the 'majority' ones with voter percentage 40 per cent and above number only 24. How does the percentage of Muslim voters in a particular constituency category influence the probability of a Muslim candidate being elected? The election results of five recent General Elections (1999, 2004, 2009, 2014 and 2019) are analysed here to answer this question (Table 3.11).

In the last five elections a total of 145 Muslim MPs were elected translating to 5.34 per cent of the totally elected. The marginal Muslim constituencies have contributed only five Muslim MPs which is 3.45 per cent of all Muslims elected and 0.34 per cent of all MPs elected. This indicates that the probability of a Muslim candidate winning from these constituencies is extremely low. This

TABLE 3.11: PCs AND THEIR CONTRIBUTION TO MUSLIM REPRESENTATION IN PAST FIVE ELECTIONS

Type of Constituency	*Seats in each type of Constituency*	*Total Seat in 5 elections*	*Muslims Elected*					*Total Muslims elected in 5 years*	*% of Elected in PCs*	*% to Total Muslims elected in 5 years*
			1999	*2004*	*2009*	*2014*	*2019*			
Marginal (up to 10%)	291	1,455	2	2	1	0	0	5	0.34	3.45
Medium (10 to 20%)	165	825	6	10	7	4	5	32	3.88	22.07
Sizeable (20 to 30%)	42	210	4	8	1	1	2	16	7.62	11.03
Near Majority (30 to 40%)	21	105	4	2	4	4	4	18	17.14	12.41
Majority (40% & above)	24	120	16	14	15	14	15	74	61.67	51.03
TOTAL	543	2,715	32	36	28	23	26	145	5.34	100

Sources: Information provided by CSDS and ECI websites.

is due to low nomination from mainstream parties for these constituencies, communalization of politics and non-Muslim voters not voting for the Muslim candidates. The percentage of Muslims elected in the marginal, medium, sizeable, near majority and majority Muslim constituencies are 0.34, 3.88, 7.62, 17.14 and 61.67 per cent respectively, which indicates that as the proportion of Muslim voters in a constituency goes up, the chance of Muslim to win also goes up.

In the sizeable and near-majority Muslim constituencies which have generally not returned Muslims, the Muslim votes get divided due to multiplicity of candidates. The atmosphere in these constituencies is communally charged during elections and Hindu votes get consolidated behind non-Muslim candidates. The easiest ploy is to portray Muslims as a threat to Hindu interests. Communal parties also raise the imaginary and totally baseless issue of Muslim appeasement.

MUSLIM-MAJORITY CONSTITUENCIES

Constituting 14.2 per cent of the total population, Muslims deserve to be represented by at least 77 MPs. The community is present in every state and regions, but not uniformly distributed. In some PCs, they are an insignificant number, while in few others they are in absolute majority positions. In marginal constituencies (voters up to 10 per cent), Muslim voters are not valued and thus, not counted. As discussed above, these constituencies have contributed only 3.45 per cent of all the Muslims elected. In the 2014 and 2019 elections, such PCs did not contribute a single Muslim MP. The medium constituencies (165) have also not contributed satisfactorily to the Muslim MPs' count.

Therefore, it becomes imperative to study the pattern of Muslim sizeable, near-majority and majority constituencies. There are 42 sizeable Muslim constituencies, wherein Muslim voters are between 20 and 30 per cent. Out of these, seven seats are reserved for the SCs and one for the STs category. This means that in 34 seats, Muslims are in a comfortable position to decide the candidate of their choice. In these seats, by aligning with SC, ST or Other

Backward Class (OBC) voters, Muslims can aim at winning and increasing their representation (Table 3.12).

There are 21 PCs wherein Muslim voters are between 30 and 40 per cent (Table 3.13). Nagina and Bahraich, both in UP, are reserved for the SC category, thus, and in 19 PCs, Muslims are effectively in near-majority. The arithmetic of polled votes in these PCs show that in most of the seats non-Muslim candidates are elected due to division of community votes among many Muslim candidates put up by various parties and consolidation of Hindu votes due to communal campaigns.

Let us examine the performance of these constituencies as far as winnability of Muslim candidates are concerned from 1967, when the election was held for the first time in the state of Jammu & Kashmir.

Nagina, a SC-reserved PC, was created in 2008 from the Bijnor seat and I have not considered it here. The performance of near-majority Muslim constituencies is extremely poor as these have returned only 19.46 per cent Muslim members and the deprivation is 80.54 per cent (Table 3.14). Leaving Barpeta (71.43 per cent), Katihar, Gurgaon, Kairana, Bahraich and Basirhat, the performance of other PCs is abysmally low. Udhampur, Kasaragod, Vadakkara, Palakkad, Bijnor, Krishnagar, and Birbhum have not returned a single Muslim MP.

Ironically, this could be due to a case of drought on one hand, and plenty on the other: Muslims not being given tickets in these PCs by the mainstream parties and the division of Muslim votes due to several Muslim candidates of various mainstream parties. While the first reason is valid for PCs in Kerala, Jammu & Kashmir and West Bengal, the second is valid for Bihar, Assam and UP.

There are 24 PCs wherein Muslims constitute a majority and absolute majority position. In these PCs Muslim voters constitute 40 per cent and above and are in complete control to decide the fate of a candidate. Two constituencies, namely Karimganj in Assam and Jayanagar in West Bengal are reserved for SCs. Karimganj was reserved for a SC candidate in 1952, while Jayanagar was constituted in 1962. It supports the observation of the Sachar

TABLE 3.12: SIZEABLE MUSLIM CONSTITUENCIES
(MUSLIM VOTERS BETWEEN 20 AND 30 PER CENT)

Sr. No.	*State ID*	*State Name*	*PC ID*	*PC Name*
1.	3	Assam	2	Silchar
2.	3	Assam	7	Guwahati
3.	3	Assam	8	Mangaldoi
4.	3	Assam	11	Kaliabor
5.	4	Bihar	6	Madhubani
6.	4	Bihar	12	Purnia
7.	4	Bihar	14	Darbhanga
8.	7	Haryana	10	Faridabad
9.	9	J&K	6	Jammu
10.	11	Kerala	2	Kannur
11.	13	Maharashtra	2	Dhule
12.	13	Maharashtra	19	Aurangabad
13.	13	Maharashtra	26	Mumbai North
14.	13	Maharashtra	29	Mumbai North-Central
15.	24	UP	10	Meerut
16.	24	UP	11	Baghpat
17.	24	UP	13	Gautam Buddha Nagar
18.	24	UP	14	Bulandshahr (SC)
19.	24	UP	15	Aligarh
20.	24	UP	23	Badaun
21.	24	UP	24	Aonla
22.	24	UP	26	Pilibhit
23.	24	UP	27	Shahjahanpur (SC)
24.	24	UP	35	Lucknow
25.	24	UP	53	Barabanki (SC)
26.	24	UP	57	Kaiserganj
27.	24	UP	59	Gonda
28.	24	UP	60	Domariyaganj
29.	24	UP	65	Kushi Nagar
30.	25	WB	1	Coochbehar (SC)
31.	25	WB	6	Balurghat
32.	25	WB	17	Barasat
33.	25	WB	20	Mathurapur (SC)
34.	25	WB	21	Diamond Harbour
35.	25	WB	22	Jadavpur
36.	25	WB	26	Uluberia
37.	25	WB	38	Bardhaman Purba (SC)

Contd.

TABLE 3.12: *Contd.*

Sr. No.	State ID	State Name	PC ID	PC Name
38.	25	WB	41	Bolpur (SC)
39.	30	Delhi	1	Chandni Chowk
40.	30	Delhi	2	North-East Delhi
41.	33	Jharkhand	1	Rajmahal (ST)
42.	35	Uttarakhand	5	Hardwar

Note: SC or ST written in bracket against a constituency indicates that the constituency is reserved for SCs or STs.

TABLE 3.13: NEAR MAJORITY MUSLIM CONSTITUENCIES (MUSLIM VOTERS BETWEEN 30 AND 40 PER CENT)

Sr. No.	State ID	State Name	PC ID	PC Name
1.	3	Assam	6	Barpeta
2.	3	Assam	10	Nowgong
3.	4	Bihar	9	Araria
4.	4	Bihar	11	Katihar
5.	7	Haryana	9	Gurgaon
6.	9	J&K	5	Udhampur
7.	11	Kerala	1	Kasaragod
8.	11	Kerala	3	Vadakara
9.	11	Kerala	8	Palakkad
10.	24	UP	2	Kairana
11.	24	UP	4	Bijnor
12.	24	UP	5	Nagina (SC)
13.	24	UP	8	Sambhal
14.	24	UP	9	Amroha
15.	24	UP	25	Bareilly
16.	24	UP	56	Bahraich (SC)
17.	24	UP	58	Shrawasti
18.	25	WB	12	Krishnanagar
19.	25	WB	18	Basirhat
20.	25	WB	42	Birbhum
21.	36	Telangana	8	Secunderabad

Note: SC written in bracket against a constituency indicates that the constituency is reserved for SCs.

30 AND 40 PER CENT) SINCE 1967 ELECTION

Sr. No.	State	PC Name	Total Elections held since 1967	No. of Times Muslim Elected	Years in which Muslims Elected	Total Score	Percentage Performance
1.	Assam	Barpeta	14	10	Not elected in 1980, 1989, 1991, 1996	10/14	71.43
2.	Assam	Nowgong	14	1	1996	1/14	7.14
3.	Bihar	Araria	14	1	2014	1/14	7.14
4.	Bihar	Katihar	14	5	1980, 1991, 1996, 1998 & 2014	5/14	35.71
5.	Haryana	Gurgaon[1]	6	2	1967 & 1971	2/6	33.34
6.	J&K	Udhampur[2]	13	0	–	0/13	0.00
7.	Kerala	Kasaragod	14	0	–	0/14	0.00
8.	Kerala	Vadakara	14	0	–	0/14	0.00
9.	Kerala	Palakkad	14	0	–	0/14	0.00
10.	UP	Kairana	14	6	1967, 1971, 1984, 1996, 1999 & 2009	6/14	42.85
11.	UP	Bijnor	14	0	–	0/14	0.00
12.	UP	Sambhal	14	2	2009 & 2019	2/14	14.29
13.	UP	Amroha	14	4	1967, 1971, 1999 & 2019	4/14	28.57
14.	UP	Bareilly	14	2	1980 & 1984	2/14	14.29
15.	UP	Bahraich (SC)[3]	11	5	1980, 1984, 1989, 1998 & 2004	5/11	45.45
16.	UP	Shrawasti (Old)[4]	14	3	1989, 1998 & 1999	3/14	21.43
17.	WB	Krishnanagar	14	0	–	0/14	0.00
18.	WB	Bashirhat	14	6	1967, 1971, 1977, 2009, 2014, 2019	6/14	42.86
19.	WB	Birbhum[5]	3	0	–	0/3	0.00
20.	Telangana	Secundarabad	14	3	1967, 1971, & 1977	3/14	21.43
TOTAL			257	50	–	50/257	19.46

Performance of this set of constituencies: 19.46 per cent; Deprivation: 80.54 per cent.

Notes: 1 Gurgaon PC existed till 1977 and came into existence again in 2008.

2 Elections not held in Jammu & Kashmir due to Kashmir insurgency.

3 Reserved for SC in 2008.

4 Balrampur is the old name of Shravasti constituency, newly created in 2008.

5 Birbhum had been reserved for SC till 2004.

Committee that many of Muslim-dominated constituencies are reserved for SCs (Table 3.15).

As far as these constituencies (22) are concerned, they have performed very well with 198 Muslim members being elected out of 281 constituency elections. Thus, the overall performance is 70.46 per cent since 1967 and over 14 elections. The deprivation of Muslims in these constituencies amounts to 29.54 per cent. Dhubri, Baramulla, Srinagar, Malappuram, Murshidabad and Lakshadweep have given 100 per cent results in favour of Muslim

TABLE 3.15: MUSLIM-MAJORITY CONSTITUENCIES (VOTER PERCENTAGE FROM 40% AND ABOVE)

Sr. No.	*State ID*	*State Name*	*PC ID*	*PC Name*
1.	3	Assam	1	Karimganj (SC)
2.	3	Assam	4	Dhubri
3.	4	Bihar	10	Kishanganj
4.	9	J&K	1	Baramulla
5.	9	J&K	2	Srinagar
6.	9	J&K	3	Anantnag
7.	9	J&K	4	Ladakh
8.	11	Kerala	4	Wayanad
9.	11	Kerala	5	Kozhikode
10.	11	Kerala	6	Malappuram
11.	11	Kerala	7	Ponnani
12.	24	UP	1	Saharanpur
13.	24	UP	3	Muzaffarnagar
14.	24	UP	6	Moradabad
15.	24	UP	7	Rampur
16.	25	WB	5	Raiganj
17.	25	WB	7	Maldaha Uttar
18.	25	WB	8	Maldaha Dakshin
19.	25	WB	9	Jangipur
20.	25	WB	10	Baharampur
21.	25	WB	11	Murshidabad
22.	25	WB	19	Jaynagar (SC)
23.	31	Lakshadweep	1	Lakshadweep (ST)
24.	36	Telangana	9	Hyderabad

Note: SC or ST written in bracket against a constituency indicates that the constituency is reserved for SCs or STs.

candidates. Only in 1989, was a non-Muslim candidate Pyare Lal Handu elected on a NC ticket in Anantnag. In Kishanganj in Bihar, Lakhan Lal Kapoor of the PSP had won in 1967 as four Muslim candidates were in the contest and Muslim votes were divided. If we take the example of Kozhikode, Wayanad, Ponnani of Kerala, Jangipur, Baharampur, Raiganj and Maldaha Dakshin in West Bengal, it is observed that these constituencies could not return Muslims in a few elections when the mainstream political parties did not put up Muslim candidates. The example of Baharampur in West Bengal is worth mentioning here.

Baharampur is a Muslim-dominated PC with all its seven assembly segments being located in Murshidabad district, which is a Muslim-dominated area. It was created in 1951, but not a single Muslim candidate has gone to the Parliament since Muslims candidates were not fielded from this seat. From 1952 till 1984, it was represented by Tridib Chaudhuri of the Revolutionary Socialist Party (RSP). Promothes Mukherjee, also of the RSP, represented it from 1994 to 1999. The former Congress Lok Sabha leader Adhir Ranjan Chowdhury has been representing the constituency since 1999. This is a sharp illustration of how the non-nomination of Muslim candidates in this PC has not sent a single Muslim MP despite being heavily Muslim dominated. Rampur, Saharanpur, Muzaffarnagar, and Moradabad of UP have not returned Muslim candidates in few elections. In Moradabad, (40 per cent Muslim voters), Muslim candidates could not be returned in 1967, 1971, 1999, and 2014. In all the other 10 elections Muslim candidates won on different non-denominational secular party tickets. The arithmetic of votes polled shows that their loss in all the four elections was owing to the division of community votes among several Muslim candidates of various parties. The case of Saharanpur and Muzaffarnagar can be explained in the same way as both the constituencies returned 50 per cent Muslim MPs (Table 3.16).

Again, to buttress my argument, I analyse the returning of Muslim candidates from Rampur constituency, which has almost 50.57 per cent Muslim population as per the 2011 Census (Table 3.17).

TABLE 3.16: PERFORMANCE OF MUSLIM-MAJORITY CONSTITUENCIES SINCE 1967 ELECTION

Sr. No.	*State*	*Constituency*	*% of Muslim Voters*	*Total elections held since 1967*	*No. of Times Muslims Elected*	*Year in Which not Elected*	*Total Score*	*Percentage Performance*
1.	Assam	Dhubri	55.0	13*	13	–	13/13	100.00
2.	Bihar	Kishanganj	53.9	14	13	1967	13/14	92.36
3.	J&K	Baramulla	97.0	13**	13	–	13/13	100.00
4.	J&K	Srinagar	90.0	13	13	–	13/13	100.00
5.	J&K	Anantnag	95.5	13	12	1989	12/13	92.30
6.	J&K	Ladakh	46.0	13	4	Elected in 1989, 1998, 1999 & 2009	4/13	30.76
7.	Kerala	Wayanad[1]	42.7	3	2	2019	2/3	66.67
8.	Kerala	Kozhikode	40.8	14	3	Elected in 1967,1971 & 1977	3/14	21.43
9.	Kerala	Malapuram[2]	69.9	14	14	–	14/14	100.00
10.	Kerala	Ponnani	66.0	14	12	1967 & 1971	12/14	85.71
11.	UP	Saharanpur		14	7	1967,1971,1984, 1996, 1998,2009, 2014	7/14	50.00
12.	UP	Muzaffarnagar		14	7	1971, 1984, 1991, 1996, 1998, 2014 & 2019	7/14	50.00
13.	UP	Moradabad	40.0	14	10	1967,1971,1999 & 2014	10/14	71.43
14.	UP	Rampur	42.0	14	9	1977,1991,2004, 2009 & 2014	9/14	64.29
15.	WB	Raiganj	44.5	14	5	Elected in 1977, 1980,1984, 1989 & 2014	5/14	35.71

16.	WB	Maldaha Uttar[3]	45.4	3	2	2019	2/3	66.67
17.	WB	Maldaha Dakshin	57.1	14	11	1967, 1971&197711/14	78.57	
18.	WB	Jangipur	62.6	14	10	1977, 2004, 2009 & 2014	10/14	71.43
19.	WB	Baharampur	53.0	14	0	Not elected in any year	0/14	0.00
20.	WB	Murshidabad	70.1	14	14	–	14/14	100.00
21.	Lakshadweep	Lakshadweep	95.0	14	14	–	14/14	100.00
22.	Telangana	Hyderabad	48.0	14	10	1967, 1971, 1977 & 1980	10/14	71.43
Total		22 PCs		281	198	–	198/281	70.46

Performance of these constituencies: 70.46 per cent; Deprivation: 29.54 per cent.

Notes: [1] Wayanad was created a new constituency through delimitation in 2008.

[2] The constituency was formed after delimitation when the erstwhile 'Manjeri' constituency was renamed Malappuram in 2008.

[3] Maldaha was bifurcated through delimitation in 2008 and Maldaha Uttar and Maldaha Dakshin were created. For this study, Maldaha Dakshin is considered as Old Maldaha PC, while Maldaha Uttar a new one since 2009.

* Election was not held in Assam in 1989.

** Election was not held in J&K in 1991 due to insurgency.

TABLE 3.17: PERFORMANCE OF RAMPUR IN RETURNING MUSLIM CANDIDATES FROM 1952 TO 2019

Year	*Rampur PC*	*Elected*	*Party*
1952	Rampur-Bareilly	Muslim	INC
1957	Rampur	Muslim	INC
1962	Rampur	Muslim	INC
1967	Rampur	Muslim	SWA
1971	Rampur	Muslim	INC
1977	Rampur	R.K. Sharma	BLD
1980	Rampur	Muslim	INC(I)
1984	Rampur	Muslim	INC
1989	Rampur	Muslim	INC
1991	Rampur	R.K. Sharma	BJP
1996	Rampur	Muslim	INC
1998	Rampur	Muslim	BJP
1999	Rampur	Muslim	INC
2004	Rampur	Jaya Prada	SP
2009	Rampur	Jaya Prada	SP
2014	Rampur	Dr. Naipal Singh	BJP
2019	Rampur	Muslim	SP
TOTAL		12	

Source: https://eci.gov.in

On 12 occasions Muslims were returned, their performance is 70.59 per cent and deprivation 29.41 per cent. The case of 1977, 2004, and 2009 can be explained in terms of Muslims not being nominated as candidate from the dominant political parties, such as SP. The case of 1991 and 2014 when BJP candidates were returned can be explained in terms of the presence of more than one Muslim candidate supported by secular parties like the SP, BSP, and Congress. A similar study can be done for the other PCs of UP like Saharanpur, Muzaffarnagar and Moradabad. The study shows that if a Muslim candidate is supported by a dominant political party, Muslims decide to vote unitedly in his/her favour and prevent the division of votes, only he/she can win.

According to reports, some based on facts and some on speculation, there are many PCs where either Muslims can win or decide the winning candidate. Syed Zahid Ahmad, a consultant on Islamic finance, says that there are as many as 150 PCs, where

Muslim voters decide the result of the Lok Sabha elections therein. According to him, there are 45 such seats in UP, 17 in Bihar, 14 each in Maharashtra and West Bengal, 10 each in Kerala and Karnataka, seven each in AP (including Telangana) and Assam, six in Jharkhand, five each in Jammu & Kashmir and Gujarat and two each in Uttarakhand, Delhi, Rajasthan, MP, and Haryana, where only Muslims can decide the fate of a candidate (TCN: 5 February 2014). The Muslim community in Maharashtra is around 11 per cent of the state's total population and can play a decisive role in 14 out of the 48 PCs. In these PCs Muslims make up between 14 and 25 per cent of the total voters. These seats are: Dhule (24 per cent), Aurangabad (20 per cent), Bhiwandi (17 per cent), Nanded (over 15 per cent), Parbhani (over 16 per cent), Latur (over 15 per cent), Akola (over 19 per cent), Thane (over 15 per cent) and 6 seats of Mumbai (each over 18 per cent voters). Since 1998, the state sent only two Muslims MPs—Antulay in 2004 and Imtiyaj Jalil in 2019.

Muslims have traditionally backed the Congress-NCP combine, but these two parties have given negligible number of nominations to Muslims. In 2009, the Congress put up Antulay and the NCP Pansare; both lost. The Congress gave only one ticket to Hidayat Patel from Akola in both years, 2014 and 2019.

In West Bengal, Muslims constitute over 27 per cent of the state population and deserve 12 seats in the Lok Sabha. There are 10 PCs, where Muslims are in absolute majority and only they can win and 10 others, where the inclination of Muslim voters decide the fate of the candidate. Due to the BJP's repeated claims of implementing the National Register of Citizens (NRC) and the Citizenship Amendment Act (CAA), which go against the interest of Muslims, they generally vote for the secular parties like the TMC, Congress and CPI(M). However, these three parties have failed to nominate fair numbers of Muslim candidates. There are seats like Baharampur, Maldaha Uttar, Raiganj, etc., which are Muslim-dominated and deserve to be represented by Muslims.

Syed Ali Mujtaba, a Chennai-based journalist says that out of the overall 543 Lok Sabha seats, Muslims can actually influence 196 seats. Experts have identified that out of 80 seats in UP, Muslims can actually influence 54 seats. These are: in Bihar 29 out of

40, in West Bengal 28 out of 42, in Karnataka 15 out of 28, in Kerala 14 out of 20, in Maharashtra 13 out of 48, in AP (including Telangana) 12 out of 42, in Assam 9 out of 14, in Gujarat 6 out of 26 and in Rajasthan 6 out of 25 seats. As a matter of fact, Muslims have a significant influence over 10 states out of the total 28 in India. In the Lok Sabha elections, the contesting sites for Muslims are UP, Bihar and West Bengal where Muslims account for 20 per cent of the overall population. Out of 162 seats in these states, there are 111 seats where Muslims can make a significant impact. The other states that are equally important to Muslims are: AP, Telangana, Karnataka, Kerala, Assam and Maharashtra. Combining these two groups of states, Muslims can make significant impact altogether in 165 PCs. Mujtaba observes that the Muslim vote has been the most effective where it is around 10 per cent of the electorates; big enough to sway the result in a multi-cornered contest by choosing a single candidate. However, where Muslim presence is 20 per cent and above, their votes have been mostly ineffective because the votes are divided among several Muslim candidates. In such constituencies, there is often counter-polarization of Hindu votes that ensures victory of a non-Muslim candidate. In this situation the leadership must convey to Muslims that where they are over 20 per cent they must vote for a single candidate, even if there are various Muslim candidates.[4]

NOMINATION OF MUSLIMS

Political scientists have enumerated multiple reasons for the 'representation deficit' of Muslims, under-nomination in elections being the most important among them. Under-nomination by national parties like the Congress, BJP, CPI, CPI(M), etc., and also by the OBC based parties and various regional parties within their regional stronghold is the main reason for their under-representation. In most of the states—including Muslim-majority Jammu & Kashmir—the percentage of Muslim candidates is far below the share of Muslims in the general population. In Assam, where Muslims constituted 31 per cent of the population, they were 19 per cent; in UP, where they were 18.5 per cent, they had

11 per cent of candidates; a similar proportion was seen in Bihar, where Muslims were 16.5 per cent of the population (2009 General Elections). More importantly, in most of the states, a majority of the Muslim candidates are independents. In the 2009 elections these were the share of independents: Maharashtra, 52 per cent, Gujarat and MP, 54 per cent each, Haryana, 66 and Rajasthan, 80 per cent. This reflects the reluctance of the parties, specially national parties, to nominate Muslim candidates.[5]

The Congress contested all elections from 1952 to 2019, but provided a low number of nominations to Muslims (6.83 per cent). During 17 elections, it gave tickets to 555 Muslims out of its total of 8,131 and 248 Muslims were elected. This puts the ratio of total elected to total nominated at almost 1:2. The nomination of Muslims peaked at 8.33 per cent in 1980. The Congress' average nomination of Muslims during 1952-71 was 5.34 per cent, 7.83 per cent during 1977-91 and 7.14 per cent during 1996-2004. It was 7.32 per cent during 2009-19. As per Table 3.18, with some exceptions, the number of Muslims elected is proportional to the number of tickets given by the Congress. From 2009 till 2019, the number of Muslims elected on Congress tickets has reduced substantially which is due to the onset of the shrinking base in the northern states, emergence of BJP and strong mobilization of Hindu identity. Iqbal A. Ansari points out,

> This pattern establishes the conclusion that given favourable political climate for a national secular party like the Congress in the common national domain, and there being no strong Hindu identity mobilization, the number of Muslim members elected will largely depend on the number of candidates nominated by the party though their chances of success will be more favourable in constituencies having fair to sizeable percentage of Muslim voters.[6]

The BJP's ideology of Muslim exclusion and its deliberate attempt to deprive them of their socio-political rights gets reflected in its 1.08 per cent nomination. Since 1952 till 2019, the BJP/BJS out of its total 4,622 nominations gave only 50 tickets to Muslims of which only four could get elected. In 2009, 2014 and 2019, five, seven and six tickets respectively were given from the constituencies where chance of their victory was pathetically low.

In 2014 and 2019, when Narendra Modi returned to power with a thumping majority, there was not a single Muslim MP in the ruling party, a sad state for Indian democracy. The CPI and CPI(M) are also national parties which have contested almost all Lok Sabha elections and given fair number of tickets to Muslims. The CPI gave 5.06 per cent nomination which is far below the share of Muslims in population. So far, only five have reached the Lok Sabha on CPI tickets and since 1971 no Muslim could get elected on its ticket. On the contrary CPI(M) has given 10.02 per cent of its nomination to Muslims, and 41 of them have been elected; mostly from Kerala and West Bengal, especially from the latter (Table 3.18).

Nominations by the PSP from 1957 to 1971 had been 5.2 per cent of which only three Muslims could get elected. This shows it had little appeal to Muslim voters. Nomination by the Janata Party formations (JP, JNP, BLD, etc.) from 1977 till 2004 was 5.44 per cent only. In 1977, when the party enjoyed popularity among Muslims only 16 got elected out of total nominations of 22. Later on, only one Muslim was elected in 1984 out of a total nominations of 15. In subsequent elections the Janata Party got eclipsed under the second coming of the Congress (1980-4) and later by its rechristened Janata Dal (1989) and its proliferations. The Janata Dal which was initially popular amongst Muslims, nominated 9.03 per cent Muslim candidates in four elections from 1989 till 1998. This shows the party nominated a fair number of Muslims, slightly lower than their due share. During these four elections 22 Muslims were elected bringing the success ratio to almost 1:4 (Table 3.19).

The nomination of Muslims by the JD formations (RJD, JDU, JDS, LJP and RLD) since 1998 till 2019 has amounted to 13.13 per cent, which is almost proportionate to population. The highest nomination of 17.36 per cent came from the RJD with nine Muslims getting elected, all from Bihar. The JDU, JDS and LJP nominated 9.54, 13.49 and 12.93 per cent candidates respectively, while the RLD has not given ticket to any Muslim. The success rate of the JDU, JDS and LJP has been poor; not a single Muslim got elected on the JDS ticket. Not only the JD, but its other

TABLE 3.18: NOMINATION OF MUSLIMS IN GENERAL ELECTIONS BY INC (INCI), BJP (BJS), CPI AND CPI(M)

		INC (INCI)				*BJP (BJS)*				*CPI*				*CPI(M)*			
Election	Year	Total Nomination	Muslims Nominated	% of Total	Muslims Elected	Total Nomination	Muslims Nominated	% of Total	Muslims Elected	Total Nomination	Muslims Nominated	% of Total	Muslims Elected	Total Nomination	Muslims Nominated	% of Total	Muslims Elected
I	1952	479	21	4.38	19	94	0	0.00	0	49	1	2.04	0	–	–	–	–
II	1957	490	27	5.51	19	130	0	0.00	0	110	7	6.36	1	–	–	–	–
III	1962	488	28	5.74	18	196	0	0.00	0	137	8	5.84	1	–	–	–	–
IV	1967	516	29	5.62	13	251	1	0.40	0	106	7	6.60	2	62	1	1.61	1
V	1971	441	24	5.44	21	160	1	0.63	0	87	6	6.90	1	85	3	3.53	2
VI	1977	492	37	7.52	14	–	–	–	–	91	6	6.59	0	53	5	9.43	0
VII	1980	492	41	8.33	32	–	–	–	–	48	1	2.03	0	63	6	9.52	5
VIII	1984	517	41	7.93	32	229	3	1.31	0	66	1	1.52	0	64	6	9.38	4
IX	1989	510	37	7.26	12	226	1	0.44	1	50	4	8.00	0	64	6	9.38	4
X	1991	505	39	7.72	12	477	4	0.84	0	42	1	2.33	0	63	6	9.52	4
XI	1996	529	39	7.37	12	471	1	0.21	0	43	2	4.65	0	75	9	12.00	3
XII	1998	477	32	6.71	7	388	7	2.07	1	58	1	1.72	0	71	6	8.45	4
XIII	1999	453	33	7.29	10	339	5	1.48	1	54	1	1.85	0	72	11	15.28	5
XIV	2004	417	30	7.19	10	364	9	2.47	0	34	1	2.94	0	69	11	15.94	5
XV	2009	439	30	6.83	10	433	5	1.15	1	56	6	10.71	0	82	8	9.76	1
XVI	2014	464	35	7.54	4	428	7	1.64	0	67	2	2.98	0	104	14	13.46	2
XVII	2019	422	32	7.58	3	436	6	1.38	0	49	3	6.12	0	81	9	11.11	1
TOTAL		8,131	555	6.83	248	4,622	50	1.08	4	1,147	58	5.06	5	1,008	101	10.02	41

Sources: Iqbal A. Ansari, *Political Representation of Muslims in India: 1952-2004* and General Election results of 2009, 2014 and 2019.

TABLE 3.19: NOMINATION OF MUSLIMS IN GENERAL ELECTIONS BY PSP, JP FORMATIONS AND JD

		PSP				*JP Formations*				*Janta Dal (JD)*			
Election	Year	Total Nomination	Muslims Nominate	% of Total	Muslims Elected	Total Nomination	Muslims Nominate	% of Total	Muslims Elected	Total Nomination	Muslims Nominate	% of Total	Muslims Elected
II	1957	189	7	3.70	2								
III	1962	168	9	5.36	0								
IV	1967	109	7	6.42	1								
V	1971	63	5	7.94	0								
VI	1977					405	22	5.43	16				
VII	1980					432	21	4.86	0				
VIII	1984					219	15	6.84	1				
IX	1989					156	7	4.49	0	243	18	7.41	9
X	1991					–	–	–	–	311	30	9.65	8
XI	1996					102	5	4.90	0	196	20	10.20	5
XII	1998					–	–	–	–	191	17	3.90	0
XIII	1999					26	3	11.54	0				
XIV	2004					58	3	5.17	0				
TOTAL		529	28	5.29	3	1,398	76	4.80	17	941	85	9.03	22

Source: Iqbal A. Ansari, *Political Representation of Muslims in India: 1952-2004* and https://eci.gov.in

formations have enjoyed considerable support among Muslims. The community was inclined to these parties as they not only ensured their security but also provided respectable share in politics. These formations have also realized that the claim of secularism would not be effective by simply wooing Muslim voters with promises related to their security, but by also ensuring their equitable share in elected bodies (Table 3.20).

The BSP nominated 12.39 per cent Muslims from 1989 to 2019, whereas the SP did 18.12 per cent from 1996 to 2019. The BSP, an avowedly Dalit party, has good record of nominating Muslims for LS elections. So far 17 Muslims got elected on its ticket which means success ratio is almost 1:19. The SP which came into existence by breaking away from the Janata Dal, has also nominated a good number of Muslims, close to their due share in UP. In 1999 the nomination of Muslims by SP at 21.19 per cent reached the highest peak of any party. So far 19 Muslims have been elected and thus the success rate is almost 1:10 (Table 3.21).

The regional parties, mostly secular in nature and popular among Muslims, have not given Muslims a fair share in party nominations. Ten regional parties mentioned in Table 3.22(A) and 3.22(B) gave only 93 tickets in three elections which is 6.89 per cent. The Biju Janata Dal (BJD) gave 60 tickets out of which only one ticket to Muslims. Shiv Sena and Akali gave respectively 68 and 30 tickets, with no ticket to Muslims. If these three parties are included then the share of Muslim nomination for 13 parties drops to 6.23 per cent. The NCP and TMC have given a good number of tickets, which is 8.82 and 13.77 per cent respectively. Other parties have performed dismally in this regard including the TMC, despite the population of Muslims in West Bengal being 27 per cent. So far, only 16 Muslims have been elected on tickets of regional parties. Only the NCP, TMC, DMK, and AIADMK have contributed to winning candidates while rest of the parties did not sending a single Muslim to the Lok Sabha. One noticeable factor is that in 2019 most of the regional parties did not give tickets to Muslims indicating the growing Hindu mobilisation and resultant margi-nalization of Muslims in Indian politics.

TABLE 3.20: NOMINATION OF MUSLIMS IN GENERAL ELECTIONS BY JD FORMATIONS

		RJD				*JDU*				*JD (S)*				*LJP*				*RLD*			
Election	Year	Total Nomination	Muslims Nominated	% of Total	Muslims Elected	Total Nomination	Muslims Nominated	% of Total	Muslims Elected	Total Nomination	Muslims Nominated	% of Total	Muslims Elected	Total Nomination	Muslims Nominated	% of Total	Muslims Elected	Total Nomination	Muslims Nominated	% of Total	Muslims Elected
XII	1998	114	18	15.79	3																
XIII	1999	61	10	16.39	2	60	4	6.67	0	96	17	17.71	0								
XIV	2004	41	5	12.19	3	73	6	8.22	1	43	4	9.30	0								
XV	2009	45	10	22.22	0	55	5	9.10	1	33	7	21.22	0	103	13	12.62	0	8	0	0.00	0
XVI	2014	29	6	20.69	1	92	11	11.96	0	34	1	2.94	0	7	1	14.29	1	10	0	0.00	0
XVI	2019	21	5	23.80	0	24	3	1.25	0	9	0	0.00	0	6	1	16.67	1	3	0	0.00	0
TOTAL		311	54	1,736	9	304	29	954	2	215	29	1.349	0	116	15	12.93	2	21	0	0.00	0

Sources: General Election results for 2009, 2014 and 2019 & Iqbal A. Ansari, *Political Representation of Muslims in India: 1952-2004.*

TABLE 3.21: NOMINATION OF MUSLIMS IN GENERAL ELECTIONS BY BSP AND SP

		BSP				*SP*			
Election	*Year*	*Total Nomination*	*Muslims Nominated*	*% of Total*	*Muslims Elected*	*Total Nomination*	*Muslims Nominated*	*% of Total*	*Muslims Elected*
IX	1989	245	25	10.20	0				
X	1991	243	16	6.58	0				
XI	1996	210	27	12.86	1	111	22	19.82	4
XII	1998	251	23	9.16	2	166	25	15.06	3
XIII	1999	225	28	12.44	3	151	32	21.19	2
XIV	2004	435	52	11.95	4	237	38	16.03	7
XV	2009	499	61	12.22	4	193	35	18.13	0
XVI	2014	501	57	11.38	0	197	40	20.30	0
XVII	2019	380	38	10.0	3	49	8	16.33	3
TOTAL		2,989	327	12.39	17	1,104	200	18.12	19

Source: Iqbal A. Ansari, *Political Representation of Muslims in India: 1952-2004* and https://eci.gov.in

TABLE 3.22(A): NOMINATION OF MUSLIMS IN GENERAL ELECTIONS BY REGIONAL PARTIES: 2009, 2014 AND 2019 ELECTIONS

		AAP				*CPI (ML)L*				*NCP*				*TMC*				*JMM*			
Election	Year	Total Nomination	Muslims Nominated	% of Total	Muslims Elected	Total Nomination	Muslims Nominated	% of Total	Muslims Elected	Total Nomination	Muslims Nominated	% of Total	Muslims Elected	Total Nomination	Muslims Nominated	% of Total	Muslims Elected	Total Nomination	Muslims Nominated	% of Total	Muslims Elected
XV	2009					80	2	2.50	0	69	6	8.70	0	30	3	10.00	2	42	2	4.76	0
XVI	2014	427	39	9.13	0	81	3	3.70	0	35	3	8.57	2	60	9	15.00	4	21	1	4.76	0
XVI	2019	35	1	2.86	0	21	0	0.00	0	32	3	9.38	1	48	7	14.58	5	13	0	0.00	0
TOTAL		462	40	8.66	0	182	5	2.75	0	136	12	8.82	3	138	19	13.77	11	76	3	3.95	0

Source: General Election results for 2009, 2014 and 2019.

TABLE 3.22(B): NOMINATION OF MUSLIMS IN GENERAL ELECTIONS BY REGIONAL PARTIES: 2009, 2014 AND 2019 ELECTIONS

		TRS				*TDP*				*YSRCP*				*DMK*				*AIADMK*			
Election	Year	Total Nomination	Muslims Nominated	% of Total	Muslims Elected	Total Nomination	Muslims Nominated	% of Total	Muslims Elected	Total Nomination	Muslims Nominated	% of Total	Muslims Elected	Total Nomination	Muslims Nominated	% of Total	Muslims Elected	Total Nomination	Muslims Nominated	% of Total	Muslims Elected
XV	2009	9	2	22.22	0	30	2	6.66	0	–	–	–	–	22	1	4.54	1	23	1	4.35	0
XVI	2014	17	1	5.88	0	30	1	3.33	0	38	3	7.89	0	35	2	8.69	0	40	1	2.50	1
XVI	2019	17	0	0	0	25	0	0	0	25	0	0	0	23	0	0	0	22	0	0.00	0
TOTAL		43	3	6.98	0	85	3	3.53	0	63	3	4.76	0	80	3	3.75	1	85	2	2.35	1

Source: General Election results for 2009, 2014 and 2019.

The Muslim base parties like the AIMIM, AIUDF, IUML, NC and PDP which operate in Muslim-dominated areas/regions and enjoy considerable support among Muslims, have been giving a majority of their tickets to them. During the last three elections these five parties have jointly given 76.15 per cent of tickets to Muslims. The NC has given all its tickets and the IUML 91.2 per cent to Muslims. In three elections, 24 Muslim candidates were elected from these parties, thus, their success ratio was as high as 2:7. These parties especially the AIMIM, AIUDF and IUML have been reaching out to other deprived groups such as the SCs, STs and OBCs and other non-Muslim group to expand their base (Table 3.23).

Political scientists have argued that the community's deprivation in Parliament is due to their low nomination. If one excludes independent candidates, the percentage of Muslim candidates in all elections and by all parties has been 7.4 per cent. The national parties like the Congress, BJP, CPI, etc., regional and the OBC based parties (with some exceptions) have not given due share in nominations. It is only the small Muslim base parties like the AIUDF, AIMIM, IUML, NC, PDP and Peace Party that have been nominating Muslims. But they are not in a position to win many seats. Some regional parties, such as the SP, CPI(M), BSP, RJD and TMC tend to distribute a good number of tickets to Muslim, but the catch is that with some exceptions, a majority of these seats are outside their regional strongholds. For example, in 2014 the SP lined up six Muslim candidates in Gujarat. The TMC, had fielded 23 Muslims out of its total of 130 in 2014, that is, 17 per cent of the total but the number in WB was only five despite greater chances of victory there. It is distressing to note that Muslims are given tickets by regional parties outside their regional strongholds with the intention of garnering Muslim votes in order to boost their party's status to a national party.[7] Basically, these parties wish to get status of 'national party' with the help of Muslim votes.

REASONS FOR THE REPRESENTATIONAL DEFICIT

Political scientists and experts on Muslim issues point out several reasons for 'representation deficits' of Muslims in India, a majority

TABLE 3.23: NOMINATION OF MUSLIMS IN GENERAL ELECTIONS BY MUSLIM BASE PARTIES: 2009, 2014 AND 2019 ELECTIONS

		AIMIM				*AIUDF*				*IUML*				*NC*				*PDP*			
Election	Year	Total Nomination	Muslims Nominated	% of Total	Muslims Elected	Total Nomination	Muslims Nominated	% of Total	Muslims Elected	Total Nomination	Muslims Nominated	% of Total	Muslims Elected	Total Nomination	Muslims Nominated	% of Total	Muslims Elected	Total Nomination	Muslims Nominated	% of Total	Muslims Elected
XV	2009	1	1	100.0	1	22	14	63.6	1	18	17	94.4	2	3	3	100.0	3	6	4	66.7	0
XV	2014	5	1	20.0	1	18	11	61.1	2	14	12	85.7	2	3	3	100.0	0	5	4	80.0	3
XVI	2019	3	3	100.0	2	3	2	66.7	1	2	0	100.0	3	3	3	100.0	3	3	3	100.0	3
TOTAL		9	5	55.6	4	43	27	62.8	4	34	31	91.18	7	9	9	100.0	6	14	11	78.6	3

Source: Results for General Elections of 2009, 2014 and 2019.

of which are of administrative nature that can be resolved by the central government while some are social and geographical in nature. These causes/factors are discussed here in brief to know why Muslims are so poorly represented in Lok Sabha.

Under-nomination

The shrinking number of Muslims in Lok Sabha is mainly due to under-nomination or less nomination as candidate during general elections. National, regional, OBC or Dalit centric parties from across the political spectrum—whether right, left and centre—whether professing secular polity or not—have been quite reluctant to give ticket to Muslims. National parties like the Congress, CPI, etc., have maintained the average nomination of 6 to 7 per cent. The BJP which professes exclusionary politics towards Muslims has given around 1 per cent tickets, mainly in areas where it had little chances of winning. Regional and OBC base parties offer a good number of tickets to Muslims, but mainly in the areas which fall out of their regional strongholds.

The Presidential Order of 1950

The Constitution (Scheduled Castes) Order, 1950 is also responsible for pitiable Muslim representation. This was issued by the President on 10 August 1950, under Article 341 of the Constitution, in criminal violation of the secular Constitution of India, as it restricted the benefit of reservation (in job and politics) to Hindus only. It has been amended twice in 1956 and 1990 to include Dalit castes belonging to Sikh and Buddhist religions respectively. Thus, Dalits of Hindu, Sikh and Buddhist religions can avail benefits of reservation, while Dalit castes belonging to Islam and Christianity are denied of it. As per the recent Delimitation Commission, 84 seats are reserved for SCs, 47 for STs and 412 for General. This means Dalit castes of Muslims (along with Christians) are not allowed to contest 84 Lok Sabha seats reserved for SCs. If this order is made religion-neutral and Dalits of Muslims and Christians are included in it, Muslims would be able to contest from these seats (or from higher seats if the base of reservation gets expanded) which would increase their seats in the Lok Sabha by at least 12 (in commensurate with presence of Dalits in Muslims).

One more point to be noted here is that the Constitution (Scheduled Tribe) Order, 1950 was passed by the President of India, under Article 342 of the Constitution. Unlike the Constitution (SC) Order, 1950, the Order for STs is religion-neutral. This means STs of Muslims are also given reservation (in job and politics). However, barring Lakshadweep, Muslims do not contest LS elections from any other constituency reserved for ST communities. There are several reasons for this: A majority of Muslim castes who have qualified as ST have not been declared STs; mainstream parties do not give tickets to ST Muslims because of low share in voters and; non-Muslim voters do not support ST Muslim candidates. Hence, Muslims can only contest 412 seats out of total 543 seats. This way for Muslim, the 'starting line' is much behind than others when the race begins.

Dalits irrespective of all religions and STs have been subjected to atrocities down the years under the Varnashram Dharma. They have been denied social, economic and other rights till India became independent in 1947. Both Dalits and Tribals must be given reservation to improve their condition and compensate the historical injustices committed against them. However, if the SC Order of 1950 is amended suitably to include Dalits belonging to Islam and Christianity and ST Order of 1950 is implemented properly, Muslims can be in position to increase their share in Lok Sabha.

Notification of Reserved Constituencies

The Sachar Committee Report (SCR) pointed out that during its consultation with the public many alleged that political participation was denied to Muslims through variety of mechanisms, mainly through the reservation of Muslim-dominated constituencies for SCs. The Committee says, 'Attention of the Committee was drawn to the issue of Muslim concentration assembly constituencies being declared as "reserved" constituencies where only SC candidates can contest elections. By this move, it was argued that

Muslims are being systematically denied political participation.' The Committee could not analyse the issue of reserved PCs, but it did analyse the issue of assembly constituencies reserved for SCs in three states of UP, Bihar and West Bengal. These states had relatively a large share of the Muslim population in India. The analysis indicated that constituencies which had been declared reserved for SCs by the Delimitation Commission in these states were by and large those constituencies, where Muslims lived in greater numbers often more than 50 per cent as well as their proportion in the population was higher than that of SCs. On the other hand, there were quite a large number of other constituencies within the respective states, where the share of SCs was large, often closer to or even more than half but those were declared as 'un-reserved'. This is seen as discriminatory in nature and intended effort by the Delimitation Commission to cut the chances of Muslims of being elected to democratic institutions. Hence, the constituencies from where Muslim candidates have better chance to win are the ones where they cannot even contest. The Committee pointed out this anomaly and the issue had been followed up by Muslim NGOs especially by the Zakat Foundation of India. Sadly, the government has not set up any fresh delimitation commission to correct the issue. This issue has been fully discussed in the community which hopes that the next delimitation commission, which is due in coming few years, may consider the issue and give justice to it.

Non-Muslim Voters do not Support Muslim Candidates

There are only few seats (about 15), where Muslims are in absolute majority and can decide the winner on their own. To maintain a due share in Lok Sabha, they must take support of other segments. The result of a Muslim candidate is contingent on his capacity to rally the support of non-Muslim voters. One may hypothesize that in the context of polarization in the majority community, Muslim candidates fail to win elections. Muslim voters support even non-Muslim candidates over their own to preserve secularism and strengthen democracy. But non-Muslims, especially the majority of Hindu OBCs and UCHs do not support Muslim candidates even though they deserve to be elected. It is all due to polarization and consolidation of Hindu voters on communal lines though some Dalits, Tribals and other minorities, especially Christians, Sikhs and Buddhist support Muslim candidates. In such a situation it becomes difficult for them to get elected. This fact is also cited by secular parties, while denying tickets to deserving Muslims.

BJP's Communal and Exclusionary Politics

The BJP openly portrays itself as anti-Muslim and has been against all forms of their empowerment. By depriving them of a just and equitable share in education, economy and politics, the party intends to push them into becoming second class citizens. So far, it has given only 50 Lok Sabha tickets to Muslims out of a total of 4,622, which is just 1.08 per cent and only four of these managed to get elected. In the 2014 and 2019 elections, the party gave seven tickets out of a total of 428 and six out of 436 respectively, which is far below the national average of about 7 per cent. It gives tickets to Muslims in those PCs where their chances of winning are extremely low. Moreover, the party fields its Muslim candidates in such a manner that they disturb the chances of established and the most suitable Muslim candidates fielded by other parties. It normally fields candidates in Kashmir regions of Jammu & Kashmir, West Bengal, Bihar, Lakshadweep, etc. Another strategy employed by the party is communalization of political space to consolidate the Hindu voters. The BJP, before or during the election, rakes up the fake or imaginary issues of cow slaughter, religious conversion, 'Love Jihad' and the slogan of *Hindu khatre mein hain* (Hindus are in danger!). Due to this the entire political situation gets communalized and Hindu voters are consolidated around non-developmental issues and also against Muslims. In this situation, it becomes difficult for a Muslim candidate to get Hindu votes and win the elections. Even communal tensions are deliberately created to consolidate Hindu votes. In polarized situation even the secular parties deny tickets citing consolidation of Hindu votes and their inability to win elections.

Absence of a Legal/Constitutional or Government Safeguards

A participatory democracy requires fairer participation of all socio-religious and ethnic groups and equitable share in legislative bodies. When India started its democratic journey, all segments of society-religious minorities, the poor, deprived sections and other disadvantageous groups—hoped that they would be properly represented in politics and governance. However, the functioning of our democracy presents a very sad picture. While some groups are disproportionately represented in legislatures, the deprived groups—mainly Muslims—have been facing a huge political deprivation. There is no set process to review the working of democracy vis-à-vis representation of minorities and other deprived sections. The report of the National Commission to Review the Working of the Constitution (NCRWC) of 2002, annual reports of National Commission for Minorities (NCM), the Law Commission Report (May 1999), reports published by the ECI, etc., are some reports which have highlighted the political deprivation of Muslims. However, there is no legal or constitutional provisions to correct this issue. The successive central governments have not made any attempt to address the political marginalization of deprived groups.

The FPTP system has drastic impact upon the representation of Indian Muslims. First, the candidate who wins in a constituency hardly gets 50 per cent polled votes. In some cases in multi-concerned contest a winning candidate gets even 30 per cent of votes. This means the system has been failing to provide a popular government. This way governments in India are being formed with less than 50 per cent of the vote share. Second, the system has failed to provide a proper representation to minorities particularly Muslims. Alternative systems, such as the PR system or the preferential voting system/ranked choice voting system have potential to force political parties to be more inclusive. It will ensure the proper representation of all segments of society. However, the government has shown no inclination to adopt either PR or other alternative electoral system.

CONCLUSION

The average Muslim representation in the Lok Sabha at 5.78 per cent, has been significantly less than their share in population. Except in 1980 and 1984, when the percentage share were 9.26 and 8.48 respectively, their share has been very low in all other years. Since 1989, when the share was 6.24 per cent, we have been witnessing a gradual decline reaching its lowest level of 4.42 per cent in 2014. Under-nomination of Muslims by all parties seems to be the main reason behind this. Political scientists have been arguing that communalization of voters leading to Muslims not getting non-Muslim votes is also a reason. Low winnability of Muslim candidates and fear of consolidation of Hindu votes is the reason for parties not offering proper share to Muslims in nominations. Since independence, Muslims have largely backed secular parties like the Congress, SP, BSP, RJD, TMC, etc. But while these parties have talked about protecting Muslim interest, they have been less forthcoming in giving due representation. Since 2014, we have been witnessing a strange and grave situation. India's electoral politics seems to be confronted with new sets of challenges posed by the rise of majoratarian nationalism. With its exponential rise in 2014, it has changed the trajectory for Muslims and made them electorally vulnerable. According to political scientist Gilles Verniers, the anti-Muslim sentiments stoked by the BJP have led to the deprivation of tickets for Muslim candidates even outside the BJP. Fear of being tagged 'anti-Hindu' has forced the Congress and other parties including the regional ones to field less and less number of Muslim candidates.[8] Political scientist Christophe Jaffrelot in his *Majoritarian State: How Hindu Nationalism is Changing India* writes that 'the formation of Hindu vote bank by the BJP, which in particular aimed to sideline minorities in the political arena, prompted other parties as well no longer to nominate Muslim candidate, except in areas with high Muslim concentration'.[9] Due to hyper-nationalism and triumph of Hindu right-wing populism, even the national secular and regional parties have oriented themselves and have been side-lining Muslim candidates given the compulsion of polarization. Starting with the 2014 general elections, political parties including Muslim-friendly ones are showing increasing disinclination to engage with the Muslim community. It is disturbing to note that even those political parties whose success depends on minority votes are denying tickets to eligible Muslim candidates for fear of being tagged anti-Hindu; thus robbing the largest minority community of its due right to take part in national policy making as equal citizen.

Back in 2006, the SCR documented how the under representation of Muslims in India's governance structure had harmed the entire community on the social, economic and educational fronts. Moreover, their gradual political isolation poses a greater challenge to the world's largest democracy. Muslims are the second largest religious groups and their political isolation is not good for our democracy in the interest of the nation. Certain constitutional, legislative or administrative measures to improve the political participation of Muslims must be adopted in the interest of the nation.

NOTES

1. *Report of the NCRWC*, 2002, Chapter 10, 'The Pace of Socio-Economic Change and Development', para 10.11.2 (b).
2. *Inquilab*, Mumbai, 18 May 2014.
3. *The Indian Express*, Pune, 24 May 2019.
4. http://www.ummid.com/news/2014/March/09.03.2014/muslim-factor-in-ls-polls.html
5. http://www.ummid.com/news/May/16.05.2009/looking-for-the-muslim-mp.html
6. Iqbal A. Ansari, *Political Representation of Muslims in India: 1952-2004*, New Delhi: Manak Publications, p. 96.

CHAPTER 4

Representation in State Assemblies

No Sufficient Voice to Influence State Government Policies

In my book, *Denial and Deprivation: Indian Muslims after the Sachar Committee and Rangnath Mishra Commission Reports*, I assessed the community's status on various social, economic, educational and other indicators and the tokenistic attitude of the governments towards it. Time and again, this form of superficial attempts to deal with the community's issues have only paid lip service to the plight of the Muslims in India. For instance, the Maharashtra government set up the Mehmoodur Rahman Committee to study the condition of the Muslim community in the state in 2008. It was tasked with studying the educational, social and economic backwardness of Muslims and suggesting measures to improve their condition. The Committee advocated reservation for Muslims in the state cabinet. It says,

> A lot of times political parties have got away by giving token representation to Muslims. The absence of Muslims in positions to influence policies is one of the reasons for their present situation. If it wants to uplift the community, the government should give proportional representation to Muslims in the cabinet.[1]

The Committee submitted its report in October 2013 to then Chief Minister Prithviraj Chavan, who promised to consider its recommendations. The report was neither made public nor presented in the assembly for discussion.

One of the key reasons why the community's plight can be ignored so wilfully is its poor representation in state legislative assemblies. Central government schemes are generally implemented by state departments. Similarly, law and order and security issues are also the domain of states. This is, indeed, damaging socio-economic, educational and security conditions as most of the subjects of governance are in hands of states.

In this chapter I will assess the presence of Muslim MLAs, or rather their absence, in the state legislative assemblies, present a brief analysis of their deprivation, nomination by political parties and presence of Muslim-dominated assembly constituencies.

PRESENCE IN STATE ASSEMBLIES

Except for Jammu & Kashmir, Muslims are poorly represented in all other states. Out of a total of 4,123 MLAs in all the 31 legislative assemblies (29 states and two UTs), only 296 are Muslims, i.e. just 7.18 per cent of the total. However, Muslims constitute 14.24 per cent of the total population in these states.

As per the population share, Muslims deserve 587 MLAs on the national level and thus they face 49.57 per cent deprivation. There is not a single Muslim MLA in the 147-member Odisha Assembly. Same situation is also mirrored in Arunachal Pradesh, Goa, Himachal Pradesh, Mizoram and Sikkim. The extent of underrepresentation in other assemblies is colossal. In major states such as Andhra Pradesh, Bihar, Chhattisgarh, Gujarat, Jharkhand, Karnataka, Madhya Pradesh, Maharashtra, Punjab, Rajasthan, Uttarakhand, and Delhi, the number of Muslim MLAs is meagre compared to their share in the state's population. There are just two Muslim MLAs in the 230-member MP, one in the 90-member Chhattisgarh and three in the 70-member Uttarakhand assemblies, respectively (Table 4.1). Apart from Jammu & Kashmir the only Muslim-majority state in India, representation of Muslims is a little better in Assam, Bihar, Kerala, Uttar Pradesh and West Bengal, though not commensurate with their population share.

TABLE 4.1: REPRESENTATION OF MUSLIMS IN STATE ASSEMBLIES AND STATE CABINETS

S. No.	*States/UTs*	*MLAs*			*% of Muslims in Population**	*Expected Muslim MLAs*	*% Deprivation*	*Ministers in Cabinet*	
		Total	*Muslim*	*% of Muslim*				*Total*	*Muslim*
1.	Andhra Pradesh	175	4	2.29	7.32	13	69.23	26	1
2.	Arunachal Pradesh	60	0	0.00	1.95	1	100.00	12	0
3.	Assam	126	31	24.60	34.22	43	27.90	14	0
4.	Bihar	243	19	7.82	16.87	41	53.66	33	5
5.	Chhattisgarh	90	1	1.12	2.01	2	50.00	13	1
6.	Goa	40	0	0.00	8.63	3	100.00	12	0
7.	Gujarat	182	1	0.55	9.67	17	94.12	19	0
8.	Haryana	90	3	3.34	7.02	6	50.00	12	0
9.	Himachal Pradesh	68	0	0.00	2.18	2	100.00	9	0
10.	J&K**	90	62	68.89	68.31	61	0.00	23	14
11.	Jharkhand	81	4	4.94	14.53	12	66.67	11	2
12.	Karnataka	224	9	4.02	12.92	29	68.97	34	2
13.	Kerala	140	33	23.57	26.56	37	10.81	21	3
14.	Madhya Pradesh	230	2	0.87	6.57	15	86.67	31	0
15.	Maharashtra	288	10	3.47	11.54	33	69.70	29	2
16.	Manipur	60	3	5.00	8.40	5	40.00	12	0
17.	Meghalaya	60	2	3.34	4.38	3	33.33	12	1
18.	Mizoram	40	0	0.00	1.36	1	100.00	12	0
19.	Nagaland	60	1	1.67	2.48	1	0.00	12	0
20.	Odisha	147	0	0.00	2.27	3	100.00	22	0

Contd.

TABLE 4.1: *Contd.*

S. No.	*States/UTs*	*MLAs*			*% of Muslims in population**	*Expected Muslim MLAs*	*% Deprivation*	*Ministers in Cabinet*	
		Total	*Muslim*	*% of Muslim*				*Total*	*Muslim*
21.	Punjab	117	1	0.85	1.93	2	50.00	15	0
22.	Rajasthan	200	8	4.00	9.07	18	55.56	25	1
23.	Sikkim	32	0	0.00	1.64	1	100.00	12	0
24.	Tamil Nadu	234	6	2.56	5.86	14	57.14	35	2
25.	Telangana	119	8	6.72	12.76	15	45.67	18	1
26.	Tripura	60	2	3.34	8.60	5	60.00	9	0
27.	Uttar Pradesh	403	34	8.44	19.26	78	56.41	52	1
28.	Uttarakhand	70	3	4.29	13.95	10	70.00	9	0
29.	West Bengal	294	43	14.63	27.01	79	45.57	41	5
30.	Delhi	70	5	7.14	12.86	9	44.44	8	1
31.	Puducherry	30	1	3.33	6.09	2	50.00	6	0
TOTAL		4,123	296	7.18	14.24	587	49.57	599	42

Source: Wikipedia (Information downloaded and updated till August 2023).

Notes: * 2011 Census Data.

** J&K figures are based on 2016 elections, before the revocation of the Article 370.

In Delhi, Rajasthan, MP and Chhattisgarh, Muslims constituted 7.03 per cent of the cumulative population, but in the 2013 assembly elections in these states had only eight Muslims out of 589 MLAs (1.35 per cent). Following the 2008 elections in these same states there were 20 Muslim MLAs out of 590 amounting to 3.39 per cent of the total.[2] In 2014, Maharashtra was down from three Muslim ministers and 11 MLAs in the previous assembly to nine MLAs and not a single minister in the government formed by the BJP. Haryana was down from five Muslim MLAs, and one minister to three MLAs and not a single minister. The situation in these two states was similar to other seven states where the BJP was either in power or in a ruling alliance—MP, Chhattisgarh, Rajasthan, Gujarat, Goa, AP, and Punjab. These nine states, which accounted for over a third of India's population had only 22 Muslims among the total 1,359 MLAs. This implies that Muslims made up 8 per cent of the population of these states, but accounted for less than 2 per cent of the MLAs.

The community finds mininal representation in state government cabinets, irrespective of which party is ruling. There are only 42 Muslim ministers out of a total of 599, which includes 14 Muslim ministers in Jammu & Kashmir. It constitute 7.01 per cent of the total ministers, and if ministers from Jammu & Kashmir are not taken into account, the number falls to 28 which is 4.86 per cent of the total. There is not a single Muslim minister in 16 states: Arunachal Pradesh, Assam, Goa, Gujarat, Haryana, Himachal Pradesh, Punjab, MP, Manipur, Puducherry, Mizoram, Nagaland, Odisha, Sikkim, Tripura and Uttarakhand. Other seven states: AP, Chhattisgarh, Meghalaya, Rajasthan, Telangana, UP, and Delhi each have only one Muslim minister. Of the 11 states with a BJP governed chief minister, UP is the only one to have a Muslim minister Danish Azad Ansari, who found his way in via the legislative council. In the 2017 and 2022 assembly elections the BJP chose not to field a single Muslim candidate. In 2016, there was just one Muslim among the 151 ministers in the nine BJP ruled states.[3] Except Jammu & Kashmir, Muslim ministers do not hold high-profile portfolios, such as Home, Finance, Idustries, Revenue, etc.

ANDHRA PRADESH

The share of Muslims in AP was 9.17 per cent (2001 Census) but dropped to 7.32 per cent due to formation of the new state of Telangana (2011 Census). Over the 15 assembly elections, 128 Muslim MLAs were elected out of 4,052. The share of Muslims in the Andhra Pradesh Assembly has thus stood at 3.16 per cent, whereas as per share in population 336 Muslim MLAs should have been elected. Thus, Muslims here faced almost 62 per cent deprivation (Table 4.2).

In the first assembly, eight Muslims were elected on Congress and two on People's Democratic Front (PDF) tickets, and one as an independent. The Hyderabad Assembly had 11 Muslim MLAs, whereas on the basis of population, there should have been 14.

TABLE 4.2: REPRESENTATION OF MUSLIMS IN ANDHRA PRADESH ASSEMBLY

Year	*Total MLAs*	*Muslim MLAs*	*% of Muslim MLAs*	*% of Muslims in Population*	*Expected MLAs as per Population*	*% Deprivation*
1952	175	11	6.29	7.75	14	21.43
1955-7	301	12	3.98	7.75	23	47.83
1962	300	8	2.67	7.75	23	65.22
1967	287	7	2.44	7.75	22	68.18
1972	287	12	4.18	8.09	23	47.83
1978	294	7	2.38	8.09	24	70.83
1983	294	8	2.72	8.47	25	68.00
1985	294	8	2.72	8.47	25	68.00
1989	294	9	3.06	8.47	25	64.00
1994	294	9	3.06	8.91	26	65.38
1999	294	10	3.40	8.91	26	61.54
2004	294	9	3.06	9.17	27	66.67
2009	294	11	3.74	9.17	27	59.26
2014	175	3	1.71	7.32	13	61.54
2019	175	4	2.29	7.32	13	69.23
TOTAL	4,052	128	3.16	8.23	336	61.90

Sources: Iqbal A. Ansari, *Political Representation of Muslims in India: 1952-2004* and ECI website.

Given the post-Partition communal polarization in Hyderabad, the 6.29 per cent share of Muslims in the first assembly, i.e. about 80 per cent of what could be ideally expected was a remarkable achievement of secular politics in India.

Earlier, the state's political scene was dominated by the Congress and Telugu Desam Party (TDP). The AIMIM entered during the 1980s, and after the partition of the state, the TDP and Yuvajana Sramika Rythu Congress Party (YSRCP) are now the main parties. In 2009, 11 Muslim MLAs were elected, seven on AIMIM, three on Congress and one on TDP tickets. In 2009, Muslims constituted 3.47 per cent of the total MLAs thus suffering a deprivation of 59.26 per cent. Nineteen candidates finished as runners-up out of which six belonged to the Congress, four to the TDP, three to the Telangana Rashtra Samithi, which is now the Bharat Rashtra Samithi (BRS), two to the Majlis Bachao Tehreek (MBT), two to Praja Rajyam Party (PRAP) and one each to the CPI and CPM. In 2014, the first election after Partition of the state witnessed election of mere three Muslims on YSRCP tickets. Muslims constituted 1.71 per cent of the then assembly. As per proportional share, they could have expected 13 members, thus the deprivation was 62 per cent. In 2014, the TDP contested elections in alliance with the BJP. The polarization that was engineered was so high that none of the Muslim candidates could finish as even runners-up. In 2019, four Muslims got elected on YSRCP tickets constituting 2.29 per cent of the total MLAs; four candidates, three from TDP and one from YSRCP were runners-up.

Since 1952, the Congress nominated 15 or less candidates in all the 15 assembly elections that followed. The TDP has been less generous in giving tickets to Muslims, and since 1984 it has nominated less than 10 in each of the elections. The CPI and CPM never fielded more than one in all the elections. In 2009, the Congress nominated 11 Muslims, the TDP just seven, the TRS three, and CPI and CPM fielded one each.[4] The YSRCP's record too has not been very different in the 2014 and 2019 elections.

According to a study, there were almost 29 constituencies (in the undivided state), where Muslims constituted 30 to 80 per cent of the voters, plus another 30 constituencies where Muslims were 15 to 30 per cent. In these 59 constituencies, the united Muslim votes could guarantee victory for any candidate who could also garner some votes from other sections of the population. As per the central government data, the community constitutes over 10 per cent of population in as many as six districts: Krishna, Guntur, Nellore, Kadapa, Kurnool and Anantapur, and about 10 per cent in Prakasam and Chittoor. The data also shows that Muslims constitute 25 per cent or more in 13 assembly constituencies (AC) in the Rayalaseema region of the state: Kadapa, Rayachoti and Praddatur in Kadapa; Adoni, Kurnool and Nandyal in Kurnool; Guntakal, Hindupur, Kadiri and Tadipatri in Anantapur; Madanapalle in Chittoor; and Chilakaluripet and Narasaropet in Guntur. In 2014, the YSRCP won nine of these 13 seats and the TDP four. There are pockets of Muslim concentration in seven more seats: Tadikonda in Guntur, Udayagiri in Nallore, Pileru in Chittoor and Nandikotkur, Atmakur, Srisailam and Allagadda in Kurnool.[5] With tickets from main political parties and a little support from other sections of society, Muslims may be able to win 13 to 15 seats.

ASSAM

Muslims constitute 34.22 per cent of this state's population, the highest after Jammu & Kashmir and Lakshadweep. There are many Muslim-majority pockets in Assam. After five new districts were announced in 2015, and two more in 2016, there are now 34 districts in Assam, of which nine are Muslim-majority ones.

Although Assam has the higher proportion, Muslims have always been the most vulnerable and politically exploited section in the state. A majority of them are socially, economically and educationally lagging behind the majority with poor representation in public and private sectors. This is generally caused by political underrepresentation and hate mongering that brands them as illegal Bangladeshi immigrants.

Assamese Muslims have a rich and long history dating back to the thirteenth century when the local tribal chieftain Ali Mes converted to Islam at the invitation of Muhammad bin Bakhtiyar Khalji in 1205. The subsequent Mughal invasions on Ahom Kingdoms and later British rule brought many Muslims to Assam as labourers, officials and traders. During the British rule, Muslims from then East Bengal were brought to work in Assam's tea gardens and farmlands. With time most of these migrants got assimilated with the local Assamese population and adopted the indigenous language and culture. However, the post-Independence era's large influx of Hindu minorities from the then East Pakistan in 1970s and before resulted in Assamese agitation against the immigrants. This agitation was later given communal overtones and turned into Muslim bashing by collectively singling out the community as illegal Bangladeshis. Under the leadership of the All Assam Students Union (AASU) leaders like Samujjal Bhattacharya and Sarbananda Sonowal, the students' wing then started to put all its effort into branding every Muslim as a foreigner. The National Register of Citizens (NRC) containing details of all Indian citizens enumerated during the 1951 Census was started after the 2003 amendment of the Citizenship Act, 1955. The purpose of the 2003 amendment is to list 'illegal immigrants' and has only been implemented in Assam from 2013 onwards.

Post-NRC, it is quite evident that both Hindus and Muslims are out of the NRC. The issue is still not settled and is pending due to discriminatory and hateful attitude of the BJP. The issue of 'illegal immigrants' has been overwhelmingly communalised in the state thus ensuring that Muslims are simply not able to participate in politics.

In the 14 assembly elections after 1952, a total of 1,699 MLAs were elected out of which 319 were Muslims (18.78 per cent). As per proportional share, they deserved 471 MLAs, so the deprivation amounts to 32.27 per cent. Assam has had the distinction of being among the states where the deprivation has been the least. In 1983, the representation (with 32 MLAs) was almost equal to their proportional share. Except for 1978 and 1985, the Congress has been the major political party representing Muslims. One noticeable feature of representation in Assam is that it has been going up from 11.43 in 1952 to 24.60 per cent in 2021 with the

TABLE 4.3: REPRESENTATION OF MUSLIMS IN ASSAM ASSEMBLY

Year	*Total MLAs*	*Muslim MLAs*	*% of Muslim MLAs*	*% of Muslims in Population*	*Expected MLAs as per Population*	*% Deprivation*
1952	105	12	11.43	22.6	24	50.00
1957	108	13	12.04	22.6	24	45.83
1962	105	14	13.33	24.7	26	46.15
1967	125	16	12.80	24.7	31	48.39
1972	126	22	17.46	24.03	30	26.67
1978	126	23	18.25	24.03	30	23.33
1983	126	32	25.40	26.23*	33	3.03
1985	126	19	15.08	26.23*	33	42.42
1996	122	27	21.43	28.43	35	22.86
2001	126	26	20.64	30.92	39	33.33
2006	126	27	21.43	30.92	39	30.77
2011	126	28	22.22	34.22	43	34.88
2016	126	29	23.02	34.22	43	32.56
2021	126	31	24.60	34.22	43	27.90
TOTAL	1,699	319	18.78	27.72	471	32.27

Source: ECI and various reports.
Note: *No Census was held in Assam in 1981. Muslim percentage is calculated by taking average of 1971 and 1991 Census.

average nomination by the Congress being between 17 and 18 per cent.

In 1952, out of a total 105 members, 12 Muslims got elected, seven belonged to the Congress and five were independents. In 1957, of the 13 Muslim MLAs, nine belonged to the Congress, three to the PSP and one was independent. In 1962, of the 14 Muslim MLAs 12 belonged to the Congress, one to the PSP and one was independent. In 1983, of the 32 MLAs 24 belonged to the Congress, two to the Indian Congress Socialist (ICS), and six were independents. In 2006, of the 27 Muslims, 10 MLAs belonged to the Congress, nine to the AIUDF, three to the Asam Gana Parishad (AGP), one to the Loko Sanmilon (LKS) and one was independent. In 2006, 25 candidates finished as runners-up, 13 of them belonged to the Congress and nine to the AIUDF. In 2016, of the 29 MLAs, 15 belonged to the Congress, 12 to the

AIUDF and two to the AGP. In 2016, 23 candidates finished as runners-up, seven belonged to the Congress, 11 to the AIUDF and five were independents. In 2021, a total 31 MLAs got elected, 15 beloned to the AIUDF and 16 to the Congress. None beloned to the ruling BJP.

From 1952 till 2001, the Congress had near monopoly over Muslim voters. This uninterrupted monopoly was broken in 2005 when the AIUDF was founded. Its objectives were to raise issues related to identity, protection and development of Assam. In 2006, the first time the party contested, it won 10 seats and its seven candidates finished as runners-up. Two of its MLAs were Hindus. In 2011, the party had 16 Muslim MLAs out of a total of 28 Muslim MLAs. Nine of its Muslim candidates finished as runners-up. In 2016, the party had 12 Muslim MLAs out of a total of 29. Eleven of its Muslim candidates finished as runners-up. In 2021, the party won 16 seats, 15 being Muslims. The party has thus become a prominent political force in Assam.

As per proportional share, Muslims deserve 43 seats in the Assam Assembly. The Muslim-majority constituencies are situated in Lower Assam (western part), which has a large section of Bengali-origin Muslims and Barak Valley. Karimganj South, Badarpur, Hailakandi, Katlicherra, Algapur, Barkhola, Katigorah, Bokajan, Mankachar, Salmara South, Dhubri, Gauripur, Golakganj, Bilasipara West, Abhayapuri North, Goalpara East, Goalpara West, Jaleswar, Bhabanipur, Barpeta, Jania, Baghbar, Sarukhetri, Chenga, Chaygaon, Hajo, Dalgaon, Biswanath, Laharighat, Dhing, Ruponihat, Samaguri, Jamunamukh, Naoboicha, Tinsukia, Bijni, Sonai and Bilasipari East are some of the Muslim-dominated Assembly seats in the state.

BIHAR

From 1952 till 2020, the average representation of Muslims in the Bihar Assembly has been about 7.3 per cent, while their average share in population is 14 per cent, according to which they deserved 674 MLAs. Only 353 got elected and thus they suffered a deprivation of about 48 per cent (Table 4.4).

TABLE 4.4: REPRESENTATION OF MUSLIMS IN BIHAR ASSEMBLY

Year	*Total MLAs*	*Muslim MLAs*	*% of Muslim MLAs*	*% of Muslims in Population*	*Expected MLAs as per Population*	*% Deprivation*
1952	330	23	6.97	11.28	37	37.84
1957	318	26	8.18	11.28	36	27.78
1962	318	22	6.92	12.45	40	45.00
1967	318	17	5.35	12.45	40	57.50
1969	318	20	6.29	12.45	40	50.00
1972	318	22	6.92	13.48	43	48.84
1977	324	24	7.41	13.48	44	45.45
1980	324	24	7.41	13.48	44	45.45
1985	324	29	8.95	14.13	46	36.96
1990	324	17	5.25	14.13	46	63.04
1995	324	21	6.48	14.81	48	56.25
2000	324	29	8.95	14.81	48	39.58
2005	243	17	7.00	16.53	40	57.50
2010	243	19	7.82	16.53	40	52.50
2015	243	24	9.88	16.87	41	41.46
2020	243	19	7.82	16.87	41	53.66
TOTAL	4,836	353	7.30	14.06	674	47.63

Source: ECI.

Unlike many other states (including Assam, UP and West Bengal) one singular feature of the Bihar Assembly is the relative steadiness of the share of Muslim MLAs, which ranged between 5.35 per cent (1967) and 9.88 per cent (2015). On many occasions, it went above 8 per cent. The Congress again had near monopoly over Muslim voters as in 1952 and 1957 out of total Muslim MLAs of 23 and 26 respectively, 22 and 24 were from the party. The 1962 elections marked the beginning of Muslims' political diversification. In 1977, the Janata Party secured 13 and the Congress 8 MLAs, out of the total 24. In 1980-5, the Congress staged a comeback like in the rest of the country. This was a period of Muslim-friendly electoral trend all over the country and Bihar Muslims secured the highest representation of 29 MLAs in 1985.

From 1990, the Janata Dal formations have been the major parties representing Muslims.

In the 2005 Bihar elections, the first after bifurcation (creation of Jharkhand in 2000), only 17 Muslims got elected. As per share in population, they deserved 40 seats and thus, they suffered a deprivation of 23 seats, i.e. 57.50 per cent. These 17 MLAs were from seven parties. The RJD, and Congress had jointly fielded 46 Muslims out of whom nine won: four on RJD and five on Congress tickets. The Lok Janashakti Party (LJP) fielded 47, but only one won. The JDU fielded nine of whom four won. Of the others, the winners were one each from the CPI(ML) and NCP, and one was an independent. A surprising, but important fact of the 2005 elections was that 42 Muslim candidates finished as runners-up, many of them with thin margins that were in some cases less than a thousand votes. The reasons could have been anti-incumbency against the RJD (many of its Muslim candidates lost due to this), and low number of Muslim nominees from the JDU. The third reason could be the division of Muslim votes as the JDU and BJP contested elections together and Muslims substantially voted for the JDU.

In 2010, 19 Muslims were elected amounting to 7.82 per cent of total seats and a deprivation of 52.5 per cent. Of those 19, the party-wise distribution was: JDU 7, RJD 6, Congress 3, LJP 2 and BJP 1. Interestingly, three of the four Congress and two of the three LJP MLAs were Muslims. Thirty-six candidates ended as runners-up. The Congress fielded 46 candidates, the RJD 26 the JDU 14, the LJP 10 and the BJP one. The division of votes among these four parties was another significant factor for the poor performance of the Muslim candidates. Chief Minister Nitish Kumar won the trust of Muslims due to the reopening of the Bhagalpur riot cases, conviction of accused through speedy trials, keeping Bihar free from communal troubles and sending a message that he would not compromise on issue of secularism despite sharing power with the BJP.

In 2015, the grand alliance of the RJD, JD(U) and Congress led by Nitish Kumar achieved a landslide victory. It witnessed 24 Muslim MLAs which was 9.88 per cent of the total and the party-wise share was: RJD 12, Congress six, JDU five, CPI(ML) one and 16 others as runners-up. Muslims unequivocally and overwhelmingly voted for the grand alliance. However, they felt betrayed when Nitish Kumar withdrew from this alliance and shifted his loyalty to the BJP without providing substantial reasons for the move. In the 2020 elections, 19 Muslim candidates won amounting to 7.82 per cent. The party wise distribution was: RJD 8, Congress 4, AIMIM 5, BSP 1 and CPI(ML) 1. This was the first election in which the AIMIM won a good number of seats. Twenty-three candidates finished as runners-up: RJD 8, JDU 8, Congress 5 and CPI(ML) 2. The noticeable feature of the 2020 elections was that not a single Muslim candidate of the JDU won since Nitish was allied with the BJP.

Likewise in the other states, the main reason for the political underrepresentation of Muslims in Bihar is the failure of mainstream parties to nominate them. Over the years, the Congress gave 9 to 10 per cent tickets to Muslims, and which was inadequate in proportion to population. Similarly, the RJD gave 10 per cent and the CPI and CPM an average of 7 and 8 per cent tickets, respectively. The second reason is the reservation of Muslim-dominated constituencies for the SCs and STs. Third, denying tickets to Muslim candidates from many Muslim-dominated constituencies and pushing them to constituencies with low Muslim presence.

This, then, is the scenario in Bihar even though the community can decide the winner in about 50 constituencies in Kishanganj, Purnea, Araria, Katihar, Madhubani, Sitamarhi, Bhagalpur, Darbhanga, Siwan, Gopalganj, West Champaran and East Champaran.

CHHATTISGARH

After the bifurcation of Madhya Pradesh in 2000 and creation of Chhattisgarh, the latter has 90 Assembly Constituencies (AC): 35 reserved for STs and 11 for SCs. Muslims are just 2.01 per cent of the population, mostly concentrated in urban pockets. Population-wise they deserve two MLAs. In 2008, the state had two Muslim MLAs, Badruddin Qureshi from Bhilainagar and

Mohammad Akbar from Pandariya. Both ACs do not have more than 10 per cent of Muslim voters (Table 4.5).

During the past four elections, Muslims deserved eight MLAs but only four were elected, all on Congress tickets thus witnessing a 50 per cent deprivation. Mohammad Akbar and Badruddin Qureshi were the only two leaders who have been given tickets by the Congress. Bilaspur, Raipur City North, Raipur City South, Patan and Dharsiwa have a good number of Muslim voters. Besides Congress, the BSP and SP have been giving tickets to Muslims but have failed to win any seat.

TABLE 4.5: REPRESENTATION OF MUSLIMS IN CHHATTISGARH ASSEMBLY

Year	*Total MLAs*	*Muslim MLAs*	*% of Muslim MLAs*	*% of Muslims in Population*	*Expected MLAs as per Population*	*% Deprivation*
2003	90	1	1.11	1.97	2	50.00
2008	90	2	2.22	1.97	2	0.00
2013	90	0	0.00	2.01	2	100.00
2018	90	1	1.11	2.01	2	50.00
TOTAL	360	4	1.11	1.99	8	50.00

Source: ECI.

DELHI

Delhi is one of the two UTs with legislative assembly which has 70 seats. During 11 elections to the Delhi Assembly, out of 700 MLAs only 49 were Muslims, which is 7 per cent though the community deserved 71 MLAs. They faced almost 31 per cent deprivation. In the first assembly they had four members, three elected on Congress and one on Socialist Party tickets. In 2003, the Congress nominated six Muslims, the SP 12, the RJD two out of seven, and the BSP six out of the total 40 candidates. The JD(S) and JD(U) had also given tickets to Muslims. Five candidates got elected, four belonged to the Congress and one to the JD(S). In 2008, five Muslim candidates won translating to 7.14 per cent of the total and a deprivation of 37.5 per cent. Of those five, three belonged to the Congress and one each to RJD and LJP. In that year, three Muslims finished as runners-up; one each belonging to the Congress, RJD and BSP. In 2013, five Muslims got elected; four from the Congress and one JD(U) (Shoaib Iqbal from Matia Mahal). Besides this, four Muslims stood at second position, two from the Congress and two from Aam Aadmi Party (AAP). In 2015, when AAP won 67 seats, only four MLAs were Muslims, and all belonged to AAP. Two Muslim candidates of the Congress finished as runners-up. In 2013, Muslims comprised a total of 108 candidates out of the total 810. In 2008, 92 Muslims were in the fray. AAP's victory in 2015 was a watershed in that, Muslim voters shifted their loyalty from the Congress to the AAP like the mainstream voters. In 2020 five Muslim candidates all belonging to AAP, were elected. None of the Muslim candidates finished as runners-up (Table 4.6).

There are seven Muslim-dominated ACs, where only Muslims can decide the winner: Okhla, Seelampur, Matia Mahal, Ballimaran, Mustafabad, Babarpur and Chandni Chowk. Sadar Bazar

TABLE 4.6: REPRESENTATION OF MUSLIMS IN DELHI ASSEMBLY

Year	*Total MLAs*	*Muslim MLAs*	*% of Muslim MLAs*	*% of Muslims in Population*	*Expected MLAs as per Population*	*% Deprivation*
1951	42	4	9.52	5.71	2	-100.00
1972	56	4	7.14	6.47	4	0.00
1977	56	2	3.57	6.47	4	50.00
1983	56	5	8.93	7.75	4	-25.00
1993	70	5	7.14	9.44	7	28.57
1998	70	5	7.14	9.44	7	28.57
2003	70	5	7.14	11.72	8	37.50
2008	70	5	7.14	11.72	8	37.50
2013	70	5	7.14	12.86	9	44.44
2015	70	4	5.71	12.86	9	55.55
2020	70	5	7.14	12.86	9	44.44
TOTAL	700	49	7.00	9.75	71	30.99

Source: ECI.

and Kirari too have a good presence of Muslim voters. As per the 2011 Census, Muslims constitute 12.86 per cent of Delhi's population, and accordingly they deserve at least nine MLAs. But since 1983, the figure has not gone beyond five MLAs.

GUJARAT

Gujarat is among the states where political deprivation of Muslims has always been the highest. During the past 16 elections, a total of 2,699 MLAs were elected, 45 of them were Muslims which is 1.67 per cent. Going by the average population (8.85 per cent), they deserved 231 MLAs, and have faced almost 81 per cent deprivation. Over the years, Muslim representation in Gujarat has only decreased. Despite accounting for nearly a tenth of the state's population, their representation has reduced from three in 2002, and five in 2007 to two in 2012, and one in the current Assembly (Table 4.7). In the 2002 elections conducted just after the Godhra communal carnage, three Muslims were elected, two belonged to the NCP, one to BSP, and none to the Congress. In 2007, the Congress had put up six Muslim candidates of whom five were elected and one finished as runner-up. In 2012, the Congress had given tickets to six Muslims out of whom two were elected, from Dariyapur and Wankaner. Four candidates finished as runners-up. In 2017, the party fielded five Muslims of whom three emerged victorious: Shaikh Gyasuddin Habibuddin from Dariyapur, Imran Yusufbhai Khedawala from Jamalpur-Khadia and Mohamad Javid Pirzada from Wankaner. Two Congress candidates finished as runners-up, Sulemanbhai Patel from Vagra and Iqbal Daud Patel from Surat West. In 2022, the Congress fielded six Muslim candidates, including three sitting MLAs. Of these only Imran Khedawala won from Jamalpur-Khadia seat. For the first time the AAP fielded three and AIMIM 12 Muslim candidates. The BJP did not field a single Muslim candidate. The dismal state of Muslim representation is reflected in the following figures:

- In 1967, only one MLA got elected against the expected 14.
- In 1990, only one MLA won against the expected 16.
- In 1995, one independent got elected against the expected 16.

TABLE 4.7: REPRESENTATION OF MUSLIMS IN GUJARAT ASSEMBLY*

Year	*Total MLAs*	*Muslim MLAs*	*% of Muslim MLAs*	*% of Muslims in Population*	*Expected MLAs as per Population*	*% Deprivation*
1952**	60	2	3.33	8.92	5	60.00
1957	118	3	2.54	8.92	8	62.50
1962	154	5	3.25	8.46	13	61.54
1967	168	1	0.60	8.46	14	92.86
1972	168	3	1.79	8.42	14	78.57
1975	181	4	2.21	8.42	15	73.33
1980	182	5	2.75	8.42	15	66.67
1985	182	3	1.65	8.53	16	81.25
1990	182	1	0.55	8.53	16	93.75
1995	182	1	0.55	8.73	16	93.75
1998	182	3	1.65	8.73	16	81.25
2002	182	3	1.65	9.06	16	81.25
2007	182	5	2.75	9.06	16	68.75
2012	182	2	1.10	9.67	17	88.24
2017	182	3	1.65	9.67	17	82.35
2022	182	1	0.55	9.67	17	94.11
TOTAL	2,699	45	1.67	8.85	231	80.52

Source: ECI & Various other reports.
Notes: * Gujarat was part of Bombay state till 1957.
** 1952 election result deal only with Saurashtra.

- In 2022, only one MLA won against the expected 17.
- Only on two occasions, 1980 and 2007, were five MLAs elected, the highest number so far.

Of the total 45 Muslim MLAs, 39 belonged to the Congress indicating it has been the only party representing Muslims in Gujarat. Therefore, the responsibility of the gross underrepresentation lies squarely on the party for not nominating enough Muslims regardless of the political compulsions. The average Muslim nomination by the Congress from 1952 to 2022 has been 3.86 per cent which was very poor. The JD's 5.71 per cent in 1990-5; BSP's 4.3 and SP's 4.76 per cent nomination in 1995 did not bring any success. While the Patels, Baniyas, Brahmins and Kshatriyas are given a big share in nominations, Muslims and OBCs are routinely ignored.

Muslims constitute a 9.67 per cent of Gujarat's population and thus, deserve 17 MLAs. The statistics show that they can influence election outcome in more than 30 ACs. In 34 ACs, Muslim voters comprise over 15 per cent and there are 20 ACs where they constitute more than 20 per cent of total voters. Of the latter, four are in Ahmedabad and three each in Bharuch and Kutch districts. Of the 34 seats with more than 15 per cent Muslim voters, the BJP won 21 in 2012, the Congress 12 and NCP one. In 20 ACs, where Muslim voters comprise more than 20 per cent of all voters, the BJP won 12 seats, while the Congress could won eight.[6] The Muslim-dominated ACs of Gujarat with percentage of Muslim voters in brackets are as follows:

1. Jamalpur-Khadia (61)
2. Vagra (44)
3. Bharuch (31.53)
4. Modasa (11.94)
5. Bhuj (27.45)
6. Anjar (14.66)
7. Dhoraji (15.38)
8. Jamnagar (37.20)
9. Godhra (17.9)
10. Surat East (22)
11. Abdasa (27.71)
12. Wankaner (27.44)
13. Somnath (18.77)
14. Mandavi (21.29)
15. Junagadh (13.94)
16. Bapunagar (23)
17. Mangrol (16)
18. Rakhial (Above 30)
19. Vejalpur (35)
20. Vatva (17)
21. Khambhalia (16)
22. Nadiad (15)
23. Limbayat (27)[7]

These seats can return Muslim candidates, if they are nominated by mainstream parties there, the candidates adopt a proper strategy, and the elections are focussed on secular issues. However, the community faces the same paradox in these constituencies: that of Muslim-dominated seats electing BJP MLAs. There are various reasons for this odd situation. Muslims are sidelined in ticket allocation by the Congress. Statistics shows that although they deserve 17 seats barely five or six tickets have been allocated to them in recent assembly elections. Moreover, they are given tickets from seats where the share of Muslim voters is low. On the other hand, ACs having between 30 to 50 per cent Muslim voters are given to the non-Muslim candidates. Third, the BJP's success in Muslim-dominated seats has largely been due to consolidation of Hindu votes in its favour and split in Muslim votes among many Muslim independent candidates. This phenomenon arises when the combined vote share of non-Congress Muslim candidates is more than the margin between the BJP and Congress candidates. These 'spoiler candidates' take away a significant chunk of votes that would have gone to the Congress, thereby helping the BJP to win. The spoilers are also a factor in seats where the Muslim population is not significant, but there is a close contest between two parties and even a slight split in votes can affect the result. For example, the Jamalpur-Khadia AC in Ahmedabad district has 61 per cent Muslims. However, in 2012, the BJP candidate Bhushan Ashok Bhatt won the seat with 38.63 per cent vote share. Samirkhan Sipai of the Congress secured 33.54 per cent votes; six other Muslim candidates jointly secured 26.9 per cent. Just one independent Sabirbhai Kabliwala secured 24.52 per cent, making it possible for BJP to win the seat.

Another factor is provided by the high number of Muslim candidates leading to consolidation of Hindu votes for the BJP. This is particularly evident in urban areas that have a history of communal violence, such as Ahmedabad. For example, the Vejalpur AC of Ahmedabad district has 35 per cent Muslim population, but the BJP secured 58.2 per cent vote share in 2012 which was almost equal to the Hindu population there. There were six Muslim candidates in the fray.[8] This illustrates how Hindu votes get consolidated behind the BJP as a matter of course, when there are multiple Muslim candidates.

During the 1980s, the Muslim community was one of the four constituents of the Congress' famed KHAM (Kshatriyas, Harijans, Adivasis and Muslims) which ensured its political domination in Gujarat. Muslims carried political weight as some Muslim MPs and MLAs were elected from seats with low Muslim presence. In the 1980s and 1990s, the the Congress addressed the concerns of the Muslims. However, the Gujarat riots of 2002 and consequent polarization of the state has completely marginalized the Muslims.

At present, they are missing from the conversation around elections in Gujarat and feel neglected. The most serious concern of Muslims is the increasing communalization of political space and their consequent insecurities. The communal polarization has gone hand in hand with their electoral marginalization. In 2002, 57 Muslim candidates jointly received just 2.87 lakh votes, 1.4 per cent of total votes polled. In 2007, 116 candidates received 4.13 lakh votes, whereas in 2012, 192 candidates got 6.51 lakh votes. In 2017, 203 Muslim candidates who constituted 11.1 per cent of the total 1,828 candidates, together received 5.04 lakh votes, i.e. 1.6 per cent of the total valid votes polled.[9]

The BJP has totally ignored Muslims not only in terms of an equitable political share, but also other developmental indicators like education and employment. On the other hand, the Congress has been giving token nomination to Muslim candidates. In 2017, when all political parties were discussing the Dalit, OBC, and Patel votes, there was not even a whisper about the concerns of the Muslim community. In the polarized atmosphere even the Congress chose to remain silent about them in its election campaigns. This has contributed to their disillusionment with the political process. Hanif Lakdawala, a social activist said in 2017, 'I think no Muslim goes to the political parties and no political parties approach the Muslims. This is generally true and is so at this time too.'[10]

HARYANA

Haryana was carved out of East Punjab on 1 November 1966 on linguistic and cultural basis. Since 1967, 13 elections to the Haryana Assembly have been held and out of the total 1,143 MLAs only 43 were Muslims (3.76 per cent). They constituted an average 4.86 per cent of the total population and deserved 55 MLAs and thus faced 21.82 per cent deprivation (Table 4.8).

In 1967, there were only two Muslim MLAs out of the total 81; one from the Swatantra Party and the other was an independent. Although a majority of the Muslim MLAs have been elected on Congress tickets, several belonged to the JP, JD, Indian National

TABLE 4.8: REPRESENTATION OF MUSLIMS IN HARYANA ASSEMBLY

Year	*Total MLAs*	*Muslim MLAs*	*% of Muslim MLAs*	*% of Muslims in Population*	*Expected MLAs as per Population*	*% Deprivation*
1967	81	2	2.47	3.80	3	33.33
1968	81	3	3.70	3.80	3	0.00
1972	81	2	2.47	4.0	3	33.33
1977	90	3	3.33	4.0	4	25.00
1982	90	4	4.44	4.1	4	0.00
1987	90	4	4.44	4.1	4	0.00
1991	90	5	5.56	4.6	4	-25.00
1996	90	3	3.33	4.6	4	25.00
2000	90	3	3.33	4.6	4	25.00
2005	90	3	3.33	5.78	5	40.00
2009	90	5	5.56	5.78	5	0.00
2014	90	3	3.33	7.02	6	50.00
2019	90	3	3.33	7.02	6	50.00
TOTAL	1,143	43	3.76	4.86	55	21.82

Sources: ECI website and the SCR (2006).

Lok Dal (INLD), independents, etc. In 2009, five MLAs were elected: one belonged to Congress, three to the INLD and one to the BSP. Three candidates finished as runners-up, one each was from the Congress and BSP and one was an independent. In 2014, of the three MLAs that won, two were from the INLD and one was an independent. Four candidates finished as runners-up, one each from the Congress, BSP and INLD and independent. In 2019, the three MLAs that were elected all belonged to the Congress, while four candidates finished as runners-up of whom two belonged to the BJP, one to the Congress and one was an independent.

In Haryana too, the familiar story is repeated. The BJP gave tickets to two Muslims in 2014, and three in 2019 while the Congress put up four and six Muslim candidates in 2014 and 2019 respectively. Overlooked by the mainstream players, a majority of Muslim candidates turn to either smaller parties such as the SP, BSP, other regional parties or prefer to contest as independents.

Muslims constitute 7.02 per cent (2011 Census) of Haryana's total population, and accordingly deserve at least six to seven MLAs. There are a few Muslim-dominated seats in Haryana such as Nuh, Punhana, Firozpur-Jhirka, Hathin, Jagadhari, Sohana, Faridabad, Hodal, Badshahpur (SC), Palwal and Ballabhgarh, and a majority are located in the Mewat region. As per the 2011 Census, 79.2 per cent of Mewat's population is Muslim. The region faces socio-economic, educational and political deprivation because all successive governments have failed to address these issues.

JHARKHAND

After Jharkhand was created in 2000 the four elections have witnessed only 15 Muslim MLAs elected out of total of 324 (4.63 per cent). As per the average population of Muslims there (14.19 per cent), they deserved 46 MLAs. The community has thus faced 67.39 per cent deprivation. In 2005, Alamgir Alam and Mohammed Izrail Ansari were elected from Pakur and Bokaro respectively; both on Congress tickets. Nine Muslim candidates finished as runners-up, three belonged to the RJD, two to Congress and one each to CPI, JD(U) and Jharkhand Mukti Morcha (JMM) while one was an independent. In 2009, the number increased to five MLAs: Congress two, JMM two and Jharkhand Vikas Morcha (JVM) one. Six candidates finished as runners-up, four belonged to the Congress and one each to the JMM and JVM. In 2014, again two members got elected from Pakur (Alamgir Alam) and Jamtara (Irfan Ansari), both on Congress tickets. Six candidates finished as runners-up of whom three belonged to the JMM, two to Congress and one to JVM. In 2019, there were four MLAs: two each from the Congress and JMM. The contest in the Rajmahal constituency proved suicidal for the Muslim candidates there. The collective votes of Ketabuddin Sheikh of the JMM and Md Tajudding of the All Jharkhand Students Union (AJSU) were more than that procured by Anant Kumar Ojha of BJP. But in a stark illustration of my argument earlier this only ended up paving the way for Ojha's victory. Three candidates finished as runners-up, one each from the Congress, BSP and AJSU (Table 4.9).

TABLE 4.9: REPRESENTATION OF MUSLIMS IN JHARKHAND ASSEMBLY

Year	*Total MLAs*	*Muslim MLAs*	*% of Muslim MLAs*	*% of Muslims in Population*	*Expected MLAs as per Population*	*% Deprivation*
2005	81	2	2.47	13.85	11	81.81
2009	81	5	6.17	13.85	11	54.55
2014	81	2	2.47	14.53	12	83.33
2019	81	4	4.94	14.53	12	66.67
TOTAL	324	13	4.63	14.19	46	67.39

Source: ECI website.

The share of Muslims in Jharkhand is 14.53 per cent (2011 Census), and they deserve 12 MLAs. However, the figure has never crossed five. There are many Muslim-dominated ACs, which have a 20 per cent and above Muslim voters and are thus capable of sending Muslim MLAs to the Assembly. Some of these constituencies are: Pakur, Jamtara, Madhupur, Mahagama, Koderma, Ramgarh, Gandey, Bokaro, Dhanbad, Tundi, Garhwa, Rajmahal, Dhanwar, Bhawanathpur, Jamshedpur (West), Hatia, Hazaribagh, Mandar, Godda, Giridih, Panki, Lohardagga, Sarath, Bishrampur and Mandu. Muslims have always supported the cause of tribals in the state. Together with the tribals and Christians, they form a huge vote bank. Here again, nominations from the mainstream parties and unity with the tribals and other marginalized sections can easily yield at least 12 to 15 seats.

KARNATAKA

From 1952 till 2023, a total of 116 Muslim MLAs were elected out of the total 3,411 (3.40 per cent), whereas the average Muslim population in the state has been 11.23 per cent. They deserve a total of 387 MLAs and have faced deprivation of over 70 per cent. Karnataka is among the states where Muslims face huge political deprivation (Table 4.10).

In 1952, only two Muslim MLAs were elected; neither belonged to the Congress. In 1957, seven were elected all on Congress tickets;

TABLE 4.10: REPRESENTATION OF MUSLIMS IN KARNATAKA ASSEMBLY

Year	*Total MLAs*	*Muslim MLAs*	*% of Muslim MLAs*	*% of Muslims in Population*	*Expected MLAs as per Population*	*% Deprivation*
1952	99	2	2.02	10.05	10	80.00
1957	208	7	3.37	10.05	21	66.67
1962	208	3	1.44	9.87	21	85.71
1967	216	3	1.39	9.87	21	85.71
1972	216	9	4.17	10.63	23	60.87
1978	224	15	6.70	10.63	24	37.50
1983	224	2	0.89	11.21	25	92.00
1985	224	4	1.79	11.21	25	84.00
1989	224	9	4.02	11.21	25	64.00
1994	224	7	3.13	11.64	26	73.08
1999	224	13	5.80	11.64	26	50.00
2004	224	6	2.67	12.23	27	77.78
2008	224	9	4.02	12.23	27	66.67
2013	224	11	4.91	12.92	29	62.07
2018	224	7	3.13	12.92	29	75.86
2023	224	9	4.02	12.92	29	68.97
TOTAL	3,411	116	3.40	11.23	387	70.02

Sources: Iqbal A. Ansari, *Political Representation of Muslims in India: 1952-2004* and ECI.

the party had nominated nine Muslims out of its total 206 candidates. In the 1978 elections, the Congress (I) nominated 16 candidates of whom 12 were elected; the JNP fielded 12 of whom two won. With one Independent winning from Gulbarga, the total tally peaked at 15, the highest so far.

In 1978, as per share in population, Muslims expected to have 24 MLAs versus the 15 they had. In 1989, there were nine Muslim MLAs; eight from the Congress, and one from IUML. The JD and Janata Party (JP) which fielded five and eight Muslims respectively did not have any success. In 1983, the Congress nominated 17 Muslims of whom only one won. One Muslim candidate won on the JP ticket. With two members, Muslims with more than 11 per cent share in population had less than 1 per cent representation. In 1999, 13 Muslims were elected, 12 belonging to the Congress and one to the JD(S). In 2004, while JD(S) improved its tally from one to two, of the 15 Muslims nominated by the Congress only four won. Thus, there were only six Muslim MLAs and the community faced almost 80 per cent deprivation. In 2008, nine MLAs won, eight of them from the Congress and one from JD(S). Nine candidates finished as runners-up of whom seven belonged to the Congress, and one each to the JD(S) and BSP. In 2013, 11 MLAs were elected, nine belonging to the Congress and two to the JD(S), while another 11 candidates finished as runners-up of whom six belonged to the Congress, three to the JD(S) and one each to the Social Democratic Party of India (SDPI) and Karnataka Janata Party (KJP). In 2013, the Congress had fielded 18 Muslims while the JD(S) gave tickets to 20 Muslim candidates in a bid to eat into Muslim votes from the Congress. In 2018, all winning seven MLAs belonged to the Congress while eight candidates of the party finished as runners-up. In 2018 the Congress and JD(S) had given 17 and eight tickets respectively to Muslims. In 2023, the Congress handed over tickets to 15 Muslim candidates and 9 of them emerged victorious. The JD(S) fielded 23 such candidates, but none could secure a victory. The AIMIM contested two seats and secured only 0.02 per cent of the votes polled. The SDPI met a similar fate as none of its 16 candidates could open their accounts.

Muslims constitute 12.92 per cent (2011 Census) of state and deserve 29 seats in 224-member Karnataka assembly. They faced a deprivation of 20 MLAs (68.97 per cent) in 2023. As in other states, the reasons for the political deprivation of Muslims are familiar: low nomination by the main parties (Congress and JD(S)), division of votes among various Muslim candidates in Muslim-dominated ACs, non fielding of Muslim candidates in Muslim-majority ACs and polarization of voters on communal lines. Muslims constitute almost 13 per cent of Karnataka's total voters and can elect at least 30 MLAs. There are several Muslim-majority seats where either Muslims can win or only they can decide the winner. Afshan Yasmin writes, 'Muslims constitute 12.91 per cent of Karnataka's population and are electorally significant in at least 20-odd urban seats. Informal estimate by political parties indicate that they are capable of changing the fortunes in at least 90 seats across the state.'[11] Calculating the assembly seat-wise Muslim population proportion from district-wise data and approximated use of GIS tools, Yasmin concludes that there are 35 ACs with a Muslim voter percentage between 16 and 20, and 15 ACs with more than 20 per cent Muslims.

Ajay Jha, writer on Politics, Security and Economy of South and West Asia says,

> Muslim voters constitute between 13 to 14 per cent of Bangalore's population and their numbers will play an important role in several constituencies in the city. Of the 28 Constituencies in Bangalore city, Muslims form 20 and 50 per cent of voters in seven Constituencies, 10 to 20 per cent in six, and five to 10 per cent in 12 Constituencies.[12]

Jha concludes that of the total 224 assembly segments, Muslim voters can decide the fate of candidates in not less than 65. There are at least seven to eight ACs including Mangalore (50.7 per cent), Pullakeshinagar in Bangalore (49.3 per cent), Gulbarga (49.7 per cent), Bijapur City (47.3 per cent), Narasimharaja in Mysore (44 per cent), Sarvagnanagar, previously known as Bharthi Nagar in Bangalore (40 per cent), and Chamrajpet (43 per cent) in Bangalore City, where Muslim voters dominate. Similarly, there are at least 12 ACs including Kudachi in Chikkodi (30 per cent), Belgaum North (34.7 per cent), Humnabad in Bidar (33.4 per cent), Raichur (31.4 per cent), Bidar (31.8 per cent), Shiggaon in Dharwad (30 per cent), Kolar (36.2 per cent), Hebbal in Bangalore (37.6 per cent), Shivajinagar (32.9 per cent) and Jayanagar (34.8 per cent) in Bangalore apart from Ramanagaram (30 per cent), and Bidar City (30 per cent), where Muslim voters are the decisive factor.

As per another report, Muslims comprise 13 per cent of the state's 5.27 crore population and can determine the outcome in 38 out of 224 ACs. Most Muslim voters are in Bengaluru's Sarvananagar constituency. Nearly a third of the 300,000 voters in this constituency are Muslims. Pulakeshinagar, Shivajinagar, Jayanagar and Padmanabhanagar ACs in Bangalore have major Muslim concentration. Tumkur, Raichur, Bidar, Bijapur and Gulbarga, are other Muslim-dominated seats.[13]

As per the estimate done by Nisar Ahmad, IPS (Retd.) of Karnataka, there are 57 ACs which have more than 21 per cent Muslim voters. Based upon the above estimates, it is clear that Muslims can influence election results in 30 to 40 ACs. But Muslims have never been represented proportionately. This may be also due to 'over representation' of certain powerful communities, such as Lingayata and Vokkaliga which have nearly 60 and 50 MLAs respectively in every assembly (Table 4.10 (A)).

TABLE 4.10 (A): MUSLIM-DOMINATED CONSTITUENCIES IN KARNATAKA

S. No.	*% of Muslim Voters*	*Name of ACs*
1.	40 to 50	Chamrajpet, Sarvagnanagar, Gulbarga Uttar, Davanagere South, Bijapur City and Shivajinagar
2.	35 to 40	Kolar, Belgaum Uttar, Bidar, Sira, Hebbal, Mangalore City South, Mangalore, Narasimharaja
3.	30 to 35	Humnabad, Bhatkal, Chikmagalur, Bantwal, Chikkodi Sadalga, Bidar South, Raichur, Shiggaon, Bellary City, Tumkur City, Ramanagaram, Gangawati, Haliyal, Hangal
4.	25 to 30	Sirsi, Chitradurga, Shimoga, Hubli-Dharwad-West, Hubli-Dharwad-Central, Jevargi, Shahapur, Yadgir, Sindhanur, Dharwad, Vijayanagara, Davanagere-North, Bhadravati, Shanti Nagar, Madikeri, Mangalore City North, Koppal, Padmanaba Nagar, Virajpet, Gadag, Kadur, Shikaripura, Sidlaghatta
5.	21 to 25	Jayanagar, Hunsur, Piriyapatna, Bangalore South, Puttur and Muddebihal

Source: Data collected by Nisar Ahmad, IPS (Retd.) of Karnataka Cadre (data not verified).

KERALA

Kerala has the highest literacy rate (96.2 per cent) in India. Along with socio-economic and educational development, the state has created a society which is rational, tolerant and accommodating. It considers the interest of all segments of society without raising communal issues. The state accommodates all significant social and religious segment as well as various shades of political ideology without causing any division in the society. It presents a model of liberal democracy where representation of various socio-religious groups is ensured in politics. The people of Kerala have built institutions on the principle of acceptance of social and religious pluralism. There are different political parties representing different socio-religious groups which advocate for the interest of a particular group without causing any harm to others. In Kerala, electoral politics is a medium of building viable collusion for accommodating diverse interests and opinions. Kerala Muslims are the only group in India who have their own political party. This party shares power with the Congress and other secular parties and have done tremendous work for socio-economic development in the state. The state, so far, has remained immune to the divisive and sectarian politics of the BJP and other right-wing groups.

From 1957 to 2021, in the 16 assembly elections, a total of 2167 MLAs were elected of whom 388 were Muslims (17.9 per cent). As per their average share in population, Muslims deserved a total of 473 MLAs. Since they had 388 MLAs, they suffered a deprivation of 17.97 per cent. Kerala is among the few states where Muslims are almost proportionately represented and their political deprivation is low. In 1957, 11 Muslim MLAs were elected two each from the Congress and CPI and seven were independents. The Muslim League did not put up any candidate in this election. In the 1960 elections, 16 MLAs were elected; 10 belonged to the Muslim League, five to Congress and one to CPI. The deprivation got reduced from 45 per cent in 1957 to 20 per cent in 1960. The deprivation was further reduced to NIL in 1980, when 27 Muslim MLAs were elected. The deprivation started picking up from 1982 and reached to almost 26 per cent in 2001 and 2006 (Table 4.11).

In 2006, 26 Muslim MLAs were elected of whom seven belonged to the Muslim League, five to Congress, nine to CPI(M), one each to the Indian National League (INL) and RSP and three were independents. Twenty-four Muslim candidates finished as runners-

TABLE 4.11: REPRESENTATION OF MUSLIMS IN KERALA ASSEMBLY

Year	*Total MLAs*	*Muslim MLAs*	*% of Muslim MLAs*	*% of Muslims in Population*	*Expected MLAs as per Population*	*% Deprivation*
1957	114	11	9.65	17.53	20	45.00
1960	114	16	14.04	17.53	20	20.00
1965	133	18	13.53	17.91	24	25.00
1967	133	21	15.78	17.91	24	12.50
1970	133	15	11.28	17.91	24	37.50
1977	140	25	17.85	19.50	27	7.40
1980	140	27	19.29	19.50	27	0.00
1982	140	28	20.00	21.25	30	6.67
1987	140	23	16.43	21.25	30	23.33
1991	140	27	19.29	23.33	33	18.18
1996	140	26	18.57	23.33	33	21.21
2001	140	26	18.57	24.70	35	25.71
2006	140	26	18.57	24.70	35	25.71
2011	140	34	24.29	26.56	37	8.11
2016	140	32	22.86	26.56	37	13.51
2021	140	33	23.57	26.56	37	10.81
TOTAL	2,167	388	17.90	21.63	473	17.97

Source: ECI website.

up; 11 belonged to the IUML, four to Congress, three to the CPI and one each to the CPM, Muslim League Kerala State Committee (MLKSC), Inidan National League (INL), JDS and Democratic Indira Congress (DIC) and one was an Independent. In 2011, 34 MLAs were elected of whom 19 belonged to the IUML, six to the Congress, six to the CPM, one to the Revolutionary Socialist Party (RSP) and two were Independents. Twenty-two candidates finished as runners-up with the majority of them belonging to the CPM. In 2016, 32 MLAs were elected which was 22.86 per cent and thus, Muslims faced almost 14 per cent deprivation. Of the 32 MLAs, 18 belonged to the IUML, six to CPM, two to the Congress, one to National Secular Conference (NSC) and four were independents. Thirty-two candidates of 11 different parties finished as runners-up. In 2021, 33 MLAs were elected which is 23.57 per cent. As per share in population, they deserved 37 seats and faced 11 per cent deprivation. Of the 33 MLAs, 15 belonged to the IUML, nine to CPM, three to Congress, one each to the CPI and INL, and four were independents. Of the 33 candidates who finished as runners-up, a majority belonged to the Congress, CPM, Muslim League and Independents. From 1957 to 2021, a total of 388 Muslim MLAs were elected out of whom 199 (51.29 per cent) belonged to the IUML. In all elections, more than 50 per cent of Muslim MLAs belonged to the Muslim League. The CPM and Congress also have a significant share. The distribution pattern indicates a major allegiance of Muslims to the IUML followed by the Congress and CPM.

These assembly election results indicate that Muslims have had a fair share in the nominations of all the political parties. Since the IUML is a part of the UDF along with the Congress, it fields Muslim candidates from most of the Muslim-majority ACs. A majority of the Muslim League tickets go to Muslims. The Congress also fields some Muslim candidates from its quota. The CPM, which is the main constituent of the Left Democratic Front (LDF) gives a fair share of nominations to Muslims. The figures are not available but it is clear that Muslims do not get proportionate nomination by the main parties like the Congress, CPM, CPI, etc.

Muslim-Dominated Assembly Constituencies

As per the 2011 Census, Muslims constitute 26.56 per cent of state population, and they deserve at least 37 seats. They are mostly concentrated in northern Kerala and that is why a majority of the Muslim-dominated ACs are situated here. Several ACs have more than 50 per cent Muslim voters. There are others where the Muslim population is between 30 and 40 per cent, or 40 and 50 per cent. Although the share of Muslim voters in each AC is not available, election results indicate those that are Muslim-dominated. Following are such seats:

1. Manjeshwar
2. Malappuram
3. Kuthuparamba
4. Kasargod
5. Vengura
6. Peravoor
7. Azhikode
8. Vallikkunnu
9. Perambra
10. Kannur
11. Tirurangadi
12. Tarur
13. Thalassery
14. Tanur
15. Aroor
16. Kalpetta
17. Tirur
18. Punalur
19. Kuttiady
20. Kottakkal
21. Chadayamanglam
22. Koilandu
23. Thavanur
24. Payyanur
25. Kozhikode South
26. Pattambi
27. Manalur
28. Beypore
29. Shornur
30. Kaipamangalam
31. Kunnammanyalam
32. Mannarkad
33. Elathur
34. Koduvally
35. Palakkad
36. Ottapalam
37. Thiruvambady
38. Kunnamkulam
39. Thrikkara
40. Kondothy
41. Guruvayur
42. Changanassery
43. Eranad
44. Ativa
45. Kazhakottam
46. Nilambur
47. Kalamassery
48. Aruvikkara
49. Manjeri
50. Ambalappuzha
51. Kovalam
52. Perinthalmanna
53. Eravipuram
54. Varkala
55. Mankada
56. Taliparamba

From the point of view of political representation Kerala is a unique state as Muslims have their own party, and have near proportional share in the assembly as well. If due nomination is given by the mainstream parties like the Congress, CPI and CPM, and they contest all Muslim-dominated seats, Muslims can achieve proportional representation.

MADHYA PRADESH

In the 15 elections from 1952 to 2018, a total of 4,238 MLAs were elected to the MP Assembly of whom 50 were Muslims (1.18 per cent). The community's share in the state has been 4.98 per cent and they deserved 206 MLAs. Thus, they faced 75.83 per cent deprivation. MP is among the states where the political deprivation of Muslims is high and they are totally marginalized in state politics. In 1952 only six Muslim MLAs were elected, all belonged to the Congress. In 1962, six Congress Muslim candidates and one from the CPI were elected. Except for 1967 when three MLAs were elected on tickets of three parties, i.e. Congress, CPI and Samyukta Socialist Party (SSP), the 1977 elections in which all four MLAs belonged to the Janata Party and 1990 in which one BJP and one Independent won, in the other elections the Congress has been the sole or major party representing Muslims and contributing 38 out of 50 MLAs. In the 1990 elections when the BJP first came to power the number of Muslim MLAs came down to two and post-Baburi demolition, no Muslim was elected in 1993, despite the Congress wresting power from the BJP. In 1998, four MLAs, all belonging to the Congress were elected from Bhilai, Satna, Birendranagar and Bhopal North. In 2003, the count went down to two; one belonged to the Congress and the other to the NCP who got elected from Bhopal North and Burhanpur, respectively. In 2003, the Congress had nominated three out of 229 (1.31 per cent). Though the BSP, SP and NCP nominated Muslims liberally, only one candidate (from the NCP) had won (Table 4.12).

In 2008, the Congress put up five Muslim candidates, and the BJP none. Only Arif Aqueel of the Congress won from Bhopal North. Four candidates finished as runners-up, two belonged to the Congress and one each to the NCP and BSP. In 2013, the Congress gave tickets to five Muslims and the BJP to one, Arif Baig from Bhopal North. Only one Congress candidate, Aqueel, could win from Bhopal North defeating Baig. In 2013, four Muslim candidates finished as runners-up, three belonged to the Congress, and one to the BJP. In 2018, the Congress fielded three Muslim candidates: Aqueel from Bhopal North, Arif Masood from Bhopal Central and Masarrat Shahid from Sironj. The BJP fielded only one candidate, Fatima Siddiqui, from Bhopal North. Siddiqui is the daughter of the (Late) Rasool Ahmed Siddiqui, a former state minister. Two candidates, Aqueel and Masood, won while two

TABLE 4.12: REPRESENTATION OF MUSLIMS IN MADHYA PRADESH ASSEMBLY

Year	*Total MLAs*	*Muslim MLAs*	*% of Muslim MLAs*	*% of Muslims in Population*	*Expected MLAs as per Population*	*% Deprivation*
1952	232	6	2.59	4.03	9	33.33
1957	288	3	1.04	4.03	12	75.00
1962	288	7	2.43	4.07	12	41.67
1967	296	3	1.01	4.07	12	75.00
1972	296	6	2.03	4.36	13	53.85
1977	320	4	1.25	4.36	14	71.43
1980	320	5	1.56	4.36	14	64.29
1985	320	4	1.25	4.80	15	73.33
1990	318	2	0.63	4.80	13	84.62
1993	320	Nil	0.00	4.96	16	100.00
1998	320	4	1.25	4.96	16	75.00
2003	230	2	0.86	6.37	15	86.67
2008	230	1	0.44	6.37	15	93.33
2013	230	1	0.44	6.57	15	93.33
2018	230	2	0.86	6.57	15	86.67
TOTAL	4,238	50	1.18	4.98	206	75.83

Source: ECI.

candidates, one from the Congress and one from the BJP, finished as runners-up. There were seven MLAs in 1962 in the state, but since the past two decades it has become difficult for a Muslim to win outside the old city of Bhopal. Muslims constitute 6.57 per cent of population and accordingly deserve at least 15 MLAs. However, they have only two MLAs and are facing a huge 86.67 per cent deprivation. Political marginalization of Muslims in MP is impacting their socio-economic, educational and security conditions.

Experts say there are three major reasons for the sharp decline in Muslim representation in the state: first, polarization of votes following the Baburi Mosque demolition; division of Muslim population after delimitation of constituencies during the Congress rule and most importantly the low nomination of Muslims by the main political parties, i.e. the Congress and BJP.

NOMINATION BY NATIONAL PARTIES

National parties like the Congress, BJP, CPI, CPI(M) and BSP together account for almost 94 per cent MLAs in MP. These parties have around 98 per cent of seats in the 2018 Assembly (225 out of 230). In 15 elections from 1952 to 2018 an average 2.32 per cent Muslim candidates were nominated by these national parties (Table 4.12 (A)).

During this period, the BJP nominated only 15 Muslim candidates out of a total 3,691 (0.4 per cent). The Congress which claims to represent Muslims in the state has given only 100 tickets out of its total of 4,093 (2.44 per cent). In terms of nomination, the

TABLE 4.12 (A): NOMINATION OF MUSLIMS BY NATIONAL PARTIES (1952-2018)

Year	*Total MLAs*	*National Parties MLAs*	*Candidates by INC*		*Candidates by BJP (JS), (BJS)*		*Candidates by other National Parties*	
			Total	*Muslim*	*Total*	*Muslim*	*Total*	*Muslim*
1952	232	207	225	8	76	0	631	14
1957	288	256	228	9	127	0	594	14
1962	288	233	228	11	195	1	794	16
1967	296	272	296	7	265	0	886	16
1972	296	278	289	6	260	1	753	16
1977*	320	314	320	9	319	5	691	16
1980	320	311	320	10	310	3	1,142	35
1985	320	314	320	7	312	2	1,002	25
1990	320	307	318	6	269	1	914	25
1993	320	298	318	5	320	0	974	24
1998	320	303	316	5	320	0	1,035	15
2003	230	215	229	4	230	0	747	22
2008	230	221	228	5	228	0	724	16
2013	230	227	229	5	230	1	789	19
2018	230	225	229	3	230	1	717	14
TOTAL	4,240	3,981	4,093	100	3,691	15	12,393	287

Source: https://www.thehinducentre.com/the-arena/current-issues/article25991277.ece
Note: *In 1977, BJP was part of Janata Party; Muslim candidates inflated numbers could not be considered as only BJPs' candidates.

highest (3.06 per cent) was in the elections of 1980, when 35 were nominated, 10 belonging to the Congress, three to BJP, one to CPI and remaining to other parties. In 2018, these parties together nominated 14 candidates out of a total of 717, which is just 2 per cent. Three candidates belonged to the Congress, one each to CPI and BJP and nine to the BSP. In short, although Muslims constitute 6.57 per cent of the population, in the nomination of national parties, their share is only 2.32 per cent. Even the Congress gave only 2.39 per cent of its tickets to Muslims which is pathetically low.

Muslim-Dominated Constituencies

Although Muslim representation is not proportionate to their numerical strength, the community's electoral power cannot be underestimated. They constitute almost 6.6 per cent of the state's population (nearly 48 lakh), and are mostly concentrated in Western MP, Malva region and Central region including Bhopal division. Districts with large Muslim population include Bhopal, Indore, Shajapur, East Nimar, Jabalpur, Mandsaur, West Nimar, Ratlam, Dewas, Vidisha, Gwalior, Sehore, Raisen, Dhar, Chhindwara, Morena and Sagar. The ACs where Muslim candidates have won in the past include Bhopal North, Bhopal South, Sironj, Burhanpur, Sehore, Indore-3, Jaora, Ujjain, Satna, Khandwa, Jabalpur, Ratlam, Seoni and Tarana.

According to Ibrahim Qureshi, former Madhya Pradesh Minorities Commission's Chairman, there were 82 ACs where minorities accounted for more than 20 per cent votes, 121 ACs where it was between 5-10 per cent and the rest had 2-4 per cent. The ACs with large minority votes are Bhopal North (60 per cent), Burhanpur (50 per cent), Bhopal South (35 per cent), Indore-1 (35 per cent), Indore-3 (30 per cent), Ujjain North (35 per cent), Jabalpur Central (35 per cent), Khandwa (25 per cent), Ratlam (25 per cent), Jaora (22 per cent), Lashkar West (20 per cent), Jabalpur East, Kurwai, Narsinghgarh, Sironj, Khategaon, Dewas, Budhni, Shujalpur (18 per cent each), Shajapur, Mandla, Neemuch, Indore-5, Maheedpur, Mandsaur, Nasrullahgunj, Icchawar, Ashta,

Ujjain South (16 per cent each), Govindpura, Sarangpur, Mungaoli (15 per cent each), Surkhi-Rahatgarh, Chhindwara, Mhow, Vidisha, Guna, Bhind and Ashok Nagar (14 per cent each).[14]

As per another estimate, besides Bhopal North and Bhopal Central, Muslim voters influence the result of more than 25 seats. These ACs are Narela, Burhanpur, Shajapur, Dewas, Ratlam City, Ujjain North, Jabalpur North, Jabalpur East, Mandsaur, Rewa, Satna, Sagar, Gwalior South, Khandwa, Khargone, Indore-1, Depalpur, etc.[15] Aqueel, a five-time MLA from Bhopal North says, 'There are nine seats in which Muslims are around 50 per cent of the population, and there are 10 seats in which they have population of 40,000 to 50,000 and can prove to be decisive during elections.'[16]

Despite many Muslim-dominated seats, they have never been proportionately represented. L.S. Herdenia, a political expert, says that Muslims account for 6.57 per cent of the state's 7.27 crore population as per 2011 Census. So, their representation in the assembly should be between 15 and 20. He says, 'We must try to increase Muslim representation in the Parliament and state assembly. For this, political parties must encourage Muslims to participate in political activities and give tickets to them.'[15]

MAHARASHTRA

In 15 assembly elections in the state so far a total 4,395 MLAs were elected and out of which 145 were Muslims. The overall share has been 3.30 per cent, whereas average share in state population is 9.19 per cent. As per share in population, they deserved 404 seats and so the deprivation amounts to 64.10 per cent. In the first assembly, 13 Muslims got elected which was 4.13 per cent, causing 45.83 per cent deprivation. In the second assembly, 10 Muslims were elected. Nine of these belonged to the Congress and one to the PSP (Table 4.13).

In 1957, the representation was 2.53 per cent and deprivation 66.67 per cent. The share peaked to 12 in 1978 and 13 in 1980 which was in line with the national trend favourable for Muslims during that period. In 1999, out of 30 candidates put up by main parties (15 by Congress, eight by SP, five by NCP and two

TABLE 4.13: REPRESENTATION OF MUSLIMS IN MAHARASHTRA ASSEMBLY

Year	*Total MLAs*	*Muslim MLAs*	*% of Muslim MLAs*	*% of Muslims in Population*	*Expected MLAs as per Population*	*% Deprivation*
1952	315	13	4.13	7.61	24	45.83
1957	396	10	2.53	7.61	30	66.67
1962	264	9	3.41	7.67	20	55.00
1967	270	5	1.85	7.67	21	76.19
1972	270	9	3.33	8.40	23	60.87
1978	288	12	4.27	8.40	24	50.00
1980	288	13	4.51	8.40	24	45.83
1985	288	9	3.13	9.25	27	66.67
1990	288	7	2.43	9.25	27	74.07
1995	288	6	2.08	9.67	28	78.57
1999	288	11	3.82	9.67	28	60.71
2004	288	11	3.82	10.60	31	64.51
2009	288	11	3.82	10.60	31	64.51
2014	288	9	3.13	11.54	33	72.73
2019	288	10	3.47	11.54	33	69.70
TOTAL	4,395	145	3.30	9.19	404	64.10

Source: ECI website.

by Shiv Sena), only 11 were elected of whom six belonged to Congress, two each to SP and NCP and one to Shiv Sena. In 2004, among the 11 Muslims elected, seven belonged to the Congress and four to NCP. Eight Muslims finished as runners-up: two from Congress, and one each from the NCP, JD(S), SP, Shiv Sena, and Bharipa Bahujan Mahasangh (BBM), and one was independent. In 2009, when the Congress-NCP combine came to power for the third time, of the 11 Muslims elected, five belonged to the Congress, three to the SP, two to the NCP and one to the Jan Surajya Shakti (JSS). Seven candidates finished as runners-up: four Congress, two NCP and one was independent. In 2014, when the BJP came to power for the first time, nine Muslims were elected of whom five belonged to Congress, two to the AIMIM, and one each to the SP and NCP. Ten candidates finished as runners-up; four of them belonged to the Congress, three to the AIMIM, two to the NCP and one to the BBM. This was the lowest representation since 1999. In 2014, the Congress gave tickets to 17 Muslims, NCP to 14, BJP to two, Shiv Sena to one, MNS to six and the SP to 17. AIMIM which entered the state for the first time gave tickets to 18 Muslims. In 2019, when a fractured verdict was delivered and three parties—the Congress, NCP and Shiv Sena formed the government, 10 Muslims were elected. Of these, three belonged to the Congress, two each to NCP, SP and AIMIM and one to the Shiv Sena. Eleven candidates finished as runners-up of them five belonged to the Congress, four to AIMIM, one to Vanchit Bahujan Aghadi (VBA) and one was independent.

In 2019, Muslim MLAs constituted only 3.47 per cent of the total. As per their share in population, they deserved 33 seats whereas only 10 got elected. Thus, they faced deprivation of almost 70 per cent which is more than average deprivation. This means the share of Muslims in the state assembly has been decreasing over the years. Before the formation of the NCP and entry of other parties into state politics, and even after that, the Congress has enjoyed a near monopoly over Muslim voters. Of the 145 Muslim MLAs elected from 1952 to 2019, 95 belonged to the Congress, and the remaining to the other parties. This shows that had the Congress nominated more Muslims, their representation would certainly have been better.

The record of the mainstream parties in the state has been poor in giving nomination to Muslims. The Congress nominated only 3.96 per cent from 1952 to 1999, which is less than a half of the Muslims' population share. In 1980, it nominated 18 which got reflected in the result as 12 of them were returned. Even after 1999, the Congress has been giving close to four per cent nomination which is far below the share in state population. Other parties like the SP, BSP, JD, etc., have been generous in giving tickets. The BSP has given overall 8.58 per cent nomination, 13 tickets (8.97 per cent) in 1995. The JD gave 7.67 per cent nomination. The SP entered Maharashtra in 1995, and gave tickets to six Muslims (27.27 per cent) followed by eight (53.33 per cent) in 1999. The average nomination by the SP till 1999 has been almost 36 per cent. Even after 1999, the SP has given almost

40 per cent tickets. The AIMIM entered the state in 2014, and gave total 24 tickets out of which 18 went to Muslims (75 per cent). In 2019, it gave total 44 tickets out of which 31 went to Muslims (70.45 per cent).

Various reasons are attributed to the pathetically low political representation of Muslims in Maharashtra, but most of them are similar to those prevailing in all the states we have looked at:

1. Very low nomination by the main parties likc the Congress, NCP, BJP and Shiv Sena.
2. Communalization of the political space.
3. Fielding of non-Muslim candidates from Muslim-majority ACs.
4. Putting up Muslim candidates from seats which are not Muslim-dominated.
5. Division of votes among several candidates in Muslim-dominated constituencies.

There are many Muslim-dominated seats, but Muslim candidates lose due to 'multiplicity of candidates' causing division of votes. For example, in the 2014 Assembly elections there were 17 Muslim candidates in Malegaon, and 20 in Nanded South. In the same year, seven constituencies with high Muslim population had eight or more candidates. A situation like this always leads to splitting of votes between Muslim candidates. In the end, only two of those eight seats elected Muslim MLAs.[17]

Muslim-dominated Constituencies

Maharashtra's 1.3 crore Muslims constitute 11.56 per cent of its total 11.24 crore population and thus deserve 33 MLAs. The community is slightly more concentrated in northern Konkan, Khandesh, Marathwada and western Vidarbha. They play a decisive role in about 40 ACs, including seats in Mumbai where they make up over 20 per cent of the total electorate. These seats are: Dhule City, Chopda, Raver, Malegaon Central, Jalgaon City, Balapur, Nagpur Central, Amravati, Karanja, Akola West, Nanded City, Kinwat, Nanded South, Parbhani, Jalna City, Aurangabad

Central, Aurangabad West, Aurangabad East, Majalgaon, Beed, Udgir, Latur City, Osmanabad, Bhiwandi West, Bhiwandi East, Mumbra-Kalwa, Versova, Mankhurd-Shivajinagar, Chembur, Kurla, Sion-Koliwada, Wadala, Byculla, Mumbadevi, Chandiwali, Malad, Sangli and Miraj.[18] The percentage of Muslim voters in these ACs are not known, but interested individuals can calculate it from the voter lists of these seats.

RAJASTHAN

In the 15 assembly elections in Rajasthan, a total of 2,880 MLAs were elected and 94 of these were Muslims (3.07 per cent). As per average share in state population (7.45 per cent), Muslims deserved 217 seats and thus faced 56.68 per cent deprivation. In 1952, five got elected, all from the Congress (the deprivation was 50 per cent). In 2008, the community deserved 17 seats, but 12 were elected, 10 from the Congress and two from the BJP. That year the deprivation was 29.41 per cent. In 2013, only two MLAs were elected while the population proportionate number was 18 seats. The community faced the highest deprivation of 89 per cent. Except for the post-Emergency 1977 election and the 1990 election, in all others the Congress has been the major political party representing Muslims. Out of the total 94 Muslim MLAs from 1952 to 2018, 68 were from the Congress. Other parties providing representation to them in this state are BJP (BJS), JNP, Lok Dal, JD and BSP (Table 4.14).

The 2008 elections witnessed the community's highest share in the Rajasthan Assembly. Eight candidates were runners-up; five of them belonged to the Congress, two to the BJP and one to BSP. In 2013, there were only two Muslim MLAs, both belonged to the BJP. The Congress gave tickets to 15 Muslims all of whom were defeated due to various factors including the anti-incumbency working against the Congress government. Of the 15 runners-up, 12 belonged to the Congress and one each to the BSP and National People's Party (NPP) and one was an independent. In 2018, of the eight Muslim MLAs, seven belonged to the Congress and

TABLE 4.14: REPRESENTATION OF MUSLIMS IN RAJASTHAN ASSEMBLY

Year	*Total MLAs*	*Muslim MLAs*	*% of Muslim MLAs*	*% of Muslims in Population*	*Expected MLAs as per Population*	*% Deprivation*
1952	160	5	3.13	6.21	10	50.00
1957	176	4	2.27	6.21	11	63.64
1962	176	3	1.70	6.52	11	72.73
1967	184	6	3.26	6.52	12	50.00
1972	184	5	2.72	6.9	13	61.54
1977	200	9	4.50	6.9	14	35.71
1980	200	8	4.00	6.9	14	42.86
1985	200	7	3.50	7.28	15	53.33
1990	200	8	4.00	7.28	15	46.67
1993	200	4	2.00	8.01	16	75.00
1998	200	9	4.50	8.01	16	43.75
2003	200	4	2.00	8.47	17	76.47
2008	200	12	6.00	8.47	17	29.41
2013	200	2	1.00	9.07	18	88.89
2018	200	8	4.00	9.07	18	55.68
TOTAL	2,880	94	3.07	7.45	217	56.68

Source: ECI website.

one to BSP and of the eight runners-up, seven belonged to the Congress and one to BJP. Muslims in Rajasthan constitute around 9.07 per cent of the state population, and deserve at least 18 seats. While many reasons are cited for the massive political deprivation, lower nomination by mainstream parties is the main reason.

Muslim voters have been loyal to the Congress because a majority of their MLAs belong to the party. Not surprisingly, the community lays great store by the nomination by Congress. The party's nomination of Muslims, however, has not always been very heartening. Its average nomination from 1952 to 2003 was about 5 per cent. In 2003, the party nominated 15 Muslims (7.57 per cent) following mounting pressure from the community for a fair share. In 2008, the party nominated 17 Muslims (8.5 per cent), out of whom 10 won. In 2013, of the 16 nominations, none were elected. In 2018, it fielded 15 candidates, seven of whom won. This shows that since 2003, it has been giving a fair share of nominations, almost close to the Muslims' share in population. Though the BJP's overall nomination of Muslims is less than 1 per cent, it has made its presence felt by having one MLA elected in five assemblies (1962, 1985, 1990, 1998 and 2003) each, and two members each in 2008 and 2013. In 2008, it nominated four, of whom two were elected and two finished as runners-up. In 2013, it again gave tickets to four candidates, two of whom Yunus Khan from Deedwana and Habibur Rahman from Nagaur won. In 2018, it nominated only one Muslim, Yunus Khan from Tonk, who lost to Sachin Pilot of the Congress. The CPI gave 10.52 per cent nominations though only one candidate won in 1977. The CPI(M) with 6.24 per cent nominations did not have any success. The JD gave five tickets in 1990, four of whom were elected. The success of this party was not repeated again. Its overall nomination has been 7.49 per cent. The BSP entered the state in 1990 and gave 9 per cent nomination, while the SP entered the state in 1998 with 11.76 per cent nomination. Although the SP and BSP have been generous in nominating Muslims these two parties do not enjoy much mass support in the state.

Muslim-dominated Assembly Constituencies

There are 20 ACs in Rajasthan, where Muslim candidates can easily win if all other factors are accounted for. Besides, there are many other seats where they can tilt the balance with their numerical strength. These 20 Muslim-dominated seats are: Churu, Fatehpur, Kishanpole, Adarshnagar, Sawai Madhopur, Pushkar, Nagaur, Makrana, Pokaran, Ramgarh, Sheo, Kaman, Soorsagar, Ladpura, Tijara, Tonk, Nagar, Bikaner East, Dholpur and Deedwana. Besides, there are some other seats which have a fair number of Muslim voters. These seats are: Jaisalmer, Jhalrapatan, Sardarpura, Sangaria, etc. Rajasthan's politics has so far been dominated by the Congress and BJP without any other serious contender. In this situation due share of Muslims in the state assembly can be ensured if these two political parties offer a fair share of nominations.

TAMIL NADU

Tamil Nadu's political space has always remained secular and inclusive; accommodating the interests of minorities and other deprived groups.

In the 16 assembly elections so far, a total 3,644 MLAs have been elected of them 93 were Muslims (2.55 per cent). During this period they constituted an average of 5.25 per cent of the state population, and thus deserved 193 MLAs. They have faced a deprivation of almost 52 per cent. In 1952, when only two MLAs were elected, the deprivation was the highest. Both these MLAs belonged to the Congress. In 1957 again, all the four Muslim MLAs belonged to the Congress and the deprivation dropped to 60 per cent. The highest number of Muslims (11) was elected in 1989 and 1996. In 1989, as they expected 12 MLAs, their deprivation was the least (8.33 per cent). Of those 11 MLAs, eight belonged to the DMK and one each to the Congress and CPI(M) and one was independent. In 1996, they were expected to win 13 seats and thus faced 15.33 per cent deprivation. In 2001, seven MLAs were elected, three from the DMK, two from the AIADMK, one from the TMC and one was independent. Of the seven runners-up, six belonged to the DMK and one to the IUML. In 2006, of the seven Muslim MLAs five belonged to the DMK and one each to the AIADMK and Congress. Of the six runners-up, three belonged to the AIADMK and one each to the DMK and MDMK and one was Independent. In 2011 when the AIADMK came to power only five Muslims were elected; two from the AIADMK, one from DMK and two from the Manithaneya Makkal Katchi (MAMAK). Of the 12 runners-up, six belonged to the DMK, two each to the Congress and DMDK and one each to the MAMAK and Viduthalai Chiruthaigal Katchi (VCK). In 2016, when AIADMK again retained power only four MLAs got elected, two belonged to AIADMK, and one each to the DMK and IUML. Of the 16 runners-up, four each belonged to the AIADMK, IUML and MAMAK, three to DMK and one to the Congress. Muslims again faced a huge deprivation of 71.43 per cent. In 2021, they improved their tally with six MLAs; three from the DMK, two from the MAMAK and one from the Congress. Of the six runners-up, three belonged to the IUML, two to AIADMK and one to Makkal Needhi Maiam (MNM), the new party floated by Kamalahaasan, a famous Tamil and Bollywood film actor who failed to win any seat for his party. He was defeated in the Coimbatore (South) constituency by his BJP rival by a margin of 1728 votes. His defeat was due to division of votes among other candidates as Congress's state working president Mayura Jayakumar contested on the DMK front, polling 41,426 votes. Muslims improved their tally, but the deprivation amounted to 57.14 per cent (Table 4.15).

Both key parties in Tamil Nadu, the DMK and AIADMK have secular credentials and are sympathetic to minorities and the deprived groups. Both parties along with the Congress offer fair

TABLE 4.15: REPRESENTATION OF MUSLIMS IN TAMIL NADU ASSEMBLY

Year	*Total MLAs*	*Muslim MLAs*	*% of Muslim MLAs*	*% of Muslims in Population*	*Expected MLAs as per Population*	*% Deprivation*
1952	191	2	1.08	4.73	9	77.78
1957	205	4	1.95	4.73	10	60.00
1962	206	4	1.94	4.60	9	55.56
1967	234	4	1.71	4.60	11	63.64
1971	234	6	2.56	5.10	12	50.00
1977	234	7	2.99	5.10	12	41.67
1980	234	6	2.56	5.10	12	50.00
1984	234	6	2.56	5.2	12	50.00
1989	234	11	4.70	5.2	12	8.33
1991	234	3	1.28	5.5	13	76.92
1996	234	11	4.70	5.5	13	15.38
2001	234	7	2.99	5.56	13	46.15
2006	234	7	2.99	5.56	13	46.15
2011	234	5	2.14	5.86	14	64.29
2016	234	4	1.71	5.86	14	71.43
2021	234	6	2.56	5.86	14	57.14
TOTAL	3,644	93	2.55	5.25	193	51.81

Source: ECI website.

number of nominations to Muslims. These parties also give fair number of seats to Muslim base parties which contest elections in alliance with them. For example, in 2016, the DMK allotted ten seats to Muslim parties. However, here too Muslims do not receive proportional nominations by the main parties.

Muslim-dominated Assembly Constituencies

In Tamil Nadu, Muslims form about 6 per cent of the state population and are scattered across the state. The Muslim pockets are Vellore, Ramanathapuram, Nagapattinam and Coimbatore. They do not form a majority in any of the ACs, but certainly act as a force to impact the outcome of elections. As per the 2016 election results, there were 10 assembly segments where the winning margin was less than 1,000 votes and 25 constituencies where the margin was less than 3,000 votes. In a state where the Muslim population is between 2,000 and 80,000 in every assembly constituency, their votes could be a game-changer in a closely contested election.[19]

Although the share of Muslims in ACs here is not available, on the basis of nominations and election results of 2011, 2016 and 2021, one can say that there are more than thirty ACs, where Muslims are either in dominant position or in a position to influence the election outcome. These ACs are: Ramanathapuram, Palayamkottai, Ambur, Triplicane, Papanasam, Chidambaram, Vaniyambadi, Kadayanallur, Nagapattinam, Avadi, Manapparai, Velachery, Alandur, Tiruchirapalli (West), Thiruvarur, Madurai, Krishnagiri, Sankarapuram, Thousand Lights, Ulundurpettai, Thanjavur, Tiruvadanai, Harbour, Ranipet, Chepank-Thiruvallikeni, Ambattur, Vellore, Villupuram, Coonoor, Thondamuthur, Dindigul, Pumpuhar, Gingee, Cumtrum, etc. If they are given tickets by the main parties like the DMK, AIADMK and Congress in the Muslim-majority seats, and these parties ensure votes from other communities, Muslims can achieve a proportional share.

More than a millennium ago, Islam reached the shores of the Tamil country through active maritime trade links. The Arab traders who brought considerable wealth into the Tamil country in lieu of spices and pearl, found a special place for themselves in the country that they called Ma'bar. As the Tamil Muslim community evolved out of this trade contacts, it found active patronage from rulers of the Tamil country that lasted into the beginning of colonial rule. During the colonial era the considerable literary output of Muslims firmly cemented their place in Tamil society. It was in this milieu that the Dravidian movement took shape in the early twentieth century, with Muslims as an integral part of it. In 1920, C.V. Venkatramana Iyengar introduced legislation demanding that certain posts in the police force be given to Indians too. Dr. C. Natesa Mudaliar of the Justice Party argued that the motion had to be reformed as, 'Non-Brahmin Indians' and went onto explicate that the term non-Brahmin 'means such as Mohammedans, Indian Christians, non-Brahmin Hindus, Jains, Parsees and Anglo Indian'. This understanding was the basis on which the Muslims and the Dravidian movement crafted their relationship. The Justice Party not only ensured political representation in the legislature but also in various offices of the state and was sympathetic to the needs of the community.[20]

Due to the Islamic principles of equality and social justice, and Tamil Muslims' love for the Tamil language and culture, they have always been part of the Dravidian movement, which has been a composite, inclusive and secular.[21] Both the parties, the DMK and AIADMK, have ensured reservation for Muslims and started schemes for their development. A majority of Muslim MLAs belong to these parties. Tamil Muslim parties like the IUML and MAMAK do not win seats on their own and contest elections on symbols of these parties. In this situation it becomes imperative for both parties to give due nomination to Muslims and also to ensure due representation in legislature.

TELANGANA

After the creation of Telangana in 2014, assembly elections were held in 2014 and 2018. In these elections a total 238 MLAs were elected, 16 of them being Muslims, forming 6.72 per cent of the total. As per share in population, Muslims deserved 30 MLAs and thus, faced deprivation of 46.67 per cent. Incidentally, in both elections eight Muslims were elected and their share in the assembly and deprivation have remained the same (Table 4.16).

TABLE 4.16: REPRESENTATION OF MUSLIMS IN TELANGANA ASSEMBLY

Year	*Total MLAs*	*Muslim MLAs*	*% of Muslim MLAs*	*% of Muslims in Population*	*Expected MLAs as per Population*	*% Deprivation*
2014	119	8	6.72	12.76	15	46.67
2018	119	8	6.72	12.76	15	46.67
TOTAL	238	16	6.72	12.76	30	46.67

Source: ECI website.

In the first elections of 2014, eight Muslim MLAs were elected; seven belonged to the AIMIM and one to the Telangana Rashtra Samithi (TRS now BRS). The AIMIM MLAs were: Ahmed bin Abdullah Balala (Malakpet), Jaffer Hussain (Nampally), Kausar Mohiuddin (Karwan), Syed Ahmed Pasha Quadri (Charminar), Akbaruddin Owaisi (Chandrayangutta), Mumtaz Ahmed Khan (Yakutpura), and Mohammad Moazam Khan (Bahadurpura). The only TRS MLA Shakil Amir Mohammed was elected from Bodhan seat of Nizamabad district. All the seats held by the AIMIM are within the jurisdiction of the Hyderabad city. Of the six runners-up one belonged to the Congress, three to the TDP and one each to the AIMIM and MBT. Out of these six, only two were defeated by non-Muslim candidates from Kamareddy and Nizamabad (Urban) ACs. In the second elections of 2018, of the eight MLAs seven were from AIMIM and one from the TRS. All winners of 2014 repeated their success in 2018 with one or two changes in seats. Again, seven were elected from Hyderabad city and one from Bodhan of Nizamabad. Of the six runners-up, three belonged to the Congress and one each to the TRS, TDP and BJP. Only two candidates, Mohammed Ali Shabbir and Taher bin Hamdan (both Congress), were defeated by non-Muslim TRS candidates.

From the Muslim nomination point of view, the main parties in the state are the then TRS (now, the BRS), AIMIM, Congress and TDP. The TRS was aware of the BJP's politics of polarization and, realised that there was a huge Hindu-Muslim divide in the state. Muslim candidates therefore had poor chance of winning the elections. So, in 2014 TRS leader K. Chandrasekhar Rao openly apologised to the Muslims for not nominating a good number of candidates from their community. Although Rao had to drop his electoral representation promise due to strategic reasons in a meeting with a community delegation, he reiterated that he was committed to appointing a Muslim as the first Home Minister of Telangana. The party gave four tickets to Muslims. Only one candidate, Shakil Aamir Mohammed registered a victory. Thus, the nomination by TRS was just 3.36 per cent. In 2018, the party fielded eight candidates which translated to just 6.72 per cent of total nominations by the party. The AIMIM can directly influence voters in more than 20 constituencies, in seven of which it has been winning in the last two elections. In 2014, the party contested 20 seats. However, in 2018 it contested only eight seats even though it had initially filed nominations for 21 seats.[22] In 2018, all parties together fielded 26 Muslim candidates in 119 seats. The BJP fielded one Shehazadi Syed who lost to Akbaruddin Owaisi at Chandrayangutta. The Congress fielded nine Muslims and the TDP one. All these candidates lost.[23]

Muslim-dominated Assembly Constituencies

Muslims constitute 12.7 per cent of the state's population (2011 Census), and deserve at least 15 MLAs. They are scattered in almost all districts of Telangana, but are highly concentrated in Adilabad, Mahabubnagar, Nizamabad, Nalgonda, Ranga Reddy, Hyderabad, Medak and Karimnagar districts. Of 119 ACs, in seven segments, Muslims account for 50 to 90 per cent of the voters. In the other segments their distribution is as follows: 20 to 50 per cent in 10, 15 to 20 per cent in 12, 10 to 15 per cent in 13, 5 to 10 per cent in 42, and 2 to 5 per cent in remaining 35 segments. There is not a single AC, which does not have at least 2 to 3 per cent Muslims. The top seven ACs that have over 50 per cent Muslim voters are: Bahadurpura, Chandrayangutta, Charminar, Yakutpura, Nampally, Karwan and Malakpet. Other ACs with 20 to 50 per cent Muslim voters include Nimzabad (Urban), Jubilee Hills,

Rajendranagar, Zaheerabad (SC), Bodhan, Goshamahal, Mahabubnagar, Khairatabad, Sangareddy and Adilabad. Another 12 seats, Amberpet, Warangal East, Karimnagar, Banswada, Tandur, Musheerabad, Vikarabad, Nirmal, Mudhele, Maheshwaram, Secunderabad and Sanathnagar have between 15 to 20 per cent Muslim voters.[24]

While the AIMIM dominates the electoral scene in the top seven constituencies, many prominent leaders from the BRS, Congress-TDP alliance and BJP are engaged in tough contests in most of the 35 ACs with Muslim vote share of 10 to 15 per cent. It is obvious that securing a sizeable chunk of Muslim votes is crucial for the main contenders from BRS, Congress and TDP. This raises concerns about underrepresentation of Muslims in Telangana. As per the present population share, there should be at least 15 Muslim MLAs. But the actual number of Muslims elected to the assembly from Telangana region, since 1951 has ranged between five and eight. From the 2014 and 2018 elections results, it is clear that the BRS is the main party in Telangana along with the TDP and Congress.

The AIMIM is a dominant force which can expand its sphere of influence much beyond Hyderabad City, where it is presently focussed. The BJP has tried to profit by polarising the majority community on slogans of 'minority appeasement' and 'unconstitutional reservation' for Muslims, but has failed so far. If the AIMIM expands its base beyond Hyderabad and the BRS and Congress-TDP nominate a fair number of Muslims, their share in the assembly can go up sub-stantially.

UTTAR PRADESH

In 18 elections to the UP Assembly, a total 7,544 MLAs were elected of which 668 were Muslims (8.85 per cent). During this period, Muslims formed 16.53 per cent of the state population, and deserved 1,246 MLAs. They faced 46.39 per cent deprivation, which is higher than Assam (32.27 per cent) and West Bengal (42.67 per cent), but lower than Bihar (47.63 per cent). In the first elections of 1952, the Congress nominated 41 Muslims of which 40 were elected which shows that initially the party had monopoly over Muslim voters, who trusted it for their safety and security. The Socialist Party nominated 14 Muslims of whom only one was elected while two candidates of the CPI failed to register a victory. Thus, in the first Assembly there were 41 Muslim MLAs translating to 9.53 per cent. As per their population share Muslims deserved 61 seats, and thus faced 32.79 per cent deprivation. The Congress gave 9.56 per cent tickets, which got reflected in 9.53 per cent representation (Table 4.17).

In 1957, the Congress nominated 48 (11.6 per cent) of whom 27 were elected. Out of the 22 Muslims that the PSP nominated only two were elected. Eight more Muslims were elected as

TABLE 4.17: REPRESENTATION OF MUSLIMS IN UTTAR PRADESH ASSEMBLY

Year	*Total MLAs*	*Muslim MLAs*	*% of Muslim MLAs*	*% of Muslims in Population*	*Expected MLAs as per Population*	*% Deprivation*
1952	430	41	9.53	14.28	61	32.79
1957	430	37	8.84	14.28	61	39.34
1962	430	30	6.98	14.63	63	52.38
1967	425	23	5.41	14.63	62	62.90
1969	425	23	5.41	14.63	62	62.90
1974	424	25	5.90	15.48	66	62.12
1977	425	49	11.53	15.48	66	25.76
1980	425	47	11.06	15.48	66	28.79
1985	425	49	11.53	15.93	68	27.94
1989	425	38	8.94	15.93	68	44.11
1991	419	17	4.06	17.33	73	76.71
1993	422	25	5.92	17.33	73	65.75
1996	424	33	7.78	17.33	73	54.79
2002	403	47	11.66	18.50	75	37.33
2007	403	56	13.90	18.50	75	25.33
2012	403	69	17.12	19.26	78	11.54
2017	403	25	6.20	19.26	78	67.95
2022	403	34	8.44	19.26	78	56.41
TOTAL	7,544	668	8.85	16.53	1,246	46.39

Source: ECI website and http:// censusindia.gov.in.

independents. Thus, in the second election 37 Muslims were elected (8.84 per cent), and faced 39.34 per cent deprivation. In the third election of 1962, there were 30 MLAs; 24 belonged to the Congress, and three each to the CPI and Republican Party of India (RPI). They constituted 6.98 per cent of MLAs and faced 52.38 per cent deprivation. When a series of bloody communal riots occurred in the state and the Congress seemed woefully inadequate in protecting their lives and dignity, Muslim voters drifted away from the party. In the three elections of 1967, 1969 and 1974, 16, 19 and 15 Muslims were elected respectively on Congress nominations. Their total strength also reduced to 23, 23 and 25 respectively, and as a result, they faced more than 62 per cent deprivation in all those elections.

In 1977, Muslims overwhelmingly voted in favour of the Janata Party as per the national trend, which paid dividends in the form of 49 Muslims getting elected 38 of whom belonged to the Janata Party. Their representation was 11.53, and deprivation 25.76 per cent, which was the lowest since 1952. In 1980 and 1984, respectively 47 and 49 got elected which was again in tune with the Muslim-friendly trend of 1980-5. Though the Congress staged a comeback the party could not win back the trust of Muslim voters as before.

It is generally said that the emergence of the BJP is always accompanied with the political marginalization of Muslims. In UP, it has been clearly proved by the election results of 1991 and 2017 when BJP emerged victorious with clear majority. In 1991, the Ramjanmabhoomi agitation was at its peak and voters were completely polarized on religious lines. When assembly elections were held, BJP emerged victorious with 221 seats in 425-member Assembly. Only 17 Muslim MLAs got elected, three belonged to the Congress, one to BSP and 13 to parties like JD and JNP. Muslims constituted 4.06 per cent of total MLAs and faced 76.71 per cent deprivation, the highest ever. This shows that whenever elections are fought on religious issues, voters get polarized and Muslims do not get their due share of representation. From 2002 onwards political scenario for Muslims started to improve as the effect of polarization has receded. In 2002, 47 MLAs got elected,

23 belonged to SP, 14 to BSP, 4 to the Congress and six to other parties and independents.

The 2007 elections were held against the backdrop of simmering communal tensions, as the Sangh Parivar worked overtime to provoke Muslims and portray them as terrorists and traitors. But the community leadership was acutely aware that a polarized election would benefit the BJP and advocated restraint from all possible forums. Muslims held their peace and maintained calm and thus were rewarded: the BJP's tally dipped from 89 to 51, while number of Muslims climbed to 56, the highest since 1952.[25] Their representation was 13.9 per cent and deprivation as low as 25.33 per cent. 29 MLAs belonged to the BSP, 21 to SP, 3 to RLD, one to Uttar Pradesh United Democratic Front (UPUDF) and two to independent. 48 candidates finished as runners-up, 21 belonged to SP, 18 to BSP, 6 to the Congress, 2 to RLD, and 1 to UPUDF. The noticeable feature of 2007 elections was that none of Congress Muslim candidates got elected and winners were almost equally divided in two parties: SP and BSP.

During the election of 2012, the issues of education, employment and speedy implementation of the recommendations of Sachar Committee was uppermost in the minds of Muslim voters. The community was also disturbed by the persistent victimization and arrest of innocent Muslim young men by security agencies, and the Batla House encounter, which it considers a fake encounter to date. In July 2011, the then CM Mayawati faxed a letter to the then PM Manmohan Singh, and demanded a Constitutional Amendment to expand the quota for backward sections amongst Muslims. An alarmed Congress announced 4.5 per cent sub-quota for OBCs among minorities. When the announcement backfired, Salman Khurshid announced that the sub-quota would be raised to 9 per cent after the election. Mulayam Singh Yadav, for his part, announced 18 per cent reservation for Muslims, if voted back to power. Yadav also promised that Urdu medium schools would be set up in every Muslim locality, and that recommendations of the SCR and Ranganath Mishra Commission would be implemented. Besides, he announced speedy trial in cases related to terror charges. When election results were declared, it became clear that Muslims had put their faith in SP, and voted overwhelmingly in its favour and the party returned to power with a clear majority. A record 69 Muslim MLAs were elected constituting 17.12 per cent almost close to share in population (19.26 per cent). Of those MLAs, 43 belonged to the SP, 16 to BSP, four to Congress, three to Peace Party, two to Qaumi Ekta Dal (QED) and one to Ittehad-e-Millat Council (IEMC). A record 66 candidates finished as runners-up, 13 belonging to SP, 39 to BSP, 10 to Congress, three to RLD and one to Apna Dal (AD). Muslims deserved 78 seats, thus they faced 11.54 per cent deprivation, the lowest since 1952. SP had fielded 78 candidates against 58 in 2007, and 43 of them registered win. BSP gave tickets to 85 against 61 in 2007, and only 16 could register the win. Riding on Rahul Gandhi's Mission-2012 euphoria, the Congress fielded 62 candidates, against 49 in 2007, but only four could win. The RLD had fielded nine in the Western UP region, but all of them lost. The victory graph of these parties showed the same trend in 140 Muslim-dominated constituencies across the state. SP won 72, BSP 27, while BJP and Congress bagged 25 and 11 seats respectively.[26] The majority of Muslims votes went to Mulayam as Muslims did tactical voting and gave almost 75 per cent of their votes to him.

In 2017, the BJP registered a massive victory, and came to power with 321 MLAs. Muslim representation fell drastically. Only 25 Muslims were elected; 17 of them belonged to the SP, six to BSP, and two to the Congress, forming just 6.2 per cent and facing huge deprivation of 67.95 per cent. The BJP and its ally Apna Dal, which together won a whopping 321 seats, did not field a single Muslim candidate and used communal rhetoric during the election campaign, as well to polarize Hindu votes. In 2012, Muslims had performed very well and five years later their representation drastically fell to one-third of what should have been.

Political scientists have tried to find valid reasons for this turn around. Between 2010 and 2015, UP witnessed a five-fold increase in communal violence and polarization was evident in villages, towns and cities *IndiaSpend* reported in February 2017. The communal riots of Shamli and Muzaffarnagar played a major role in polarizing the voters not only in Western UP, but also in whole of it and other parts of India. Even during the election campaign voters were polarised on issues like *shamshan* (cremation crowd) and *qabristan* (graveyard). Polarization worked in favour of BJP as it registered massive win. The second factor was division of votes among secular parties/alliances. Experts pointed out at data which showed that SP-INC alliance, and the BSP had jointly polled more votes than the BJP in 370 of 403 ACs. In several ACs, the split in Muslim votes between these two alliances helped the BJP. In more than two dozen seats the division of Muslim votes benefited the BJP, even in the communally polarized areas of Muzaffarnagar and Shamli, Muslims failed to judge the winning candidate. Nowhere was this more obvious than Meerapur, the AC in Muzaffarnagar which was the epicentre of the 2013 communal riots. In the three-way division, the SP lost to the BJP by 193 votes, while the BJP's Avtar Singh Bhadana got 69,035 votes and SP's Liyakat Ali got 68,842 votes. These results belie assumptions that Muslims vote en mass in communally polarized areas. Eighty-four Muslim candidates were runners-up, 35 each belonged to the SP and BSP, 13 to the Congress, and one to the AIMIM.

In 2022, when the election was again fought on communal lines through slogans of 80 per cent *vs* 20 per cent, Jinnah, Buldozer baba and in the backdrop of atrocities inflicted on Muslims, the BJP returned to power winning 255 seats. Muslims won 34 seats, 31 belonged to the SP, two to the RLD and one the Suheldev Bharatiya Samaj Party (SBSP). BSP fielded 88 Muslim candidates, while the SP 64 and AIMIM more than 60 candidates.

In UP, the mainstream parties except the BJS/BJP have given a fair number of tickets to Muslims often close to their due share. In the first elections of 1952, the Congress nominated 41 Muslims (9.56 per cent), the Socialist Party 14 and CPI two. In 1957, Congress nominated 48 (11.16 per cent) and the PSP 22. Till 1980, the Congress had been nominating almost 10 per cent in all elections. The average Congress nomination from 1980 to 1993 had been about 11 per cent. During this period, Muslims did not vote for the Congress in UP hurt, and upset as they were especially after the events of 1992 and the aftermath. Following this the

Congress reduced its nomination to just 13 (3.14 per cent) in 1996, which is the lowest since 1952. The 1989 elections marked the entry of the BSP as a Muslim-friendly party, which nominated 75 Muslims (20.16 per cent) in its first election. The SP entered electoral politics in 1991 and gave almost 16 per cent tickets. The BSP, SP, and JD had nominated about 20, 14 and 17 per cent Muslims respectively, while the LKD nominated 14 per cent in 1996. In the 2002 elections, the BSP, SP and Congress respectively nominated 82, 46 and 61 Muslims. Overall, the Congress has given close to 10 per cent nomination, which has increased in recent times as the party wants to attract Muslim voters. The BSP and SP have given close to 20 and 16 per cent nominations respectively. Both these parties have been forming the government in rotation in UP. The nomination of Muslims by the Congress, BSP, and SP in Muslim-dominated ACs has caused division in Muslim votes resulting in the victory of non-Muslim candidates. This is one of the most serious issues that UP Muslims are facing today.

Muslim-dominated Assembly Constituencies

Muslims make up 19.26 per cent of UP's population (2011 Census) and they deserve at least 78 MLAs. Political analysts argue that due to their large population, Muslims can influence elections in 140 to 150 ACs. Gilles Verniers, a prominent political scientist, in his report published in 2014 by The Hindu Centre for Politics and Public Policy (a think tank) says that Muslims of UP are mostly concentrated in Upper Doab, Rohilkhand, Awadh, and the North of Poorvanchal. Twenty districts and around 100 *tehsils* have a Muslim population of over 20 per cent. The Muslim vote is a determining factor in 34 out of 80 PCs, and in 130 out of 403 ACs. As per another report, there are 21 minority-concentrated districts (MCD), identified as those where at least 25 per cent of the population comprises minorities, especially Muslims. These 21 MCDs account for 133 assembly seats.[29] Ali Zafar, a prominent Muslim voice in UP says, 'There are as many as 143 seats in UP where it has traditionally been believed that Muslims can make or mar the fortunes of political parties. Of those, in 70 seats Muslims have 20-5 per cent, and in the remaining 73, they account for 30 per cent or more of the population.'[30] Besides, there are other reports, which suggest there are roughly 130 to 140 seats where only Muslims can win or decide the winner.

To conclude, Muslims in UP, as per their numerical share deserve at least 78 MLAs. This is not difficult to achieve as there are at least 130 to 140, seats, where Muslims are in dominant position and only they decide the winner. If the main political parties especially the SP, BSP, and Congress give proper share in nominations, ensure that Muslims vote do not get divided due to multiplicity of candidates and also fetch few votes from other marginalized communities, Muslims can easily achieve their due share in the UP Assembly.

UTTARAKHAND

Uttarakhand was formed on 9 November 2000 as the 27th state of India by carving out the Northern hilly regions of UP. Since its formation, five elections have been held in which only 13 Muslim MLAs were elected out of a total of 350 (3.71 per cent). During this period, the Muslim population share in the state has been 13.14 per cent, and they deserved 46 MLAs. As only 13 MLAs got elected, they faced 71.74 per cent deprivation. Uttarakhand is among the states, where political deprivation of Muslims is excessively high (Table 4.18).

In 2002, only three MLAs were elected which was just 4.29 per cent. These three MLAs belonged to the BSP and were elected from Manglaur, Bahadrabad and Laldhang. Of the four runners-up, two belonged to the Congress and one each to SP and BSP. In the second elections again, there were three MLAs all of whom belonged to the BSP and elected from the same constituencies as in 2002. Four candidates finished as runners-up, two belonged to the SP, one to Congress and one was an independent. In 2012, only two MLAs, Furkan Ahmed of the Congress from Pirankaliyar, and Sarwat Kareem Ansari of the BSP from Manglaur were elected forming only 2.86 per cent. Six candidates finished as runners-up, three each belonging to the Congress and BSP. In 2017, again two MLAs got elected, Ahmed from Pirankaliyar and Qazi

TABLE 4.18: REPRESENTATION OF MUSLIMS IN UTTARAKHAND ASSEMBLY

Year	*Total MLAs*	*Muslim MLAs*	*% of Muslim MLAs*	*% of Muslims in Population*	*Expected MLAs as per Population*	*% Deprivation*
2002	70	3	4.29	11.92	8	62.50
2007	70	3	4.29	11.92	8	62.50
2012	70	2	2.86	13.95	10	80.00
2017	70	2	2.86	13.95	10	80.00
2022	70	3	4.29	13.95	10	70.00
TOTAL	350	13	3.71	13.14	46	71.74

Source: ECI website.

Mohammad Nizamuddin from Manglaur, both on Congress tickets. Of the three runners-up, two belonged to the BSP and one to the Congress. In 2022 when the BJP retained power, only three Muslim MLAs got elected: two belonged to the BSP and one to the Congress. The Congress fielded two Muslim candidates, while the BSP fielded three and SP eleven. The AIMIM which entered first time in the state provided four tickets to Muslims.

There is no data in the public domain to help draw a clear picture about the nomination of Muslims by the main parties like the Congress, BJP, BSP and SP. The Congress and BSP have near monopoly over the Muslim votes. But they have not given due nomination to the Muslims. The number of successful Muslim candidates, and runners-up suggest that the Congress has been giving only four to five tickets to Muslims in every election. The BSP and SP have been giving seven to eight tickets which are not proportionate to population. The BJP simply does not nominate Muslim candidates in the state. In 2012, the party had given just one ticket to a Muslim candidate, Kaleem Ansari who lost from Mangalaur.

Muslim-dominated Assembly Constituencies

Muslims constitute almost 14 per cent of the state's population. Of the total 1.1 crore voters, over 15 per cent are Muslims. Minority communities can influence poll outcome in at least 34 of 70 ACs. The share of Muslim voters goes up to between 15 and over 50 per cent in 23 out of the 70 ACs that are spread across Haridwar (10 ACs), Udham Singh Nagar (8 ACs), Dehradun (3 ACs), and Nainital (2 ACs).[31] In all the 11 ACs in Haridwar, Dalits and Muslims are jointly in a position to decide the winner. According to 2011 Census, of the total population of 18,90,422 in Haridwar district, there are 6,48,119 Muslims (34.28 per cent). There are 13,05,266 voters in 11 ACs and Muslims, on an average constitute 20 to 50 per cent of the voters in each AC. There are more than 6 ACs such as Roorkee, Piran Kaliyar, Bhagwanpur, Manglaur, Khanpur, Jwalapur, etc., where percentage of Muslim voters is from 25 to 50 per cent.[32] Of 11 lakh voters in Udham Singh Nagar, between 2 to 2.5 lakhs voters are Muslims, about 2 lakh Dalits and 1.8 lakh are Sikhs. Similarly, Nainital district has almost 1 lakh Muslim voters. In Udham Singh Nagar, Muslims are deciding factor in at least six ACs. Jaspur and Kiccha are two most important ACs as they have sizeable Muslim population. Thus, the 15 ACs where only Muslim candidates can win or decide the winner are: Piran Kaliyar, Sahaspur, Manglaur, Laksar, Haridwar (Rural), Jaspur, Kiccha, Khatima, Khanpur, Chakrata, Bhagwanpur, Jwalapur, Roorkee, Sitarganj and Jhabrera.

State's political space is primarily dominated by two Hindu upper castes: Brahmins and Thakurs, who respectively constitute 22-5 and 35 per cent of state population. Most of chief ministers so far have been from these two upper castes. The 19 per cent SC population is close to UP's 20-1 while Muslim's 14 per cent is nowhere near UP's 19 per cent. The OBCs constitute less than 5 per cent, while STs constitute 3 per cent.

Because of the dominance of the Brahmins and Thakurs, political parties do not bother to appeal to Dalits and Muslims. Except in pockets in the plains, these parties mostly nominate candidates from the upper castes.[33] It is also an established fact that whenever politics is dominated by the UCHs, especially Brahmins, Thakur and Baniyas, the Hindu OBCs and Muslims are bound to suffer politically. According to the Indian Council of Social Science Research (ICSSR), the Muslims of Uttarakhand face acute poverty, unemployment and lack of development as compared to their Hindu counterparts. Only 69 per cent Muslims in age group of 5-16 were enrolled in formal educational institutions compared to 86 per cent of Hindus. Communal elements in the state are freely spreading hate and threatening Muslims to further marginalize them socio-economically and politically. In this situation, main parties like the Congress and BSP must think about how to improve representation. A fair number of nominations, prevention of division of Muslim and Dalit votes and ensuring a non-polarised political space can improve share of Muslims in the state's political scene.

WEST BENGAL

From 1952 to 2021 a total 4,801 MLAs have been elected of them 644 were Muslims (13.41 per cent). During 70 years, their average share in state population has been 22.47 per cent, and they deserved 1,080 MLAs. Thus, they have faced 40.37 per cent deprivation which is lower than of Bihar (47.37 per cent) and UP (46.39 per cent), but higher than Assam (32.27 per cent). Presently, Muslims constitute 27.01 per cent of population, which is almost double than the national population share (14.2 per cent), and they deserve 79 MLAs. In 1952, 22 MLAs got elected and they faced 52.17 per cent deprivation, which is the highest so far and the only occasion deprivation was above 50 per cent. Deprivation has been high in elections of 1957, 1971 and 2001. The lowest was noted in 2011 and 2016, when 59 got elected in both years: share was the highest at 20.07 and deprivation the lowest at 25.32 per cent. In 2021, 43 MLAs got elected and deprivation rose up to 45.57 per cent, which is higher than the average (Table 4.19).

In the first election of 1952, the Congress nominated 24 Muslims out of its total 236 (10.17 per cent) nomination, whereas Muslim population share was 19.46 per cent. Twenty of these canditates alongwith two independents were elected. They constituted 9.24 per cent of the first assembly facing a huge deprivation of 52.17 per cent due to under-nomination by the Congress, whatever the social constraints and political compulsions might

TABLE 4.19: REPRESENTATION OF MUSLIMS IN WEST BENGAL ASSEMBLY

Year	*Total MLAs*	*Muslim MLAs*	*% of Muslim MLAs*	*% of Muslims in Population*	*Expected MLAs as per Population*	*% Deprivation*
1952	238	22	9.24	19.46	46	52.17
1957	252	25	9.92	19.46	49	48.98
1962	252	27	10.71	20.00	50	46.00
1967	280	35	12.50	20.00	56	37.50
1969	280	36	12.86	20.00	56	35.71
1971	279	29	10.39	20.46	57	49.12
1972	280	35	12.50	20.46	57	38.60
1977	294	37	12.59	20.46	60	38.33
1983	294	36	12.24	21.51	63	42.86
1987	294	35	11.91	21.51	63	44.44
1991	294	42	14.29	23.61	69	39.13
1996	294	40	13.61	23.61	69	42.03
2001	294	39	13.27	25.25	74	47.30
2006	294	45	15.30	25.25	74	39.19
2011	294	59	20.07	27.01	79	25.32
2016	294	59	20.07	27.01	79	25.32
2021	294	43	14.63	27.01	79	45.57
TOTAL	4,801	644	13.41	22.47	1,080	40.37

Source: ECI website.

be. In 1957, the Congress increased its nominations to about 12 per cent, 21 Muslims got elected. Together with two CPI MLAs and two independents, the total was 25 (9.92 per cent) and they faced 48.98 per cent deprivation. In 1962, 1967, and 1969, 27, 35 and 36 Muslim MLAs respectively got elected. In 1969, 36 MLAs were divided among 11 parties and 6 independents. The Congress still enjoyed monopoly over Muslim voters as it had 12 Muslim MLAs. In 1971, the CPI(M) with 11 Muslim MLAs became a major challenge to the Congress which still had 16 MLAs. In 1977, the CPI(M) became the major party representing Muslims by winning 22 seats for them. Although CPI(M) had increased its monopoly over the Muslim voters, the INC was not wiped out as it had good number of Muslim MLAs in every election. In 2001, a total of 39 MLAs were elected, which was one less than in 1996. Muslims constituted 13.27 per cent of all MLAs and faced 47.3 per cent deprivation. The CPI(M) had 17 MLAs, while Congress with 10 was in the second position. Rest of the MLAs were distributed among several parties. The TMC which entered the elections in 2001 had only two Muslim MLAs.

In 2006, 45 MLAs were elected: 25 belonging to CPI(M), 7 to Congress, 3 each to the TMC and All India Forward Bloc (AIFB), four to Revolutionary Socialist Party (RSP) and one each to CPI, RJD and West Bengal Socialist Party (WBSP). They constituted 15.3 per cent of total MLAs and faced almost 40 per cent deprivation. Of the 51 runners-up, 22 belonged to the TMC, 18 to the Congress, 8 to the CPI(M), 2 to the AIFB and 1 to the CPI. Although the TMC could manage to win only three seats for Muslims, its 22 members featuring at the second position gave an indication that the party would be a major political force popular among Muslims. In 2011, the TMC-Congress alliance came to power with 226 MLAs, ending 35 years-rule of the CPI(M). The Left Front could win only 61 seats (CPI(M) 40, CPI 2, AIFB 11, RSP 7 and SP 1). In this election, 59 Muslim MLAs got elected: 26 belonged to the TMC, 14 to Congress, 13 to CPI(M), two each to AIFB and RSP and one each to SP and independent. Muslims constituted around 20.07 per cent of all MLAs, and faced the least deprivation of 25.32 per cent. Of 59 MLAs, 15 had been elected from Murshidabad district alone. As high as 57 candidates finished as runners-up, 27 belonged to CPI(M), 10 to the TMC, 7 to Congress, 5 to AIFB, 4 to RSP, 1 each to CPI, and the Revolutionary Communist Party of India (RCPI) and two independents. This was the first occasion when the representation of Muslims went above the 20 per cent mark. Even this strength was less than 7 per cent compared to 27.01 per cent share in population. The findings of the SCR and their pathetic socio-economic condition was one of the factors Muslims shifted their support from the CPI(M) to the TMC. They also hoped that Mamata Banerjee would implement the SCR to improve their socio-economic and employment conditions. In 2016 elections, the Muslim representation remained at 59 as in 2011, constituting

20.07 per cent of the total, 32 belonging to the TMC, 18 to Congress, 8 to CPI(M), and 1 to the AIFB. The Congress managed to increase its count to 18 from the previous 14, reaping the benefits of an alliance with the Left Front whose total strength reduced to 9 from 18, five years before. Of the 61 runners-up, 26 belonged to the CPI(M), 19 to the TMC, 9 to the Congress, 2 to the AIFB, 1 each to the RSP, CPI and DCP(PC) and 2 were independents.

The 2021 elections were basically contested between two parties: the TMC and BJP. While the former struggled to regain the mandate for the third time, the BJP tried aggressively to dislodge the former by polarizing the elections on basis of a range of communal and sectarian issues. It accused Mamata Banerjee for playing the politics of minority appeasement but failed. Of 292 seats for which results were declared, the TMC bagged 213, while BJP managed to win 77 only. 43 Muslim MLAs got elected: 42 belonged to the TMC and one to the Indian Secular Front (ISF). None of the Muslim candidates of the Congress and CPI(M) could win as Muslim votes fully consolidated behind the TMC. Nineteen candidates finished as runners-up, five belonged to the BJP, four each to the Congress and ISF, three to CPI(M), two to TMC, and one independent. The main reason behind the decline in the number of Muslim MLAs is the rise of BJP on the electoral scene of the state and decline of the Congress and Left Front. As opposed to 2016, when 53 Muslims had been nominated by the TMC, this time only 47 were nominated. This is one of the reasons for decline in number of Muslim MLAs. Due to emergence of BJP, its polarization politics and consequent fear of losing majority community votes among the secular parties resulted in less nomination of Muslims. Consequently their representation fell from 20.07 in 2016 to 14.64 per cent in 2021.

From 1952 to 1972, the Congress was the major party representing Muslims in the state. In 1952, it nominated 24 Muslims out of 236 seats that it contested (10.17 per cent), half of Muslims' share in population. Twenty of them got elected. In 1957, it nominated 27 out of 251 which amounted to 10.76 per cent. The Congress' nomination of Muslims hovered between 8.93 (1969) and 15.28 per cent (1996). Its average nomination during 1952 and 2001 has been 12.48 per cent, whereas in the same period the Muslims' average share in population was 21.21 per cent, which shows that it did not give due nomination. Average nomination by the CPI and CPI(M) had been respectively 7.51 and 12.48 per cent, which were also lower than population share of Muslims. Two other constituents of the Left Front, RSP and AIFB respectively nominated 6.98 and 6.57 per cent till 2001. The present ruling party, the TMC entered electoral politics in 2001 and nominated 24 Muslims out of total 226 (10.62 per cent) while they constituted 25.25 per cent of state population. In 2011, 39 Muslims were fielded by the party. In 2016, 53 were fielded which was about 18 per cent of total nomination. To counter the Muslim appeasement charge by BJP, it fielded only 47 Muslims (12 per cent) in 2021 which is much less than their population share. Analysing Muslim nomination by major parties like the Congress, CPI, CPI(M), TMC, etc., it is clear that they have not been given their due share which is the chief reason for their political deprivation.

Muslim-dominated Assembly Constituencies

Approximately, one-third of 294 ACs in WB have over 30 per cent Muslim electorates. Maldah, Murshidabad, North Dinajpur, South 24-Parganas, North 24-Parganas, Nadia, Birbhum and South Dinajpur have higher share of Muslims in district's total population. As per the 2011 Census, Murshidabad has 66.27 per cent Muslim share, whereas Maldah's population includes 51.27, and North Dinajpur 49.92 per cent Muslims. In 2011, of the 59 Muslim MLAs, 15 got elected from Murshidabad district alone. There are 79 ACs, where Muslims population percentage is 20 to 30 of which 13 are reserved for SCs and three for STs. There are 33 ACs, where the Muslims account for 30 to 40 per cent, and of which three are reserved for SCs. In the range of 40 to 50 Muslim population percentage, there are 15 ACs of which six are reserved for SCs. There are 13 ACs where Muslims' share in population is from 50 to 60 per cent, of which two are reserved for SCs. There are 31 ACs, where Muslims account for over 60 per cent of electorates, of which none is reserved. To conclude, there are 44 ACs where Muslims are in absolute majority and only they can win the elections.[34]

As per the 2011 Census, Muslims constitute 27.01 per cent of population, and they deserve 80 seats in the assembly. Unfortunately, they have never been able to reach close to this and have faced 40 per cent deprivation. Less nomination by main parties and reservation of Muslim-dominated seats for SCs are the main reasons. In 2021, the TMC fielded 79 SC candidates whose share in the state population is 23.5 per cent, and 17 ST candidates who constitute 5.8 per cent. It fielded only 47 Muslims although they constitute 27.01 per cent. West Bengal is communally less polarized where elections are contested normally on secular issues. If Muslims are given proper share in nominations, they would in turn be able to achieve due share in the assembly. Secular parties which wish to ensure social and political justice in the state must nominate fair number of Muslim candidates.

REASONS FOR LOW REPRESENTATION IN STATE ASSEMBLIES

Demographic Distribution

Uneven distribution of population restricts the political strength of Muslims to specific sub-regions. For example, Muslim voters in UP are mostly concentrated in Upper Doab, Rohilkhand, Awadh and the North of Poorvanchal. In Bihar, they are concentrated in Seemanchal and North-Western districts, and in Assam in Lower Region. The geographical distribution of Muslim MLAs roughly matches the demographic distribution, though it does not entirely equal it. Combined with the effect of the FPTP system, chances of winning electoral seats is usually determined by their voting strength at the constituency level. In ACs, where Muslim voters are in low numbers, their strength is not even counted. They can think of winning seats, where their proportion is more than

30 per cent of the total electorates. In ACs, where Muslim voters are between 10 to 25 per cent, they can decide the winner by leaning towards a particular candidate, but they cannot elect a candidate. In ACs, where they are between 25 to 40 per cent, election space is communalized and one observes strong consolidation of Hindu voters in favour of Hindu candidates, in most cases belonging to the BJP. Muslim candidates can think of winning seats where their voters are 30 to 40 per cent. Besides this, the ground experience tells us that due to gerrymandering of Muslim-dominated constituencies many of which have been so carved out that Muslims are not in position to decide the winner. It is a deliberate act of the delimitation authorities to reduce them to minority in many constituencies. Before the Gujarat elections of 2012, three ACs of Ahmedabad were carved in such a way that Muslim voters became a minority in their previous Muslim-dominated constituencies.[35]

When such doubtful gerrymandering is done, local Muslim leaders must move the courts against the unreasonable and biased act of the Delimitation Commission. When such policies were being adopted in Hyderabad, the AIMIM had moved the court. The government must set up an all-representative Delimitation Commission, which is not prejudiced about any religious, social and ethnic groups.

Low Nomination by Mainstream Parties

Mainstream parties that enjoy the support of Muslims do not provide due nomination to them. The Congress' nomination of Muslims varies from state-to-state, but it has been about 60 to 70 per cent of what they deserve. Regional parties like the SP, BSP, RJD, DMK, TDP, TMC, AAP, JD(U), etc., relatively give higher number of tickets, but still less than due share. Communist formations are also not much interested in improving representation of Muslims in politics, and used to offer limited nomination. Muslim-based parties like IUML, AIMIM, AIUDF, Peace Party, ISF, etc., have been providing much more nomination often higher than due share. The BJP normally does not offer tickets to Muslims, due to its majoritarian and exclusionary political agenda. In the 2017

UP elections, the party did not nominate a single Muslim candidate. The perception that Muslim voters split their votes locally could discourage parties to nominate less number of Muslims. Consolidation of Hindu votes, Muslim candidates not being able to get votes of other communities, communalization of politics, etc., are other main reasons, which discourage mainstream parties to give due nomination to Muslims. In recent years, however, mainstream parties, barring the BJP, have made more explicit appeals to Muslim voters with the hope of adding their support to their core electorates. However, a quick glance at ticket distribution shows that the number of tickets to Muslims has indeed recently increased, but not very substantially, and currently it is lower than what it was in the early 2000s.

It has also been observed that an increased number of Muslim candidates do not necessarily translate into increased number of Muslim MLAs. Since 2014, due to the politics of polarization of BJP, mainstream parties shy away from giving tickets to Muslims, which is evident from nominations in many state elections.

Reservation of Muslim-dominated Constituencies for SCs

In many states, several constituencies, where Muslims are in a majority and SCs/STs in minority have been reserved for the SCs/STs. In these seats, Muslims have a greater possibility of winning due to their numerical strength. The SCR conducted a study on delimitation in Bihar, UP and West Bengal and found 27 reserved ACs, where Muslims were more in number than Dalits. It also pointed to 28 general seats where the Dalit population was more than that in the reserved ACs, while Muslims were fewer in number.

Zafar Mahmood, a retired bureaucrat, has been arguing that there are many ACs reserved for SCs that have substantial Muslim population. As these seats fall in the reserved category, Muslims are not allowed to contest. He says, 'Section 9(1)(c) of the Delimitation Act mandates that those Constituencies be reserved in the Parliament and Assemblies where the SC concentration is the highest in the state. That law has been violated in the last seven decades and the loser in the process is the Muslim community.'

The SCR had recommended that the matter be referred to the Delimitation Commission asking it to fix the anomaly but the government has not done anything so far. Community organizations and activists have been writing to successive Prime Ministers, including Narendra Modi on this issue, but with no success.

Division of Votes

Division of votes among several Muslim candidates is one of the reasons for their defeat in elections. When there are several Muslim candidates in a constituency, voters fail to judge the strongest candidate. This leads to a split in votes and the loss of seats, often to the benefit of the BJP. For example, ten seats were lost in this manner in the 1996 assembly elections in UP to the sole benefit of BJP. In 2002, the BJP won 13 seats in the same way, while six other seats were lost due to the dispersion of Muslim votes in constituencies, where sometimes Muslims were in absolute majority. This situation arises also when a non-Muslim candidate of a secular party contests election from a Muslim-dominated seat. Several ambitious Muslim candidates also contest as 'spoilers' or 'vote-cutters'. In states other than UP, the BSP and SP candidates have got defeated several Congress/regional party candidates in Muslim-dominated seats. This has happened even in seats, where a secular party fielded Muslim candidates. This has resulted in a paradox: Muslim dominated seats elect BJP candidates without Muslim votes. This has happened in Gujarat as well. In this situation, the combined vote share of non-Congress Muslim candidates is more than the margin between BJP and Congress in a state where these parties are main contenders. The spoiler candidates take away significant votes that would have gone to the Congress, thereby helping the BJP to win.

Fielding non-Muslim Candidates from Muslim-dominated Constituencies

The secular/regional parties that enjoy Muslim support do not give tickets to them in many Muslim-dominated ACs, and they are asked to contest elections from seats which have low percentage of Muslims. This is evident from the analysis of assembly elections in many states like Bihar, UP, Maharashtra, MP, WB, Rajasthan, etc. In 2020, elections of Bihar, the Congress had given tickets to non-Muslim candidates from many Muslim-majority ACs. However, strong Muslim candidates were asked to fight from seats that had low share of Muslim voters. This indicates parties are not interested in improving representation and Muslims are given few tickets just for formality. Parties that are really interested in improving the representation of Muslims must give tickets to them from Muslim-majority constituencies, and also arrange party votes from other non-Muslim communities.

SOME IMPORTANT OBSERVATIONS

Muslim MLAs Mostly Emerge from Regional Parties

With a few exceptions, Muslim MLAs mostly come from regional parties. A few of the MLAs also belong to the Congress in states, such as MP, Rajasthan, Assam, Chhattisgarh, Karnataka, Gujarat, etc. Most of the MLAs belong to SP and BSP in UP, RJD and JDU in Bihar, TMC in West Bengal, AIUDF in Assam, BRS and AIMIM in Telangana, TDP and YSRCP in AP, DMK and AIDMK in Tamil Nadu, AAP in Delhi, IUML in Kerala, NC and PDP in Jammu & Kashmir, etc. In assembly elections of four states and one UT held in March-May 2021, Muslim candidates emerged winners in TMC, AIUDF, IUML, DMK and handful of little known regional parties. Muslim candidates also won on Congress and CPI(M) tickets in Assam and Kerala. Urmilesh, a senior journalist and author, says,

> Traditionally, for the minorities, Congress was the large umbrella platform, which offered them opportunities as an all-India party. With the decline of the Congress and the BJP less than welcoming, it is the regional parties that are offering them the opportunity to win elections from general constituencies. Parties like the RJD and SP in Bihar and UP have always offered them a platform. The regional parties now constitute the real opposition to the BJP.[36]

Regional parties are more secular in nature and provide not only socio-economic justice, but also ensure security to Muslims. These parties offer a platform to the minorities for their political empowerment. It is also true that they have aspirations to be a part of the national political scene.

BJP's Strong Show Tied to Lesser Muslim MLAs

Wherever the BJP and its alliance partners have performed well, the number of elected Muslim MLAs has reduced. Conversely, where non-BJP parties have done well, Muslim representation has generally gone up. For example, in UP in 2017, the BJP did exceptionally well and returned to power with three-fourth mandate. The number of Muslim MLAs dropped from 69 in 2012 to 25 in 2017. Percentage-wise it dropped from 17 to 6. In Karnataka elections of 2018, number of Muslim MLAs fell from 11 to 7. In the Bihar Assembly Elections of 2020, the BJP and its allies came to power and Muslim MLAs dropped from 24 to 19. In the state elections of Rajasthan, MP, Chhattisgarh, Delhi, Maharashtra, Odisha, and Jharkhand, the BJP was uprooted from power and Congress and regional parties came to power. Muslim representation grew marginally in some cases. The biggest increase was in Rajasthan, from two in 2013 to eight in 2018, where the Congress wrested power from BJP. In Chhattisgarh and MP, where the Congress ended 15 years of continuous BJP rule, the Muslim MLA count went up from NIL to one and one to two, respectively. Maharashtra and Jharkhand are interesting as number of Muslim MLAs increased little. The exceptions to this trend are some states where the number of Muslim MLAs increased while they were ruled by the BJP.[37]

Muslims' Vote Share in a Constituency Decides Issues of the BJP's Election Campaign

In the North Indian states, the election campaign issues taken up by the BJP are mostly decided by the percentage share of Muslims in that particular constituency. Ground realities often corroborate this observation. In areas, where Muslims form a majority (more than 50 per cent), fear of the BJP is relatively muted. The election issues here focus on land and livelihood, governance and delivery, development, etc. Even the BJP candidates are compelled to raise issues related to health, education, employment, infrastructure, etc. In contrast, where Muslims have moderate to sizeable presence (20 to 35 per cent), the BJP rakes up non-existent imaginary and communal issues and fosters prejudices to polarize Hindu voters. It does not raise the issue of beef ban in Goa and the North Eastern states due to fear of losing the majority votes. Whereas beef ban and cow protection issues are raised only in the Hindi-belt states.

Growing Concern for Community's Political Empowerment in States

Muslims have never been duly represented in the Parliament. Secondly, Muslim MPs are distributed among various national and regional parties and have not raised unified voice and compelled the government to frame laws for protection, progress and dignity. On the other hand, issues related to education, health, employment, economic progress, security, etc., are in the hands of states. There are serious discussions in the community and growing concern for political empowerment in states. Due to the hostile attitude of the BJP on the one hand and the half-hearted attempts of the Congress on the other, Muslims are turning towards regional and Muslim-base parties.

Unfortunately, while Muslims are making every effort to get due political representation due to the polarization effect, the regional parties are also not fulfilling their demands. Many politicians claim that putting up a Muslim candidate in a mixed locality is a losing proposition. Finally, Muslims are turning to Muslim base parties, such as AIMIM, AIUDF, ISF, IUML, etc. The emergence of these parties can be seen in this context. These parties are not growing in a vacuum. Muslim parties have fed off the growing feeling of political disempowerment among the Muslims, and the realization that it is increasingly becoming difficult for a Muslim candidate to get support outside the community.

NOTES

1. *The Indian Express*, Pune, 31 October 2013.
2. Ibid., Pune, 11 December 2013.
3. https://theprint.in/india/no-muslim-minister-in-15-of-indias-28-states-one-each-in-10-other/343623/
4. https://www.news18.com/blogs/india/do-we-need-a-muslim-party-0-744212.html
5. *The Indian Express*, Hyderabad, 10 April 2019.
6. *India Today*, New Delhi, 3 December 2017.
7. http://www.catchnews.com/politics-news/gujarat-polls-how-bjp-wins-muslim-dominated-seats-without-getting-muslim-votes-89475.html
8. Ibid.
9. *The Indian Express*, Mumbai, 20 December 2017.
10. https://thewire.in/politics/irrelevance-muslims-gujarat-elections
11. *The Hindu*, Bengaluru, 8 May 2018.
12. https://enarada.com/wooing-muslim-voters-in-karnataka
13. https://www.rediff.com/news/2008/may/07kgovt1.htm
14. https://zeenews.india.com/home/muslims-hold-key-in-onethird-seats_131494.html
15. https://www.newsclick.in/madhya-pradesh-polls-38-lakh-muslim-voters-only-4-candidates
16. *Hindustan Times*, Bhopal, 10 November 2018.
17. https://scroll.in/article/685289/in-numbers-new-maharashtra-assembly-has-lowest-number-of-muslims-ever
18. *The Indian Express*, Mumbai, 7 October 2019 (Additional information provided by Zeeshan Shaikh of *The Indian Express*).
19. *The Times of India*, Chennai, 30 December 2020.
20. https://www.india-seminar.com/2018/708/708-s-anwar.htm
21. https://www.newsclick.in/Why-BJP-Hindutva-Runs-Into-Tamil-Wall
22. *Business Standard*, Hyderabad, 2 December 2018.
23. *The Indian Express*, Pune, 14 December 2018.
24. *Telangana Today*, Hyderabad, 5 December 2018.
25. https://www.thehindu.com/news/states/article/2806264.ece
26. *The Times of India*, New Delhi, 14 March 2012.
27. *The Hindu*, New Delhi, 13 March 2017.
28. https://www.thehinducentre.com/verdict/commentry/article5886847.ece
29. *The Indian Express*, Pune, 7 March 2012.
30. *The Financial Express*, Lucknow, 13 March 2017.
31. *Hindustan Times*, New Delhi, 5 January 2017.

32. *The Times of India*, New Delhi, 12 January 2017.
33. *The Indian Express*, New Delhi, 15 February 2017.
34. Information compiled by Association SNAP (Social Network for Assistance to People).
35. *Inquilab*, Mumbai, 8 December 2012.
36. https://www.moneycontrol.com/news/trends/6868131.html.
37. *The New Indian Express*, New Delhi, 23 November 2020.

CHAPTER 5

Policy Issues Related to Political Representation

The term 'appeasement of minorities' is often heard one in Indian politics; it is an allegation regularly hurled at any party that even mentions taking up an issue relating to the minorities. The outcome is that the main political parties have taken fright and steer clear of taking up the concerns of the minorities. However, the irony is that while the minorities, especially the Muslims, face huge political and other forms of deprivation, we find that every party is trying to appease the Hindu voters. And within that, it is the UCHs who are being pandered to.

India has always been what Christophe Jaffrelot calls an 'ethnic democracy'; a system where the majority Hindus are privileged, and minority Muslims are discriminated against. Appeasement of the majority especially in religious matters is creating a sense of majoritarianism which is harming the political rights of minorities and tarnishing the image of our democracy at the international level.

Governments, mainstream political parties, the media and intellectuals blissfully ignore the political deprivation suffered by the weaker sections. Even today, there is no fixed mechanism to monitor and review the political participation of weaker sections and minorities in the Indian democratic process. Other allied issues like funding of elections, election expenditure, criminalization of politics, under representation of smaller parties, shifting to EVMs, etc., have been discussed by governments and Election Commission of India (ECI) appointed committees and commissions.

Even more pertinently—as we shall see below—a number of state level committees delved into the backward socio-economic situation of the Muslims, but failed to emphasize their political deprivation or recommend measures to mitigate it.

NON-INCLUSIVE FUNCTIONING OF INDIAN DEMOCRACY

Indian Muslims have been the victims of the non-inclusive functioning of Indian democracy since Independence. The political philosopher John Stuart Mill observed that 'the first principle of democracy is representation in proportion to population'. India is a signatory to the International Covenant on Civil and Political Rights, which binds the nations to ensure proper and equal representation of the minorities in every spheres of the government. However, Muslims, other religious minorities, OBCs and marginalized sections are in conspicuously negligible numbers in the Indian Parliament, state assemblies and cabinets.

From 1952 to 2019, Muslims constituted only 5.78 per cent of all elected MPs and faced 51.4 per cent deprivation. As mentioned in the previous chapter, they constituted 7.18 per cent of all MLAs in states and faced 49.57 per cent deprivation. Along with Muslims, other religious minorities, the poor and OBCs are also not proportionately represented in politics. Due to political reservations, the SCs and STs are represented in politics as per their share in population. Then who is cornering the benefits of politics in India at the cost of the deprived communities? The obvious answer is the UCHs. They have been enjoying disproportionate political benefits depriving Muslims, other minorities, OBCs, etc.

We Indians claim that ours is the largest democracy, which is secular and liberal in nature. However, since the first general elections, it has been facing genuine problems. Due to communalization of politics, use of money and muscle power, casteism, the weaker sections particularly the minorities and OBCs are deprived of the political right to be represented proportionately. The widespread use of communal issues and polarization of voters on religious lines, has made it difficult for Muslim candidates to get elected from mixed constituencies. Communal and caste propaganda during elections has cast its shadow on our democratic process. Similarly, issues related to progress, peace and development have been sidelined.

Political parties, democratic institutions like the ECI, various parliamentary committees, academic institutions, etc., are aware of the issue of political deprivation that Muslims and other groups are facing, but there is no honest attempt to improve the situation. Even the assurances given at the time of framing of the Constitution have not been fulfilled by successive governments. While scrapping provisions on reserved quota, the rights of Muslims and other minorities to fair share in legislatures and cabinets was not questioned in principle. These sections were assured that even without Constitutional guarantees they would be ensured their due share. In spite of such categorical assurances by Nehru, Patel, and other leaders to the minorities and Hukum Singh's sound proposal that after ten years of its functioning, the system of non-reservation of seats for minorities should be reviewed, no mechanism was created to monitor and review the situation.

Hamid Ansari, the former Vice-President of India points out, 'Democracy means that when decisions are made, I am a participant. If I am not a part, then exclusion follows.'[1] In India, minorities constitute almost 20 per cent of the total population, and if they are not participants in decision-making, and do not benefit from the democratic process, exclusion is an obvious result. This aspect of non-inclusive functioning of Indian democracy has caused huge political loss to religious minorities, especially Muslims, leading to security concerns, socio-economic and educational backwardness and a feeling of exclusion.

REPORTS ON ELECTORAL REFORMS

Several reports on electoral reforms have been published by a number of academic institutions, political observers and analysts, scholars, journalists, academicians and committees and commissions appointed by governments. These reports are:

1. V.M. Tarkunde Committee Report (1974-5)
2. The Study conducted by Centre for Policy Research (Lok Raj Baral on Party Reforms, 2000)

3. Dinesh Goswami Committee Report (1990)
4. The Indrajit Gupta Committee on State Funding of Elections (1998)
5. Justice V.R. Krishna Iyer Committee (1994)
6. 170th Report on 'Reform of the Electoral Laws' (1999) of the Law Commission
7. The Election Commission's comments on the recommendations of the various reports based on experience of ground realities.
8. Proposal of the Election Commission on Electoral Reforms (1998-2000)

These reports have covered general issues of electoral reforms, such as funding of elections, disproportionate vote-seat balance, stability of the Centre, criminalization of politics, etc. None of them has directly addressed the issue of underrepresentation of weaker sections, especially Muslims and OBCs. Despite being aware of these issues the ECI, successive governments, academic circles and other institutions have neglected to bring the issue into the public domain and suggest concrete steps to resolve it. On the contrary, deliberate attempts have been made to hide the facts.

The NCRWC's Consultation paper on 'Review of Election Law, Processes and Reform Options' has considered the FPTP system as undermining the representative character of our elected legislatures. The paper says:

> The multiplicity of political parties, combined with our Westminster based first-part-the-post system results in a majority of legislatures and parliamentarians getting elected on a minority vote. In other words, they usually win by obtaining less than 50 per cent of the votes cast i.e. with more vote cast against them than in their favour. There are states where 85 to 90 per cent of the legislatures have won on a minority vote.[2]

The paper recommends that there should be a run-off contest held the very next day or soon thereafter between the top two candidates so that one of them will necessarily win on the basis of 50 per cent plus one votes polled. However, the NCRWC left it to the government at the centre and the ECI to discuss this important issue: 'The commission recommends a careful and full examination of this issue by the Government and the Election Commission of India'.[3]

The NCRWC in its chapter on the 'Pace of Socio-Economic Change and Development' has clearly recognized the fact of under-representation of minorities, especially the Muslims:

> At present the political representation of minority communities in legislatures, especially Muslims, has fallen well below their proportion of population. The proportion of BCs among them is next to nil. This can lead to a sense of alienation. It is recommended that in situation of this kind, it is incumbent for political parties to build up leadership potential in the minority communities, including BCs, SCs and STs among them, for participation in political life. The role of the state for strengthening the pluralism of Indian polity has to be emphasised.[4]

However, the Commission failed to make any concrete suggestion to correct the representational deficit. The SCR underlines the political deprivation of Muslims thus:

> The participation of Muslims in nearly all political spaces is low which can have an adverse impact on the Indian society and polity in the long run. The marginalized either have inadequate numbers that comes in the way of making their presence felt in the normal course of governance or they are not politically empowered.[5]

The people, with whom the Committee interacted, said that political participation and representation in governance structures were essential to achieve equity. They alleged that participation was denied to Muslims through a variety of mechanisms.

The SCR cited two specific instances: First, non-inclusion of names of many Muslim voters in the voter-list in many states, and second, reservation of assembly/parliamentary constituencies for the SCs despite these being numerically dominated by Muslims. To further enhance participation of minorities in local bodies, the Committee recommended that appropriate state-level laws could be enacted on the lines of the AP government's initiatives of formulating and implementing new nomination procedures. The Committee recommended a more rational delimitation procedure to de-reserve Muslim-dominated constituencies. It also advocated that apart from these two initiatives, it was important to evolve other methods to enhance political participation of the community. As the Committee focused mainly on social, economic and educational conditions, it did emphasize political participation, but did not suggest specific measures to improve the political share of Muslims.

Other reports on the socio-economic conditions of Muslims in various states have highlighted their political deprivation, and its fallout on their socio-economic, educational and security conditions. 'Socio-Economic and Educational Backwardness of Muslims in Maharashtra: A Report', popularly known as the Mehmoodur Rahman Committee (MRC) report said that the Muslim community lagged behind severely in political representation. During that period, Muslims had 11 MLAs and five MLCs, although they deserved at least 30 MLAs. The MRC too failed to recommend anything to improve the situation. The Commission of Inquiry (CoI) constituted by the Telangana government in 2015 did not comment on political representation of Muslims in the state either. The report confined itself to social, economic, educational, security, exclusion and housing conditions of Muslims. Likewise, several states set up committees to investigate the socio-economic and educational backwardness of Muslims and suggest remedial measures. These committees/commissions neither analysed the issue of political underrepresentation nor did they suggest anything to improve it. The post Sachar Evaluation Committee, constituted to evaluate and review the implementation of recommendations of the SCR in 2013, submitted its report in 2014. The Committee Chairman, Prof. Amitabh Kundu and other eminent members made strong recommendations about giving SC status to Muslim and Christian Dalits, bifurcation of OBC category and other path-breaking measures. However, they did not analyse the political deprivation and could not suggest any remedial measures.

Political scientists and leaders have been highlighting the several issues directly related to policy and implementation, which adversely affect Muslim representation. I have no doubt that if the government or the ECI take serious note of these pertinent issues and devise corrective measures, political representation of Muslims would improve to a satisfactory level.

UNDER-NOMINATION BY POLITICAL PARTIES

It has been pointed out time and again that one of the main reasons responsible for political deprivation is under-nomination or inadequate nomination of Muslims by the main political parties. And this state of affairs holds true for parliament, state assemblies or the local bodies. They face discrimination and injustice at the very first stage. National secular parties like the Congress, CPI, CPM, etc., have given only 6 to 7 per cent tickets to Muslims in all the Lok Sabha elections. The OBC base parties and some regional parties provide slightly higher nominations, but still lower than their proportional share. The BJP which thrives on a 'hate Muslim' agenda tries to exclude them totally. Since 1980, the party has put up only 20 candidates in the Lok Sabha elections; just three of whom have won. Due to the rise of the BJP, Muslims are finding it even more difficult to get tickets from secular parties in today's political climate, and the anti-Muslim sentiments aroused by some leaders in the BJP has led to fewer Muslim candidates outside it. Secular parties fear being categorized as 'anti-Hindu', if they promote Muslim candidates.

The idea of 'inclusive democracy' requires that the composition of political parties and their electoral participation is genuinely inclusive. Judged by this standard, no political party in India is, indeed, inclusive. Political and social scientists have been advocating that the political parties must reflect 'social diversity' in their affairs: both in organization as well as nomination of candidates. In this context, they suggest that the People's Representation Act (PRA) should be amended to direct political parties to compulsorily reflect social diversity in their party organization, as well as in nomination of candidates to all elective bodies. This may be easily applicable to all national and state-level parties, but not to smaller parties which contest only few seats. Unless this is done, dominant caste/ communities would perpetuate their hegemonic control over affairs of political parties including most importantly nomination of candidates. Through the amendment, the national and state parties would be forced to reflect social diversity in their organizational structure, as well as in nomination of candidates to all type of elections. Under this provision all parties must annually submit community-wise break up of their candidates for election to the central and state legislatures and local body held during the preceding year. The ECI must scrutinize the party's community-wise nomination during the previous five years under the social diversity provisions. The parties must be required to offer an explanation for persistent underrepresentation of any social group, especially those like Muslims and Hindu OBCs, who have suffered political deprivation over a long period. However, it needs to be noted that nominating a fair number of Muslims by national/state parties will continue to remain unproductive unless parties take responsibility to get them elected by helping them on the ground level. This is also not going to produce any result, unless the single member constituency and FPTP system is replaced by multi-member constituencies and other vote counting methods.

DENIAL OF SC STATUS

As per Articles 330 and 332 of the Constitution, seats for SCs and STs are reserved respectively in the parliament and state assemblies in proportion to their share in population of the respective states/UTs. According to the recent Delimitation Commission, 84 seats are reserved for SCs, 47 for STs and 412 for general candidates. It is pertinent to note that under Article 341(1) of the Constitution, the President of India passed the President (Scheduled Castes) Order, 1950 granting SC status to Dalits, who professed only Hindu religion. The said Order was modified in 1956 and 1990 to include Sikh Dalits (Mazhabi Sikhs) and Buddhist (neo-Buddhist) religions respectively. As a consequence, the Dalit castes of Christian and Muslim communities are deprived of SC status and cannot avail the benefit of reservations in jobs, education and politics. Constitutional experts, scholars and politicians have been persistently arguing that the Order of 1950 discriminates against Dalits on the basis of their religion, and thus it is unconstitutional. It is anathema and a black spot on the Constitution. Muslims cannot contest the 84 seats reserved for SCs. If the order is made religion-neutral and SC status is extended to Dalits of the Muslim community, they may be able to increase representation by 12 Lok Sabha seats as per their 14.2 per cent share in national population. Muslims would also be able to increase seats in state assemblies according to their share in state population. The denial of SC status to Muslim Dalits is also an important factor for the pitiable number of Muslims in the parliament and state assemblies.

Dalit Christians and Muslims have been fighting legal and political battles to get SC status since 1950. They have been denied their genuine rights and the ruling parties must correct this injustice. The Supreme Court also must expedite the long pending petition and pronounce judgement in light of Article 14 of the Constitution, Indian caste realities and persistent injustice faced by Christian and Muslim Dalits.

DISCRIMINATION AGAINST MUSLIM STs

Unlike the Constitution (SC) Order, 1950, the category of ST is religion-neutral, which means castes of tribal origin in Muslims have also been granted ST status. In other words, Muslim STs are also given benefits of reservation in jobs, education and politics. As per the Delimitation Commission, 47 PCs and proportionate assembly seats in states are reserved for STs. This means Muslim groups, who qualify as ST can contest election from constituencies reserved for STs. However, it is disturbing to note that barring Lakshadweep, Muslim STs do not contest parliament election from any other PC reserved for STs due to several reasons. Muslim tribal groups are not properly counted during census operations and their number is always contested. Secondly, many Muslim tribal groups who qualify as STs are included in the OBC category, while their Hindu counterparts are in ST category. Thirdly, political parties do not give tickets to Muslim STs because of their low share in voters of reserved ST constituency. Fourthly, seats where Muslim STs are in good numbers have not been reserved for STs. Finally, non-Muslim voters do not support a Muslim candidate in a ST-reserved constituency.

Thus, it is suggested that if a sub-quota is carved out for Muslim STs, they may be able to win at least six to seven seats out of 47 reserved for all STs on national level. Identification of these six to seven seats does not require much effort and would be useful in improving the political representation of Muslims. This would also help in mainstreaming of tribal groups present in Muslim community.

RESERVATION OF MUSLIM-DOMINATED CONSTITUENCIES FOR SCs

Political scientists have pointed out that one of the reasons for low political representation of Muslims is the reservation of Muslim-dominated constituencies for SCs. The predominantly Muslim populated seats are reserved for SCs even though the SC voter percentage is insignificant there. On the other hand, constituencies having less Muslims, but high voter percentage of SCs are not reserved for the SCs. This blocks Muslims from getting elected from constituencies where they are in good numbers. In 2006, the issue was first highlighted by the Sachar Committee. The SCR said,

> Another issue emphasized before the Committee was that a number of Parliamentary and Assembly Constituencies with substantial Muslim voter population are reserved for SCs while the SC population was not high there. Certainly, constituencies with comparatively lesser Muslim voter population remain unreserved even though they have sizeable SC population.

From the reserved constituencies, only SC candidates can contest elections. The Committee analysed data of some ACs from Bihar, UP, and West Bengal and concluded that there was truth in the allegations submitted before the Committee. The Committee also said:

> Data relating to the reserved constituencies for SC candidates in three states of Uttar Pradesh, Bihar and West Bengal was analysed by the Committee. These states have a relatively large share of the Muslim population in India. The data shows that constituencies which have been declared reserved for SCs by the Delimitation Commission in these three states are by and large

those constituencies where Muslims live in greater numbers often more than 50 per cent as well as their proportion in the population is higher than that of SCs. On the other hand, there are quite a large number of other constituencies within the respective states, where the share of SCs is large, often closer to or even more than one half but these are declared as 'non-reserved'. Arguably, this can be seen as discriminatory and certainly reduces the opportunities that Muslims have to get elected to democratic institutions.[6]

After publication of the SCR, many community leaders and intellectuals demanded that the government correct the anomaly. Prominent among them is Dr. Syed Zafar Mahmood, an ex-bureaucrat and the president of the Zakat Foundation of India. According to him, in Assam for example, the Karimganj Lok Sabha constituency has 52 per cent Muslims (as per Census), and 13 per cent SC, but it is reserved for SCs. Yet, Jorhat and Dibrugarh are not reserved even though Muslim population there is only 5 per cent. Likewise, the Bahraich AC is reserved for SCs which has 35 per cent Muslims, and only 16 per cent SCs. But Raebareli is not reserved, although it has 30 per cent SCs and only 6 per cent Muslims. In state after state this trend continues.[7] As the chief editor of *Restoration of Representational Justice to Muslims in India: Case of De-reservation of Illegally Reserved Electoral Constituencies*, Mahmood has been fighting a long battle to restore Muslim-dominated constituencies. He, along with other activists, plans to approach the court for a constitutional remedy to curb the violation of law and to assure justice to the underrepresented Dalits and Muslims. According to the report, there are constituencies across the country, where restoration of justice is required for Muslims and Dalits. Citing an example from UP, Mahmood said that the Nagina PC has 43.21 per cent Muslims, and 22.05 per cent SCs but is reserved for SCs. Similarly, Nagina AC too has 56.8 per cent Muslims, and 26.7 per cent SC but is also reserved for SCs. On the other hand, Dhaurahra and Unnao PCs have more than 30 per cent SC population and much less Muslim presence, but these are not reserved. Chail, Maholi, Manikpur, Sirathu, Harchandpur, Hardoi, Purva, Marihan, Bakshi Ka Talab and other ACs have more than 30 per cent SC and negligible Muslim presence, but these are not reserved for SCs.[8]

Section 9(1)(c) of the Delimitation Act, 2002 reads as: 'Constituencies in which seats are reserved for the SCs shall be distributed in different parts of the state and located, as far as practicable, in those areas where the proportion of their population to the total is comparatively large'. However, this provision has been openly violated by the Delimitation Commission, while reserving parliament and assembly constituencies for SCs in all States/UTs. In fact, this has also been violated in reserving wards in municipal areas for different weaker sections of the society.

The SCR recommended a more rational delimitation procedure that did not reserve constituencies with high minority population shares for SCs and that would improve the opportunity for minorities, especially Muslims, to contest and get elected to the Indian parliament and the state assemblies. The UPA-I government, in principle, had accepted all recommendations of the SCR, but this vital recommendation has not been implemented so far. The Committee recommended the reference of this anomaly by the government to the Delimitation Commission which was in session then. But the Commission did not implement it, and the problem still persists. The government, on its part, neither communicated with the then Delimitation Commission nor did it constitute a fresh one with the clear mandate to correct the anomaly.

Muslim community leaders have been raising the issue before the government without any success. Dr. Mahmood, along with other community leaders, met the then PM Dr. Manmohan Singh on 16 September 2013, and apprised him about the situation. He said, 'We would earnestly urge you to kindly appoint the next Delimitation Commission immediately giving to it the clear mandate of looking into wrongful allocation of constituencies with large Muslim presence, for Scheduled Castes.'[9] Later on, he wrote a letter to Dr. Singh requesting the same. In January 2014, he met Rahul Gandhi while he was preparing for the General Elections of 2014. So far nothing positive has ensued. Had the UPA government in 2007-8 referred the recommendation of the SCR to the then Delimitation Commission which had been in session those days, this anomaly would have been corrected. But sadly, it failed to implement the SCR recommendations. As is obvious, this is a very important decision which calls for a strong political will on the part of the government. The government must discard the imaginary fear that the majority community will be antagonistic to such a move.

ADVERSE GERRYMANDERING OF CONSTITUENCIES

During the CAD, Mahatma Gandhi had proposed that certain constituencies be redrawn in such a way that they would become favourable to Muslims, so that they could increase their political representation. However, this positive intention has never been implemented. On the contrary, successive Delimitation Commissions have drawn the constituencies in such a way that the voting strength of Muslims has been reduced. Whether due to intended or unintended gerrymandering, these Commissions have been working against the political interests of Muslims. This can be easily noticed on the national level in cases of creation of PCs and ACs.

There are many districts in India where Muslim population is high in the administrative units. By adverse gerrymandering, the respective parliamentary constituencies are carved out in such a way that percentage of Muslim voters is much less than the percentage of Muslims in the districts. The modus operandi is to cut the Muslim-dominated areas in more than one part and every part is then attached to some other seats, where Muslims are in minority. Consequently, Muslims are in a minority in all the seats that are created. Similarly, assembly constituencies are drawn intentionally in such a way that voting strength of Muslims gets reduced. There are many small towns where Muslims are in majority. However, these towns are bifurcated and attached to two or more assembly constituencies thus making Muslims a minority in all. For example, in West Champaran district of Bihar, Devraj region has 22 villages with combined population of more than one lakh. After name of every village, 'Devraj' is added and these are majorly Muslim-dominated villages. These 22 villages are bifurcated and attached to three assembly constituencies: Ramnagar, Bagaha and Narkatiaganj, finally reducing the percentage of Muslims in all assembly constituencies. Such adverse gerrymandering can be seen in every state in India. This is done with the sole intention of reducing Muslim representation in elective bodies.

Adverse gerrymandering has also been applied in drawing boundaries of municipal wards in all big cities. This has resulted in low representation of Muslims in municipal corporations and councils. The common Muslim citizen in a city perceives that his or her voting strength is deliberately reduced by adverse carving out of the wards. This is difficult to recognize on the PC or AC level, but quite easy to see and understand in case of municipal wards because of small area and composition of voters.

Although the data presented in Table 5.1 is from 1991 Census and earlier Delimitation Commissions, the case of adverse gerry-

TABLE 5.1: ADVERSE GERRYMANDERING IN CASES OF SOME PARLIAMENTARY CONSTITUENCIES

S. No.	*State*	*PC*	*Percentage of Muslims in Population of the Votes*	
			District	*Constituency*
1.	AP	Hyderabad	39.35	32
2.	Assam	Barpeta	56.07	38
3.	Assam	Dhubri	70.45	55
4.	Assam	Karimganj (SC)	49.17	33
5.	Assam	Nowgong	47.18	28
6.	Bihar	Araria (SC)	40.42	28
7.	Bihar	Katihar	39.85	37
8.	Bihar	Purnea	34.53	29
9.	Haryana	Gurgaon	34.40	3
10.	MP	Bhopal	23.96	18
11.	Rajasthan	Jaisalmer (Barmer)	24.12	13
12.	UP	Bahraich	29.20	23
13.	UP	Bareilly	32.68	28
14.	UP	Bijnore	40.35	38
15.	UP	Gonda	25.35	17
16.	UP	Muzaffarnagar	34.52	27
17.	UP	Pilibhit	23.12	19
18.	WB	Maldah	47.00	40

Source: Iqbal A. Ansari, *Political Representation of Muslims in India: 1952-2004*, p. 394.

mandering is clearly visible. In Barpeta of Assam, the population of Muslims in the district was 56.07 per cent while in Barpeta PC the voter percentage had reduced to 38 per cent. If the constituencies are drawn with honest intention, keeping in mind Mahatma Gandhi's advice, Muslim voter percentage can increase and result in better representation of Muslims.

SUB-QUOTA IN WOMEN'S RESERVATION BILL

The Women's Reservation Bill was first introduced in Rajya Sabha in May 2008 and immediately referred to a Standing Committee. In 2010, it was passed in the Rajya Sabha and transmitted to the Lok Sabha. However, the Bill lapsed with the 15th Lok Sabha. There has always been talk on empowerment of women through political representation keeping in mind the fundamental right to self-representation and self-determination. The original idea for the Bill came from a constitutional amendment which was passed way back in 1993, which mandated that one-third of seats in local bodies, gram panchayat and nagarpalikas, should be reserved for women. The Bill was introduced and conceived as a long term plan to extend same reservation to women in Lok Sabha and state assemblies for political empowerment. The Bill sought to reserve 33 per cent seats for women in Lok Sabha and state assemblies on rotation basis. Reservation for women shall cease to exist 15 years after the commencement of the Act.

Whenever a debate was initiated on the Bill in the parliament, OBC leaders, particularly, Lalu Prasad Yadav, Mulayam Singh Yadav, Sharad Yadav, etc., expressed apprehension that all the reserved seats would be cornered by women of upper-caste category, and they demanded a proportionate sub-quota for women of OBC, Dalit, Adivasi and Muslim groups. Even political scientists argued that women belonging to Muslim, Dalit, Tribal, and OBC groups were less educated, economically weak and not many of them were participants in politics. If the Bill was passed and implemented most of the seats would be cornered by upper-caste women. They advocated sub-quota for women of deprived sections. Muslim organizations have also strongly demanded a sub-quota in the women's Bill.

Muslim women have been vocal and demanded that benefit of reservation must be ensured to the deprived sections. During a conference of the National Women's Front, its Secretary Fareeda Hasan said,

> We believe that a mere implementing 33 per cent reservation will not be sufficient as the women belonging to Muslims, Dalits and OBCs are the most backward sections, most marginalized in women. We want a sub-quota within the women's reservation because we feel that most of the places/posts would be occupied by women from the upper-caste and there won't be anybody to represent the Muslims, Dalits and Tribals.[10]

These concerns expressed by OBC leaders and women of deprived sections seem genuine, and it would be in the interest of social justice if sub-quota for women belonging to Muslims, Dalits, Tribals and OBCs is created in the Bill. National parties and governments always seem to be ready to ensure gender justice, then why do they hesitate to ensure social justice to women of all deprived groups?

PROPORTIONAL REPRESENTATION SYSTEM

PR is one of the electoral systems in which divisions in an electorate are reflected proportionately in the elected body. The PR system mainly ensures two types of proportionality: geographical and political. There are many administrative units/states in a country and seats for each state in the national parliament are reserved in proportion to population share. This is geographical PR, which is easy to achieve. Political PR basically ensures seats to all competing parties in proportion to votes received in elections. When N per cent of the electorates support a particular political party or set of candidates as their favourite, then roughly N per cent of seats is allotted to that party or those candidates. The essence of political PR is that all votes contribute to the result, and not just a plurality, or a bare majority. This is entirely different from FPTP system in the sense that every vote cast is counted and contributes in elected representation. The most prevalent form of PR all require the use of multi-member constituencies (also called super-districts), as it is not possible to fill a single seat in proportional manner. Multi-member constituencies with large number of seats tend to provide higher level of proportionality in PR systems. Widely used variants of PR electoral systems are: party-list PR, Single Transferable Vote (STV) and Mixed-Member PR (MMP).

In party-list PR system, political parties decide the candidate lists and voters vote for a list. The relative vote for each list determines how many candidates from each list are actually elected. Lists can be 'closed' or 'open'. Closed lists are determined before the elections, usually by the party or through primary elections. Open lists allow voters to indicate preferences for individual candidates during the elections. Party-list PR is the most widely used PR system, and currently being used in 85 countries. In STV, voters can rank individual candidates, rather than just vote for a single 'best' candidate. During the count, as candidates are elected or eliminated, surplus or discarded votes that would otherwise be wasted are transferred to other candidates in order of preferences, forming consensus groups that elect surviving candidates. STV is used only in two countries: Ireland and Malta, and also in Australian senate. Mixed-Member PR (MMP) is a two-tier mixed electoral system which combines FPTP/majoritarian election and a compensatory regional or national party-list PR election. Voters typically have two votes, one for their single-member constituency and another for the party list. Parties that are underrepresented by constituency elections are compensated by additional members, so that total representatives of each party are proportional based on the party-list vote. MMP is used in seven lower houses.

The principle of democracy professes equality as its very root and foundation. It tries to give justice to all segments of society. John Stuart Mill, in his 1861 essay, 'Considerations on Representative Government wtites', 'In a really equal democracy, every or any section would be represented, not disproportionately, but proportionately.'[11] In other words in a democracy, every segment of society must be represented proportionately. If majority community gets maximum seats and minorities low number of seats, it becomes a rule of majority over the minority. In this situation, protection and preservation of rights of minorities become secondary and minorities basically become subject of the majority rule. Many political theorists agree with Mill, that in a representative democracy, the representatives should represent all substantial segments of society. People also argue that PR system can be applied not only to achieve geographical or political PR, but also to get proportional representation for all segments of society especially weak, women, minorities, etc. In fact, many countries have been using some variants of PR or mixed-PR system to ensure fair share for minorities and other numerically weak racial groups.

In the Indian political scenario, some variants of PR, or mixed PR system can be applied to give justice to women, OBCs, Muslims and other minorities. India has had the experience of multi-member constituencies in the General Elections of 1952 and 1957. Out of 487 seats of the first Lok Sabha, 314 were single-member constituencies and 72 SC and 26 ST seats. There were 86 two-member and one three-member constituencies. For 494 seats, in the second Lok Sabha, there were 312 single-member and 91 double-member constituencies. After two Lok Sabha elections, the system of multi-member constituencies was abolished citing frivolous reasons. India is a diverse country and for giving proper representation to all segments of society, the scope of multi-member constituency would have been expanded.

Women, OBCs, Muslims and other minorities are not represented properly in elected bodies, and are politically deprived. Some variants of PR system or mixed variants may be used to ensure fair share. Political scientists argue that constituencies with high share of Muslims, says, between 21 to 50 per cent be constituted as multi-member constituencies. Similarly, this can be done to provide representation to OBCs and women. The said groups are politically marginalized, but, still there is no effort on government level to ensure fairer share to these groups. During the rule of the Congress, there was no mention of the excessive political deprivation that

Muslims and OBC faced. In the present goernment, however, there seems to be an all-out effort to further marginalize these groups and grant an excessive share to the UCHs. As regards to adoption of a suitable variant of PR, it entirely depends on the will of the governments and consensus among political parties.

REVIEW OF ELECTION RESULTS

The Lok Sabha and state assembly election results give a clear picture about political representation of every religious group, caste or class of people as well. Some religious groups are overrepresented, while some are underrepresented. Even in a religious group some dominant castes are represented higher than the average while weak and deprived castes are diminished.

In the Indian context, generally it is observed that SCs and STs are proportionately represented as seats are reserved for them in proportion to their population. The UCHs are disproportionally represented at the cost of the OBCs, Muslims and other minorities. A 'review committee' can be set up after every Lok Sabha and assembly elections of all states to review the representation of all religious groups, tribes, castes, classes, etc. The committee may have members from all parties and if possible from every section of the society. It may analyse the representation of different groups, over and underrepresentation of some groups, and also give possible reasons for uneven share. It should also suggest remedial measures to correct the political deprivation of some groups, and also how to make the parliament/state assemblies more representative. It may be asked to submit the report within three months of formation of the government. Detailed discussions must be held and every party should be given sufficient time to express their views about it. After discussion, findings and recommendations may be accepted, and must be applied in the next elections to give political justice to all segments of society to make elected houses more representative. This may be given constitutional status and separate laws may be enacted by the Lok Sabha, and all state assemblies keeping in mind the local situation. This step may not only ensure PR, but also establish peace and brotherhood in the society and would also ensure equitable distribution of economic benefits to all segments of society. Framers of the Constitution foresaw this situation and thus they included 'political justice' in the preamble of the Constitution.

AFFIRMATIVE ACTION IN ELECTORAL DEMOCRACY

Variants of PR, or combination of these with multi-member constituencies have several limitations. The chances of adopted system not yielding desirable results will always be there, especially when a sizeable section of the majority becomes unsympathetic to minorities, as is the case at present in India. Considering the present political condition of Muslims and the assurances given to them at the time of framing of the Constitution, there is an urgent need to improve the situation. Provision of fixed quota (as practiced for SCs and STs) must be made to Muslims along with OBCs according to their share in population. Provision of fixed quota of seats may be made in the parliament, all state assemblies and local bodies. Small steps and cosmetic changes to improve the political representation, if any, are not going to serve the purpose; strong steps with the backing of the Constitution are required to improve it. A fixed quota is a strong step in providing political justice to all deprived sections, including Muslims. In order to take this step, a debate, political consensus and sympathetic attitude towards minorities are needed.

NOTES

1. *India Today*, New Delhi, 11 July 2018.
2. *Report of NCRWC,* Chapter 4, para 4.16.1.
3. Ibid., Chapter 4, para 4.16.6.
4. Ibid., Chapter 10, para 10.11.2(b).
5. The Sachar Committee Report, 2006, p. 241.
6. Ibid., p. 25.
7. http://twocircles.net/2014apr09bsp_promises_delimitation_commission_after_ polls_dereserve_predominantly_muslim

8. https://www.news18.com/news/india/illegal-reservation-of-lok-sabha-constituencies-leading-to-low-muslim-percentage-in-parliament-report-2146701.html
9. http://twocircles.net/2013sep30appoint_delimitation_commission_zafar_mahmood.html
10. http://twocircles.net/2014nov19/1416393600.html
11. https://en.m.wikipedia.org/wiki/Proportional_representation

CHAPTER 6

Ground Level Factors Affecting Muslim Representation

In the previous chapter, I have already discussed how some policies adopted by political parties, and a few implemented by the government at the Centre have adversely affected the political prospects of Muslims. It is perhaps only in the recent past that these issues are being debated, and written upon by Muslim community leaders and intellectuals. I dare to hope that this attempt to awaken the common Muslim citizen has started bearing fruit. There is no doubt that, if the mainstream and prominent regional political parties seriously assess and think about the issues that Muslims face, we would be able to see the beginnings of change. At the same time, governments too must review, and correct their stance on certain policy issues to help improve Muslim representation.

Besides policy issues, there are conditions at the ground level that contribute directly to the political deprivation of Muslims. These are the following: the BJP's hostile attitude towards Muslims, several Muslim candidates contesting in the same Muslim-dominated constituencies, division of votes among secular parties in Muslim-dominated constituencies, issue of leadership in the community, deletion of names of eligible Muslim voters from the voter lists, disunity between the Muslims and Dalits, etc. These issues tend to invariably come up during elections. A closer look at all these factors reveals that these are the result of mismanagement among secular parties, a lack of prudence among the Muslims regarding political representation, and the discriminatory attitude of officials, especially at the lower levels of the government bureaucracy.

I feel strongly that if the leaders of the Muslim community create awareness about the complexities of politics, these issues would be handled in a better way and Muslim representation would improve.

BJP's EXCLUSIONARY ATTITUDE

The BJP's perspective on the political representation of Muslims is mainly guided by the RSS, which makes no secret of its objective to establish a sectarian nation where minorities will be second class citizens and the Dalits and OBCs will act as 'foot soldiers'. Its conception of an exclusionary nation is totally against the secular, democratic and inclusive nature of present-day India. The party's policy is deeply rooted in the ideology of 'Hindu nationalism' that regards Hindus alone to be the deserving citizens of the country. Those citizens who profess the 'foreign religions' namely Christianity and Islam are regarded as a threat to the Hindu nation. M.S. Golwalkar, the RSS chief ideologue, outlined this in his book, *Bunch of Thoughts.* The BJP's ideological foundations are on the similar lines of the Nazi ideology advocated by Adolf Hitler. Appreciating Hitler's genocide of the Jews, Golwalkar writes,

> . . . To keep up the purity of nation and its culture, Germany shocked the world by her purging the country of Semitic races—the Jews. National pride at its highest has been manifested here. Germany has also shown how neigh impossible it is for races and cultures, having differences going to the root, to be assimilated into one united whole, a good lesson for us in Hindustan to learn and profit by (*We or Our Nationhood Defined*, p. 27, 1938).[1]

The BJP harbours a deep hatred for the religious minorities in India and has been against their political empowerment. Since its inception, the party has not thought about Muslims as equal citizens of this country. Instead, it has worked tirelessly to antagonize a community which is the second largest majority. It has demanded that Muslims abandon their places of worship, tried to provoke, engineer communal riots, and when in power failed to act against goons who attacked them. In fact, the party has even asked Muslims to abandon their many constitutionally granted rights.

The BJP is uninterested in accommodating minorities, especially Muslims in its agenda of political empowerment. The party has nominated hardly any Muslims in the parliamentary and assembly elections. From 1952 to 2004, the BJP gave only 0.82 per cent of its nominations to them. Since 1980, it gave only 20 tickets in the Lok Sabha elections, out of which only three candidates got elected. The BJP's ideology of Muslim exclusion, and its deliberate attempt to deprive them from political participation was reflected in its 1.08 per cent nomination of Muslim candidates from 1952 till 2019. During this period, out of a total 4,622 nominations, it gave only 50 tickets, and out of these candidates only four were elected. In 2009, it gave five tickets, seven in 2014 and six in 2019, while the party distributed more than 400 tickets in all these elections. Moreover, those tickets were given in Jammu & Kashmir and in Muslim-dominated seats of Bihar, West Bengal and Lakshadweep, where the chances of the BJP Muslim candidates were very low. In 2014 and 2019, when Narendra Modi returned to power with an absolute majority, he did not have a single Muslim MP in his party a first since Independence. This is not only shocking in itself, but unfortunate for Indian democracy.

Similar situations exist in assembly elections. In Rajasthan, Madhya Pradesh and Delhi, where assembly elections were held in 2013, the party gave only six tickets to Muslims, out of more than 500 nominations although these states had about 50 Muslim-dominated ACs, and 17 Muslim MLAs in the previous assemblies. Even top leaders of the BJP Minority Cell were not given tickets. It gave only one ticket in MP, and four in the 200-member Rajasthan assembly. Only one candidate was fielded in Delhi which had 70 seats and 12 per cent Muslim population. The BJP fields Muslims only in those ACs where they are in majority, and there is very little chance of winning the seat with a non-Muslim candidate. In January 2018, out of 1,418, BJP MLAs elected in northern and western states, only four were Muslims. When elections were held in 2018 in Madhya Pradesh, Rajasthan and Chhattisgarh, it lost power in those states and representation of Muslim increased significantly. In the Gujarat assembly elections of 2012, 2017 and 2022, not a single Muslim candidate was fielded. In 2012 and 2017 assembly elections of UP, no Muslim was fielded. In 2014 assembly elections of Maharashtra only two Muslims were nominated and none in 2019. 'The BJP doesn't want Muslims in the assembly and parliament. It is against political empowerment of the community and denial of seat to a Muslim is part of the same agenda,' points out F.M. Thakur, who heads the Maharashtra Muslim Sangh, an umbrella outfit of several Muslims (*The Times of India*, 13 October 2019). The BJP has no use for inclusive politics. By not fielding Muslims in most of the states, the party has also sent clear signals that Muslim votes cannot influence its winnability. In fact, its electoral prospects increase when it defines itself in opposition to Muslims.

From the above statement we can draw several conclusions. First, the BJP's rise results in limited political space for Muslims. Wherever the BJP performed well, the Muslim representation went down. Between 1980 and 2019, number of Muslim MPs, and their percentage witnessed a gradual decline by more than half, while Muslim's share in population has risen. As a result, the gap between their share of population and representation in Lok Sabha increased rapidly. The responsibility for this trend lies primarily with the BJP which has endorsed fewer Muslim candidates, and is amplifying the same more than any other parties, because it occupies more political space than other parties. In states where BJP is either ruling or one of the major ruling alliance partners, one finds reduced share of Muslims in assemblies. UP returned the highest number of Muslim legislators in the 2012 assembly elections, when the BJP was relegated to the third position winning only 47 seats. In 2017, it returned to power with 312 MLAs, the number of Muslim MLAs dropped to 25. This trend is clearly visible in all the states as well as on the national level. The emergence of the BJP has negative consequences for Muslims' due share in politics and power.

Second, the BJP plays the politics of communalism and majoritarian nationalism to appeal vast majority of Hindus. It raises communal issues and emphasizes the religious divide in order to take advantage of communal consolidation. It used to raise various imaginary religious issues to appease, and to consoldate Hindu voters. It uses this method to divert the attention of common masses from life-related issues. It promotes communal divide among various communities to garner votes, which is destroying communal harmony and common fabric. India's electoral politics seems to be confronted with new sets of challenges posed by the rise of majoritarian nationalism. With its exponential rise in 2014, it has changed the trajectory of Muslims, and made them electorally vulnerable. The Hindu nationalism has totally sidelined all minorities and questioned their allegiance and contribution to India. Majoritarian nationalism and culture constitute as a sole nationalism and national culture. In the Indian context, the dominance of the BJP's brand of Hindu nationalism has called into question the future stability of Indian plurality and viable presence of Muslims in electoral politics. Hindu nationalism undoubtedly represents one of the major challenges Indian democracy has faced in all its years of existence.

Third, due to majoritarian politics played by the BJP, the Congress and other secular parties shy away from giving tickets to Muslim candidates. It is important to note that the overall drop of Muslim share in politics has come from regional parties in the elections held between 2014 and 2023. Regional parties are refraining to give tickets to Muslims in the wake of strong majoritarian politics. According to Gilles Vernier, the anti-Muslim sentiments stoked by the BJP have led to the deprivation of tickets for Muslim candidates even outside the BJP. Fear of being tagged 'anti-Hindu' has forced the Congress and other parties to field less and less number of Muslim candidates.[2] Jaffrelot, in his *Majoritarian State: How Hindu Nationalism is Changing India* writes that 'the formation of a Hindu vote bank by the BJP, which in particular aimed to sideline minorities in the political arena, prompted other parties as well no longer to nominate Indian Muslim candidate, except in areas with high Muslim majority'.[3] Since Independence, Muslims have largely backed secular formations like the Congress, SP, BSP, TMC, RJD, etc. In this situation they have been less forthcoming in giving them due representation. There is no doubt that this indifference towards Muslims has been caused by the triumph of Hindu right-wing populism. The so-called minority-friendly parties have re-oriented themselves, sidelining potential Muslim candidates in the name of 'winnability' given the compulsion of 'polarization'.

The BJP aims to liberate the party entirely from the 'Muslim vote' that it accused other parties of wooing for electoral gains at the expense of Hindu majority. In fact in election campaigns, the BJP candidates have publicly announced that they do not need Muslim votes. The above facts and discussion show that the BJP aims its strategies and objectives against the political empowerment of Muslims.

SEVERAL CANDIDATES IN THE SAME MUSLIM-MAJORITY CONSTITUENCIES

The presence of several Muslim candidates in Muslim-dominated constituencies divides Muslim votes, and reduces the chances of the one who is most likely to win. More damagingly this leads to the defeat of the most suitable Muslim candidate fielded by secular parties and non-Muslim candidates (mostly fielded by the BJP), win in this situation. In such situations, besides the most powerful candidate, other Muslim candidates behave as 'spoilers' or 'vote-cutters' and the result, is a paradox: Muslim-dominated seats elect BJP candidates.

Even though Muslims account for 25 per cent or more of the population in 90 PCs and are able to influence the elections, they are not united in voting. Several Muslim candidates from secular parties contest from a constituency, thereby dividing their votes. That often results in the win of BJP candidate. The outcome of UP's Rampur PC in 2014, where nearly 50 per cent of voters are Muslims, is one of several such examples. Of the 12 candidates, seven were Muslims. All major parties, except the BJP nominated Muslim candidates. But the BJP candidate won with a vote share of a little over 37 per cent. Similarly, there are a few PCs in UP where Muslim voters are over 50 per cent. However, in 2014, not a single Muslim could reach the Lok Sabha due to division of votes among Muslim candidates of Congress, SP, and BSP. In 2014, all Muslim-dominated PCs elected BJP candidates.

In fact, it is relatively more visible as the margin of win in assembly elections remains low. Every state has Muslim-dominated ACs. Two or three secular parties give tickets to Muslims from most of these seats and apart from these, some independent Muslim candidates also contest from the same seat. Due to the split in Muslim votes, the non-Muslim candidate not supported by Muslims, wins the seat. Secondly, the victory of BJP candidates from Muslim-dominated seats becomes easy as margin of votes is less in assembly elections. Parties, such as BSP, SP, RJD, etc., have caused defeat of several Congress candidates in Muslim-dominated seats situated in MP, Rajasthan, Chhattisgarh, Gujarat, Haryana, etc. This happened even in seats, where the Congress had fielded Muslim candidates. For example, the four-time MLA and former minister in Maharashtra Mohammad Arif Naseem Khan was defeated in the 2019 assembly elections in Chandivali by 409 votes. Khan secured 85,470 votes against Shiv Sena nominee Dilip Lande's 85,879, while AIMIM candidate Mohammad Imran Qureshi secured 1,117 votes which was more than the margin of defeat. There are numerous examples of such defeats in UP, Bihar, Haryana, Rajasthan, MP, Gujarat, Maharashtra, Karnataka, etc., particularly caused by Muslim candidates fielded by parties like SP, BSP, RJD, AIMIM, Dalit based parties and Muslim independent candidates. There are two ways in which the presence of Muslim independents or party candidates of smaller parties help the BJP: vote-splitting and Hindu vote consolidation.

Vote-splitting

This occurs when the combined vote share of independent, and candidates supported by smaller parties is more than the margin between the BJP, and the main secular party candidates. The spoiler candidates take away big chunk of votes that would have gone to the strongest Muslim candidate, thereby helping the BJP win. The spoilers also help on seats where the Muslim population is not significant but the seat is closely contested between two parties and even a small split in votes can change the result. In the 2012 Gujarat elections, here is an example of the constituency describing the larger votes given to the BJP in a Muslim-majority constituency:

Jamalpur-Khadia Constituency

Muslim population: 61 per cent
Bhushan Ashok Bhatt (BJP): 38.63 per cent votes
Samirkhan Vajirkhan Sipai (INC): 33.54 per cent votes
Margin of BJP's victory: 5.09 per cent
Other Muslim candidates (combined vote share): 26.9 per cent.

In this constituency, there were as many as six Muslim candidates other than that fielded by the Congress. Just one independent, Sabirbhai Kabliwala, secured 24.52 per cent of the vote, making it possible for BJP to win a seat, where Muslims constituted 61 per cent. Incidentally, the BJP's vote share was almost exactly the same as proportion of Hindus in the constituency, which meant it was possible for the party to have won without getting a single Muslim vote.[4] Several Muslim-dominated assembly seats have been lost to BJP candidates due to presence of large number of Muslim candidates: independents and small party candidates.

Hindu Vote Consolidation

The second way in which Muslim candidates help the BJP is not easy to express quantitatively. It has been observed that the presence of numerous Muslim candidates leads to consolidation of Hindu votes in favour of the BJP. This is particularly evident in urban areas with a history of communal violence. In areas where communal polarisation is less, the presence of large number of Muslim candidates does not necessarily have a bearing on the Hindu voting pattern. Such consolidation is particularly visible in ACs, where Muslim voters' percentage is above 20 per cent but below 40 per cent. Some examples from Gujarat assembly elections of 2012 are given here.

1. Vejalpur (Dist: Ahmedabad)
   Muslim population: 35 per cent
   Number of Muslim candidates: 6
   BJP vote share: 58.2 per cent
2. Vagra (Dist: Bharuch)
   Muslim population: 44 per cent

Number of Muslim candidates: 5
BJP vote share: 51.13 per cent

3. Surat East (Dist: Surat)
Muslim population: 22 per cent
Number of Muslim candidates: 7
BJP vote share: 53.39 per cent
4. Limbayat (Dist: Surat)
Muslim population: 26 per cent
Number of Muslim candidates: 6
BJP vote share: 53.06 per cent.[5]

In all the above ACs, due to a large number of Muslim candidates, almost all Hindus voted for the BJP, as its vote share was almost equal to the share of Hindus in the population.

Political observers point out that multiple Muslim candidates in Muslim-dominated seats, and the consequent fall in political representation could be a reflection of their growing indifference towards political parties and Muslim leaders who have represented them so far. There are a number of reasons for this dismal state of affairs. First, secular parties give tickets to Muslims only in Muslim-dominated seats, which are limited in number. Naturally, all the deserving candidates do not get tickets from the most powerful secular party. Other deserving leaders or new aspirants tend to smaller secular parties for tickets or contest as independent. The second reason which is observed even by common people is plenitudes of Muslim candidates basically promoted by BJP to cause split in Muslim votes, make them ineffective and thus, ensure the win of BJP candidates. There are two Muslim-dominated seats in Surat district: Limbayat and Surat East. In 2017, there were 76,000 Muslim voters in Limbayat and 67,000 in Surat East which could have played major role in deciding winner from those ACs. However, there were too many independent Muslim candidates from both the ACs. Ordinary Muslim voters openly said that these candidates contested elections to squeeze out money from other candidates. Some even said that a majority of such candidates were lured by the BJP to contest and split Muslim votes.[6] Moreover, Muslims have failed to create a political space for themselves due to various reasons. Most of these candidates lack political understanding and do not have a record of working for the ordinary people. And yet, they clamour to contest elections.

An examination of their profile shows that these are Muslim doctors, engineers, businessmen, graduates, etc., with no experience in politics. It has been observed that they contest elections only to see their names in the ballot papers and end up with a few votes. This reflects the political immaturity of a community which is struggling to improve its share in politics.

This aspect can be minimized to a large extent, if there is a will to do so. In the assembly elections of UP and Bihar, states with large Muslim voters, they have tried 'tactical voting'. Leaders, community members and organizations gauge the winning ability of non-BJP candidates in every PC through feedback received from the ground and then announce the names of secular party candidates, who seem capable of defeating the BJP candidates. Even if the strongest candidate is non-Muslim and there is another Muslim candidate contesting against him, Muslim leaders advise the community to vote for the former. In case the strongest candidate is a Muslim, they advise other weak Muslim candidates to withdraw their nominations. Frequently this advice is conveyed to ordinary Muslims in cities through word of mouth, called *pudia* (packet). During the 2014 general elections, the Joint Committee of Muslim Organizations led by the late Syed Shahabuddin, a renowned Muslim leader, sent out its recommended 'tactical voting' list of candidates. Throughout UP and Bihar, some Muslim candidates who were not strong and whose candidature in 2009 elections resulted in the division of community votes, were withdrawing from contest in 2014. It was to prevent division of Muslim votes. If the community leaders and organizations decide the strongest Muslim candidate based on input received from the ground, communicate it to voters and persuade the weak candidates to withdraw nominations, this problem can be minimised to a large extent.

DIVISION OF SECULAR VOTES

Division of votes between two or three secular parties is responsible for Muslim candidates not being elected from Muslim-dominated seats. It is also a clear reason for success of BJP candidates from such seats. In some constituencies where Muslim voters are almost 60 to 70 per cent of the total voters, strong Muslim candidates from two or three parties divide votes and the BJP candidate wins with 35 to 40 per cent votes. In this way, Muslims lose many seats in parliament and state assembly elections. The phenomenon is visible in states where at least two secular parties have been active which are equally powerful such as UP, Bihar, Delhi, etc. In the 2014 general elections, there was division of votes between the SP, BSP, and Congress and thus, Muslim candidates lost in all Muslim-dominated seats. Not a single Muslim got elected from UP in 2014 due to this reason. Likewise, many Muslims lost elections due to division of votes between SP and BSP during the 2017 assembly elections. SP and BSP cause defeat of many Muslim candidates from other secular parties (mostly Congress) in Delhi, Rajasthan, Haryana, Maharashtra, Gujarat, MP, Chhattisgarh, Karnataka, Bihar, etc. Besides UP, division of votes between AAP and Congress in Delhi, BRS and Congress in Telangana, TDP and YSRCP in AP, DMK and AIADMK in Tamil Nadu, CPI(M) and Congress in Kerala, Congress and JDS in Karnataka, Congress and NCP in Maharashtra, Congress and INLD in Haryana, Congress, CPI(M) and TMC in West Bengal, Congress and AIUDF in Assam, etc., have caused defeats in Muslim-dominated constituencies.

In the Kairana AC, Muslims account for 63 per cent of the total population. Yet, in the 16 elections held since 1957, it has returned only five Muslim MLAs. Even in the assembly elections of 2012, the community was not able to send its MLA because all the votes got divided between candidates of two secular parties. In mid-term poll of 2014, the situation got improved. In Moradabad's Thakurwara, Muslims constitute 52 per cent of population, yet out of the 17 elections, they were able to elect their candidates only on six occasions. In 2012, the Muslim candidate lost due to division of votes between two secular parties. Here too, the situation improved in the mid-term elections of 2014. Despite one-third Muslim population in Bithari Chainpur (Bareilly), Bilaspur (Rampur), Deoband and Barkhera (Pilibhit), Mehdawal (Sant

Kabir Nagar), Biswanthpur (Partapgarh), Chaproli (Gonda), Sheikhpur (Badaun), Lucknow East and Mahasi (Bahraich), in 2012 assembly elections, neither did any Muslim candidate win nor anyone was even number second. In Rudauli, in spite of the one-third population being Muslim, the Muslim candidate lost the election by a few votes.[7] The Prakash Ambedkar-led VBA had spoiled the Congress-NCP alliance's chances in several Lok Sabha seats in Maharashtra in 2019. The VBA wrecked the prospects of at least 22 candidates of the Congress-NCP alliance in the 2019 Maharashtra assembly elections. It was nowhere in the race in seats, where, the VBA seemed to have ruined the chances of the alliance candidates. But the votes it secured were more than the margin of victory. The VBA was supposed to attract mainly non-BJP and non-Shiv Sena votes. In Akola West, BJP candidate G.M. Sharma polled 72,838 votes, while Congress candidate Sajid Khan got 70,469. The margin was roughly 2,400 votes but the VBA candidate polled 20,563 votes.[8]

Our discussion supported with figures above clearly shows that for the division of votes and consequent success of BJP candidates from Muslim-dominated seats, it is the secular parties that are directly responsible. Each of these parties sacrifice the principles they pay lip service to because of their selfish ambitions. If secular parties strive to form an alliance, this issue could be solved easily. However, to do so every secular party needs to set aside its selfish interests.

In parallel, it must be pointed out that senior members of the Muslim community do not pay attention to the seriousness of the situation. They make no effort and spend no time to unite the community and form a consensus and thus allow their votes to be devalued. Community leaders and organizations have to fulfil their *milli* (community) and constitutional obligation with full sense of responsibility. Community activists should be aware about political situations. They have to collect information, scrutinize prospects of each Muslim candidate, and identify the strongest one. Religious leaders must spread the information and try to unite Muslim voters. To persuade weak candidates to withdraw from the contest is also important.

LACK OF LEADERSHIP

In a democracy, leaders contest elections from a particular seat and the most popular, most appropriate and strongest one emerges victorious. Good leaders who work for the people and fulfil their aspirations mostly win the elections. The contribution of any caste or religious group in politics or elective bodies is dependent on the quality of its leaders. Some social groups, especially the UCHs, have a disproportionate share in politics as they have produced suitable leaders or have been given proper opportunity to grow in politics. The political backwardness of Muslims is seldom pinned on the leadership or lack of it. The community's current situation is mainly due to the absence of leadership within its ranks and at all levels.

After Independence, except for a few prominent personalities, the community has not produced good leaders who can be termed as grassroots leaders or win elections on their own. The Muslim leaders who were cultivated in the past were not effective because they lacked ability to get elected on their own. They generally lacked charisma, mass support, money and muscle power—all needed to win elections. There are Muslims who desire to be leaders and have access to money and muscle power, but lack respectability and acceptability. There is huge lack of effective and progressive leadership in the community. Unfortunately, there are Muslim leaders in the Congress and some regional parties who are so designated only because they completely propped up by these parties. These so-called leaders do not have any mass appeal in the community and depend entirely on the mercy of the parties they belong to. They do not advocate socio-economic and constitutional rights of Muslims, and generally toe the line of the party leadership. Besides such leaders, there are Muslim religious leaders (*ulema*/*maulvis*) that talk about religious and identity issues only and have no idea of socio-economic, human rights, educational and security issues. Leaders of progressive mindset who are well-informed and work on the ground for all communities, and have a political base are normally not found in the community.

Let us turn to the *ulemas*. They are generally *madrasa*-educated who dress up in a particular way and normally talk on religious, spiritual, emotional and identity based issues. Their overall mindset is conservative, and they don't take up issues of socio-economic progress, discrimination, human rights and justice for other deprived groups. In the Mughal Empire, whenever hereditary dynasties took over governance, the kings maintained the façade of being guided by divine law. *Ulema* were also part of the imperial court. When the Empire fell, the *ulema* effortlessly moved into the role of community leaders, as a kind of bridge between the state and the people. Noted journalist and writer Ghazala Wahab writes:

> Subsequently, when non-religious Muslim politicians emerged in the beginning of the twentieth century their focus was the political representation of their class of Muslims, which was the *Shurafa*, rather than the uplift of the downtrodden. To discredit them as representatives of the larger community, the 'nationalist Muslims', essentially members of the INC, turned to the *ulema*, mainly from the Darul Uloom Deoband and its Delhi-based associated group, Jamiat Ulama-i-Hind, to steer the Muslim masses towards the Congress and its politics. Explaining this paradox of supposedly liberal politicians seeking Muslim support through its least liberal entity, the *ulema*, Salman Khurshid says that once the educated class—the AMU crowd and the landed gentry—drifted towards the Muslim League, thereby according it legitimacy, the Congress party had to find a new class of grassroots leaders whom the masses could identify with. In their perception, the *ulema* had that sort of persuasive power to steer the masses towards the Congress.[9]

This is how the *ulema* was represented in the Congress. There are *ulemas* in various regional and OBC based parties as well. Besides, there are *ulema* who are not associated with any political party, but issue political statements and attempt to guide the community during elections. Although Muslims at large ignore them, they insist on portraying themselves as the 'guardians' of the community. They are inherently incapable of leadership, for they lack its core essentials: a mass base, political understanding and even rudimentary acceptance of democratic processes. The needs of the community have always been education, employment, socio-economic progress and preservation of their fundamental rights, but the *ulema* has practiced politics of 'religious difference' preoccupied with tokens and empty symbolism. A simple case of alimony for Shah Bano was projected as an existential threat to the religious and cultural rights of Indian Muslims. The legislation in the aftermath of the SC judgement is cited as an appeasement by the right-wing forces even today. The *ulemas* have not only proved consistently useless in safeguarding the constitutional rights of Muslims, but have also been complicit in the erosion of these rights. They rarely rake up issues pertaining to prejudice in the government department, harassment by security agencies, indiscriminate arrest of Muslim youths in the name of terrorism and equal distribution of resources. The *ulema* have done great harm to Muslims by playing politics in the name of religion, identity and token benefits. They never tried to prepare Muslims for how to be part of an inclusive and plural society, and to learn the art of mutual coexistence. When religion and politics are mixed, it causes a greater damage. In a secular and democratic state, Muslims should separate politics from religion. Politics in a secular democracy should always be secular at all levels. There should be clear division of religion and politics in India, thus, helping to safeguard the constitutional rights of minorities. The *ulema* must understand the dynamics of politics and reorient themselves, and their thoughts in a state that is fast moving towards majoritarianism.

The inefficient leaders that form another category have been created by mainstream political parties. After Independence, for decades, India was ruled single-handedly by the Congress, which thrived on the support provided by Muslims and other minorities. Since the party lacked inner party democracy, the leadership was entirely based on a nomination process which was at the whim and mercy of the party high commands. Often Muslim leaders were selected and groomed based on the loyalty factor and imposed on masses in quest to gain maximum mileage during elections. In this process, where loyalty was the sole criteria, genuine grassroots leaders were sidelined to give way to the sycophants, who were there for their self-interest. As a result, the interest of the common people became a casualty. Genuine issues of Muslims were sidelined as these leaders toed the line of the party. Such was the moral bankruptcy of the Muslim leadership that they were scared to raise socio-economic and security issues in legislative bodies, because they thought that this act will chastize them for working against the party line. This is still going on and has created leaders who have become MPs, MLAs, ministers, and even occupied the posts of the President and Vice-President. For political parties, it has worked very well, cemented secular credentials, and caught the imaginations of the world. But unfortunately, it has created leaders who are suave and soft in manner, but do not have the courage to raise the issues of Muslims in the public domain. They are not leaders by virtue of their following among the masses but because of the access they have to powerful leaders of the party.

A similar situation exists in regional parties. Either Muslim leaders in the party are out of touch with their constituencies or stand on such shaky foundations that they dare not speak their mind on Muslim issues. As a result, other non-Muslim leaders in the party venture out to take up the issues of the Muslim masses. Muslim leaders lack mass following, and are more concerned about securing positions with help of big leaders. Lack of a 'tall' Muslim leader is a deliberate creation of sinister design by the political parties, who are eager for Muslim votes, but do not want to share power. Any Muslim leader that is in a position to ask for more is kept on the sidelines and has to be contented with insignificant positions in the power structure. A Muslim leader with mass following who can stand on his own is despised by political parties. On the other hand, those who toe the party line and are silent on serious Muslim issues are rewarded by the parties. The typical Muslim leaders of all political parties rarely rake up the genuine problems of Muslims. Instead, they dabble in the same issues that the *ulema* do, such as the protection of Islam, Urdu language, Muslim Personal Law, AMU and so on.

Once in interaction with Muslim youth Congress leaders, Rahul Gandhi said, 'We do not even have five (Muslim) leaders who have pan-India appeal from Kashmir to Kerala.' Gandhi also said, 'After Maulana Azad, we have not had a leader with a national stature.'[10] When some among the audience named Ghulam Nabi Azad and Salman Khrushid, Rahul dismissed the suggestions saying that Muslims, say, in Andhra Pradesh would not identify themselves with those leaders. This means the party has failed to develop a giant Muslim leader who has a national appeal. Gandhi's statement was a candid admission of his party's failure to develop minority especially Muslim leaders. The question arises, who do you blame if such leaders have not emerged? It is the responsibility of the party leadership to promote and project mass leaders. Instead, it has done just the opposite. With few exceptions, a similar situation exists in regional and OBC base parties. They have developed leaders who have low ambition, do not raise vital issues, have no mass base and are totally at the party's mercy.

The traditional belief in the Congress and other secular parties has held that 'only a Hindu can be a Muslim leader'. As already observed Muslim leaders stand on shaky foundations and dare not speak their mind. Leaders like Khurshid, Azad and those of other secular parties can take up the challenge, but, since they lack mass following, they do not want to meddle in community issues. They are more concerned about securing positions for themselves. As a result other leaders in the party venture out to take up the issues of Muslims. High profile leaders like H.N. Bahuguna, Arjun Singh, Digvijay Singh, Lalu Prasad Yadav, Mulayam Singh Yadav, etc., have carefully cultivated the secular image. These leaders can raise Muslim issues easily. They believe that a Muslim's backing of minority issues in a country with the ghost of the Partition would draw charges of 'communalism', which in itself is absurd. In India, every caste, community, group has its leadership for advocacy of their needs and concerns, for example, Mayawati for Dalits, Lalu and Mulayam for OBCs, BJP leaders for UCHs, but there is no one to speak exclusively for the rights and dignity of Muslims. If any one does so, he or she immediately branded as a communal and extremist. Even Hindu leaders in secular parties do not like Muslims advocating for their own community. In fact these parties fear that they may be blamed for appeasement by right-wing groups and lose the majority community's votes. In reality, these are imaginary fears which these parties have to overcome to prepare Muslims for leadership roles.

So what is the kind of leadership that the Muslim community needs? Ali Nadeem Rezavi, who teaches history at AMU, says, 'They need a forward looking secular leadership which can understand the social, economic and political interests and aspirations of the masses.'[11] K. Rahman Khan, Congress leader and former Union Minister, reiterates the need for emergence of genuine leadership in the community. In his book, *Indian Muslims: The Way Forward*, he writes:

> Today, the Indian Muslims require leaders who can provide them guidance for advancing economically, educationally, socially and of course, spiritually, as well as for promoting harmony and good relations between Muslims and members of other communities. They need leaders who can provide them an authentic understanding of their faith, which meaningfully addresses issues of great contemporary relevance, such as gender justice, social equality, individual rights, freedom of thought and expression, interfaith understanding and inter-community harmony, religious pluralism, environmental protection, dialogue and harmony between different Muslim sects, democracy, secularism and so on. They need leaders who can help them contribute positively in a rapidly-changing, cosmopolitan world.[12]

In today's scenario, what are the qualifications of a Muslim leader? The latter must be educated, widely travelled and should have vision to look beyond the spoils of power. He must keep his personal interests aside and inspire for change and generate hope. He must be aware of the different issues of Muslims in all the states and cultivate a balanced perspective on these. He must know the socio-economic, educational and security issues of minorities, deprived groups, such as the SCs, STs and OBCs and maintain a constitutionally approved approach to social justice. The leader must be able to win the trust of the impoverished, labourers, migrant workers, farmers, landless workers, etc., in his ability to alleviate their plight. One should be equally comfortable in the company of the educated class and intellectuals, and the not so well-educated constituents. Muslims must look for this kind of ideal leader or their leaders must try to acquire these qualities. Their institutions, NGOs, educated class and elders must inspire confidence in younger generations, educate and train youths to become such leaders.

So far, the majority of Muslim leaders have hailed from elite groups and upper-castes that were better educated than the socially, educationally and economically weaker sections, such as OBCs,

Dalits and tribal Muslims. These leaders were educated and cultured, but generally not effective, as they had no mass base and survived on the mercy of party leaders. Mostly, they had no clear understanding of many issues, nor did they ever attempt to understand the pain and sufferings of the common Muslim masses. As a consequence, they were not in position to work for the betterment of 85 per cent of the Muslims in the first place. Like *ulema*, they raised issues like the *sharia* laws, Urdu, *madrasas*, the AMU, etc., but not about poverty, employment, social justice, safety and security and an equitable share in government schemes. The leadership of the weaker sections had gained momentum with the advent of the All India Momin Conference, but gradually with the passage of time and due to lack of foresight, this movement fizzled out. Now, various political and social organizations like the All India Pasmanda Muslim Mahaz, the All India Backward Muslim Morcha, etc., have emerged and are trying to make place for the deprived sections. Even regional secular and OBC base parties are turning to leaders of deprived groups to get majority votes in Muslims.

It is disturbing that the deprived sections amongst the Muslims have no say in politics. In India, votes are cast on the basis of caste affiliations and some of the electoral gains made by the parties and leaders are on the basis of the numerical strength of the castes they are affiliated to. Similarly, the person aspiring to lead Muslims must be in a position to associate himself with the caste that has an advantage over others in the number game. In spite of the fact that Islam preaches equality and prohibits divisions based on caste and creed, Muslims in India practice caste system, which is basically adopted from the Hindu caste system. Although the severity of the caste system is relatively less, there are OBCs, Dalit castes and many tribal castes within the Muslim community. These deprived sections which constitute 82 to 85 per cent of the total Muslim population, are poor, educationally weak and are considered to be at the bottom of the Muslim social hierarchy. Despite constituting the bulk of Muslim population, politically, they have been marginalized. If someone from their ranks can become a leader, they would enjoy a tremendous advantage over others as he belongs to the majority section, since he would get mass support. Since democracy is a game of numbers, this approach will not be inconsequential and will pay rich dividends. This dividend can be in the form of a Muslim Mulayam, Lalu Prasad or another Muslim Mayawati. This act will not only create leaders from the deprived sections, but Muslims' share in politics will also go up. Not only the Muslim community, but all parties including the Muslim base parties must adopt this approach to create leaders from the deprived sections.

There is no denying that there is acute lack of leadership in the Muslim community, which is responsible for its political deprivation. Muslims must create and nurture leaders who could boldly raise their issues in the general public. This will be possible only through hard work and persistent struggle. Those who are bold and courageous, ready to work hard, seen among people during their bad times and attempt to ensure justice to the people are always accepted as leaders.

MISSING NAMES FROM VOTER LISTS

There are numerous newspaper reports and complaints by politicians and activists saying that names of genuine voters belonging to Muslim and Dalit communities are either not included or deleted from the voter lists citing frivolous reasons. Deleting names in bulk affect the electoral prospects of Muslims and Dalits. Election officials claim that the deletion of names of Muslim voters is unintentional. However, Muslims doubt their intentions and in some cases discrimination is clearly noticed as similar incidents are not reported from Hindu localities. It is the fundamental right of any citizen to get the name enrolled on the electoral rolls. It is also a fundamental right of every voter to cast votes during elections. Deleting names in bulk reduces the strength of Muslim voters which is cited as a key factor for Muslims low share in politics.

There are various methods to estimate missing number of voters from voter list. RayLabs Technologies has been able to carry out data analysis of publicly-available electoral rolls and built household size reports for 800 ACs across the country. Khalid Saifullah, who heads a small team of professionals and has worked for the enrolment of the missing voters in various parts of the country, says,

> It identified that the percentage of households having only one voter in all SRCs is eleven per cent. But as per voter rolls, it is 20 per cent in Muslim and Dalit communities. As per 2011 Census, the percentage of single person household should be less than 5 per cent. There is variation between the two databases, so we consider 80 per cent of the household with one voter as missing voter households and started a field survey.[13]

Due to high fertility rate in Muslims and Dalits, household size is bigger. But here one voter household is shown at 20 per cent in Dalits and Muslims. Theoretically, it must be less than 11 per cent. This hints to conspiracy against Muslims and Dalits.

As per data compiled by the Centre for Research and Debates in Development Policy (CRDDP), there are 150 to 180 million Indian citizens that have been left out of the electoral rolls and therefore, would be unable to exercise the right to vote. According to the same data, more than three crore Muslim and four crore Dalit voters are missing from electoral rolls across India. The organization and its allies had started a countrywide campaign to include such 'missing voters' on electoral rolls. In a bid to address the issue, CRDDP had initiated 'Mission 2019—no voter Left Behind' to include name of genuine voters in the voter list.[13]

When the then Harbour MLA P.K. Sekar Babu of the DMK received petitions (March 2019) alleging that the names of several Muslims in his constituency in Chennai were missing, he decided to verify it. He found the complaints to be valid. According to his estimate, more than 10,000 Muslim voters had been removed from the rolls. Shahul Hameed, a voter in Harbour AC, said that more than 500 names, including his, were missing from the rolls in his residential neighbourhood. Former Chennai Corporation Council Floor Leader V. Sukumar Babu claimed that more than 7,000 Dalit voters resettled from slum along the river Cooum in the Chepauk-Tiruvallikeni AC. The government had used force to resettle Dalits from slums in Chennai to locations about 40 km away. He said election officials ought to have visited new homes of the resettled Dalit families and included their names in voter lists.[13]

In March 2013, H.D. Deve Gowda, the former PM and national president of the JD(S) met then Chief Election Commissioner (CEC) in Delhi and submitted a petition alleging about Muslim voters' name being dropped on large-scale from voter lists in the then state government of BJP. He complained that more than 20,000 names of Muslim voters had been deleted from every AC and thus they had been deprived of right to vote. He also complained that that act had been done 'intentionally'. He appealed to the ECI to intervene in the matter on urgent basis.[14] In April 2013, Karnataka JD(S) leader Abdul Azeem claimed that about 50,000 names had been deleted from the draft list in Hebbal AC in Bangalore, out of which 20,000-25,000 were Muslim voters. He had filed a complaint with the ECI in December 2012, about huge inaccuracies in voter names and details and about missing names from the list. He also alleged that there was a deliberate attempt by a few BJP politicians, especially, Katta Subramanya Naidu to sabotage election in their favour as the contract to print the voters name had been given to a printer who had links to those BJP politicians. In reply, the ECI had stated that electoral roll of the Hebbal AC would be revised on furnishing valid identity and address proof.[15]

The problem in Karnataka started again before its assembly election of 2023. Shivajinagar, which is in the heart of Bengaluru, has around 1.91 lakh voters, 40 per cent of whom are Muslims. The constituency has been represented by a Congress MLA since 2008. The row started with a private complaint filed by a BJP sympathiser listing out 26,000 voters as fake which included mostly Muslim and Dalit names. The ECI started the inquiry on the complaint and issued notices to 9,159 voters in January 2023, as they had eiher died or shifted their homes. As per Standard Operating Procedure (SOP) of the ECI, *suo-motu* deletion can not be made in the six months prior to the term of an assembly ending. Here, the ECI violated its own SOP. The ECI justifed its action by invoking clause which said that deletion can be done under 'special circumstances'. But the question arises, how is a complaint filed by a private party that too with enmass names can compel the ECI to swing into action. The opposition parties blamed that the ECI should not have acted in haste as the complaint was 'malicious' and 'communally motivated' (https:// thenewsminute.com).

In April 2014, the All India Milli Council (Mumbai) and other organizations held a press conference and alleged that names of Muslim voters had been deleted on a large scale from voter lists in Muslim-dominated pockets, such as Rashid Compound (Mumbra), Bharatnagar, Kausa, Nalasopara, Mira Road, etc. They also alleged discrepancies such as residing Muslims were shown as transferred, many had found their addresses as only the area name whereas many males were listed as females. There were thousands of Muslim residents of Rashid Compound area of Mumbra, whose names had been missing from the area voter list. They complained that this could not be a simple mistake because while there were many Muslims who were residing at their noted addresses the voter list said they had moved away and many others found their gender changed. They alleged that the voter list must show the new addresses of persons whose status is marked 'shifted'. They claimed that there had to be a conspiracy behind manipulation of voter list so that Muslims were held back from voting. Backing the allegations they said that most of non-Muslims living in the same area did not face such problems. A corporator from Mumbra said that he had sent 17,000 completed forms, but only 2,500 names were included and the rest were left out. They made a written complaint to the Chief Electoral Officer (CEO), Maharashtra and attached many documents to support their claim. They alleged that a similar situation was faced by Muslims at the national level to deprive them of their voting rights. In Moradabad, 15,800 names of Muslim voters were disappeared. In Ayodhya, total 84,650 voters increased after revision of the roll and 2,711, 2,699, 1,778, and 1,314 voters were listed in some households of the city. However, Faizabad which was a Muslim-dominated area registered an increase of just 690 voters. In Lucknow, the number of voters increased to 30,000 after revision of the roll. When proper verification was done, it was found that only 6,000 voters had increased.

Finally, they alleged that all that was done was 'intentional' and under a broad 'conspiracy' which should have been investigated deeply.[16] According to newspaper reports, 10,585 voter names were deleted from electoral rolls in Mumbra-Kalwa (149) AC in Maharashtra and a majority of deleted voters were Muslims and Dalits. Officials said that the dropped voters did not live on the mentioned address. The MLA from the constituency and former Housing Minister Jitendra Awhad alleged that names of Muslim and Dalit community voters had been deleted intentionally. Several people had been living on the same address for the last many years were also included in the list of deleted voters. He warned that if the deleted names were not restored, he would take to the streets and agitate before the collector's office and the election department.[17] I have mentioned only a few of many such cases that have been reported and noticed by activists; there are hundreds of others that have been either not reported or reported but did not come to public notice. There are numerous such claims from across India, which need to be inquired deeply and corrections be made. Malafide intentions of election officials should be punished.

Inadequate manpower in the district election offices across India is said to be the key challenge in handling the issue of arbitrary deletion of name of voters. Many data entry operators and other personnel associated with the process of inclusion or deletion of voters' names are found to be untrained. A majority of data entry operators are non-Muslims, who do not spell Muslim names correctly and commit mistakes. At many places, the personnel deputed for update of the electoral rolls do not cooperate with the public in collecting information and entering it. Ignorance of the process is yet another challenge. For example, a majority of Muslims and SCs are poor and stay in rented houses. While shifting homes they do not change the address on the voter card. When booth level officers come for verification, they do not find the voter on the mentioned address and delete the names.

Illiteracy among the Muslims and Dalits are another factor. As per the 2011 Census, 68 per cent Muslims and 65 per cent SCs are literate. This means one-third of each of Muslims and Dalits are illiterate, and thus unable to read and write. A majority of them remain unaware of the process of deletion and inclusion of names on electoral rolls. Also, according to a CRDDP study, misuse of Form 7 has also been found to be on increase in many constituencies. Political parties reportedly check Form 20 to know party-wise break-up of votes in a polling booth. After analysing this, they select the households which they assume to be 'other party votes' and apply Form 7 online to delete the names who do not vote for them. It is expected that proper verification is done before deleting names of voters, but in a majority of cases, verification is not done and names are deleted without consent of the voter. Local leaders and community activists must be alert about this.

Every citizen who completes 18 years of age will be eligible to apply for voter identity card and entitled to vote. First-time voters and those whose names have been left out of the electoral rolls must enrol to be able to exercise their franchise. There are citizen facility centres for the guidance of first-time voters, and those whose names are deleted or are transferred. Voters must come forward to register themselves.

Useful Forms

Form 6: New Registration
Form 6A: Overseas voters
Form 7: Objecting inclusion of names or seeking deletions from electoral roll.
Form 8 : Change in name/address
Form 8-1: Change in address in the constituency

Eligibility Criteria

- 18 years of age
- Citizen of India
- Registered in the same area of residence

Documents Required

- Address proof (passport, electricity bill, driving licence, PAN card, etc.)
- Age proof (birth certificate, school/college marks sheet, school leaving certificate, Aadhar, etc.)
- Passport size photo

Submission of Forms

- Deputy DEO's office, Tehsil offices
- All polling kendras
- Voters' help centres
- Ward offices, electoral registration offices

Online Application

- http://eci.nic.in/eci/eci.html
- State CEO websites (such as www.ceo.maharashtra.gov.in etc.)

Election officials in every district must be proactive in including names of all voters particularly those belonging to the weaker sections, on the rolls. They should adopt a multi-pronged strategy to reach out to voters for registration of their names and approach to housing societies, colleges, NGOs and political parties as part of the special drive for voter registration. The Systematic Voters' Education and Electoral Participations (SVEEP) programme is taken up during every election to maximise enrolment of voters. The administration must implement it honestly particularly in areas of the poor.

ATTEMPT TO DISENFRANCHISE

In democratic countries where various groups, races and religious communities reside, but do not share harmonious relations, there are persistent attempts by the majority (dominant) groups to disenfranchise the dominant minority group. The level of literacy, conviction in petty criminal cases, citizenship issues, etc., are used to block people of certain groups from voting during elections. Communal riots/ethnic violence, forced evictions, intimidation, forceful snatching of voter identity cards, etc., are also used to disenfranchise minorities. The Jim Crow system of mass disenfranchisement deserves to be mentioned here. In addition to the separate and unequal treatment to blacks in southern states of the USA, they were systematically denied the right to vote in most of the rural South through selective application of literacy tests and other racially motivated criteria. The Jim Crow system was upheld by local government officials and reinforced by acts of terror perpetrated by vigilantes. One sees similar methods being adopted to disenfranchise Muslims, as well as Dalits.

Our Constitution has given every citizen, irrespective of one's caste, community or religion, etc., the right to vote. As a citizen of India, Muslims too have equal right to vote. They are numerically strong and in position to win many seats of Lok Sabha on their own. Out of 543 PCs in India, in 125 seats Muslims make up 20 per cent or more of the voters, enough to tilt the electoral balance in elections. In states too, they can win many seats or influence the outcome of elections on several ACs. Along with Dalits, they have been able to block the communal leaders to become MPs or MLAs and the path of communal parties for several decades from gaining power at the Centre. The electoral strength of Muslims and Dalits has been a thorn in the sides of the communal parties and conservative elements within the Congress. They have cited lack of education, the number of children in a household, criminal cases, conviction in petty crimes, communal riots, evictions, intimidation, violence, etc., to disenfranchise Muslims and Dalits.

Some leaders of the BJP, Shiv Sena, etc., have openly threatened Muslims that their voting rights would be taken away. In April 2015, the Shiv Sena said that the voting rights of Muslims should be 'revoked' as the community has often been used for 'vote bank politics'. 'If Muslims are only being used . . . to play politics, they can never develop. . . . Muslims will have no future till they are used for vote bank politics. . . . Balasaheb (Thackeray) had once said voting rights of Muslims should be withdrawn. What he said is right,' said in the party mouthpiece *Saamna*.[18] Although the controversial remark drew sharp criticism from other parties, no criminal action was taken against the newspaper. In India every caste/community is used as a vote bank by one or other party. Dalits, Tribals, Brahmins, Kshatriyas, Baniyas, Jats, Yadavas, Reddys, Nairs, etc., have been used as vote bank by some or the other party(ies). The BJP thinks that the Muslim population has played a major role in keeping the party out of power until 2014. For a long time, the party and its leaders have been campaigning against Muslims and urging that they should be disenfranchised. The BJP's anti-Muslim policies including the citizenship policies, which mirror the Jim Crow system of mass disenfranchisement, point to communal violence and community-based schism set to define India's national politics. In 2016, running a polarising election campaign in a bid to form its first government in Assam, the party vowed to disenfranchise millions of Muslim immigrants there. After NRC, when it could not find many Muslims out of NRC and found substantial number of Hindus out of NRC, it brought CAA to grant citizenship to immigrant Bangladeshi Hindus while denying the same to Muslims. During the West Bengal Assembly election campaign, the BJP declared that it would throw out the illegal Bangladeshi immigrants from West Bengal which created fear and anxiety among Muslims. When the NRC exercise failed to achieve its objective in Assam, BJP leader Himanta Biswa Sarma said the NRC could not find foreigners in Assam because a large number of Bangladeshis migrated to other parts of the country. In other words, it was then necessary to hunt for them in the rest of India.[19] In fact, he gave an indication to nation-wide NRC. This created fear and anxiety among the Muslims. They argue that through NRC combined with CAA, the BJP wants to disenfranchise a large number of Muslims. Communal violence, mob lynching and targeted violence by vigilante groups, rampant discrimination and subsequent alienation are basically used by the BJP to disfranchise Indian Muslims.

In Assam, Muslims make up 34.2 per cent of the total population, forming majority in nine districts. The state has now been electing Muslim MPs and a good number of MLAs. The AIUDF has become the main opposition party in assembly. Several communal riots including the Nellie have been engineered to intimidate, alienate and disenfranchise them. The BJP and other right-wing outfits in the state have been demanding that Bangladeshi immigrants coming after the creation of Bangladesh should be identified and deported. Sarma said in 2016 that if the party was elected to power it would try to bar Muslims of Bangladeshi origin that had entered India between 1951 and 1971, from voting. They could stay but would have to re-apply for citizenship.[20] When the NRC exercise could not find substantial Muslims out of NRC, the local extremist outfits are trying to make the exercise redundant.

Besides this, the central government brought the Citizenship Amendment Act (CAA) to grant citizenship to illegal Hindu immigrants. This is basically a deliberate act to disenfranchise Muslims. Now the BJP govt. in Assam has adopted the method of forced evictions. On 23 September 2021, police used force to evict families from their land in Dholpur village of Darrang district. The authorities said that 1,200 families were evicted as part of a plan to start an agricultural project. The authorities freed a land of 4,500 *bighas* (6 sq. km) of land. Nearly 5,000 people (mostly Muslims), were forced to live in the open. During the forced-eviction drive and protest by Muslims, two people, Moinul Haque and Shaik Farid, were killed.[21] The eviction drive highlighted the BJP's explosive community politics, which attempted to disenfranchise and uproot Muslims in Assam.

The CAA was passed in December 2019 and fear persists that it would be used to disenfranchise and revoke the citizenship of Muslims. It grants citizenship to all non-Muslim immigrants coming from Pakistan, Afghanistan and Bangladesh up to 31 December 2014. The Act clearly violates the Article 14 of the Constitution and discriminates against Muslims. The Modi government has repeatedly said that it would conduct nation-wide NRC and then apply CAA. This means post-NRC, people belonging to Hindu, Sikh, Christian, Jain, and Parsi communities falling out of NRC will be granted citizenship on application by applying CAA. Muslims falling out of NRC would face trauma, go to detention centres and finally lose their right to vote. This act has been brought to traumatise and disenfranchise Muslims.

The BJP is even trying to snatch away the voter identity cards of Muslims. Five BJP activists of the women's wing were arrested by police in a Muslim-dominated area of Bengaluru in August 2015 after locals accused them of trying to steal their voter ID cards. Shamsunnisa, a voter of Siddapura locality in Bangalore said, 'Five women came into my house around 5 p.m. and told me they were from the census department. They asked me to show them my voting card. When I showed them the card, they said it was no longer valid and tried to take it away.' When some people of the locality gathered and asked the women for their ID cards, there was confusion. After a few minutes the women started crying and confessed that they were BJP workers. Finally, the police arrived, escorted them to safety and lodged an FIR saying the women were trying to con voters into parting with their voting cards.[22]

The right-wingh elements have been trying hard to disenfranchise Muslims as they are the biggest stumbling block in their bid to gain political power. The UCH leaders even try to disenfranchise OBCs and Dalits. Their action is guided by the fear of deluge of OBCs, Dalits and Muslims in legislative bodies which would end their dominance in politics and governance.

DALIT-MUSLIM UNITY

While we have examined the inherent anti-Muslim nature of the BJP, it is equally true that the party is averse to Dalits. Both communities have a shared history of discrimination and exclusion and both have also suffered due to their own leaders bending to lures of vested political interests. Again, militant Hindutva often goes against the interests of the marginalized castes and concerns and its objectives are more in tune with the ambitions and aspirations of the upper castes. The BJP makes token and superficial gestures of appointing a Dalit in an official position to mislead Dalits but does not address their genuine problems. Dr Ambedkar observed,

> There are many lower orders in the Hindu society whose economic, political, and social needs are the same as those of majority of Muslims and they would be far more ready to make a common cause with the Muslims for achieving common ends than they would with the high caste Hindus who have denied and deprived them of ordinary human rights for centuries.
>
> Dr. Babasaheb Ambedkar (*Writings and Speeches*, vol. 8, p. 359)[23]

A key factor for poor representation of Muslims and weak leadership in Dalits is lack of unity between them. But despite similarities in socio-economic and cultural milieu, they are not united on political fronts. Because of this both the communities have suffered losses in the political field. There are many Muslim-dominated PCs and ACs where Muslims' share in population is

30 to 40 per cent. They need the support of Dalit voters to win these seats. If they unite with Dalit parties and procure Dalit votes in these Muslim-dominated seats, their representation would certainly go up. Political parties, that are genuinely working for Dalits, have also suffered politically due to lack of Dalit-Muslim unity. There is no national level Dalit party and the majority of Dalit parties in states either have been assimilated or become adjunct to main parties. Aside from the BSP in UP, most other Dalit parties have been subsumed by mainstream political parties or become their adjunct, negotiating for a small share of political power pie. Due to reservation in politics, seats are reserved for SCs, but those elected are actually the stooges of the main political parties. Dalit politics has actually returned to the 'chamcha age', the only difference being that Dalit leaders are pleading before the BJP and other regional parties instead of the Congress.

According to the Pew Research Centre, there were around 213 million Muslims in India in 2020, 15.5 per cent of the population, while Dalits formed around 16.6 per cent. In UP, Muslims and Dalits constitute 19 per cent and 20.7 per cent respectively of the state's population. Together they make up 40 per cent of the population, which is sufficient for getting majority in the Assembly. A combination of these two communities would be a formidable electoral alliance. Nonetheless, a Dalit-Muslim electoral alliance is a pipe dream despite the empirical data on backwardness of Muslims and Dalits being almost the same. As per the 2011 Census, while literacy rate on national level was 73.0 per cent, in Dalits and Muslims it was respectively 66.1 and 63.5 per cent, both below national level. As per the Post-Sachar Evaluation Committee report (2014), Muslims and SCs show a sharp dropout after the age of 13. While it occurs in all SRCs, it begins early in Muslims and the SC/ST. There is not much difference among them in terms of unemployment ratio or kind of work. In terms of poverty, per capita income, infrastructure and civic facilities in their residential areas which are also segregated and ghettoized besides many other socio-economic parameters, there are great similarities.

Historically, a vast majority of Muslims are thought to be descendants of Dalits, BCs and Tribals, who embraced Islam to seek liberation from centuries of Brahmanical tyranny. Some authors believe that Dalits and Muslims are brethren. Both are the victims of Hindu oppression and have a common culture that seeks justice, equality and brotherhood. In terms of cultural and lifestyle habits, there is hardly any demarcation between them. Government policies, in some cases, have equally harmed both communities. The beef ban in many states has affected both communities negatively. The Qureshis traditionally have been engaged in meat business, while the Dalits do leather business. Since 2014, the vigilante mobs have not only lynched Muslims, but also killed many Dalits on suspicion of carrying and eating beef. While one is targeted on the basis of religion, the other is marked out for its caste identity. Dalits look to Muslims as a resilient force and Islam as a movement against oppression. They look to Muslims to liberate them from shackles of oppression and inequality through united action. Dr. Ambedkar generated hope in Dalits of India and asked them to educate, organize and agitate to get their rights. Muslims look to Dalits to embrace those values. These facts alone should have ordinarily been enough to cement a strong bond of unity between them.

Unfortunately, this is not the case. Even though the urge to forge unity is prevalent among backward and Dalit castes of the Muslim community, the rich among them namely the *ashraf*, however, are not mobilised substantially in this way. The rise of the BJP to power and various atrocities committed against Muslims, have opened the eyes of even the *ashraf* section. Now, along with the *Ajlaf* and *Arzal*, Ashraf Muslims seem to be ready to forge an alliance with Dalits. These two communities can make common cause to challenge the upper castes' hegemony and even compel the government to take decisions in their favour.

Recently, there have been some efforts to bring them together on common platforms so that a political understanding could be created and future political alliances made. As pointed out, Dalits and other oppressed sections share strong historical and cultural bonds with Muslims. During much of the colonial period, they were united on various issues. They had in common a fear—often a hatred—of the dominant Brahmanism. As Dr. Ambedkar pointed out in his book *Thoughts on Pakistan*, between 1920 and 1937, it was Muslims, Dalits and other non-Brahmins who had worked on the reforms, held office in provincial assemblies and worked in alliance on programmes which included establishing water tanks, constructing roads, and schools for untouchables. In areas such as Bengal, a political alliance was formed between the Namashudra (Dalit) and Muslims, which had gained strength because both were predominantly tenants fighting anti-landlord struggles. Of late, Asaduddin Owaisi has been trying to bring them together so that both Dalits and Muslims could switch votes from one party to another forming a block of voters whose needs cannot be ignored. Keen to replace the influence of the so-called secular parties, he has been organising conferences to bring them together in areas where Muslims dominate, but need the support of Dalits. Other Muslim base parties are doing the same. When the Welfare Party of India (WPI), the political wing of Jamaat-e-Islami, was formed in 2013, its leaders stressed the need for strong Dalit-Muslim alliance to counter what they called the rule of a 5 per cent over India. Revolutionary and former Naxalite poet Gunmadi Vittal Rao, or Gaddar said Muslims should unite with other oppressed sections then only would they achieve political justice. Prakash Ambedkar the grandson of B.R. Ambedkar argued that there was a political vacuum created due to the communal and narrow casteist politics of the mainstream political parties. This vacuum can be filled by uniting Muslims with other oppressed communities on the agenda of development and justice.[24] Jignesh Mewani, an activist and MLA from Gujarat, has launched the Dalit Muslim Ekta Manch to 'uproot the fascist forces ruling the country since 2014'. He was even trying to expand the Manch to include tribals of Gujarat, and fight for basic rights of citizens beginning with Ahmedabad city and expand across the state upto national level. Similar efforts are being made by lesser-known Dalit and Muslim organizations.

Prominent Dalit and Muslim leaders have long stressed the need for a broad-based unity, seeing this as a powerful means to challenge 'upper caste' oppression that both sides regard themselves as victims. Yet, Dalit-Muslim unity project has hardly advanced beyond mere sloganeering or at best strategic political alliances at the time of elections. By and large, the moves to unite them have been confined to the political level though even that has not succeeded fully. Recent years have seen the emergence of few political parties ostensibly committed to Dalit-Muslim unity, but this cannot fructify in the absence of strong bonds between these two groups on social and justice level. In other words, a meaningful unity between them is possible only through strong contacts and close alliance at the level of civil society.

Whenever there is talk of Dalit-Muslim unity, the upper castes in right-wing organisations, and BJP try to deceive the Dalits with calls of Hindu unity. They make an all-out effort to discredit and finally break it. For Hindutva organizations, Dalits are Hindus only on three occasions: during the Census to be enumerated as Hindus, during elections to get Dalit votes and at the time of communal riots against Muslims. The Dalits have never been considered part of the *Sanatan Dharma*, the upper-caste politicians have given them nothing in return for their votes, Muslims are not their enemies and more importantly, the riot cases are registered against them. Professional competitiveness and rivalry (especially in the bovine and leather business) sometimes lead to clashes between them. Such petty quarrels have been tuned into Hindu-Muslim riots. While otherwise the Dalits are treated shabbily, atrocities committed against them and even lynched by vigilantes when there is talk of unity, the Hindutva organizations sense the threat and make every effort to disrupt it. Secondly, whenever there is any such effort, the upper castes in every party take it as a threat to their survival and use the media to do all in their capacity to concoct conflicts between Dalits and Muslims to disrupt any move towards unity.

It must be admitted that the Muslim community as a whole has never been fully sympathetic to the Dalit cause or tried whole-heartedly to forge unity. The Muslim community is not monolithic, and is divided into at least four major groups: *ashraf*, *ajlaf*, *arzals* and tribals, each with distinct socio-cultural and political interests and aspirations. An *arzal* Muslim, placed at the bottom of the caste hierarchy, has more in common with a Dalit Hindu than *ashraf* (elite) Muslim. *Ajlaf* (backward castes) Muslims share many similarities with OBC Hindus more than with *ashrafs*. The *ajlaf* and *arzals* (degraded) who constitute 85 per cent of Muslims have been sympathetic to Hindu Dalits and always in favour of Dalit-Muslim unity not only on the political level, but also on issues of social justice. The elite Ashraf who make up 15 per cent of Muslims have not supported Dalit Hindus wholeheartedly on many occasions. *Ashraf* leaders and their organizations like Jamaat-e-Islami Hind (JIH), Jamiat Ulema-e-Hind (JUH), etc., their institutions like the All India Muslim Personal Law Board (AIMPLB) have never enthusiastically supported this agenda.

I want to examine the means whereby a strong and long lasting alliance between Dalits and Muslims can be created. Sociologist and caste studies scholar Gail Omvedt says that a solid Dalit-Muslim alliance for the future should be directed to building a prosperous, egalitarian and casteist-free India. Muslims can make contribution in three major ways. First, by rebuilding a Muslim culture that regains the artistic and scientific accomplishments of the past, that stands for modernism and an understanding of Islam that brings forth its egalitarianism, as well as cultural-artistic achievements. Islam directed at maintaining its identity within a genuinely pluralistic society can be a powerful force for reconstructing the base of an Indian national community. Second, by recognizing that within Indian society, there is a special task of fighting the Brahmanism that has become dominant, and maintains casteism and feudal attitudes. Freeing Indian culture from the stranglehold of Brahmanism will provide the basis for genuine national development. It can only be done by listening to Dalit voices like Ambedkar, Phule, Periyar, Iyothee Thass, Mayawati, Kanshi Ram and others. Third, as Dalits search for a new faith, Islam should participate in this process. Dalits must be respected as an autonomous community; as they themselves break more and more decisively with Brahminism, they will go their diverse ways, and in the process some will turn to Islam.[25] In short, she advised Muslims to regain artistic accomplishment, humanitarian attitude and scientific temper of the past to create an egalitarian society, to create a common force to fight Brahmanism. They must read and listen to Dalit thinkers and assist and participate in the process of Dalits' search for a new faith.

Scholars argue that the term 'Muslim community' as conceived in the social sense has to be destroyed as it has not only failed either to protect or advance its members politically, but, as the 2014 election showed, made even its vast population irrelevant to India's electoral arithmetic. They say the community must be divided along social lines of *ashraf*, *ajlaf* and *arzals*. Pasmanda Muslims (both *ajlaf* and *arzals*) share social, cultural and historical bonds with Hindu Dalits. Pasmanda group Muslims must unite with Dalits to create a common platform not only to advance politically but also to fight a common enemy i.e. Brahmanism. Khalid Anis Ansari, sociologist and writer on Pasmanda issues, says:

> Since the express object of the Pasmanda movement has been to raise the issue of caste-based exclusion of subordinate caste Muslims, it has stressed on caste-based solidarity across religions. As Ali Anwar, the founder of Pasmanda Muslim Mahaz, says, 'There is a bond of pain between Pasmanda Muslims and the Pasmanda sections of other religions. This bond of pain is the supreme bond. . . . That is why we have to shake hands with the Pasmanda sections of other religious.'[26]

In short, the Pasmanda group of Muslims share the bond of pain with other oppressed groups, i.e. OBCs and Dalits of Hindu religion. These groups must unite to gain political rights, and also to fight injustice committed by elite upper-caste groups. Pasmandas share a widespread feeling of 'Muslimness' with the Ashraf Muslims. Generally speaking—religion-based solidarity is broken by caste and caste-based solidarity is broken by religion. Pasmanda thinkers choose to focus on caste-based solidarity and discard the solidarity that is based on religion.[27]

Dalit thinkers believe that most Islamic parties, organizations and Muslim politics embrace religion and often politics for them is subsumed within the ethical practices that religion demands from them. For them there is no sociality without religion. In great contrast to Muslim politics, contemporary anti-caste politics, in spite of its great impact and subversive potential, is very much part of a modern-life world. It has today become an extremely secular category, where moving away from Ambedkarite thought, religion itself is dismissed as not important for annihilating caste.

Given this, when there is a talk of Dalit-Muslim unity, the demand made of Muslim groups is to discard the issues of religion and subsume themselves within the secular, liberal caste category. The demand made is to discard issues related to religion and not the religion. The coming together of Dalits, with a new understanding of the attempt to appropriate them into the Hindu religion, and Muslims, with a renewed understanding of caste/social stratification among them, in common platforms of struggles will alone lead to such an endeavour.[28]

Besides the above conditions, Dalits and Muslims must unite to fight for justice in cases of atrocities committed against them and fight human rights violations, issues of social justice and economic exclusions. Breaking the barrier of religion they must stand unitedly on common platforms to raise issues of empowerment. These are the means by which political understanding will automatically follow.

NOTES

1. http://twocircles.net/2014jun10/can_modi_be_compared_hitler.html
2. https://clarionindia.net/political-marginalization-of-muslims-in-the-age-of-majoritarion-nationalism/
3. Ibid.
4. http://www.catchnews.com/politics-news/gujarat-polls-how-bjp-wins-muslim-dominated-seats-without-getting-muslim-votes-89475.html
5. Ibid.
6. *Inquilab*, 26 November 2017.
7. http://www.ummid.com/news/2017/February/12.02.2017/how-muslim-votes-get-divided-in-uttar-pradesh.html
8. *The Indian Express*, Pune, 26 October 2019.
9. Ghazala Wahab, *Born a Muslim: Some Truths About Islam in India*, Delhi: Aleph Book Company, 2021.
10. *The Indian Express*, Pune, 19 July 2012.
11. https://www.newsclick.in/Lack-Leadership-Indian-Muslims-Falling-Behind-Secular
12. https://theprint.in/pageturner/excerpt/some-clerics-think-they-are-above-quran-its-making-indian-muslims-sectarian-and-backward/761943/

13. https://www.thehindu.com/elections/lok-sabha-2019/in-tamil-nadu-muslims-and-dalits-find-it-harder-to-stay-on-the-rolls/article 26655937.ece
14. *Inquilab*, 6 March 2013.
15. http://twocircles.net/2013apr05/50000_voters_name_deleted_electoral_rolls_says_jds_leader_abdul_azeem.html
16. *Inquilab*, 4 April 2014.
17. Ibid., 18 October 2021.
18. *The Indian Express*, Pune, 13 April 2015.
19. https://www.aa.com.tr/en/analysis/opinion-new-india-law-aims-to-disenfranchise-muslims/1687520
20. https://www.reuters.com/article/india-politics-idUSKCN0WC2WR
21. https://www.newframe.com/evictions-in-india-an-ominous-message-to-muslims/
22. *Hindustan Times*, Bengaluru, 13 August 2015.
23. http://twocircles.net/2014sep24/1411548420.html
24. http://twocircles.net/2013may27/wpi_ap_launched_massive_ show_strength.html
25. https://www.laits.utexas.edu/africa/ads/731.html
26. https://www.dalitcamera.com/anxieties-surrounding-dalit-muslim-unity/
27. Ibid.
28. Ibid.

CHAPTER 7

Other Issues Concerning Muslim Representation

Among the many myths about the Muslim community that are fostered in the popular imagination, but not backed by evidence is that of the 'Muslim vote bank'. There are many factors that have led to this perception even to the point where one political party called for the curtailing of the right to vote for Muslims in order to do away with 'vote bank politics'!

There is an assumption that the Muslims constitute a homogenous and monolithic community while the reality is that it is not only sociologically diverse, but is also divided into 700 different castes. Several commission reports have testified to this. For example, the Pasmanda Muslims constitute an extremely backward community on all the social, economic and educational indicators. They are vastly different from the Ashraf Muslims. However, various sections find it helpful to foster this myth in the public perception in order to further their ambitions. Again, Muslims are spread across the country for generations and thus culturally, socially and linguistically different from their religious counterparts in other states.

In this chapter I discuss the myth of the Muslim vote bank and the various stakeholders who foster it, the politics of the Pasmanda Muslims *versus* the Ashraf Muslims, and the challenges inherent in it and the need for acknowledgment of the Pasmanda discourse by the mainstream parties, how Muslims have been used by the secular parties, the political deprivation of OBCs, the return of upper castes' politics and their appeasement by the BJP, and whether the Aam Aadmi Party (AAP) truly represents a political alternative for the Muslims in India.

MUSLIM VOTE BANK: MYTH OR REALITY?

Do Muslims vote differently from the other castes or communities? There is not much difference between Muslim voting behaviour and that of other communities. However, the right-wing groups, the BJP and even the secular parties have created and sustained the myth of the Muslim vote bank to promote their own selfish interests.

'Muslim vote bank' is defined both in a positive and negative sense. Although they constitute only 14.2 per cent of the population, it is publicized that the 'Muslim vote' is decisive in electoral politics because the 'winnability' of secular candidates or sustainability of any political coalition at the regional/national level are intricately associated with Muslim voters support. The Muslim vote bank, in this sense, refers to the collective political strength of Muslim voters. For this reason, their concerns are valued and their issues find place in manifestoes of political parties. The second argument, which is negative in nature is propagated by the BJP, right-wing groups and scholars wherein they allege that Muslims are used as political commodity during elections, particularly by the secular parties and 'appeased' for their votes. This is done primarily to raise and consciously sustain polarization of the atmosphere and consolidate Hindu votes. In 2015, the Shiv Sena's mouthpiece *Saamna* actually demanded revocation of voting rights of Muslims to stop vote-bank politics.[1]

On the other hand, several scholars, political scientists and Muslim political leaders have been arguing that a 'Muslim vote bank' does not exist in reality. In fact, say some of them, Narendra Modi's victory in 2014 clearly showed the existence of a 'Hindu vote bank'. Wajahat Habibullah, erstwhile Chairman of the National Commission for Minorities, said in 2013, 'The notion that Muslim vote *en masse* is a myth that has survived for years. Though they may unite on a certain issues, it is no thumb rule.' Asaduddin Owaisi once said, 'There has never been a Muslim vote bank in India, there has always been a Hindu vote bank. Narendra Modi shattered this myth of there being a Muslim vote bank by winning the 2014 Lok Sabha elections.'[2] Hilal Ahmed, political scientist based at CSDS, writes, 'There is ample empirical evidence in the form of electoral statistics that suggest that the 'Muslim vote bank' is indeed a myth.' Based on the election results of the 2014 Maharashtra assembly elections, the freelance journalist Jyoti Punwani pointed out, 'The Maharashtra assembly election has again proved that Muslims do not vote as a block.'[3] Muslims also believe that the vote bank myth is deliberately spread to keep the community away from the real concerns of empowerment. Just before the UP assembly elections of 2017 an educated Muslim in Firozabad told a journalist, 'The truth is that those who describe us as vote banks are the ones who block our progress so that we can be caught in their tentacles forever.'[4]

The term 'Muslim vote bank' did not originate from the Congress or the Sangh Parivar or from the Muslim community. It originated from the frequently used expression 'vote bank' in the 1950s. M.N. Srinivas, a sociologist, who conducted field work in a village in Mysore region in 1953, was probably the first political observer, who used the expression 'vote bank' to describe the relationship between politicians and the rural elites, who had a hold over the voters. He noted that locally powerful individuals emerged as 'vote banks' for politicians, as they were approached by the leaders to mobilize voters for their caste/community. In return, he argued, these patrons expected various favours from the leaders. Thus, the rural elites who had a hold over the voters were called the 'vote bank'. Politicians dealt with these vote banks without establishing a direct relationship with the voters. 'Vote bank' emerged as a universally applicable descriptive term to critique India's electoral process and political parties. It began to find concrete expression in the politics of later years.

From 1967, Muslim votes started to deviate from the Congress. In 1967 they were considered an important factor to win elections. As the non-Congress parties began to mobilize Muslims towards a winnable social coalition of minorities, SCs and OBCs (and the consequent appeal by All India Muslim Majlis-e-Mushawarat (AIMMM)), the Congress approached the pro-Congress Muslim clergy. The clergy openly asked Muslims to vote for a party especially the Congress. *Fatwas* issued by Abdullah Bukhari of

Delhi's Jama Masjid can be seen in this context. In return, religious figures got various benefits from the Congress. In the 1980s and 1990s, due to the Ramjanmabhoomi movement and widespread communal riots, the community voted unitedly in favour of some parties, primarily to defeat the BJP. Secondly, on eve of every election, the clergy issued *fatwas* to direct Muslim voters. This, in turn, created a perception that Muslims constitute a homogenous political community governed by the logic of the 'Muslim vote bank'.[5]

The myth of the Muslim vote bank has survived till today with the help of different stakeholders who try to sustain it for different political reasons. First, BJP and right-wing groups raise the issue to create an impression that Muslims have collective voting strengths, which is exploited by secular parties. This helps to scare Hindu voters and consolidate them in their favour. This is also used to create an impression that, if Hindus do not vote unitedly secular parties will come to power which will be a threat to their existence. Second, the secular parties try to sustain it, directly or indirectly, to create an impression that the participation of Muslims in electoral politics can be reduced to their Islamic identity and other related religious issues. For this reason, the secular parties address only the identity and religious issues, and do not focus on education, employment and political empowerment of Muslims. They focus on religious tokenism as if Muslims do not need material progress. Elite Muslim leaders always want to create the impression that Muslim vote is unified and they vote *en masse*. This is used to justify the convenient political package termed '*Muslim Issues*', viz., the protection of Islamic personal laws, restoration of the minority character of the AMU, Urdu language, and Baburi Masjid. The elite leaders failed to understand the sociological stratification of the community which is the reason for Dalits and backwards among Muslims being denied the reservation that they genuinely deserve. The clergy too is also responsible for creating such an impression and its sustenance for gaining personal benefits. They portray themselves as leaders of the unified Muslim community to gain political benefits like nominations to legislative bodies or commissions. The idea of a 'Muslim vote bank' has been disproven many times by those who have studied Indian voting data published after the elections. A study conducted by Rahul Verma and Pranav Gupta about Muslim voting pattern in UP is worth mentioning here. From their studies, they found that:

1. Muslim voters are *not* more politically active than the common voter, indicating that they are not disproportionately organizing themselves to grab political power.
2. Muslim voters are *not* more likely to listen to community leaders and others who wish to dictate how they vote. About half of the total electorate says they make up their mind on who to vote for, and the share is the same for Indian Muslim voters.
3. Muslim voters are *not* more loyal to a single, nor are they more likely to *never* vote for a particular party. About a third of all voters declare party allegiance; the figure is same for Muslims. About a quarter of the wider electorate say they will never vote for a particular party; the figure is same for Muslims.
4. The Muslim vote in UP is divided among SP, BSP and Congress, with each enjoying the support of different groups of Muslims. There is no unified vote bank.
5. Multiple analyses of voting patterns show that even 'strategic voting' within ACs of Muslims to defeat the BJP candidates does not occur. There is no correlation between consolidation of Muslim votes and the BJP's vote share in that particular election.
6. Comparing Muslim consolidation and fragmentation with other groups, the study found that in 2012, Muslim and Brahmin votes were comparatively more fragmented, while Yadav and Jatav votes were more consolidated; in 2014, Brahmin and Muslim votes were more consolidated, while Yadav and Jatav votes were more fragmented. All this is to say that all these groups are not all, as is imagined by some upper-caste Indians, 'vote banks' in the sense they imagine. Each of these groups is fragmented to various degrees and at various times.[6]

Nilanjan Mukhopadhyaya's analysis of the Muslim voting pattern in the 2017 Gujarat elections showed that Muslims voted along economic lines rather than consolidating to defeat the BJP across the state. The study reveals just how diverse the Muslim population in Gujarat is, and how much they voted according to their local, constituency-level concerns.[7]

Ahmed notes in his book, *Siyasi Muslims: A Story of Political Islam in India*, moments when Muslims voted for the BJP. Most significantly, it shows how percentage of Muslims voting for the BJP candidates goes up sharply when the main political contest is between only two parties. If Muslims were indeed a vote bank consolidated against the BJP, such a contest would see *fewer* Muslims voting for the BJP, not more. These reports indicate that Muslim voters exercise their voting rights just like other voters.

Muslims are not averse to voting for the BJP. According to the Lokniti-CSDS poll published after the Maharashtra assembly elections in 2014, 53 per cent of Muslims voted for the Congress, and 16 per cent for the NCP. For the first time, the BJP received 13 per cent Muslim votes, and its ally Shiv Sena, 11 per cent. These two parties jointly received 24 per cent of Muslim votes.[8] Poll analysts have indicated that the percentage of Muslims voting for the BJP has been rising. As per the CSDS studies, only 3 per cent Muslims voted for the BJP in 2007 UP assembly elections, the same rose to seven in 2012. As per the CSDS survey, 8 per cent Muslims voted for the BJP in the 2014 Lok Sabha elections, almost double the 2009 tally, enabling it to win 45 of 87 Lok Sabha seats with more concentration of Muslim voters, which included 27 seats from UP alone. This is despite the fact that the BJP generally does not field Muslim candidates.[9] Muslims not voting for the BJP cannot become the basis of allegations that Muslims vote *en masse*, or they constitute a vote bank. The BJP, as a political party, plays the politics of communalism, takes an anti-Muslim stand on every matter associated with them and is ideologically against their empowerment including political empowerment. It does not field Muslims candidate nor does it address their concerns of safety and security. The party remains silent about mob violence by right-wing elements, attacks on Muslims by the Bajrang Dal and communal riots. The party has even indicated that it would like to scrap the constitutionally guaranteed rights of Muslims. In a democracy, people vote for a party that addresses their concerns and is sympathetic to their causes. In this situation it is against logic to believe that Muslims would vote for the BJP. If the BJP behaves like a normal party in a secular democracy, Muslims would certainly vote for the BJP in the same way as they do for other parties which do politics on progress and livelihood issues and not on communal and contentious issues as the BJP does.

Broadly speaking, the notion of 'Muslim vote bank' is based on a strong assumption that Muslims form a single monolithic homogeneous group, while the reality is that Indian Muslims are as diverse as the Hindu community. They are divided not only on social group basis, such as *ashraf*, *ajlaf* and *arzal* but also on caste lines into numerous castes and into various religious sects such as Sunni, Shia, Wahhabi, Ahle-Hadees, Deobandi, Barelvi, Bohra, etc. On the national level, they are also divided on basis of language, region, class, culture, etc. This internal diversity actually determines the nature of their voting pattern which is also driven by local exigencies. Their participation in electoral politics primarily depends on issues, such as education, employment, safety and security, political empowerment, commitment of parties to secularism, etc. However, political parties are not keen to recognize the fact of diversity as well as issues of empowerment. Hilal Ahmed writes, 'The notion of Muslim vote bank, it seems, will continue to survive until and unless Muslim plurality is recognized as a political reality.' Aftab Alam, a professor of Political Science at AMU, writes:

> By not recognising the plurality of Muslim electorate political parties seem to deliberately perpetuate the imaginary and illusory 'Muslim vote bank' phenomenon to divert the attention from real issues that confront the community. Projecting Muslim voters as a monolithic community breeds majoritarian communalism. Notwithstanding the fact that the threat to their security and identity is an important consideration that shapes the voting behaviour of Muslim elites but issues like education and employment are vital determinants for the rest but the political parties are not ready to recognize this difference. There is no empirical evidence to suggest that Muslims vote differently. Conversely, there have been numerous scientific studies conducted in recent years that demolish most of these myths associated with Muslim voters.[10]

Generally, Muslim population vote for secular regional parties, national parties like Congress, CPI, CPI(M), the OBC based parties and Muslim base parties in some regions of few states. They strategically vote at the local level for the party that best serves their interests. Parties and reasons to support them vary from constituency to constituency. Some people vote considering their personal relations with the candidates and some keeping in mind their personal interests. Even among family members, there is no consensus on voting. Clearly, there is no 'Muslim vote bank'.

HAVE MUSLIMS BEEN USED BY SECULAR PARTIES?

Since Independence, secular parties received Muslim votes wholeheartedly in the name of 'protecting secularism', but the community did not get its share in politics. Many secular governments at the centre and in states were formed with Muslim votes, but in none of them did Muslims get a place in cabinets. These parties promised to protect secularism and assured security to Muslims, but did not seriously focus on socio-economic development, educational advancement and their due share in politics.

Owaisi targets political parties for using Muslims as a vote bank and says, 'The condition of Muslims has become like a "band baja party" in a marriage procession, where they (Muslims) are first asked to play music, but are made to stand outside on reaching the wedding venue.' Muslims have been discarded not only in politics, but their lives and properties have not been protected during riots or when they face rampant discrimination by these so called secular parties. Accusing governments of discrimination, Owaisi says, 'In the eyes of all other (secular) political parties, Muslims are merely a vote bank. These parties have not done justice to Muslims. Only those who have power are heard.'[11]

After the Partition, Muslims who remained in India were told both by Muslims and 'secular' leadership that, if they wanted to survive in Hindu India it was their duty to protect secularism, which in real terms meant voting for the party, which in return would keep India secular. In India's political lexicon, therefore 'secularism' became synonymous with 'Muslim vote bank'. The Sangh Parivar parties used it conveniently to mean 'appeasement of Muslims'. In real terms secularism meant protecting minorities from possible violence and discrimination, while in practical terms it meant appeasement of Muslims, especially before elections. The Congress and other secular parties have created an impression that only Muslims need secularism, and for this they need to vote for them. Muslims have been carrying the burden of secularism for the last 75 years. Owaisi further said, 'Successive governments of various political parties over the past several years have "abused" the term secularism and "used" it as an opportunistic tool to deceive the minorities.'[12] Repeated use or abuse of the term 'secularism' has done more harm to Muslims than serving any purpose. Political scientists Pradeep Chhibber and Rahul Verma say the use of the word 'secular' diverts attention from real problems faced by Muslims. Secularism as a rhetorical political tool has done more harm than good in four ways. It has flattened the diversity of the Muslim community, redefined their interests primarily in terms of religion and privileged the Muslim elite. It has given right-wing groups a political tool to mobilise voters by using the empirically questionable rhetoric of a Muslim vote bank.[13]

Post-Partition, when Muslims from the educated class, bureaucracy, army, landed gentry and big businessmen shifted to Pakistan, the Congress turned to the *ulema* to get Muslim votes. In their perception, the *ulema* had the persuasive power to steer the Muslim masses towards the Congress. The party, which claimed to be secular, looked to the *maulanas*, political *ulema* and conservative elements, instead of university educated liberals to garner Muslim votes. This was the subtle manner in which religious leadership was first promoted and then imposed on Muslims by 'secular' parties. Liberal Muslim leaders demanded socio-economic progress, educational rights while religious leaders were more concerned with Muslim personal law, protection of *madrasa* and Urdu, or perceived notions of 'Islam in danger'. From Jawaharlal Nehru to the present leadership of the Congress, this 'appeasement' of Muslim religious leadership imposed a heavy cost on the educational and economic growth of Muslims. Other secular/regional parties have been following this path of appeasing religious leadership to garner Muslim vote. Even today, party leaders are seen in religious gatherings of Muslims wearing a skull cap in *iftar* parties. But when it comes to giving Muslims an equitable share in education, job and govenment schemes, they are nowhere to be found. 'Secular' leaders made a beeline to get political *fatwas* (opinons) from the Madanis of Deoband, Ali Mian of Nadwatul uloom, Shahi Imam Bukhari of Jama Masjid to Arshadul Qadri and Tauseef Raza of Barelvi sect, so that Muslims were herded like sheep to vote to save secularism. Shahid Siddiqui, a seniour journalist, writes, 'Realising that these "secular" parties only cared for and promoted narrow-minded religious leaders, even educated liberal and secular Muslim leaders started speaking the same language.'[14] Even today educated secular leaders focus more on religious issues than socio-economic progress.

Insidiously, programmes to save secularism are organized by secular parties in Muslim-dominated areas. The intention is to create fear among Muslims which actually means that these parties are asking Muslims to vote out of fear rather than for development. They have created the perception that, if secularism perishes in India, Muslims rights would not be preserved. Muslims have no 'option' but to vote for these parties if they want India to remain secular. Siddiqui further writes:

> Any group or community without an option in a democracy is a bonded slave of certain parties and politics. There are regional alternatives like SP, Trinamool Congress, RJD and so on but their attitude is the same. They all expect Muslims to pay protection money in the form of their votes, the secular 'Jaziyah' of modern democratic India. How long and for how many more elections will this continue? When will secularism be the need for a modern state which treats its citizens equally, rather than a burden to be carried by minorities of this great nation? The enemies of secularism are not those who have opposed it but those who have manipulated it for their electoral benefit, looking to get Muslim votes out of fear rather than from conviction.[15]

After the results of the 2014 general elections, this disturbing and even scary situation has worsened further. The empty talk of protecting secularism and promises of token benefits to the Muslim community on the eve of elections is no longer heard. Today, no secular party addresses the Muslim electorates. From 2006 to 2013, almost all secular parties talked about implementing the recommendations of the SCR. They made promises on socio-economic and educational progress including giving reservation to the backward sections among Muslims. Now, even this lip service to Muslim empowerment and protection of secularism has completely stopped. Due to the growing wave of communalism and fear of loosing the majority Hindu votes, they maintain silence on Muslim issues. They do not visit Muslim areas, or announce anything on the SCR or even pose for photographs with people wearing skull caps even during election campaigns. Today Muslims have become untouchables for the secular camp.

In an article in *The Print*, D.K. Singh writes:

> The silence in most Muslim-dominated habitations in India's hinterlands is almost eerie. As if there was no election happening! Leaders stay away. Photo-ops with prominent Muslim clerics and politicians are a thing of the past. No political party has sought endorsement from the Shahi Imam of Delhi's Jama Masjid this time. There are no more talks of mob-lynching or references to 'Hindu fundamentals' or attacks on secularism. . . . Yesteryear's flag-bearers of secularism seem convinced today that the best way to protect it is to avoid Muslims.[16]

There was a time when the BJP's political rivals accused it of pursuing the agenda of making Muslims 'second-class citizens' in India. Today, it is ironical that the same secular camp is for all practical purposes treating Muslims no differently. Owaisi says this apathy would lead to marginalization and ghettoization of the minority community. Minorities see clear signs of cowardice, opportunism and lack of ideological conviction in these secular parties. These parties have utilized Muslims and banked on their votes without incorporating them into mainstream politics. Community leaders have warned secular parties that they cannot take Muslim votes for granted. If apathy or the fear of losing Hindu votes is making secular parties look away, Muslims also have other political options. The growing success of Muslim base parties can be seen in this perspective.

POLITICAL DEPRIVATION OF OBCs

There is no reservation of seats for OBCs in politics. Of the total, 15 per cent of seats are reserved for SCs and 7.5 for STs on the national level in the parliament. Muslims (mostly *ashraf*) hardly constitute 5 per cent of all MPs. Other minorities have 3 to 4 per cent share. This means 70 per cent of MPs are distributed between two groups: UCHs and Hindu OBCs. The UCHs, constitute about 15 to 20 per cent of population, however, their share in the parliament has been between 40 to 50 per cent. This means, the OBCs which constitute almost 52 per cent of the population have only 15 to 25 per cent of MPs. This means they face almost 50 per cent political deprivation making them one of the most deprived groups in politics. The obvious reason for this is that the UCHs or *savarnas* have been cornering disproportionate number of seats. Two national parties, the Congress and BJP, are *savarna*-dominated and make every effort to maintain their supremacy and to marginalize the Hindu OBCs who are disunited and ignorant of their political share. With the formation of Janata Dal, the OBCs began to organize politically and JD gave majority of its tickets to OBCs. Thus, the proportion of OBCs in the Lok Sabha jumped from 11 per cent in 1984 to almost 20 per cent in 1989. The V.P. Singh government implemented the Mandal Commission report and reserved 27 per cent of seats in the civil services and PSUs for OBCs. The upper-castes instantly mobilized to prevent this reform that would curb their job opportunities which were valuable before the economic liberalization of 1991.

Jaffrelot writes, 'Their resistance aroused indignation among the lower castes and resulted in a consolidation of OBC groups. Many OBCs stopped voting for upper-caste notables and preferred to elect representatives from their own social milieu to parliament.'[17] In the Hindi belt, the percentage of OBC MPs nearly doubled from 11 per cent in 1984 to more than 20 per cent in 1990s. In turn, the proportion of upper-caste MPs dropped from 47 per cent in 1984 to below 40 per cent in the 1990s. By 2004, upper-caste presence in the Lok Sabha had fallen to 33 per cent, while 25 per cent MPs were OBCs. This turnaround was initially possible due to the JD and later to its regional offshoots including the SP, RJD and JD(U). Though the JD disintegrated in the 1990s, it did not affect the dynamics of democratisation the party had set in motion. All parties including the Congress, by then, had realized the voting strength of the OBCs and that they could not rely on the old clientelist mechanism to get upper-caste notables elected and were thus forced to field a good number of OBC candidates. Having seen the strength of OBCs and the trend of 'social justice' already set in by implementation of Mandal Commission (Mandal I), the Congress decided to take it further. When it came to power in 2004, it passed a legislation to reserve 27 per cent of seats in educational institutions for the OBCs. The decision, also known as Mandal II, has contributed a lot in empowerment of OBCs, socially and politically. Thus, the intention of V.P. Singh to provide social justice to a large chunk of the society fructified. He had announced, 'Now that every party is wooing the deprived classes, with every round of elections more and more representatives of the deprived sections will be elected. This will ultimately be reflected in the social composition of local bodies, state governments, and the central government. A silent transfer of power is taking place in social terms.' The affirmative actions on behalf of the OBCs have not only benefited them economically and educationally, but encouraged them psychologically to achieve political power. Thus, Mandal enabled OBCs to gain political strength.

However, we saw this upward trend reversed in the general elections of 2009, when UCH representation shot up to 43 per cent, and share of the OBCs fell to 18 per cent. In 2014, the BJP which is another party that aggressively protects the UCH interests came to power with a clear majority at the expense of the OBCs and Muslims. The share of UCH MPs rose to 44.5 per cent, whereas that of OBCs dropped to 20 per cent.[18] The same trend of UCH domination was confirmed in 2019. The Hindutva politics of the BJP has fully decimated the politics of social justice. Political scientists say that whenever Hindutva/communal politics gains ground, the share of upper-castes especially Brahmins goes up and those of the deprived goes down.

The decline of OBC representation has much to do with the OBCs themselves. First, OBC politics revolves around the issue of reservation which has reached saturation point due to the 50 per cent cap put by the Supreme Court. Today no OBC leader can say 'vote for me, you will get quota' anymore. Now the politics of quota does not appeal to the OBCs. Second, the dominance of Yadavs in UP and Bihar, during the SP and RJD rule respectively, has divided the OBCs. Some OBC castes are so alienated and disenchanted that they stopped voting along with the Yadavs. In Bihar, Kurmis followed Nitish Kumar who formed the JD(U) as early as 1994. Upendra Kushwaha created a separate party called the Rashtriya Lok Samata Party (RLSP), mainly consisting of the Koiri castes of Bihar. Likewise, many OBC base parties of the lower OBCs have been formed in UP and Bihar. In these states, the BJP has started nominating non-Yadav OBC candidates and this move has paid dividends. These lower OBC castes have drifted to the BJP and started voting for it due to their resentment towards the Yadavs. This strategy was obvious in the 2019 elections when poor OBCs voted more for the BJP than for the BSP-SP alliance in UP despite the elitist image of the former. Fifty nine per cent of the 'poor' OBCs supported the BJP, against 33.5 per cent who turned to the BSP-SP alliance.[19] The Gadariyas, Kushwahas, Telis and Lodhis, etc., resent the Yadav domination and the way the latter have cornered a large proportion of reservations. These lower OBC castes now vote the BJP just to end the domination of Yadavs in politics. Besides this, by supporting Hindutva forces, they also try to sanskritize themselves in order to be accepted by the Hindu 'high tradition'. Thirdly, the fall of the OBC share in parliament is also due to the rise of the BJP, an upper-caste dominated party that has received full support of *savarnas*, precisely to contain the rise of the OBCs. The communal politics of the BJP has defused the effect of the politics of social justice and made these lower castes forget their roots and long standing exploitation. Religious mobilization has blinded the OBCs to their political deprivation.

In the recent past, one sees the revival of OBC politics through a few pending issues which are important for them. After the Rohini Commission suggested bifurcation of the OBC category into four sub-categories, OBC organizations have started demanding caste-based census to assess the actual strength of the OBCs. They have demanded relaxation of the 50 per cent cap on reservation in order to provide reservation as per share in population. The demand for caste-based census or lifting the cap of 50 per cent reservation heralds the onset of 'Mandal III'. The OBCs may think about their political empowerment after these demands are met since their share in politics is pathetically low. This may lead to the demand of proportional share in politics and that may lead to 'Mandal IV'.

RETURN OF UPPER-CASTE POLITICS

The UCHs consisting mainly of Brahmins, Kshatriyas, Baniyas, Bhumihar, Kayastha, etc., have maintained complete monopoly over politics and institutions of democracy due to historical, socio-economic and political reasons. Till the advent of Mandal politics, almost all chief ministers had been Brahmins. Their domination was visible through disproportionate share in MPs, MLAs, ministers, party nominations and monopoly over governance. Earlier this was possible through the Congress and now the BJP. These two parties are upper-caste base parties and take every care to protect not only their overall interest but also maintain their disproportionate share in politics. In 1984, the share of UCH MPs was as high as 47 per cent. When the Janata Dal gained momentum in politics, it shifted the focus and fielded a good number of OBC candidates which resulted in the reduction of UCHs representation. After implementation of Mandal Commission, OBCs stopped voting for UCH candidates and preferred to elect representatives from their own social group. As a result share of UCH MPs dropped from 47 per cent in 1984 to below 40 in the 1990s. By 2004, UCHs presence in Lok Sabha had fallen to 33 per cent, while OBC presence had reached to 25 per cent. The 2009 general elections marked reversal of the trend, as UCH representation shot up to 43 per cent and that of OBCs fell to 18 per cent. Politics around Mandal and quota started fading away. The 2014 general elections confirmed the trend of the domination of upper-caste politics, as their representation further increased to 44.5 per cent. It was the first time since Independence that the proportion of UCHs in Lok Sabha increased two times in a row. The trend was also confirmed in 2019 as share of UCH MPs was well above 40 per cent. In the Hindi belt, 45 per cent of the BJP MPs were upper castes in 2014 and 2019. The overrepresentation of the upper-castes was reflected in the BJP's ticket distribution as well. If one sets aside reserved seats, 62 per cent of the general category MP candidates of the BJP in the Hindi belt were UCHs as against 37 per cent of all the other parties combined. When Modi formed the union cabinet in 2014, out of 24 cabinet ministers, 16 were from the UCHs: nine Brahmins and seven Thakur/Rajput. In 2019 of the 55 ministers in his cabinet 47 per cent were from the UCHs, 13 per cent from the dominant castes (including Jats, Patels and Reddys), 20 per cent OBCs, 11 per cent SCs, 7 per cent STs plus one Muslim and one Sikh. This clearly indicates the return of the Aryavarta.

The return of upper-caste political domination has been possible due to various factors. First, the reservation of seats for educational institutions by the UPA-I government was seen by upper-castes as an attack on their rights. They could no longer trust the Congress which had been pursuing pro-poor and pro-deprived policies. They shifted to the BJP and now treat it as if it is their saviour. Moreover, the party is trying to create a Hindu Rashtra where their monopoly would be restored to what they claim it was in ancient times. Secondly, Modi camouflaged communalism under the slogan of development which attracted several youths who had shifted to urban localities in search of employment. According to the CSDS-Lokniti National Election Survey 2014, richer OBCs have voted for the BJP more than poorer OBCs (37 per cent against 28 per cent). In UP, poorer Yadavs had stayed faithful to the SP (82 per cent), but higher the class of Yadavs, the more they shifted towards the BJP. In 2014, 32 per cent of 'lower class' Yadavs voted for the BJP, as against 49 per cent for the SP. Thirdly, due to the Yadavization of SP in UP and RJD in Bihar, the lower OBC castes shifted to the BJP in search of political benefit. As I have mentioned earlier, the lower OBCs supported the BJP over the BSP-SP alliance in 2019. It is the same with the non-dominant SC castes. In UP, BSP is the party of Jatavs. The non-Jatav SC castes which were neglected in the BSP have shifted to the BJP.

The political domination of the UCHs has many consequences. Besides reducing the share of OBCs in politics, they have begun to fulfil their long pending dreams of hardcore Hindutva. They are making consistent efforts to make redundant the system of reservation so that it could be abolished. These include: lateral entry, reducing vacancies in the UPSC civil services and the EWS quota. Basically, they want to decimate the politics of social justice. Jaffrelot writes:

> The Modi Government has transformed the reservation system. First, the erosion of the public sector has resulted in a steady decrease in the number of jobs reserved for SCs. At the same time, the number of civil services candidates short listed by the Union Public Service Commission (UPSC) dropped by almost 40 per cent between 2014 and 2018, from 1,236 to 759. Second, the creation of a lateral entry in the Indian administration has diluted the quota system. Third, the introduction of a 10 per cent quota in 2019 for the Economically Weaker Section (EWS) has altered the standard definition of backwardness and de facto reserved such a quota to upper castes who were not that weak (By setting an income limit of Rs. 8,00,000 per annum to qualify under EWS, the government has made over 95 per cent of the upper castes eligible for this quota).[20]

Besides disturbing the reservation of SCs, STs and OBCs, the BJP leaders have even started to eulogise about the moral superiority of the upper-castes in public. The Sangh Parivar attempted enforcing the value system of the Hindu upper-castes. Vigilante groups have been let loose to attack and mob-lynch Muslims in the name of 'Love Jihad', 'killing the cow', 'eating beef', etc. Dalits and tribals are also being attacked for eating beef. Many Dalit bridegrooms have been attacked for riding on a horse in their marriage processions or growing a moustache which is seen as a sign of strong masculinity. Hard administrative restrictions have been put on those who want to convert to Buddhism, Sikhism, Islam and Christianity. Jaffrelot writes:

> The BJP's rise to power may, therefore result, not only in a post-Mandal counter-revolution that has enabled upper-caste politics and policies to stage a comeback but also in the promotion of some upper-caste orthopraxy and ethos via state vigilantism. The new dispensation exemplifies a style of control

that is as much based on political power as on the enforcement of social order, something very much in tune with the RSS's tradition.[21]

This comeback of upper-caste politics through the BJP poses a danger to democracy and democratic institutions, starting with the freedom of expression and dissent. The party wants not only to undo the affirmative actions but also to annihilate everything that empowers the historically deprived groups. They want to create a graded society as per the teachings of *Manusmriti* and finally change the Constitution.

POLITICS OF PASMANDA MUSLIMS

So far, the discussion of political representation is based on an assumption that Muslims are a unified community which is homogeneous and needs and concerns of every section is the same. However, socially, they are not a monolithic category in reality. As discussed in the SCR, the Muslim community is divided into three major categories: *ashraf* (upper castes), *ajlaf* (backward castes) and *arzals* (Dalit castes). The community consists of different categories and each category has different political share, views and aspirations. While Ashraf Muslims have a big share in politics, *ajlaf* and *arzals* are nowhere represented in politics.

Pasmanda Muslims

The word 'pasmanda' derived from the Persian word, which means left behind, refers to Indian Muslims belonging to the Shudra (backward) and *ati*-Shudra (Dalit) castes. The backward castes among Muslims are called *ajlaf* and have been categorized as OBCs. Similarly, Dalit castes in the community are called *arzals*. Thus, it can be argued that Pasmanda is an amalgamation of two sociological categories *ajlaf* (OBC Muslims) and *arzal* (Dalit Muslims) in the Indian context. The term 'pasmanda' was also adopted as an oppositional identity to that of the dominant Ashraf Muslims in 1998 by the All India Pasmanda Muslim Mahaz (AIPMM), a group which mainly works in Bihar. Since then, however, the *pasmanda* discourse has found resonance elsewhere too. Pasmanda

Muslims have historical experience of social othering, economic marginalization and poor political representation. The irony is they have suffered immensely at the hands of the *ashraf*. They face government apathy and also the neglect of mainstream political parties. Khalid Anis Ansari writes:

> As far as social sphere is concerned, Ali Anwar's *Masawat ki Jung* (2000) has documented caste-based disenfranchisement of Dalit and backward caste Muslims at the hands of self-styled Ashraf leaders in community organizations like *madrasas* and personal law boards, representative institutions (Parliament and State Assemblies) and departments, ministries and institutions that claim to work for Muslims (minority affairs, *waqf* boards, Urdu academies, AMU, Jamia Millia Islamia, etc.). The book also underlines stories of humiliation, disrespect and violence on caste grounds that various Pasmanda communities have to undergo on a daily basis, at least in northern parts of India.[22]

Sociologists and Pasmanda activists agree that Ashrafs constitute 15 per cent while the Pasmanda Muslims account for 85 per cent of the total Muslim population.

Political Representation

Although Pasmanda Muslims account for 85 per cent of Muslims, they face acute political deprivation as they are not duly represented in the Lok Sabha and legislative assemblies. Due to various historical, social and political reasons, Ashrafs corner most of the seats wherever Muslims are winners. Pasmanda Muslims who are 11.3 per cent in national population, had 0.8 per cent average share in the Lok Sabha till the 14th Lok Sabha.

> If we go through the Members of Parliament from 1st to 14th, then it appears that 400 out of 7,500 members were from Muslim community. 340 out of 400 were from the Ashraf section. According to the 2001 Census, Muslims constitute 13.4 per cent. Since Ashraf Muslims constitute nearly 15 per cent of total Muslim population, this tells that 2.01 per cent are Ashraf and their representation in Lok Sabha is 4.5 per cent. This is more than double of their share in population. At the same time, Pasmanda Muslims constitute 11.3 per cent and their representation in Lok Sabha is only 0.8 percentage'. (Translated excerpt from the undated pamphlet of All India Pasmanda Muslim Mahaz.)

In the 17th Lok Sabha (2019) there are 25 Muslims MPs—18 Ashrafs and 7 Pasmanda. This means the Ashraf caste which is 15 per cent of the Muslim population has 72 per cent of Muslim MPs and the 85 per cent Pasmanda population is represented by only 28 per cent. As per the 2011 Census, Muslims are 14.2 per cent of the total population. Thus, on the national level Ashraf constitute 2.13 per cent, while their share in Lok Sabha is 3.32 per cent while Pasmanda constitute 12.07 per cent of national population and their share in Lok Sabha is just 1.29 per cent. This speaks volumes about political deprivation of the Pasmanda castes. If we examine the Bihar assembly elections of 2020, we find Bihar returned 19 Muslim MLAs: 16 Ashraf and 3 Pasmanda. Thus, Muslims constitute 7.82 per cent of 243-member assembly which is very low vis-à-vis their population share of 16.87 per cent. On breaking it further, 2.53 per cent Ashraf have 6.58 per cent representation while 14.34 per cent Pasmanda have only 1.23 per cent share. This explains Pasmanda are hugely underrepresented in state assemblies. One could also infer that the Ashraf Muslims, an erstwhile ruling class, are politically overrepresented at the cost of Pasmanda Muslims. Hence, it is explicitly evident who is getting the benefit of Muslim politics.

Reasons for Political Deprivation

Secular regional/OBC base parties consider the community a homogeneous group and have not comprehended the internal divisions and contradictions. They consider Ashraf Muslims as the sole representative of the community and give most of the tickets to them. The non-representative nomination is the main reason for the low political share of Pasmanda Muslims. Ansari comments on general elections of 2019:

> For example, if we see the distribution of ticket for Pasmanda Muslims then only one out of seven *Mahagathbandhan's* Muslim candidates in Bihar is a Pasmanda and both the BJP-led NDA's candidates are *ashraf.* In Bihar, the population of *ashraf* community is not more than four per cent of the State's entire population, yet they got 15 per cent representation among the

Mahagathbandhan candidates. In UP, only one of the nine Muslim candidates fielded by the Congress is a Pasmanda. The BSP has fielded two Pasmanda candidates out of six Muslims and one Pasmanda is fighting on SP ticket (out of four Muslims). It is true that in the BJP, there seems to be no space for Pasmanda Muslims, but the flag-bearers of secular and social justice politics have also disappointed the Pasmanda Muslims.[23]

The second reason is the lack of leadership among them. Due to socio-economic and educational backwardness, Pasmanda are at the bottom of the social hierarchy. Therefore, they have fallen behind and few have the capacity to become leaders. On the other hand, the Ashrafs are socio-economically empowered and have created many leaders. The secular parties only want leaders in the Muslim community that they can use for their own vested interests, but do not want to take on responsibility or the hard work to ensure social justice within the community.

Key Elements of Ashraf and Pasmanda Brand of Politics

There are basic differences between two brands of politics as Ashrafs treat the Muslim community as a part of minorities which is unified and takes oppositional stand against communal elements of Hindutva ideology while the Pasmanda brand considers the community as an amalgamation of different sociological groups which have similar socio-economic condition with deprived sections across religions. The JUH and Ashraf leaders mobilize the community on the trope of religio-cultural identity based on three issues: preservation of Muslim personal laws, promotion of Urdu language and preserving the minority character of the AMU. The defence of Babri Masjid also became a key element which does not exist today. On the other hand, Pasmanda politics is based on experience of social oppression on the lines of caste-based hierarchy based on key issues such as social justice, inclusion in mainstream society and an equal share in education, job and politics. Pasmanda groups identify themselves with the deprived sections of Hindus, Sikhs, Buddhists, such as SCs and OBCs and advocate unity in the fight of social justice.

Second, the Pasmanda politics highlights the symbiotic nature of majoritarian and minoritarian fundamentalism. It says communal leaders of majority and minority communities complement and thrive on each other to take equal benefit from communal brand of politics. Ansari says,

> The *pasmanda* activists have consistently emphasized the high-caste symbiotic and co-constitutive nature of Hindu and Muslim communalism and the need to contest them simultaneously. The communal discourse benefits the pan-religion caste elite at the expense of the social justice concerns of the subjugated castes who are often the foot soldiers and victims in the violence.[24]

Pasmanda leaders oppose both Hindu and Muslim communalism and politics based on it. While one initiates it, the other party takes it to logical conclusions and the ultimate losers are the deprived sections from both communities. Waqar Hawari, a Pasmanda activist, says, 'While Muslim politicians like Imam Bukhari (Shahi Imam) and Syed Shahabuddin add the *jodan* (starter yoghurt), it is left to Hindu fundamentalists to prepare the yoghurt of communalism. Both of them are responsible. We oppose both Hindu and Muslim fanaticism.'[25] Pasmanda leaders advocate unity among depressed castes across religions. They emphasise the pan-religion solidarity of subjugated castes as encapsulated in the slogan *Dalit-Pichda ek samaan, Hindu ho ya Musalman* (Dalits-Backwards are all alike, whether they be Hindu or Muslim).

Demands

Pasmanda leaders have been making demands for inclusion and secularism. The AIPMM has put up 14-point demand charter which can be clubbed together into four categories: Fair share in politics, SC status for Dalit Muslims, socio-economic equality, and educational equality as well as share in minority dominated institutions. As regards the first demand, they ask for fair representation in the Parliament, state assemblies and ministries. In their view, all political parties mostly give tickets to the Ashrafis, while they ignore backward Muslims. Ashraf Muslims that constitue

15 per cent of the total Muslims, get the support of 85 per cent Pasmandas to get elected. Hence, the winnability and political strength of Ashrafs is entirely dependent on support of backward Muslims. On the other hand, the backward Muslims do not find any share in politics. For this, they implicitly endorse the political view of Dalit leader Kanshi Ram, where he gave the famous slogan *jiski jitni sankhya bhari, uski utni hissedari* (participation should be in proportion to the population share). As the first step, they demand proportionate share in party nominations. The second demand is related to grant of SC status for Dalit castes in Muslim and Christian communities. Initially, the 1950 Presidential Order, granted the SC status to Dalits belonging to only Hindu religion. Because of pressure from Ambedkarite and Sikh organizations, the order was amended in 1956 and 1990 to grant SC status respectively to Dalits of Sikh and Buddhist religions. Hence, the amendment shows that the SC status is reserved only for those religions that are Indic in nature. Pasmandas argue that to escape caste based atrocities and inhuman treatment Dalits converted to non-Hindu religions, but their socio-economic condition did not improve. They face inequality and deprivation even today.

The third demand relates to economic security and government policy to help artisanal groups. A majority of backward caste Muslims work in the unorganized sector where there is no economic and social security. Therefore, they demand that the government ensure economic security for these sectors. They want inclusive economic policy which could serve the interest of not only the Pasmandas but also of common masses who are working in this sector. The fourth demand relate to educational equality such as reservation for Pasmanda students in minority educational institutions. They also demand the complete implementation of the SCR, and discussion and debate on the Ranganath Mishra Commission Report in the parliament.[26]

Challenges

Pasmanda politics is a new social movement which is in its initial phase. Like other social movements, it is also facing many challenges.

First, all parties consider Muslims as a monolithic whole, which is homogenous with no internal divisions. This mindset is the biggest challenge before it. This political discourse has not been widely recognized by political parties across different political ideologies be it rightist, leftist or centrist. All political parties acknowledge Muslims as one category and their manifestoes address the problems of Muslims under the broad head of 'minority' without mentioning 'Muslims'. The word 'pasmanda' is nowhere mentioned in their manifesto. They have not paid attention to social stratification among Muslims and acute backwardness of Pasmanda section. This attitude shows that they don't acknowledge Pasmanda Muslims, their demands, political assertion and political discourse.

The second challenge lies within the Muslim community itself. First, the Ashrafs do not support the idea of Pasmanda Muslims and argue there is no casteism and class structue in Islam, and the discourse of Pasmanda has been initiated to create disunity within the Muslim community. They consider Pasmanda politics as going against the community, and are of the opinion that this kind of politics divides the community and there is no scope and future of it. There is also lack of consensus among the Pasmandas. Pasmanda activists work only in Bihar and UP and do not concentrate in pan-India presence. They are not adequately organized and lack a strategy to take the discourse forward.

The third challenge is about its location and limited expansion. The movement started in Bihar and spread to some of its districts. Later, on it expanded to several parts of UP. It also started in Maharashtra but has a limited presence. Pasmanda politics is largely a north Indian phenomenon. Although some of its committed members have been trying to educate the people and create awareness in the masses, it has not reached to the common masses especially in southeren and eastern India.[27]

The fourth challenge lies in the feasibility of Pasmanda discourse in the binary of minority/majority, or Hindu/Muslim politics. It is absolutely clear from the election outcome that whenever communal politics becomes strong, the politics of social justice takes a back seat. Pasmanda politics is basically the sub-set of a social justice movement. Today, when Hindutva politics holds sway, political parties have forgotten social justice issues since Hindutva engages parties on communal and sectarian issues. When all secular parties are trying to maintain a safe distance from Muslims, it is difficult for them to recognize and raise the issue of Pasmanda politics. Thus, communal politics is one of the biggest challenges for Pasmanda politics. Like other counter-hegemonic identity movements, Pasmanda politics also confronts many challenges such as, lack of resources and appropriate institutions, co-option of its leaders by state and dominant political parties, lack of relevant movement literature, internal power conflicts, and so on.

Discussion

Indian Muslims are not a homogeneous community and sociologically stratified into various groups. Though seldom discussed in popular spaces, the Muslim society is internally divided in about 700 castes (*biradaris*). The Kaka Kalelkar Commission, the Mandal Commission, the SCR and other reports have affirmed the presence of different sociological groups and castes. Casteism among Muslims is not a fading, but an evolving phenomenon. The contemporary caste-based mobilization, i.e. Pasmanda politics is not a temporary phenomenon. It is going to stay and gain momentum further. Pasmanda movement advocates social justice, equality in opportunity and fair share in politics. The secular parties consider the community as a homogenous whole and find it convenient to negotiate with Ashraf leaders as spokespersons of the entire community. However, the biggest challenge is that most political parties don't acknowledge the Pasmanda discourse. Shamsher Alam writes:

> However, the biggest challenge is: how to penetrate this idea into the mind of political parties and leaders as they are not explicitly acknowledging the idea of Pasmanda politics? They are focusing on Muslims by considering them as a monolithic whole. This could be done only by highlighting to them the importance of Pasmanda politics and its character, the inclusive and representative. As along as the political parties would acknowledge Muslims as one unit for political purpose, they would be haunted by the ghost of being a Muslim party, Muslim appeasement or minority appeasement. The political

parties could remove such kinds of tags by two methods. First, acknowledging the concept of Pasmanda politics. Second, by giving their due share in the form of representation in politics. By adopting these methods, the binary of Hindu-Muslim politics would cease to exist.[27]

Hence, Pasmanda politics will demolish the inter-community hatred and also give justice to centuries old backwards of the Muslim community. Pasmandas' struggle for empowerment can help democratise Indian Islam and deepen democracy in the country.

IS AAP A POLITICAL ALTERNATIVE?

The Aam Aadmi Party (AAP) emerged from Anna Hazare's Movement India Against Corruption, an anti-corruption movement to discredit the then UPA government, and disproportionately harm the Congress party. Bringing in the Lokpal Bill to curb corruption was at the centre of it. The movement was launched by Arvind Kejriwal with Anna Hazare as the face of the movement, which shook the system of the then government. It had the solid backing of the RSS in the major process of mobilization of the people, and RSS leaders have confessed that their cadres supported the Hazare's movement. It received undue media attention and discredited the government in the eyes of the public. The upsurge came to challenge the very parliamentary system, and it was touch and go for the survival of the parliament, which survived the pressure from the Anna-Kejriwal led movement. It was basically an attack on then democratically elected government and smelt of a much bigger conspiracy. Two streams emerged from it. One stream wanted to target only the Congress as articulated by the leaders like Kiran Bedi, V.K. Singh, etc., who now are comfortably settled in the BJP. The other was led by Kejriwal which broadened the base of the movement from 'corruption issues', to 'municipal issues' and formed the AAP.

Although the party published a 'Vision Document' and mentioned some issues like the Batla House Encounter, illegal arrest of Muslim youths, etc., it shied away from taking any stand on Muslims, and for a very long time seemed to shy away from clearly making its position clear on communalism and issues concerning minorities. During the elections to the Delhi assembly in 2013, it paid lip-service to some of the apprehensions of Muslims in its manifesto, but failed to make concrete promises for their socio-economic progress and security. In fact during the peak of the Delhi assembly elections of 2013, the Muzaffarnagar riots erupted and Muslims suffered a huge damage to their life and property. But AAP remained silent. This was the reason most Muslims in Delhi frowned upon the party at a time when large number of voters, including the educated middle-class, migrant Dalits, etc., shifted to it. Muslims silently rejected AAP's appeal. It fielded candidates in three Muslim-dominated ACs of Old Delhi's Ballimaran, Matia Mahal, and Chandni Chowk, along with Seelampur, Okhla and Mustafabad, but they finished in third or fourth positions.

After a poor performance in Muslim-dominated areas in 2013, AAP formed a task force in an effort to gain the community's trust before the Lok Sabha elections of 2014. It was an attempt to reach out to Muslims. That seemed to have paid some dividends as Muslim organizations like the JIH and AIMMM issued letters in support of AAP and said that it was a secular party and Muslims should vote to check communal forces. In the 2015 Delhi assembly elections, it had been careful about not raising the issues pertaining to communal violence and Muslim victimhood. It managed to convince the community to associate themselves with a new kind of politics. Unlike in 2013, when the party had issued pamphlets raising the issue of Batla House Encounter, it chose to ignore contentious and controversial issues which could have given the BJP reason to polarise the voters. The Muslims of Delhi also felt that AAP was a major force and that only AAP could defeat the BJP. Dr. Tanweer Fazal, who teaches at Centre for the Study of Social Systems, JNU said, 'In the last election, the community did not know if the AAP could defeat the BJP, but this time it is slightly different. Certainly, they will get benefit in some of the constituencies.' The party swept the election winning 67 out of 70 seats. The wholehearted support of Muslims of Delhi was also one of the factors for its spectacular performance.

The Delhi assembly elections of 2020 were held when the anti-CAA movement was at its peak and the Shaheen Bagh campaign of Delhi had become the focal point of the movement. AAP made no sympathetic approach to the movement as its key leaders rarely mentioned the apprehensions of Muslims in general and of Delhi Muslims in particular. Kejriwal had even said during the protest that if his government had control over the Delhi police, they would have cleared the Shaheen Bagh in 'two hours'. Muslims in Delhi had no choice but to vote for AAP since they saw it as a potent force which could challenge the BJP and keep it out of power. They also felt that the Congress was nowhere in the race. Finally, AAP won 62 seats, BJP 8 and the Congress none. Although Muslims voted for AAP with higher percentage in 2020 than in 2015, but the party failed Muslims miserably.

The Delhi communal riots broke out in February 2020 in which 42 people, mostly Muslims, were mercilessly killed and 200 lay injured in hospitals. Hindutva goons planned and executed the riot in broad daylight while the Delhi police merely stood by. Kejriwal's inaction and inertia during the 2020 Delhi riots which shook the capital for many days, made many people doubt his 'secular' credentials. Although the Delhi police comes under the central government it does not absolve the sitting CM of Delhi from his basic duty as a public representative. Instead of going to the ravaged *mohallas* and taking to the road to save innocent lives, he went to Raj Ghat to pray for peace. He failed miserably to express concern, ask for accountability, meet the victims, visit burned localities, announce help for victims and arrange meetings to maintain communal harmony. Even his supporters questioned his silence. AAP ditched Muslims, who now think that the party is a smaller version of the BJP and it is not an alternative for them. On 8 August 2021, some Hindutva elements gathered at Jantar Mantar and delivered hate speeches and raised slogans of genocide of Muslims. Jantar Mantar falls under the New Delhi assembly constituency which is represented by Kejriwal. He remained silent and did not demand arrest of any of the people involved in the incident. He had said that if Delhi police had come under his control he would have cleared Shaheen Bagh 'in two hours'. But he failed to make a similar statement like: 'If I had control over Delhi police, I would have arrested all those who chanted communal slogans at Jantar Mantar.'[29] These incidents clearly indicate the dual approach of AAP on issues related to Muslims and Hindus. While he has been soft on the Hindu right-wing, he vehemently raised and demanded strict action againt Muslim agitators. He has realized that Muslims have no option in Delhi and they would vote for him regardless of whether his party supports or neglects them. In 2021, the party presented a 'Deshbhakti' budget and earmarked Rs. 45 crore for installing the Tricolour at 500 locations in Delhi and also sanctioned Rs. 25 crore to provide yoga and meditation services. Experts say that during the COVID-19 pandemic the government should have prioritized unemployment and health. Experts also say that to achieve its national expansion plan, AAP is trying to copy the politics of the BJP which is closer to appeasing Hindu sentiments and neglecting the issues of overall progress.

In the process of emergence and working on national level, certain things have happened which create suspicion about its intention. During campaign of 2014 Lok Sabha elections, all other parties were completely neglected, but the BJP and AAP got full media attention. While the Congress and other regional parties were demonised by the media, BJP and AAP were equally praised. Secondly, AAP managed to marginally erode the BJP base, it severely harmed the Congress. While some BJP supporters shifted to the AAP, a large number of Congress voters went to it. Thirdly, during the 2014 Lok Sabha elections, although AAP had no national presence, it put up more than 400 candidates across India and most of them lost their deposits. Many of them became the reason for the defeat of the Congress/regional party candidates. Political observers have realized this fact. Lastly, Kejriwal and Hazare have completely forgotten the issue of corruption. While Kejriwal was harsh on corruption during the Congress tenure, he never raised the same during the BJP rule which is beyond comprehension. Hazare, who was once called the second Gandhi, suddenly left the field and has not raised the issue of corruption during BJP rule. It is clear that the party was created with the sole intention of ousting the democratically elected Congress government.

Some people realized this fact and had warned that every vote to AAP would ultimately go to the BJP. In March 2014, a group of activists in Mumbai urged the community not to vote for the AAP in the Lok Sabha elections, saying it would benefit the BJP. Shabnam Hashmi, a social and Human Rights activist said in 2014, 'I am among the strongest critics of Congress which has failed Muslims on many counts, but AAP can't be an alternative. Every vote that goes to the AAP will make the job of the BJP easier.'[30]

What is the politics of AAP? The politics of parties is judged by their actions, manifestos and pronouncements. The party's vision document is silent on most of the issues related to society, economy, social justice, protection and preservation of the rights of minorities. The party has superficial approach on majority of issues related to economy, national security, social and gender justice.[31] It has failed to assure minorities on protection and safeguard of various constitutionally guaranteed rights. Instead of becoming a party to counter the BJP, it divides the secular vote. In this scenario it definitely cannot be a political alternative for Muslims.

NOTES

1. http://twocircles.net/2015apr12/1428859676.html
2. *The Times of India*, New Delhi, 11 November 2021.
3. *The Indian Express*, Pune, 27 October 2014.
4. https://www.livemint.com/Opinion/Muslim-vote-bank-Reality-or-myth.html
5. https://theprint.in/opinion/bjp-wants-to-defeat-the-idea-of-muslim-vote-bank-by-using-muslims/181242/
6. https://www.firstpost.com/politics/the-idea-of-a-muslim-vote-bank-and-demographic-takeover-how-data-shows-up-this-narrative-as-contemporary-mythology-8041581.html
7. Ibid.
8. *The Indian Express*, Mumbai, 21 October 2014.
9. https://www.tribuneindia.com/news/archive/comment/myths-of-the-monolithic-muslim-vote-bank-367968
10. Ibid.

11. *The Times of India*, 27 September 2021.
12. *India Today Web Desk*, Chennai, 13 March 2021.
13. *The Indian Express*, Pune, 5 November 2014.
14. *The Times of India*, Pune, 8 April 2014.
15. Ibid.
16. https://theprint.in/opinion/owaisi-has-merely-let-the-open-secret-out-secular-parties-had-ditched-muslims-long-ago/234605/
17. Christophe Jaffrelot, 'What is left of the 'Mandal' moment', politically and socially, now?', *The Indian Express*, 22 August 2020.
18. Ibid.
19. Ibid.
20. Christophe Jaffrelot, 'The Return of Upper Caste Politics', *The Indian Express*, Mumbai, 10 February 2021.
21. Ibid.
22. Khalid Anis Ansari, 'Muslims that "minority politics" left behind', *The Hindu*, 17 June 2013.
23. Shamsher Alam, 'Mapping Pasmanda Politics in India: Demands and Challenges', *Mainstream*, 22 June 2019.
24. Khalid Anis Ansari, 'Owaisi Represents Only The Elitist Muslims, And Not The Entire Community', *Outlook*, 24 November 2020.
25. Ansari, 'Muslims that "minority politics" left behind', *The Hindu*, 17 June 2013.
26. Alam, 'Mapping Pasmanda Politics in India: Demands and Challenges', *Mainstream*, 22 June 2019.
27. Ibid.
28. Ibid.
29. https://www.theprint.com/news/politics/arvind-kejrival-silence-aap-jantar-mantar-communal-slogans-hindutva
30. *The Times of India*, Mumbai, 8 March 2014.
31. http://twocircles.net/2014jan12/contemporary-political-ferment-aam-aadmi-party.html

CHAPTER 8

Conclusions and Way Forward

Churning within the Community to Create Space in Mainstream Politics

Muslims are missing in the corridors of power in India. In the various state government cabinets, municipal corporations and councils, government appointed bodies and in constitutional positions—they are conspicuously absent. NDA's 78-member union cabinet currently does not have a single member from the largest religious minority. The non-BJP national and regional parties are fielding fewer and fewer Muslim candidates in order to counter the BJP even as they bank on 'captive' Muslim votes. For its part, the BJP makes no bones about its extreme antipathy to Muslims and simply ignores them as candidates as well as their issues of progress and security. The immediate impact of this state of affairs is that the relentless attack on the Muslim community on all fronts is not only gathering momentum but is allowed to do so, completely unopposed. There is no concerted attempt to stem or push back the proliferation of prejudiced myths and demonization of the community.

In this concluding chapter, I will discuss all these above aspects but also dwell on two very important issues. One, I will examine how the Muslim representatives in legislative and parliamentary bodies as also political forums have fared so far whilst representing the concerns of their community. And two, where does the Muslim community go from here? How do the ordinary Muslim citizen and community leaders see the way forward? What strategies should they adopt to achive at least a fair representation?

I believe that the mental and emotional churn within the community is aspiring towards forming a Muslim political party or an alliance of Muslim based parties on national level. I will assess the debate on this aspect and the challenges and strategies that would come into play should this come about.

CURRENT CONDITION OF REPRESENTATION

From the political representation point of view Muslims are facing a difficult situation. Currently, there is no Muslim CM in any state. Jammu & Kashmir used to have one, but not after it was converted into a union territory in 2019. The state wad deliberately converted into an UT so that Muslims could not achive the post of CM. In the current political scenario, where triumphant Hindutva and communal politics rule, Muslims are treated as 'untouchables', and are deprived of their due share in the parliament, state assemblies and local bodies.

In the 2019 Lok Sabha elections, out of 543 MPs, Muslims have only 26 (4.8 per cent) while they deserved 77 MPs as per proportional share. They suffered huge deprivation of 66.23 per cent, getting just one-third of what they actually deserve. The Congress, SP, BSP, TMC and NC are the parties which contributed to the count of Muslim MPs. The states of West Bengal and UP, contributed with six Muslim MPs each, while Kerala and J&K with three each, Bihar and Assam two each, and Tamil Nadu, Telangana, Lakshadweep and Maharashtra with one member each are other contributory states. Nineteen states and seven UTs have not contributed a single Muslim MP. Previously, the gap between the size of their population and representation in Lok Sabha was maintained quite fairly, but after 1989, the gap increased and reached its peak in 2014 which was attributed to the exponential rise of the BJP in national politics. Political space for Muslims has shrunk as more than 50 per cent of space is occupied by the BJP. Communal politics and appeasement of the majority community have aggravated the situation. Sensing the majoritarian threat created by the BJP, even secular parties have reduced the number of tickets. Muslims are trapped in a situation where they do not see any chance of recovery.

Muslims are equally deprived in state assemblies. In 29 states (including the erstwhile Jammu & Kashmir) and two UTs with state assemblies, they constitute only 7.18 per cent of total MLAs causing a huge deprivation of 49.57 per cent. In states like Assam, Bihar, West Bengal, UP, and Kerala, they are a little closer to their due share. In Odisha, there is no Muslim MLA, while in Punjab and MP their share is 0.85 and 0.87 per cent respectively. In Chhattisgarh, Gujarat, Haryana, Jharkhand, Karnataka, Maharashtra, Rajasthan, Tamil Nadu, and Uttarakhand their representation is extremely poor. Comparing the assembly elections from 2013-15 with their previous elections for 968 assembly seats in Maharashtra, Haryana, Rajasthan, MP, Chhattisgarh and Delhi, we noted the decline of due representation from 35 to 20 per cent. In 2018, only one Muslim won in Chhattisgarh, two in MP, and eight each in Rajasthan and Telangana. Representation in UP Assembly declined from 17 per cent in 2012 to just 6 per cent in 2017. Due to the expansion of the BJP in the states, Muslim representation has started to shrink.

As analysed in Chapters 3 and 4, there are several reasons for this dismal condition. I believe three reasons are responsible for the recent further decline: Low nomination of Muslims, rise of the BJP, and the present FPTP system. The fair representation of a group is directly linked with the number of nominations by the main political parties. More and more we are witnessing increased apathy of the mainstream parties in fielding Muslim candidates in all elections. The BJP gave only six tickets while the Congress maintained its tally of about 30 tickets to Muslims in the Lok Sabha elections. Interestingly, the regional secular parties who bank to a greater extent on minority votes are exhibiting the same pattern of denial and fielding of fewer Muslim candidates, evidently as a 'tactic' to counter the BJP. To counter the threat of communal polarization, the secular parties do not field Muslims even in Muslim-dominated constituencies. Verniers believes that anti-Muslim sentiment stoked by the BJP leaders has also led to fewer Muslim candidates outside the BJP. The Congress and other parties fear being tagged as 'anti-Hindu' if they promote Muslims candidates. Due to the aggressive Hindutva politics of the BJP, and consequent anti-Muslim sentiments it is likely that the number of Muslim candidates may go further down.

The researches by Jaffrelot and Verniers, who studied the issue of political deprivation of Indian Muslims, point to one major reason for their decline: rise of the BJP. The BJP plays the politics of Hindu majoritarianism which is directly linked to shrinking space for Muslims in the Indian political arena. It does not offer tickets to Muslims and as a result when the party wins a state, the share of Muslims is practically non-existent. In 2017, UP elections, the party did not put up a single Muslim candidate and as a result no Muslim MLA was elected from the ruling BJP. Also the share of Muslims drastically came down from 17 per cent in 2012 to 6 per cent in 2017. Jaffrelot makes an important observation in his book, *Majoritarian State: How Hindu Nationalism is Changing India.* He writes,

> Each time the BJP conquers a new state, the number of Muslim MLAs drops. The most spectacular example is found in UP where, in 2017, their proportion went from 17 to 6 per cent. While the figure of 17 per cent, achieved in 2012 mainly thanks to the success of the SP [Samajwadi Party], had brought the share of Muslim MLAs closer to their share of the population in UP, the figure of 6 per cent, associated with the BJP's landslide victory, reflects an underrepresentation comparable to that of 1991, when the party had already taken control of the state.[1]

The BJP does not stop at reducing the political space for Muslims, but goes on to communalize the election campaign through various sectarian issues as well. Citing the reason of communal consolidation, the secular parties do not give tickets to Muslims in respectable proportion, either. Whenever the BJP wins elections in MP, Chhattisgarh, UP, Rajasthan, Gujarat, Bihar, etc., it captures the entire political space and Muslim representation falls to its lowest level. This implies the reduced political strength or shrinking of political space for Muslims is directly linked to the rise of BJP.

Third, the FPTP system contains many flaws and is particularly disadvantageous for religious minorities which are distributed across the country. In their book, *The Verdict,* reputed journalist Prannoy Roy and editorial adviser Dorab Sopariwala call the FPTP system a 'double-edged sword' that 'hugely rewards communities if their votes are concentrated in a geographic region'. They also elaborate,

> The more geographically concentrated the community is, the better is the multiple of seats it wins for the votes it secures. Conversely, the first-past-the-post system punishes minority communities, which are not concentrated in pockets of the country, by penalising them with fewer seats per vote. The more evenly a minority is spread geographically, the lower is the bang/seats for the buck/vote.[2]

Muslims are more or less evenly distributed across the country except in a few pockets. At the same time, due to communal polarization and continuous vilification by the BJP, they do not receive Hindu votes. In this situation it has become difficult for Muslims to get elected.

In 90 out of India's total 675 districts, covering 85 PCs, Muslims account for more than 20 per cent of the population. In 35 seats, they constitute more than 35 per cent of the electorates. As per C-Voters, they could be a significant factor in roughly 70 seats. In 720 of the total 4,121 ACs, they are in a decisive number. This shows that in a good number of PCs and ACs Muslims are in a decisive number and can turn the result in favour of any candidate. Despite all these favourable factors, their representation has reached the lowest level. Muslims are not getting elected even from Muslim-dominated seats. The BJP's entire political agenda is directed against Muslims just to create fear in the majority community in order to consolidate the latter's vote. On the other hand, the secular parties do not visit Muslim areas during the poll campaign and show no enthusiasm to woo them fearing reaction from the right-wing groups. These parties believe that courting the largest minority would cost them the majority Hindu vote bank in the face of the worst-ever communal polarisation. Maulana Nadeemul Wajdi, a leading figure of Deoband, says,

> Muslims have been pushed into such a situation, where BJP knows, they will not vote, so they hardly campaign in our localities and have nothing to offer. At the same time, these secular parties, know, they [Muslims] cannot go anywhere so they also don't bother about our progress.[3]

The secular parties bank on the knowledge that Muslims will never vote for the BJP, and would cast their votes in their favour regardless of whether these parties campaign among them or not. In this situation Muslims have been reduced to mere passive players in politics.

PERFORMANCE OF MUSLIM LEGISLATORS

In a democracy every group or community should be given a fair chance to represent themselves in legislative bodies. Institutions can care about the minorities as long as they are duly represented in them. But in recent years, the number of Muslim MPs and MLAs has reached the lowest level. For redressal of the problems faced by them and to ensure justice, Muslims need a proper share in elected bodies. Muslim elected representatives are also expected to raise the concerns of the community not only in the parliament and state assemblies, but in all relevant forums in matters of safety and security, education and employment, empowerment or injustice done to them. Unfortunately, Muslim legislators have failed in their basic duty to protect the interest of Muslims. They toe their respective party lines and remain silent due to party pressure. Experts say representation is just a necessary, and not a sufficient condition to ensure relevant Muslim issues being raised in legislative bodies.

One of the criteria to measure the performance of Muslim legislators is the number of questions they ask in legislative bodies. While Owaisi has been vocal on Muslim issues, most of the other MPs choose to remain silent even on issues of safety and security. Many Muslim MPs neither ask questions nor do they participate in debates. Murshidabad, which has a huge poor Muslim population was represented by Abdul Mannan Hossain of the Congress; he failed to ask a single question in the first three sessions of the 15th Lok Sabha (2009-14). Maldah North and South constituencies are equally poor. Their MPs Abu Hasem Khan Chaudhary and Mausam Noor respectively of the Congress also created a record of sorts by not asking any question in the parliament.[4]

The type of issues and seriousness with which they are raised are also an important consideration. Saloni Bhogale, a research fellow with the Trivedi Centre for Political Data, Ashoka University, in 2019, conducted a study on questions raised in the parliament on issues concerning Muslims. She found that 1,875 unique questions were raised about Muslims between 1999 and 2017. Muslim and non-Muslim MPs had a share of 22 and 78 per cent respectively in those questions. When seen with the fact that Muslim MPs did not make up more than 6 per cent of Lok Sabha at any period, it shows that they had a larger relative share in questions concerning Muslims. However, only 2 per cent of all questions raised by Muslim MPs in the Lok Sabha were about Muslim issues. This figure was 0.3 per cent for non-Muslim MPs. Among issues concerning Muslims, questions about Hajj had the biggest share, while violence against Muslims and welfare of Muslim prisoners had the smallest share.

There is a difference between raising issues and the type of issues raised for the community. Those like the Hajj, establishment of *madrasas*, and other religious aspects find prominence in Muslim MPs' questions. Education, safety, security and issues of ensuring justice do not get much importance. The best example of this is education. The analysis shows that 44 per cent of the questions regarding Muslim education were focused on *madrasas* although only 4 per cent of the Muslim students of school going age group are enrolled there. This suggests that questions by Muslim MPs might not be highlighting the relevant issues of the community. Similarly, a survey conducted by the Bureau of Research on Industry and Economic Fundamental (BRIEF) found about 13 per cent respondents cite issues of security for Indian Muslims. However, this topic barely makes up 3 per cent of all questions pertaining to Muslims in India.[5] This shows that Muslim MPs either do not raise questions related to Muslims or raise questions of religious nature. They avoid questions related to the empowerment probably due to regressive party policies.

On many crucial occasions, Muslim MPs have remained silent. I will mention two examples here: the parliamentary debate on the Triple Talaq Bill and the reaction to the Muzaffarnagar riots (2013). During the first parliamentary debate on Triple Talaq in

December 2017, just four of the 23 Muslim MPs spoke on the Bill, although it was directly concerning Muslims. There was no one to speak from the BJP. The late Maulana Asrar-ul-Haque Qasmi, who was then MP from Kishanganj from the Congress, did not participate in the debate. He was severely criticized for not opposing the Bill. When he was asked as to why he did not take part in the debate, he said that the Congress party did not allow him to do so. Sometimes parties do this because they fear communal polarization. Often, the Muslim legislators remain silent fearing the party's disapproval. The Muzaffarnagar riot which occurred in September 2013 is considered to be one of the most horrible communal disturbances. Around 50 people, mostly Muslims, were killed and thousands displaced. The SP was in power with 40 Muslim MLAs and UP had 69 Muslim MLAs from all parties. When the riot occurred, Muzaffarnagar had two Muslim MLAs and one MP Kadir Rana. The UP assembly debates confirmed that Muslim MLAs of the SP always adhered to the arguments made by senior party leaders like Akhilesh Yadav and Mulayam Singh Yadav. In fact they did not officially participate in relief and rehabilitation works in the riot-affected areas (though many of them contributed to the relief projects led by the Jamiat-Ulama-e-Hind).[6] They followed instructions given to them by their respective parties and did not raise the issue on other platforms either. A communal riot is a situation of extreme distress when the help of representatives is urgently required. However, in a majority of such cases, Muslim representatives have failed the community.

It is natural for Muslims to have expectations from their representatives who win on their votes. These leaders must fulfil the duties and help the community in crucial times, whilst also raising issues in the parliament and other proper forums. When the issues of safety and security arise, they have to be extra cautious and partner with other secular legislators to ensure justice to victims. In order to do this they may have to go against the party lines and keep aside personal interests.

Muslim representatives must not only work for Muslims, but the general public at large and it is imperative that they should come together on a common platform, prepare the relevant questions and participate in debates. They must read about the deprivation of Muslims, comprehend and speak up.

SHOULD MUSLIMS HAVE THEIR OWN POLITICAL PARTY?

Political scientists and Muslim leaders have strongly suggested that to have due share and strong voice in politics the largest minority community must have a political party of its own. Some argue that it would improve political representation and strengthen our democracy, while others warn that it would give Hindu right-wing parties an excuse to polarize Hindu voters which would ultimately further marginalize Muslims in all spheres of life. Omar Khalidi, a US-based Indian writer gave the following advice to Muslims on overcoming political deprivation:

(a) They can join one of the parties sympathetic to them with secular orientation,
(b) They can work as pressure group with non-partisan posture and party affiliation, or;
(c) They can set up their own political party and try to be a part of secular coalition governments to take political advantage.[7]

Since Independence, Muslims have largely supported secular parties that promised security and progress to them. Earlier, they were solely with the Congress and in the recent past have begun voting for the regional parties. These parties do not give proper share to Muslims in party nominations citing the reasons of win-nability and communal consolidation. Their work as pressure groups with non-partisan stance has also not helped them achieve their targets. In fact, wherever it was adopted, it marginalized the com-munity further. They have formed political parties in Kerala, Assam, Telangana, UP and Tamil Nadu to improve political representation and socio-economic condition, which has also not helped much. Thus, Indian Muslims have tried all these approaches with not much sucess. This is largely due to their scattered population throughout India, no Constitutional safeguards for due political representation and communalization of political space where it is almost impossible for Muslim candidates to get elected from mixed localities.

There is a deep realization within the Muslim community that most political parties have stopped at symbolism in addressing its issues. All secular parties were happy to receive their votes, but betrayed their hopes and expectations on most occasions. Therefore, Muslims want to form their own political parties. The question that arises, however, is: which are the issues that the community must put on electoral agenda while forming a political party.

In my view the following should be the issues of an electoral agenda:

1. Due share in the parliament and state assemblies.
2. Huge socio-economic backwardness as indicated by the SCR and implementation of its recommendations.
3. Frequent communal riots, mob lynching, etc., and legislation to guarantee security.
4. False arrest of Muslim youths in the name of terrorism.
5. Proper share of Muslims in the system of reservations.
6. Ensuring equality, justice and dignity.

These are secular issues and it would be easy for Muslim-base parties to do politics. Besides it, other minorities and deprived sections may support such policies.

Today, Muslims seek to discover their own power of agency through politics by utilizing their numbers. There is a growing consciousness among them that they must assert themselves to create political space of their own. Now they want direct representation and do not want to be treated like a vote bank. Muslims are the only social group in India who are still to discover the power of their agency. Every other caste or religious group either has its own party or wields real power inside traditional parties. Having been cheated by every secular party, in one way or another, a majority of Muslims question whether there should be an exclusive party for the largest minority or not? There are multiple kinds of responses to this: many who say yes, and many who say no. A few years ago an overwhelming majority was not in favour of forming a separate party. But now, especially after 2014, after being neglected and sidelined by all secular parties, there is a growing consciousness for forming a separate political entity. Those who advise not to do this argue thus:

1. By this secular votes get divided.
2. This will strengthen the fundamentalist and non-secular communal parties.
3. Election cannot be contested or won in the name of Muslims only.
4. Communal organizations and parties will spread the fear of making another Pakistan.

Those who are not in favour of forming a party argue that in a democracy numbers matter and a minority must not merely survive, but exert influence or create pressure without forming any separate party. The example of Jews in the USA can be cited here as without forming any party they are running the USA. Although the situation in India is different for Muslims, they can influence the government by their numbers. By forming social alliance with regional parties Muslims have increased their representation in UP, WB and Bihar. So, instead of forming a party, they can create social alliances with secular regional parties. Lastly, they say that the days are past when Muslims could win on their own. One needs to take along all sections of society, if one wants to win elections. Being with the national or regional parties is in the interest of the community. They also want Muslim leaders to unite Muslim votes and increase their status in the secular parties and demand political benefits for the community such as increased share in politics and power.

Should Muslims heed these arguements? Due to disenchantment with secular parties on many issues, there is a growing consciousness to form a separate political party on the national level or alliance of all Muslim-base parties to protect socio-economic and political rights of Muslims. They feel that due to various apprehensions mentioned above, since 1947, Muslims blindly supported the so-called secular parties and continuously lowered their political status. But these parties did not leave a single opportunity to lower the political status of Muslims. By provoking the fear of communal parties, Muslims were exploited politically. Just as *garam masala* (a mix of dry spices) is used to flavour food, but picked and moved to the side of the plate while eating, these parties used Muslims during the elections and after success completely ignored them. This fear has occupied space in their mind. For the last 70 years, they feel that these parties received Muslims votes in bulk but haven't delivered.

Owaisi says, 'Muslims should emerge as a political force to get their rights in the country.'[8] He believes this will strengthen the country, the roots of secularism and restore confidence among Muslims. He also said that the AIMIM would continue its political journey to expand in different parts of the country despite the allegations from its rivals that it was dividing secular votes. On another occasion, he said, 'Muslims must realize that they have to have a different political identity. They must get out of the thinking that if they have a different political identity that will lead to strengthening the communal forces. This is a totally wrong understanding of the situation. This will strengthen our parliamentary democracy.'[9] He elaborates,

> We have tried and tested secular parties but they haven't come to our rescue. Despite being the Congress in power in Maharashtra, every two-three months Muslim youths are being picked up under false charges of terrorism. This can only stop when you become a political force. No one is going to come from the sky or the ground to help. . . . We have to create our own leaders under a political party.[9]

Dalit scholars also feel that Muslims must have a separate political identity. The Muslim political leadership is really weak; those who existed as Muslim leaders in the Congress were not connected to the poor and marginalized Muslim masses. The mass Muslim leadership did not get politicized. The Congress and the BJP do not want a leader who can organise his own people. Kancha Ilaiah, a famous Dalit scholar says,

> So, in my view, a time will come when Muslims will have to form their own national party or a national coalition of all the Muslim parties by retaining their political and social identity. That will give them much more strength than working from within other parties. They tried that in Congress, and

except Abul Kalam Azad, I don't think anybody else got significant space in the Congress system. There may be ministers but they were not having significant powers.[10]

Community leaders have also held the view that Muslims must have a separate political identity. Abdul Raheem Qureshi, president of Majlis Tameer-e-Millat, a socio-religious group in Hyderabad, says, 'Muslims are not satisfied with any mainstream political party. All the parties have failed to reflect the community's aspirations in parliament and state assemblies.'[11] He and many others say there is nothing wrong in forming parties to secure the rights and due share of every community, religious or otherwise. Manithaneya Makkal Katchi (MMK) then legislator M.H. Jawahirullah said in 2013, that the growing number of Muslim political parties was a natural consequence of democracy and called for coordination of all Muslim groups in India. Naiyar Fatmi, an activist in Patna, said that while there was no scope for a Muslim party in Bihar, on national level there may be. He said that Muslims had been frustrated with major political parties. Asghar Nawaz Khan, a leading Muslim in Bangalore, said, 'Yes, we are disenchanted by the mainstream parties because we don't matter to them except during the elections.'[11] Rasool Abdul of Muttahida Muslim Mahaz, a socio-religious outfit in Karnataka, complained 'We don't get any support from the Congress or JD(S) when young Muslims were harassed or arrested on fake charges.'[11] Muslim leaders feel that major issues facing the community in all parts of India are not getting addressed because of 'the absence of a political party which works for it'. The feeling of political disempowerment among Muslims, and the realization that it is increasingly becoming difficult for them to get support outside their community is leading them towards the realization that they need a party of their own.

The average votes polled by Muslim candidates is going down in every election. Many parties point to this reason for refusing tickets to them. Many politicians claim that putting up a Muslim candidate in a mixed locality is a losing proposition. Because of these developments, there is lot of churning in the community. There is no attempt to guarantee safety and security or to end day-to-day harassment and discrimination against them. Their population share is slightly less than that of Dalits. While there is lot of talk, promises and discussion about Dalit votes, Muslims have simply disappeared from the discussions during elections. They are almost 15 per cent of voters. They form the only social group in India, which is still to discover its power of agency. Every other caste or SRCs either has its own party, or wields real power inside traditional parties. Now Muslims want to take destiny in their hands. There is growing consciousness among Muslim voters that they can be a force to reckon with in regional and national elections, at least in pockets. This also means that they are not willing to play the old politics of vote banks, where they voted en block for whoever could defeat the BJP. Feeling of safety and affinity with the parties are also playing major role in creating such consciousness. Muslim MPs/MLAs sometimes may not put up a great performance, but do not sit silent on issues of the community's safety. For example, Muslims account for over 35 per cent of the population of Hyderabad and many feel that this is the only metro city where Muslims are at home. A senior journalist on anonymity said, 'Middle-class Muslims and educated Muslims do not feel highly excited with the MIM but always end up voting for them. This is because of the perception that this is the only party which represents us, the Muslims, who are a discriminated lot.' He further elaborates, 'The same logic would be applicable if there is an all-India Muslim Party.'[12]

A separate political identity of Muslims is now just a matter of time. All evidences and the mindset of the community indicate that sooner or later a Muslim political party or parties will come into existence. In the initial phase of re-discovery of identity politics as a tool of political empowerment, Muslim parties may be more regional than national in character. While it is difficult to predict now, this will reshape Indian politics over coming decades. However, one thing is clear: Muslims are no longer willing to play second fiddle to the parties they have so far voted for, whether it is the Congress or regional parties, including the Communists. Indian politics over the next decade will thus evolve to take one or two forms: emergence of a national party or a coalition of regional parties of Muslims. Political scientists also predict a coalition of caste-based (Dalit, Tribal or OBC) and community-based (Muslim, Sikh, etc.) parties.

Muslims have tried and tested many alternatives, but not formed a political party for the last 70 years. I think the time has come to explore the alternative of moving away from the path they have trodden so far. Muslim leaders, activists, thinkers, scholars, academicians, journalists, etc., must sit together and have a deliberation on this. They should also deliberate on how to minimize the division of secular or especially Muslim votes while doing this.

Whenever Muslims will establish a political party in India, even if the party is based on hardworking and honest people, in the beginning secular votes will be divided. Non-secular and communal parties will be benefited. Analysts also point to a possible reaction if an exclusive Muslim party is formed. Right-wing forces may instil fear in Hindus and try to polarize votes on religious ground, even if the Muslim party does not use religion in politics at all. This could lead to escalation of tension on the ground. Some scholars even say that this will create national disorientation. But to change the situation, one has to overcome the doubts and challenges. An elaborate strategy on the issue is vital. The timing of formation of the party, its composition, policies and issues to be taken up during the elections are important factors like policies towards other deprived sections, the poor, issues related to human rights, etc., Muslim leaders, activists, intellectuals, scholars, journalists, etc., must have an elaborate discussion on all these issues.

It will be a positive step, if Muslims form a secular party in conjunction with other oppressed minorities and deprived groups and then struggle for equal rights, socio-economic development and justice for the deprived and dispossessed while paying adequate attention to their own community. Shrill communal politics by Muslims is bound to fail as they are thinly spread in the country and dominant only in few pockets of concentration.

Political scientists argue that there is no feasibility of Muslims forming a religion-based political identity. Such identity is immediately perceived as separatists. If Indian Muslims form a religion-based political identity that would give instantaneous prominence to BJP's Hindutva ideology and even secular Hindus who are sympathetic to the cause of Muslims, would not support them or go the BJP way. As far back as 28 December 1947, S.A. Barelwi, an Indian Islamic revivalist and Maulana Ahmad Said, the vice-president of the Jamiat Ulama, had advised Muslims to dissolve communal groups. They said,

> The time has come when Muslims of all shades of opinion must take a united decision to abjure communal politics which, far from serving the real interest of the masses and affording them necessary protection and security, (tends) to encourage social and political reactions and injure national life by encouraging false and unnatural divisions and fostering hatred and suspicion among different communities.[13]

There are two important points to consider: forming a religion-based political identity and seeking votes on religious and emotional issues. If Muslims form a political party based on religion, as mentioned above. Right-wing groups as well as secular Hindus, who are generally sympathetic to Muslims on many issues would immediately term the party as separatist and blame it for the politics that the Muslim League played before Partition. The net result of religion-based shrill Muslim politics would be the consolidation of majority of Hindu votes in favour of BJP and other right-wing parties and several secular candidates, Muslims and non-Muslims, of secular parties may fail at the polls. Seeking votes in the name of religion or on emotional and sentimental issues is also not going to work. Muslims are in minority and cannot win elections by addressing only Muslim electorates. Lastly, two or three Muslim MLAs in a state are not going to serve any purpose. There is anger in Muslim youths due to many reasons. Adopting religion-based political tactics in tapping despair and anger of Muslim youths is also not going to work. This will further alienate the community in the long run. The RSS and other right-wingh groups will start targeting Muslims on various communal issues to unite Hindus under the pet slogan of 'Hindus in danger'.

Even the ordinary Muslims in India do not approve of the idea of a separate political identity based on religion. They feel it will hurt Muslims socio-economically and is going to fail in the long run. A majority of them are concerned about identity-based negative politics that focuses mostly on emotional and religious sentiments. They feel such negative and religion-based approach would severely damage the larger educational, social and economic interests. The step would alienate them further from the national mainstream.

Muslim scholars and leaders are also concerned about the Muslim parties which are big in numbers but weak in strength and spread. Three national level Muslim parties, i.e. the AIMIM, AIUDF and IUML, have been successful to some extent in sending MPs and MLAs, but failed to influence the public. Two other parties—the Welfare Party of India (WPI) and Social Democratic Party of India (SDPI)—have not made any impact in national politics although they received some votes in Muslim pockets. Besides, there are smaller regional Muslim parties. In Kerala, besides the IUML, there are two other parties: Indian National League and Peoples' Democratic Party. Tamil Nadu has Muslim Munnetra Kazhagam (MMK) to complement the rest of the OBC-based parties that currently dominate state politics. UP has a good number of smaller Muslim parties such as the Peace Party of India, Rashtriya Ulema Council, Qaumi Ekta Dal of Mukhtar Ansari, Ittehad-e-Millat Council (IMC), Rashtriya Inquilab Party, Welfare Party, Millat Party, Parcham Party, etc. Many of these parties have ceased to exist as they either merged with national mainstream parties or became redundant. The Rastriya Majlis Party (Bihar), Awami Vikas Party (Maharashtra), Indian Secular Front (West Bengal), etc., are other smaller parties.

These parties lack long-term planning, ideological coherence and are unaware of the game of politics. They are weak, limited in spread and even Muslims do not support them. They have failed to attract large Muslim voters as they do not consider them as an alternative that can fight for their rights and justice. They have failed to generate confidence in Muslim voters. These parties have a tendency to align with mainstream parties after elections and lose their distinctiveness. A Muslim voter said in 2011, 'Look at what happened to the Ulema Council candidates who later joined the Congress. Or the Majlis Party, which lost the Lok Sabha elections due to personal ambitions of people within the party. Masood and Asghar Khan of the Loktantrik Party, which was formed in 2009, merged it with the Samajwadi Party. These small-time outfits just become political bargainers.' Rana Ayyub, then assistant editor of *Tehelka,* wrote, 'To be fair, many of the smaller groups are aware of this history and baggage and are trying bridge their differences. They see strength and security in numbers.' In the same article Ayyub quoted an unnamed observer who said, 'If these parties unite and become a force to reckon with, the Muslim voters can perhaps be in a position to have a true representation and break out of the clutches of appeasement he is subjected to before every election.'[14]

People not trained in politics form political outfits to achieve personal ambitions. Some do it to extract community votes and then either merge it with mainstream parties or dissolve it and join other parties. Some use it as a tool to bargain for personal benefits. Keeping in mind the Muslim parties of UP, Manish Tiwari and Ranjan Pandey write:

> In the absence of a distinct agenda, programme or urge for betterment of their own caste voters, these opportunistic parties (like several other smaller political parties) were more like vehicles for individual leaders desperate to shape their own political careers and the voters showed little interest in helping them accomplish this objective.[15]

Fed up with the existing parties, Muslims talk about having their own party, but they do not realise what it takes to have a political party. Who amongst them has the skills, foresightedness or the patience to work at the grassroots level to create a structure that can challenge the existing parties such as Kanshi Ram? Or the strength, skill and courage to plan and create their own organization/party and sustain it with strategical thinking and hard work such as Lalu Yadav, Mulayam Singh Yadav or Mamata Banerjee?

While forming a party, Muslims must keep three objectives in mind: (a) To protect and uphold the Constitution; (b) Distance from religious ideologies and its leaders; and (c) Address all deprived sections of the society while keeping the focus on Muslims. The party must fit into the democratic set up of India and cherish the democratic values keeping in mind the diversity of the nation. Our Constitution is under attack from various sides. If some changes are made in it, rights and safeguards given to minorities would be in danger. The party must swear to safeguard the Constitution and organise itself within it. The community members must come out of the clutches of the so-called religious leadership, and let themselves develop a real political leadership, with required political approach and practical attitude. They must keep in mind that they make up just 14.2 per cent of the population and would not be able to succeed by sidelining other deprived sections. They must maintain a secular approach, while focusing on problems faced by them. Lastly, the party must also focus on problems and issues faced by other deprived sections, such as Dalits, OBCs, Tribals, nomadic tribes, landless labourers and the poor of all religions. They must fight for their rights and stand with them in the hour of need. While keeping focus on the community, it should also take up issues of human rights, social justice, environmental protection, farmers' issues, etc. It must become a political force to reckon with.

Strategically, they can adopt three important things to remain relevant in the game of politics: (a) Sympathetic attitude to OBCs and Dalits and readiness to form alliance with OBC and Dalit-base parties; (b) Development of quality leadership; and (c) Working hard for the people at the ground level. Dalits and OBCs are equally deprived and not duly represented in various fields including politics. Their asset holding is poor in comparison to their population share. Sympathetic approaches to OBC and Dalit-based parties will work because territorial dispersal as well as geographical proximity of Muslims and Dalits at pan-India level will ensure success of such an alliance. Social alliances are always helpful in furthering political objectives.

Educated and experienced Muslims should opt for politics and while self-motivated and seasoned leaders can bargain with party bosses within their respective parties over the issue of representation of Muslims, the former will judge the direction of wind and guide the community in right direction. There is no alternative to hard work at the ground level. They must serve people irrespective of caste and religion, raise local issues and acquire a fair knowledge of how administration works at the local level.

Events of the past shows whenever Muslims have tried to form their own parties or groups to put pressure on political system to get justice and equal treatment, the Congress has through its Muslim leaders, tried to scuttle or dilute those efforts. In the 1970s when Osmani, a prominent leader, formed the United Muslim Front in Assam, the Congress promised him the position of CM of Assam, and got him to merge his party with the Congress. After Osmani did so, he was made only a minister in Assam.[16] Another example is from Assam itself. A few years ago when Ajmal formed the AIUDF, and it made some headway in the Assam elections, the Congress managed to remove him from the Assam unit of JUH through the influence of the Madani family. The Congress through its Muslim leaders is again making serious attempts to create dissension in the AIUDF and get it to merge into the Congress party.[16] The AIMMM is full of senior and dedicated community leaders who have long records of service and want to keep party politics out of Mushawarat. By using the manipulative slogan of 'bringing in the new generation into Mushawarat leadership', the Congress has used every effort to introduce election in selecting the president of AIMMM. This bid was not successful. Yet, AIMMM may continue to face attempts to cause dissension in its ranks. AIMMM's determined effort to remain an independent voice for Muslims and give election-eve advisories does not sit well with the Congress. They want Musharawat to behave like the Jamiat.[16] Congress has also tried to co-opt leadership of the Pasmanda Muslim Mahaz, and its leaders like Ali Anwar and Ejaz Ali by promising them Rajya Sabha seats if they merge their groups with the Congress in Bihar and UP.[16] If Muslims form a party, there is every possibility that the Congress and other secular parties would attempt to co-opt its leaders and create pressure to either dissolve it or merge with them.

If at all a party is formed by Muslims, it must work within the Indian political and legal systems and be prepared to deal with the obstacles that will be placed in its path. The former US speaker of the House Tip O' Neill rightly used to say that all politics is local. The Muslims must forget international and national issues (to some extent) and focus on local issues and learn how to deal with the local administration by training more people in political processes. They must mobilize people, organize on rights-based issues, and join common cause with other deprived groups. They should motivate members and invest in them with training and education; teach the art of politics and develop leadership at all levels—from local to regional to national level. The party should give ample representation to different sections of Muslims, Dalits, OBCs, youths and other marginalized groups. Muslim women have been ignored in politics. They can be given due representation to develop women's leadership in the community.

DO MUSLIMS LISTEN TO *ULEMA* IN MATTERS OF POLITICS?

Before answering this, let me ask another question which is more specific. Do Muslims follow the advice of Muslim religious elites/ *ulema* or some other pressure groups? One of the long standing stereotypes about Indian Muslims is that they vote as per the advice or election-eve written advice (deliberately termed as *fatwa* by the media), and the call of religious leaders, i.e. *ulema.* This falsehood has been deliberately spread by sections of the media to serve its purpose and used by right-wingh groups to target and blame the community. Various religious leaders from Abul Kalam Azad to Syed Abdullah Bukhari to the present day *ulema* have misused their position and issued advice to influence the mood of Muslim voters. Political parties have basically exploited the influence of *ulema.* Studies show that Muslims do respect them in religious and cultural matters, but don't want them to be involved in politics. It has become tough for them, since Indian politics entered the coalition era to issue any such advice, as it has become impossible for them to do this in the era of aggressive Hindutva politics. They realize that this would hand the BJP a tool to polarize the election campaign further.

The AIMMM intervened in electoral politics as a Muslim representative body in the 1967 general elections by publishing a nine-point People's Manifesto to evolve an electoral strategy for Muslim voters to vote for candidates who could defeat the communal forces and strengthen secularism. Since then, the AIMMM has been issuing such advice to guide Muslim voters not only at the national level but also for some particular PCs. In 2014, it had advised to vote for the Congress and AAP at the national level, and various regional secular parties at the state-level to defeat the rising communal and fascist forces. In 2019, the AIMMM, which is also called an umbrella body of Muslim organizations, convened a meeting of heads of all prominent Muslim organizations including JUH, JIH, etc., and decided not to issue any election statement. The community leaders and political scholars hailed the decision. First, Abdullah Bukhari and now Ahmed Bukhari, the Shahi Imams of Jama Masjid, consciously issued election statements in support of the most powerful party/coalition. Starting with the Janata Party in 1977, the Bukharis issued advice to support different parties sensing the mood of common Muslim voters. They transformed the historic Jama Masjid into a symbolic centre of Muslim politics to bargain with political parties. Before the general elections of 2014, Ahmed Bukhari said that during the last 65 years, Muslims blindly supported the Congress, but this had yielded nothing but wounds. The Congress was responsible for the backwardness of Muslims and therefore, Muslims would not support the Congress. Bukhari also asked Muslims not to support the SP and AAP. He constituted a committee of eleven members to audit the work done by political parties for Muslims and the community's action would be based on that report.[17] Sensing the mood and aggressive communal politics of the BJP, he did not issue any statement before the general elections of 2019. However, the *ulema* of Mumbai appeared to be more vocal. Around 700 *ulema* representing different sects and sub-sects asked voters to exercise their right in favour of the 'secular parties' so as to defeat the BJP in 2019. Besides, there are state-level prominent *ulema*, organizations of *ulema*, custodians of prominent *dargah*, etc., who issue statements to support parties before assembly elections. These statements create an impression that *ulema* play a crucial role in determining Muslim voting in elections and that Muslim votes can be swayed with the help of religious leaders. However, Muslim voting patterns and political attitudes do not confirm such media-centric assumptions.

As regards *ulema*, a sizeable number of Muslims believe that they are influential in political matters. According to the Religious Attitudes, Behaviour and Practices Survey 2015 of CSDS-Lokniti, a majority of Muslims believe that *ulema* are highly influential in politics. This observation is historically valid. Since the days of Maulana Abul Kalam Azad, *ulema* have been actively participating in politics in variety of ways. The JUH's unconditional support to Congress's nation building project in the 1950s, the AIMMM's call for strategic voting in 1967, election *fatwas* of the Shahi Imams of Jama Masjid, Maulana Abul Hasan Nadwi's (Ali Mian) persuasive role in the Shah Bano case and comments of various *ulema* in matters and policies of the government, including the NRC and CAA, are revealing examples that underline the influence of ulema in politics. Some issue election *fatwas*, others extend support to political parties, while yet others extend support to government policies and programmes. Some of them play politics away from the public eye while some participate in political deals and gain personal benefits. It is thus natural for Muslims to feel *ulema* are influential in politics.

But, a majority of Muslims do not want ulema to offer support to political parties in elections. Various studies by the CSDS-Lokniti confirm that Muslims do not want religious elites to support any political party. The Religious Attitude and Behaviour Survey 2015 found that a significant majority of Muslims do not want the *ulema* to indulge in electoral mobilization. Hilal Ahmed gives two examples to elaborate. The AIMMM decided to intervene in the electoral politics as a Muslim representative body in the mid-1960s. It published a nine-point People's Manifesto to evolve an electoral strategy for Muslim voters for the 1967 general elections. Its resolution called upon Muslim voters to vote for candidates irrespective of their religion, community or party. It extended formal support to 135 candidates in different states. That appeal to Muslims paved the way for what is now called strategic voting. An analysis of the 1967 election demonstrated that out of 135 Mushawarat-supported candidates, only 42 managed to win. One also finds a similar trend in the state assemblies. The AIMMM-supported candidates did not do well in most of the cases. Their performances were not up to the mark even in the Muslim-dominated assembly constituencies.[18]

The second example is about the political *fatwas* issued by the Bukharis or the Shahi Imam of Jama Masjid of Delhi. The political role played by Abdullah Bukhari, in the 1980s, especially his 'election *fatwa*' validates the point. Indira Gandhi discovered Bukhari as a Muslim leader in the early 1970s and nurtured his political aspirations. Bukhari, on his part, made full use of his political patronage to play a political role, and transformed the historic Jama Masjid into a symbolic centre of Muslim politics to bargain with political parties. Bukhari consciously issued election-eve advisory and statements in support of the most powerful party/coalition: the Janata Party in 1977, the Congress in 1980 and 1984, the Janata Dal in 1989, and the Congress again in 1991. The strategy legitimized his status as the political *Imam-e-Hind* and consolidated the media-friendly argument that Muslims always follow the advice of the *ulema*, and vote as a block.[18] The present Shahi Imam of Jama Masjid Ahmed Bukhari declared his support for the SP in the UP assembly election of 2012, and asked Muslims to support the party and in return received many benefits. However, the fact is that the Muslim voters never listen to *ulema* and they vote as per their local requirements, socio-economic issues and security concerns.

In the past, *ulema* used to gauge the mood of common Muslim voters and then issue *fatwa* asking Muslims to vote for a particular party/coalition. They asked to vote for a party to which the Muslims otherwise would have voted. The AIMMM, Bukharis, local *ulema*, etc., used the same technique and proved themselves correct in the eyes of the political parties. Ahmed writes:

> Like any other serious observer, Bukhari seemed to evaluate the mood of the Muslim voters just before every crucial election. In order to legitimize his status as the sole spokesperson of Indian Muslims, he supported the party/coalition which, in any case, was going to secure Muslim votes. Janata Party in 1977, Congress in 1980 and 1984, Janata Dal in 1989 and Congress in 1991 received overwhelming Muslim support even in those regions where Bukhari's *fatwas* were highly irrelevant.[19]

Moreover, the clerics start with the issues of the community but settle for personal interest, being rewarded by political parties. In the UP assembly elections of 2012, Ahmed Bukhari gave a clarion call to support the SP. When it came to power, his son-in-law Umar Khan who had lost the assembly election from Behat in Saharanpur on SP ticket was made an MLC. Another relative Waseem Ahmed Khan was appointed as chairman of the UP Pollution Control Board with the rank of state minister.[20] Many *ulema* have been appointed as members of Rajya Sabha for extending their support to the Congress and other regional parties. Ahmed writes:

> The critical yet evasive Muslim response to *ulema* politics is quite instructive. Muslims seem to make a very clear distinction between religious concerns and political matters. They do recognise the importance of *ulema* as intellectuals and expect them to operate in the realm of religious knowledge. But, voting in elections is seen primarily as this-worldly affair, for which guidance of *ulema* is not required.[19]

Muslims make a clear distinction between political and religious leaders. Their understanding of political leader is also unambiguous. The concept of leadership in the community is quite similar to those in other SRCs in India. Muslims are politically awakened community, and they understand meaning of leaders and leadership. Muslim leaders are envisaged primarily as professional politicians who follow the usual rule of the game. Muslims expect their leaders to:

(a) Be educated and learned who could guide the community on socio-economic and political matters.
(b) Be progressive and work for development in their localities.
(c) Tackle everyday encounters with the police and other administrative power structures.
(d) Raise the voice in cases of injustice or discrimination with them.
(e) Provide safety and security, and in the hours of communal riots must raise voice on proper forums.

The community needs education, employment, equal treatment and preservation of its fundamental rights. On the contrary, the *ulema* practice politics of 'religious difference', preoccupied with tokens and empty symbolism such as the protection of Islam, Urdu language, Muslim personal law and so on. They have not only proved consistently useless in safeguarding the constitutional rights of the community, but have also been complicit in the erosion of these rights. The community must ask this belated question: what have the *ulema* achieved for ordinary Muslims in all these decades? Secular parties use the *ulema* to influence Muslim voters; the BJP uses them to frighten Hindu voters to consolidate and the media projects them as the Muslim voice. In fact, they are needed for the 'Muslim othering' project. Asim Ali, a scholar in political science, writes:

> If you are still not convinced about the uselessness of the Muslim religious leadership on political issues, then imagine their disappearance from the political realm for a moment. It is hard to think of a single negative impact on Muslims. However, it might be disconcerting for politicians who find it convenient to deal with these religious intermediaries and keep them in good humour, rather than having to deal with ordinary Indian Muslims directly and address their genuine grievances. It will also be troubling for the media, which is also invested in maintaining these religious leaders as the 'Muslim voice', as a cherished source of readily available soundbites, which they substitute for ground reporting on the genuine issues of Muslims.[21]

Muslims have increasingly made it clear that they don't look to *ulema* for political guidance, but need a leadership that works at the ground level and safeguards constitutional and economic rights. They want leaders who work for education, development, secularism, constitutional and human rights. They do not want a narrow-minded religious leaders. They feel that the community should be freed from the clutches of so called socio-religious leadership, and must develop real political leadership with a broadminded and practical approach. One must note that India is a secular country which prohibits religion in politics. Muslims are a minority and they cannot dictate the rule of politics. There is so much Islamophobia in the society that mere presence of the *ulema* can polarize the political atmosphere. Mohammad Adeeb, ex-Rajya Sabha member, writes:

I always hold all religious scholars in high esteem and have all regards for their services rendered for the religious causes. But I do not see any justification or even a practical need for their active involvement in politics. I oppose this trend, as I observe no real political or social will in their approach and find them, beyond all doubts, indulged in petty bouts, serving their narrow ends and ignoring Muslims' common interest, in any case. With folded hands, in all respect, I appeal to them to rise to the occasion and work for the general good of the Muslim community, otherwise, once the community is finished, they themselves would also be nowhere in sight.[22]

SUMMARY OF RECOMMENDATIONS

Political scientists, scholars and community intellectuals have suggested many steps to improve the political representation of Muslims. Rajeev Bhargava, a noted Indian political theorist, points out that any mechanism of political self-representation must remain faithful to the following three or four values: (a) it must fulfil the legitimate political demands of groups to have a fair representation, to have a powerful voice in the deliberative process; (b) as far as possible, it should not violate the individual autonomy; (c) part of what we mean by respecting individual autonomy is that Muslims retain their choice to be represented by non-Muslims; and (d) although there is a presumption that Muslims share the same life conditions and life prospects, and therefore the same interests, this cannot be an immutable assumption. Bhargava says that if all these conditions are to be met, the following recommendations may be most appropriate in the Indian context.[23]

1. Multi-member constituencies.
2. Proportional representation in the form of preference voting.
3. Intra-party quotas in proportion to population.
4. Identification by the ECI of the constituencies where intra-party quotas are to be allotted.

Based on my analysis in the earlier chapters, the following are the minimum measures required to enable Muslims and other underrepresented segments to have a fair share in politics.

1. The Representation of the People Act, 1951 must be amended to make parties accountable for any persistent underrepresentation of minorities. It may be made binding on parties to nominate fair number of minority candidates, at least in proportion to share in population.
2. Government must appoint a new Delimitation Commission with clear mandate to de-reserve those SC-reserved constituencies which have high proportion of Muslims. Seats having high share of SCs and low share of Muslims may be reserved for SCs.
3. The Presidential Order of 1950 must be amended to grant SC status to Dalits belonging to Muslims and Christians. By this Dalit Muslims and Christians can get proportional share in seats reserved for SCs.
4. An 'affirmative gerrymandering' may be done by the Delimitation Commission to enhance share of Muslim voters in some Muslim-dominated constituencies.
5. Forming multi-member constituencies and allowing cumulative voting or adopting Single Non-Transferrable Vote (SNTV) system. Constituencies with Muslim voters between 21 to 50 per cent may be constituted as multi-member constituencies.
6. Government must think of doing away with the FPTP system, and adopt some suitable form of PR so that smaller parties and unrepresented groups could get fair share.
7. Application of religion in politics has caused greater harm not only to minorities but to democracy itself. Communal polarization during elections has made it almost impossible for Muslim candidates to get elected from mixed localities. The ECI must implement the code of conduct strictly and take penal action on candidates/parties that use religion in politics. If it is not checked, survival of democracy may be in danger.

Hence, the implementation of these recommendations is not difficult for the government, if it has the will and a sympathetic attitude to the Muslim minority. For this to happen, it must first realize that minorities are an integral part of the Indian population and their persistent deprivation in politics is not good for the working of democracy. For a healthy and stable democracy due political share of minorities is necessary. So far, although the governments have been aware of the underrepresentation of minorities, particularly Muslims, in politics they have not constituted any committee or commission to investigate the issue, its reasons and possible measures to improve it. In spite of categorical assurances of fairness by Nehru and Patel to minorities, that the system of non-reservation of seats for minorities should be reviewed, no mechanism for monitoring and review has been brought into existence. If we look back and see the 75 years of democracy, the parties in power, earlier the Congress and now the BJP, have ignored the issue. In fact, these parties have deliberately kept Muslims under persistent political underrepresentation.

CONCLUDING REMARKS AND WAY FORWARD

India Needs an Inclusive Democracy

India is full of diversities whether it be religious, social, regional, linguistics, etc. Besides major religions like Hinduism, Islam and Christianity, it has other religions like Sikhism, Buddhism, Jainism, Zoroastrian, tribal religion, atheism, etc. Social divisions like upper-castes, OBCs, Dalits, Tribals, etc., are present in almost all religions and regional and linguistic diversities are easily noticeable. Our freedom fighters and framers of the Constitution had hoped that Indian democracy would ensure political justice to all religious groups, segments of society, class and different regions/states. They had also hoped that the democracy would function in such a way that all religious and social groups would have proportionate share in politics. The Preamble of the Constitution says that 'it resolved to constitute India into a Sovereign, Socialist, Secular, Democratic, Republic, which would ensure to all its citizens social, economic and political justice'. It implies secular democracy aims at proportionate share of all religious and social groups in parliament, state assemblies and corridors of power. However, functioning of democracy, so far, shows it has not ensured political justice to religious minorities and socially and economically deprived sections. While the UCHs, landlords, the rich, etc., have disproportionate share in politics, Muslims, socially deprived and the poor have been facing huge deficits. It has created huge disparity, economic inequality, distrust, heartburn and disunity in the Indian society. Political scientists have been arguing that if India wants all round progress and to become a superpower, it must ensure political justice to all segments of society. For this, India must adopt an inclusive and participative democracy. The political class and ruling parties must have the courage to take steps which could break the monopoly of the rich, powerful, UCHs and Ashrafs in politics and make India an inclusive democracy. This is possible only if the ruling party believes in inclusiveness and wants to ensure political justice to all. The government must set up a committee/ commission after every general election to map the political deprivation of all weaker sections and minorities, possible reasons of deprivation and suggest concrete measures to improve it. The suggestions may be debated in the Parliament and implemented in the next general elections.

Current Political Condition

Muslims are the second largest majority community constituting 14.2 per cent of the population. Although they have never been duly represented in politics, presently their representation in the parliament, state assemblies and local bodies has gone to an alarmingly low-level. They are marginalized and have become outcastes in politics. In the 17th Lok Sabha (2019-24), they have only 26 MPs which is 4.8 per cent of the total. As per share in population, they deserve 77 MPs and thus face a huge 65 per cent deprivation. How can a community that accounts for 15 per cent of the total population have just 4.8 per cent representation, if it is monolithic and a vote bank? It is time to call a halt to such false propaganda because it is meant to create a non-Muslim vote bank. In 2014, when Narendra Modi came to power with thumping majority, Muslims had the lowest ever representation. They had only 22 MPs forming 4 per cent of 16th Lok Sabha (2014-19) and faced the highest deprivation of 71.4 per cent. Previously, the gap between the size of Muslim population and their representation in the Lok Sabha was fairly maintained. For instance, the representation had gone up from 2 per cent in 1952 to almost 10 per cent in 1980. From 1984 to 2009, the representation remained in the ranges of 8 to 6 per cent. In the 16th and 17th Lok Sabha, it went below 5 per cent and a similar decline is noted in state assemblies. Comparing the assembly elections of 2013-15 with previous elections in Maharashtra, Haryana, Rajasthan, MP, Chhattisgarh and Delhi, the decline from 35 to 20 per cent is clearly visible. In UP, it declined from 17 in 2012 to 6 per cent in 2017 which increased to 8.4 per cent in 2022. In most of the states, Muslim political deprivation is clearly noticeable and there are states which do not have a single Muslim MLA.

Due to continuous political deprivation and visible political exclusion, their electoral marginalization is almost complete. Successive governments have done nothing to do away with their political alienation. Political scientists argue that urgent measures for political mainstreaming of Muslims are needed because the situation is going from bad to worse after the coming of the BJP to power. Lawyer and political commentator A.G. Noorani says that Muslims in India are facing the same situation that they had faced in 1857 and 1947. He observes, 'No political party, secular or "communal", has made a sincere effort to address them or simultaneously draw Muslims into the political mainstream and enlist the support of non-Muslims.'[24] Due to the aggressive Hindutva politics of the BJP, Muslims have become electorally untouchables. This party believes in total political exclusion of Muslims. In the parliamentary elections it normally gives five to seven tickets to Muslims and that too from constituencies, where it knows there are no chances of winning. It does not give tickets to Muslims even in states where Muslims account for a substantial share in population like UP, Bihar, Gujarat, Maharashtra, etc. Verniers believes that anti-Muslim sentiment stoked by some in the BJP has led to fewer Muslim candidates outside the BJP since the secular parties fear being tagged as anti-Hindu if they promote Muslim candidates. These parties, citing the reason of winnability and communal polarisation, have been denying Muslims the tickets in party nominations. The end result of this is to electorally marginalize the Muslims. Besides this trend, the BJP is raking up issues that are clearly anti-Muslim and the strategy is paying rich political dividends. Inflation, education, employment and economic downfall are not the issues in elections. Love jihad, triple talaq, *hijab*, cow protection, Pakistan, Jinnah, etc., are new election issues in India. For secular parties, Muslims have become a non-entity as they want to take their votes, but like to maintain a safe distance from them. Secular parties do not hold rallies in Muslim areas, raise their issues in elections or give them their due share in party nominations.

Hindu OBCs and Muslims Face Similar Political Deprivation

In 17 elections (1952-2019), the share of Muslims in the parliament has been at 5.78 per cent and they have faced 51.40 per cent deprivation. In the 17th Lok Sabha (2019-24), with 26 MPs, they constitute just 4.79 per cent of all MPs and face 66.23 per cent deprivation. They got just 34 per cent seats of what they deserve in the Lok Sabha. OBCs (majority are Hindus) face similar political deprivation since they constitute almost 52 per cent of the total population, but their share in the 16th Lok Sabha (2014-19) was only 20 per cent. Representation of SCs, STs, other minorities (Sikh, Christian, Jain, Buddhist, etc.) are almost fixed. The Muslims' share hovers around 5 per cent. When all groups are excluded, the representation of Hindu OBCs is inversely related to that of the UCH. A 20 per cent share for OBCs means they get only 38 per cent of what they deserve. Whenever the BJP plays aggressive Hindutva politics, the UCH share goes up. In 2014 it went up to 44.5 per cent. The conclusion is that whenever the BJP improves its tally, the UCH share goes up while that of Hindu OBCs and Muslims goes down.

While there are some academic research on the political deprivation of Muslims and efforts are being made by them to overcome it, the Hindu OBCs do not have even this limited advantage. From 1947 till 1989, the Congress government implemented due affirmative action for SCs and STs, but did not provide the same to the OBCs. The UCHs who dominate the Congress thought that the OBCs might challenge their authority. The BJP is also a party of UCHs who do not want OBCs to grow politically. There has been no official effort to map their political deprivation and suggest corrective measures. The Mandal Commission recommended quota in jobs which did not intend to equalize socio-economic conditions but to empower its beneficiaries. In his Independence Day speech on 15 August 1990, V.P. Singh said, 'We believe that no section can be uplifted merely by money. They can develop only if they have a share in power and we are prepared to provide this share. . . .' The ultimate aim of Mandal was to give the OBCs a proper share in politics and power. However, the Mandal moment is fading as the share of Hindu OBCs in politics has reached a level which was recorded before 1980.

Muslims are Politically Awakened Community

As discussed in the first chapter, Muslims have greater faith in democracy and its impact as a tool to bring socio-economic change. Over the decades, they have been contributing much to strengthen democracy, and are one of the most politically awakened community in India despite facing political deprivation. They know their share in politics, reasons for underrepresentation and also remedial measures to be taken at the community as well as official level. Community leaders, activists, intellectuals, organizations, etc., have been striving hard to get due share in politics. They know that political representation is the key to all empowerment and they must have it to have a voice in the parliament and state assemblies. The leaders of the SCs and OBCs must tell their groups how powerful they are, how huge their political deprivation is and prepare them to refuse to act at the behest of manipulative and communal forces. Eighty-four Lok Sabha seats are reserved for SCs. Very few of them have more than 50 per cent Dalit population, which means the non-Dalit voters decide the fate of

Dalit candidates in reserved PCs. A vocal or assertive Dalit leader has little chances of winning from the reserved seats, and in order to be re-elected, a Dalit MP is careful not to antagonize the non-Dalits. One way of doing this is to remain silent in the parliament. Also, the proceedings in the Lok Sabha indicate that barring a few Dalit MPs, the others do not raise issues concerning Dalits either in the legislatures or the media. Major parties especially the BJP and Congress want their Dalit leaders to play 'deaf and dumb'. These MPs do not raise their voice when Dalits are lynched by hysterical mobs and attacked due to various identity issues such as sporting moustaches, riding horses in wedding processions, etc., atrocities are committed against them, socio-economic and educational rights are encroached upon or their constitutionally guaranteed rights are attacked. According to Kanshi Ram, such politicians are just *chamchas* (stooges) of their party. The apprehension expressed by Dr. Ambedkar is being confirmed as no real Dalit leaders are being elected while only agents of the big parties flourish. The discussion for separate electorates has already come to end. The OBCs constitute 52 per cent of the population but their share in politics has been close to 20 per cent in 2014 and 2019 elections. They are politically marginalized but, happy that UCHs are ruling over them. As already discussed, their share has dropped to the lowest level and the share of UCHs has increased. Apart from some dominant castes such as Yadav, Kurmi, Jat, etc., the middle and lower Hindu OBCs face extreme political exclusion. Sadly, they are not aware of this pathetic condition and have become part and parcel of the project of building a muscular Hindu Rashtra. They have basically become foot soldiers of the BJP. They are not aware that their political, socio-economic and reservation rights are being snatched by the BJP, but are happy to attack Muslims and Dalits. A majority of the accused arrested in the lynching of Muslims belong to OBC castes. It is ironical to note that when V.P. Singh implemented the Mandal report to empower OBCs, the BJP started the Ram Mandir movement to counter it. The BJP's or Hindutva's political growth is antithetical to the empowerment of OBCs. The OBCs should understand their numerical strength and that they are the biggest stakeholders in Indian democracy and realize that no party can form a government without their support. They should be made aware that BJP is against their empowerment, and it may revoke the OBC reservation once in a position to do.

Political Strength

After our analysis above we realize that there are two type of political strengths of Muslims: right to vote and their numbers, i.e. Muslim-dominated constituencies. Muslims are respected and valued by political parties because they have the right to vote. There have been some attempts (Chapter 6) to disenfranchize Muslims, but the roots of democracy are so strong that these attempts would not succeed. Muslims must be alert, identify such attempts and fight tooth and nail to preserve their rights.

Second, Muslims have a significant presence in some constituencies which are winnable. Out of 543 PCs, Muslims can actually influence the outcome in 196. The poll analysts have identified that out of 80 seats in UP, Muslims can influence 54. Similarly, in Bihar they can do so in 29 out of 40 PCs, in West Bengal on 28 of 43 PCs, in Karnataka on 15 out of 28 PCs, in Kerala on 14 out of 20 PCs, in Maharashtra on 13 out of 48, in Andhra Pradesh on 12 out of 42, in Assam on 9 out of 14 seats, in Gujarat 6 out of 26 and in Rajasthan on 6 out of 25 seats. Muslims have a significant influence over 10 out of 28 states. There are more than 30 per cent Muslim voters in 35 PCs. In 38 other seats, they are 21 to 30 per cent. In another 145 PCs, they are 11 to 20 per cent. If all these are added, Muslim voters can influence the results of a whopping 218 PCs. Besides, there are 5 to 10 per cent Muslim voters in 183 PCs, and 5 per cent in 142 PCs. Even these voters can make significant impression on the electoral process.[25] Similarly, they can win or change the result in favour of any candidate in several ACs of many states. In the 720 of the total 4,121 ACs, they are in decisive number where they can turn the fate of candidates and parties. Muslim-dominated PCs and ACs are actual strength of Muslims. They should map the percentage of voters in each constituency by engaging people who work on elections. If the share is above 30 or 35 per cent, they must demand that the dominant secular party ensure that one Muslim candidate is put up. If the share is below 30 per cent, they should vote for a secular party candidate after proper bargaining on socio-economic and education progress, safety and work in their localities.

Suitable Political Options

As already discussed, to be better represented in state formations, the minorities, particularly Muslims have three choices: one, they can join one of the parties sympathetic to minorities or secular in orientation; two, they can work through non-partisan pressure groups that would ensure the election of sympathetic individuals regardless of party affiliation; and finally, they can form their own political party and try to get benefits by holding the balance of power in a coalition government. We have seen that since Independence, Muslims have utilized all these options at different places/states but have neither got a proper share in politics nor has their socio-economic condition improved.

When the political climate is not polarized to an extreme degree, the above options could be used in the following ways:

(i) When their share in a constituency is from 5 to 15 per cent: They can from non-partisan pressure groups and work to ensure the win of sympathetic individuals regardless of party affiliations.

(ii) When share in a constituency is from 15 to 30 per cent: join one of the secular parties sympathetic to them. In this situation, they must ask the party to give tickets to Muslims, and ensure their victory. If there is no Muslim candidate, they must vote for a single secular party to be decided by consensus.

(iii) When share is 30 per cent and above: support the candidate of a Muslim party. Muslim-base parties generally field Muslim candidates in such constituencies. After election when government is formed by a secular party, Muslim party/parties can become part of the secular coalition.

With little modifications, as per local requirements and political climate, these are political options for Muslims which could be used intelligently. In this way they can get their proportional representation without harming the secular parties.

Muslims Should be Part of the Deprived Majority

Muslims think they are in a minority and this tends to demoralize them giving them the impression that they are at the mercy of the majority. Dr. Javed Jamil, an author and community thinker, writes in his book, *Muslim Vision for Secular India* that the status of Muslims in India has three factors defining it. They are a minority with guaranteed rights given in the Constitution that make them equal citizens of the country. As a minority, they are just 19.3 per cent of the population and feel that they are numerically inferior and have to live at the mercy of the majority. Although they enjoy Constitutional protection, they have minimum role in government formation. As an ideological bloc, they are the second largest majority which must be in a position to influence the direction of all policies of the government. In this situation, the government must treat their problem as a national problem making it easier to resolve it. Thirdly, sociologically, they are part of the deprived majority. As already discussed Pasmanda Muslims (OBC+Dalit) constitute 85 per cent of the Muslims. Similarly, the Hindu deprived sections (OBC+SC+ST) constitute almost 80 to 85 per cent of the Hindu population. If Muslims want to play a meaningful role in national affairs, they need to focus on the third status. If they are part of the deprived majority, their socio-economic, educational and political rights will be preserved. This is what the Pasmanda discourse argues. They may get a meaningful share in politics as well. This could also secularize the politics and end Hindu-Muslim enmity deliberately created, and propagated by elites of both the major communities.

Muslims Should Expand Their Support Base

Secular parties refuse tickets to Muslims citing two reasons: their winnability and communal polarization. In fact, these two reasons are interrelated. Whenever there is communal polarization, the probability of a Muslim candidate winning elections goes down. It has also been pointed out that it has become difficult for them to get elected from mixed localities because Hindus do not vote for Muslim candidates regardless of suitability. To tackle this, Muslims should expand their support base. Their social location combined with habitation in rural hinterlands in proximity with Dalits and OBCs, gives an opportunity to expand the support base among them. An overwhelming majority of Pasmanda Muslims are basically converts from Hindu OBCs and Dalit castes and not only have professional interactions, but also stay side-by-side in rural areas. Muslims think only about their problems/issues and do not come out of this 'selfish mentality'. Muslims must realize that atrocities are not committed only against them, but also against Dalits, tribals and the poor. Whenever Dalits are attacked by Hindutva forces and atrocities are committed against them, Muslim organization/parties must support them in their fight for justice. They must support them in their agitations against dilution of SC/ST Prevention of Atrocities Act, and in defence of their constitutional rights. Similarly, the OBCs have been demanding the caste-based census, reservation in proportion to population and proportionate share in govt. welfare schemes. Muslims must become part of their struggle. Secondly, Hindu OBCs are being used as foot soldiers of militant Hindutva groups such as Bajrang Dal, Hindu Yuva Vahini, various vigilante groups, etc. Muslims must communicate with them to make them aware that they are being used and UCHs are reaping the benefits of communalism. They must be made aware that those arrested for inflicting violence on Muslims are mostly OBCs/Dalits. Similarly, Muslims must support the tribal rights groups. By doing the above, they will increase their social base and play a meaningful role in secularization of a majority of Hindus.

Political Space Needs to be Secular and Seen to be Secular

When BJP came to power in 2014 with an absolute majority, the number of Muslim MPs went down to 22 which is an all-time low after 1952. Whenever the BJP comes to power in states like

MP, Rajasthan, Chhattisgarh, UP, Bihar, etc., the number of Muslim MLAs falls drastically. When secular issues dominate the election campaign or secular parties win the elections, Muslims' representation goes up. So, it is advisable for Muslims to make the political space secular, keep the election on secular issues and refrain from raising or showing anything which are communal in nature. They should fight elections on planks of secular/life-related issues, such as employment, education, economy, inflation and development in the constituency; infrastructure like road, schools, hospitals, good sports complex, etc.; civic facilities like water, drainage, cleanliness, etc.; and due share in govt. welfare schemes. These issues are related to every citizen. They should not raise Muslim specific issues, such as Urdu, *shariah* and other religious issues or international Muslim issues. Secondly, during the elections, Muslim leaders and candidates should maintain a secular outlook and show broad mindedness. Emotional and controversial issues should be avoided. Right-wing groups are simply waiting to pounce upon any such issue that will help them to polarize Hindu voters.

Ground Level Planning and Training

If politics decides the fate of Muslims, why not teach them such lessons? Only on the basis of their voting strength can Muslims gain political share and overall progress. So, Muslims should be aware of the rules of the game of politics. These lessons could be given through short duration classes held in each nook and corner of Muslim localities. Muslim gram panchayat members, councillors, MLAs, MPs, leaders, activists, political science students, NGOs, etc., must design training courses for general voters according to local requirements. The aim should be to educate voters to enhance share in politics or elect candidates who are most suitable for them. Leaders and trainers must make the community aware of how to democratically assert themselves in politics.

During the training period, the community can be taught suitable lessons to face the electoral process on different levels. Every member must be advised to come out on voting day and exercise the right to vote. Community leaders must ensure that every person votes as a moral and constitutional duty. Secondly, they should vote keeping in mind the local requirements, societal needs and interest of the nation. They should vote for development, secularism, peace and prosperity, better law and order, etc. They should ask the community to vote for a single candidate where they are 20 per cent or more even if there are multiple Muslim candidates. There should be a coordination committee of all groups and organizations that should be entrusted to take decisions in selecting most suitable candidates. Creation of suitable leadership at local level should also be part of the training. It is high time for Indian Muslims to become the captain of the ship and master of their destiny and steer themselves through turbulent waters of the electoral politics in India.

Creation of Good Leaders

Even after 75 years of Independence, Muslims lack a strong political leadership which is capable of voicing their concerns without polarizing the atmosphere. The weakening of secular parties and consequent rise of the BJP has put additional burden on them to create leaders who could guide the community in turbulent days. In this situation, they need a leader like Kanshi Ram, who worked for Dalits to make them a strong community and a political force. He also voiced concerns of minorities and backward classes. He followed an inclusive policy without causing a rift in the society. Muslims also need leaders like Maulana Abul Kalam Azad who worked for the betterment of Muslims, and their inclusion in the national mainstream. He encouraged the concept of 'Composite Nationalism' which was endorsed by Maulana Husain Ahmed Madani in which Indian Muslim and nationalist Muslim identities were mutually reinforcing, and Muslims could be both at once. Today, they need a leader like V.P. Singh who sacrificed his wealth and worked for the complete empowerment of OBCs and other poorer sections of the society. They also need leaders like Lalu Prasad Yadav who struggled hard to give the deprived in Bihar a voice and did not compromise on the issue of secularism. In short, they need a socio-political leadership and not religious leadership.

They are seeking a forward-looking secular leadership to understand the social, economic and political aspirations of the masses. The community actually needs leaders who work hard on the ground level and have solid mass base.

As discussed it earlier, even in Muslim-dominated constituencies Muslim candidates need votes from other communities to get elected. So, they need a leader who has the confidence of the other communities. This can be won only through hard work and serving the people at ground level. Grassroots leaders must have core essentials like: mass base, political understanding, and full acceptance of democratic process. To understand and accept the democratic process, one should be educated and have fair knowledge of our Constitution, democracy and institutions. For political understanding, they must know the state, central and local-level politics, aspirations and demands of people. For mass base, one needs to serve the people on the ground. Leaders must be conversant with the local administration and be ready to serve the people on a daily basis and deal with their issues concerning the police, revenue, health department and local bodies like *gram panchayat*, municipality and city corporations related to various issues. Readiness to serve the people is a necessary condition.

Broad Vision: National and General Issues

As discussed earlier, Muslims have greater faith in democracy, institutions and its effectiveness to bring socio-economic change. They wish to participate in elections to enhance share in politics, but they normally raise community specific issues and also organize workshops and programmes on community's problems and its condition. This comes across as a 'selfish attitude' and 'inward looking' mentality. Muslims must come out of this closed mentality and raise issues of all especially, the deprived sections. They must formulate their vision of a democratic, secular and progressive India for which they have to create their vision document and include issues like education, employment, inflation, peace and development, infrastructural facilities, reservation issues of Dalits and OBCs, farmers' issues, etc. They should follow the concept of 'composite nationalism', and work hard for national unity and composite culture. Muslims leaders must train the masses for 'mutual co-existence' and also do something to motivate people for harmonious living. They also clearly express their vision to make India a progressive country and strong nation. Genuine concerns and honest attempts are always appreciated by the general electorates, and they value the efforts for nation building. Thus, to enhance acceptability in general public, the community leaders must come out of the ghettoized mindset, selfish attitude and community specific issues. They must contribute towards national progress and nation building.

GOAL TO ACHIEVE SOCIAL DEMOCRACY: LIBERTY, EQUALITY AND FRATERNITY

According to Dr. Ambedkar, democracy is not merely a tool to govern the people but a system of governance to serve the people equally and also to achieve socio-economic and political justice. He says that 'Democracy is not merely a form of government. It is primarily a mode of associated living, of conjoint, communicated experience. It is essentially an attitude of respect and reverence towards one's fellow men.'[26] These concerns indicate his firm faith in democracy and advocacy to use it properly to serve all sections of society and create a just and harmonious society.

In his famous speech delivered in the Constituent Assembly on 25 November 1949, Dr. Ambedkar gave out three warnings for the survival of democracy. These things are antithetical to the concept of democracy, and if not checked would ultimately put democracy in jeopardy. The first warning: Hold fast to constitutional methods of achieving our social and economic objectives, which means there is no place of violence in the society and democratic and constitutional methods could be used to achieve objectives. Second warning: Not to lay their liberties at the feet of even a great man, or to trust him with power which enable him to subvert their institutions. He elaborates that in India, *bhakti* or what may be called the path of devotion or hero-worship, plays a part in its politics unequalled in magnitude by the part it plays in the politics of any other country in the world. *Bhakti* in religion may be a road to the salvation of the soul. But in politics, *bhakti* or hero-worship is sure road to degradation and to eventual dictatorship. Elaborating on third warning. Dr. Aambedkar says, 'The third thing we must do is not to be content with mere political democracy. We must make our political democracy a social democracy as well. Political democracy cannot last unless their lies at the base of it social democracy.'[27]

On social democracy and its constituent of liberty, equality and fraternity, Dr. Aambedkar said:

> What does social democracy mean? It means a way of life which recognizes liberty, equality and fraternity as the principles of life. These principles of liberty, equality and fraternity are not to be treated as separate items in a trinity. They form a union of trinity in the sense that to divorce one from the other is to defeat the very purpose of democracy. Liberty cannot be divorced from equality, equality cannot be divorced from liberty. Nor can liberty and equality be divorced from fraternity. Without equality, liberty would produce the supremacy of the few over the many. Equality without liberty would kill individual initiative. Without fraternity, liberty would produce the supremacy of the few over the many. Without fraternity, liberty and equality could not become a natural course of things. It would require a constable to enforce them. We must begin by acknowledging the fact that there is complete absence of two things in Indian Society. One of these is equality. On the social plane, we have in India a society based on the principle of graded inequality which we have society in which there are some who have immense wealth as against many who live in abject poverty.

One cannot live the life of contradictions. On the element of contradictions in Indian society, Dr. Ambedkar said:

> On the 26 January 1950, we are going to enter into a life of contradictions. In politics we will have equality and in social and economic life we will have inequality. In politics we will be recognizing the principle of one man, one vote, and one vote one value. In our social and economic life, we shall, by reason of our social and economic structure, continue to deny the principle of one man one value. How long shall we continue to live this life of contradictions? How long shall we continue to deny equality in our social and economic life? If we continue to deny it for long, we will do so only by putting our political democracy in peril. We must remove this contradiction at the earliest possible

moment or else those who suffer from inequality will blow up the structure of political democracy which this Assembly has to laboriously built up.

Fraternity is vital for peace and harmonious living in a society. On the element of fraternity, he says:

> The second thing we are wanting in is recognition of the principle of fraternity. What does fraternity mean? Fraternity means a sense of common brotherhood of all Indians—of Indians being one people. It is the principle which gives unity and solidarity to social life. It is a difficult thing to achieve. How difficult it is, can be realised from the story related by James Bryce in his volume on American Commonwealth about the United States of America.

Political power in India has been the monopoly of a few and the many are not only beasts of burden, but also beasts of prey. The monopoly has deprived them of their chance at betterment. These downtrodden classes are tired of being governed, and are impatient to govern themselves. This urge for self-realization in the down-trodden class must not be allowed to devolve into a class struggle or a class war. It would lead to the division of the house that would indeed be a day of disaster. This can only be done by the establishment of equality and fraternity in all spheres of life. Dr. Ambedkar through these words advocated the establishment of social democracy in the country.

Political democracy is basically a numerical or mechanical democracy in which elections are held and people are elected without any consideration to due share of all sections of society. When it reflects due share of all groups of people, marginalized groups get an opportunity to govern themselves. Dr. Ambedkar's dream of social democracy has not been fulfilled so far as many groups are not truly represented. In fact in recent times, we are going in the reverse direction which could create class struggle and perpetual division in the society.

ON A FINAL NOTE

Finally, we can conclude that the Muslim community of India, has been facing a huge political deprivation at all levels: Parliament, state assemblies and local bodies. Lok Sabha has seen the upward increase of Muslim representation from 2 per cent in 1952 to 10 per cent in 1980 which dropped to 4 per cent in 2014. In 17 general elections, they have achieved just one-third share of what they deserved as per the proportional share. Muslims have never been a strong voice in the Lok Sabha and thus no concrete measures have been taken for their socio-economic development or legislation passed to ensure safety from communal riots. While a majority of Muslim MPs hail from Assam, Bihar, West Bengal, UP and Kerala there are many states with significant population of Muslims which do not return Muslim MPs, because Muslims are thinly spread all over the country. The decline is equally noted in state assemblies. In none of the states, are they represented as per share in the state population. In Assam, Bihar, West Bengal, UP, Kerala, Telangana, etc., their share of MLAs is satisfactory. In other states, it is pathetic and that is affecting their socio-economic conditions as most of the subjects are in the hands of states.

The biggest reason for this low share and high degree of deprivation is denial of tickets by secular parties and exclusionary politics of the BJP. The Congress and regional parties do not nominate Muslims in proportion to their population share. The BJP's exclusionary politics defines its electoral prospects in opposition to Muslims. The party gives five to six tickets in parliamentary elections for seats, where it has no chances of winning. It does not give tickets to them in assembly elections in many states like UP, Gujarat, Maharashtra, Bihar, etc. Moreover, it accuses secular parties of appeasement when the latter offer a few tickets to Muslims. These parties are so afraid of the BJP's brand of majoritarian politics, and so weary of loosing majority votes that they hesitate to give tickets to Muslims even though they bank on Muslim votes. The exclusionary instinct is becoming stronger even among the regional parties as a tool to contain the growth of right-wing fervour in India.

Muslims are now the new untouchables in Indian politics. The political parties do not raise their issues, do not visit their areas during the elections, and even the secular parties do not nominate Muslim candidates in Muslim-majority constituencies. These parties rest on the confidence that in an effort to check the BJP, Muslims would be forced to vote for them, anyway. This attitude has led the Muslims to seriously think about forming their own party and trying to take control of their own destiny. The burden to save Indian secularism cannot be carried by the Muslim community, alone. It is the majority community which has to decide whether it wants a secular or a theocratic state.

National leaders and successive governments at the centre have ditched Muslims on most occasions and consciously attempted to deprive them politically. In May 1949, when Muslim members Begum Aizaz Rasool and Tajamul Hussain of the Constituent Assembly moved amendments to exclude Muslims from the provision of reservation of seats in the legislature, Jawaharlal Nehru and Sardar Patel gave assurances to the minorities of fair justice. They were assured that even without constitutional guarantee minorities would be ensured their fair share. In spite of such a categorical assurance of fairness by Nehru and Patel and Sardar Hukum Singh's sound proposal that after ten years of its functioning, the system of non-reservation of seats for minorities should be reviewed.

During the last 73 years of functioning of the Constitution, the national polity has failed to honour the promises and assurances of those tall leaders, and there is no review mechanism to resolve the political deprivation of Muslims. A method has been devised by the officials of the Delimitation Commission to reduce Muslim representation by reserving Muslim-dominated seats for SCs and STs. The SCR has shown with evidence that several such seats were reserved for SCs which reduced the share of Muslims in politics. Community leaders and activists pointed out this anomaly to the then government and requested to constitute a fresh delimitation commission with the mandate to correct it. So far nothing has happened. Biased officials of the Delimitation Commission carry out demarcation of the constituencies in such a way that it reduces the number of Muslims in some constituencies dominated by them. Field experience shows that Muslim-majority localities have been divided, and attached to two or three constituencies and thus they are not in dominant position in any of them. This has also been raised on several forums but nothing has happened so far. And also, the names of several Muslims are missing in the electoral rolls. There are deliberate attempts not to enter the names of Muslim voters in electoral rolls. When Muslims shift their residence, their names are not included in the electoral roll of the new area. By other methods there is an attempt to disenfranchise Muslim voters.

Due to low economic participation, Muslims contribute only 6 per cent of the GDP. They are economically and educationally backward; they are the poorest lot; social and physical infrastructural facilities are absent in their localities; share in government employments is pathetic and social and reservation issues of Muslims are not settled so far. Recommendations of the SCR and Ranganath Mishra Commission are gathering dust. Since Independence, hundreds of big riots were engineered and lakhs of Muslims killed, but not a single legislation to ensure safety and security is passed in the parliament. Since Muslims lack political weight, the Communal Violence Bill once introduced in the parliament, has not been passed so far. On a daily basis, they face discrimination, prejudice and unfair treatment at their work place, residential areas and government offices. Some committees have recommended that a legislation on the lines of the SC and ST (Prevention of Atrocities) Act be passed to put an end to discrimination against Muslims. Unfortunately, this also has not happened. Muslims are on fast track to become neo-Dalits in India. These all are nothing but the consequences of huge political deprivation.

The pertinent question here is: what should the Muslims do? The Muslim masses, including the leaders, activists, thinkers and youths must understand the Indian political system well to know the share of Muslims in politics at all level, the deprivation faced by them and reasons for it. As already discussed, their strengths are:

(i) Greater faith in democracy and more participation in democratic processes.
(ii) Muslim-dominated seats: Parliamentary and Assembly.
(iii) Their greater commitment to the Constitution, secularism and social justice.
(iv) Youth population and an urge to serve the nation.

Similarly, as discussed in previous sections, their weaknesses are:

(i) Thinly spread in every nook and corner of India, forming majority in very few seats.
(ii) Secular parties' indifferent attitude to their due share in politics.
(iii) Inherent communal bias in the majority community.
(iv) No political awareness and short sightedness in the community.

The Muslims' greater faith in democracy and bigger participation in democratic process could be used as a basis to demand the government of the day to set up a review committee to go into the reasons for political deprivation and suggest measures to restore the system of reservation of seats as promised by our leaders at the time of framing of the Constitution. Their biggest strength is in the seats dominated by them especially where they constitute more than 30 to 35 per cent of the total voters. In these seats they must try to get their members elected with a little help from voters belonging to Dalit, Tribal or OBC groups or Hindu voters of secular orientation. Their high commitment to constitutional values, preservation of secularism and positive attitude to social justice of all deprived groups could fetch votes of deprived groups. The relatively high share of youth population, and their willingness to serve people of all castes and religions is also an added strength. They can be trained, motivated and taught to take on the roles of leaders.

The uniform spread of Muslim voters can be a strength if they work unitedly and call upon the secular candidates to work for overall progress and ensure safety and security. Secular parties are indifferent to issues of their political empowerment and give them only 40 to 50 per cent ticket of what they deserve. These parties cite winnability and communal polarization as ground for not giving tickets from mixed localities. If these parties work in a proper manner and take concrete measures to tackle communal polarization, winnability of Muslims would certainly go up in mixed localities. To reduce communalism in the majority community, Muslims must adopt the principle of mutual co-existence. They should continue to extend help to Hindus as they did during the

COVID-19 pandemic. As discussed, short courses on political awareness may be organized for educated youths. Micro-level training is a must for creating political awareness in the community. Collecting field-level data and ascertaining percentage of Muslim votes in each PC, AC and municipal ward/gram panchayat is necessary for political participation.

Muslims must try to frame their politics, as far as possible, around secular issues particularly those related to livelihood, shelter, health, education, etc., and keep away from communal and emotional issues. When the BJP fights elections on communal issues and rises to prominence in states, the representation of Muslims goes down drastically and, therefore, it is in their interest to keep the political pitch secular. The community must also focus its energy on creating secular leadership rather than religious leadership that drags the community around sentimental/religious issues which polarizes the elections further.

Creating political awareness and bridging the Hindu-Muslim gap should be on the agenda of Muslims, if they want to grow politically. Political empowerment has never been the regular discourse of the community. For several decades after Independence, it has been made to feel guilty for the Partition though it was largely the fallout of political maladjustments. Muslim leaders must work towards political awareness amongst community members, particularly the youth and women. Observers say the lack of communication with Hindus and other religious communities could continue to work against the interests of Muslims. Disunity will harm them severely. Muslims must establish communication with Hindus to improve relation. It should be on the top of their agenda and could be treated as a movement. To make the movement more inclusive and fruitful, they have to approach the politically aware youths from all sections of society. Main agenda of the movement should be to create an environment of understanding and reconciliation.

Undoubtedly Muslims have to reorient themselves to get due share in politics. The government and democratic institutions also have to ensure political justice to minorities and deprived communities. Democracy means four basic things. Firstly, there must be deliberate political moderation. Democracy cannot run if the government doesn't respect the wishes and aspirations of that section of the population, that section of the parliament which is in a minority and constitutes the opposition. Secondly, political parties must be responsible. Thirdly, the opposition is not incompatible with the warm personal relations and goodwill between the government and the opposition. Fourthly, the national interest prevails over the party interests. In a democracy the government should not ignore the wishes and aspirations of the minority communities.

Legal and constitutional characteristics of democracy as advocated by Lucien Radel in his book titled *Roots of Totalitarianism: The Ideological Sources of Fascism, National Socialism, and Communism,* also includes minority rights among its nine characteristics.[28] This means in a democracy rights of minorities, that includes their political rights as well, must be preserved. They must be given a fair chance to participate in the process of democracy. The Framework Convention for Protection of National Minorities European Council's Instrument says that the protection of national minorities is essential to stability, democratic security and peace in a nation. In any state, the faith and confidence of minorities in the functioning of the state in an impartial manner is an acid test of its being a just state. Due representation of minorities in democratic institutions gives stability to the nation and makes it an inclusive and sustainable democracy. Scholars say that political mainstreaming of religious minorities and socially deprived groups is inevitable for stability in a democratic nation.

India claims to be the largest democracy in the world. But the claim is meaningless, if due share in politics is not provided to the religious minorities, weaker sections and socially deprived such as Dalits, Tribals and OBCs. Seats in the parliament and state assemblies are reversed for SCs and STs, but Muslims (especially Pasmanda Muslims) and Hindu OBCs, have been facing huge political deprivation and are absent in the corridors of power. As a result, their socio-economic, educational and political rights are not duly preserved and consequently India is not achieving the success it truly deserves. Until a truly representative social democracy is established, our claim of being the largest democracy sounds hollow.

As far as the efforts of the ECI and governments on electoral reform are concerned, numerous reforms have been suggested by opposition parties, lawyers, jurists and academicians. Various committees/commissions were also constituted for this purpose. These issues include corrupt practices and electoral offences, electoral rolls, voting age, issue of high number of independent candidates, money power, booth capturing and intimidation of voters, EVM tampering and other allegations. It is pity to note that not a single committee was constituted to address the grave political deprivation faced by Muslims.

If the government wants to solve the problem of inadequate political share of certain religious minorities and deprived groups, it must adopt inclusive democracy and work on the methods to create a social democracy. India is full of social diversity as people belonging to various religions, caste, communities, regions, ethnicity, etc., reside here. If certain communities are not duly represented in politics, it creates social disharmony and socio-economic rights of unrepresented groups are not preserved. Consequently, it creates a social and economic inequality and ultimately the very purpose of democracy gets defeated. Merely conducting elections on routine basis and electing governments after every five years has actually become a formality which creates a numerical or mechanical democracy. To fulfil the dreams of our framers of Constitution, the government must adopt the essence of social democracy as advocated by Dr. Ambedkar which can break the monopoly of a few dominant castes/group and give political justice to minorities and politically deprived groups.

If due representation is not given to religious minorities and other socially deprived groups it creates a government of persons belonging to a few privileged castes/groups. It creates a monopoly of a few who think only about a section of the population and ignore the interests of the majority. This creates a socio-economic inequality which ultimately hampers the growth of the nation. If due representation is ensured to all, then it creates an all-representative and all-caring government which think about the interest of all citizens. An all-representative government ensures socio-economic justice to all and provides equal opportunities to every citizen of the country. This ensures the participation of every citizen in the workforce and thus, increases economic productivity of the nation. Thus, political mainstreaming and due representation of all is greatly needed for overall growth and nation-building.

NOTES

1. https://www.theleaflet.in/lack-of-muslim-representation-in-politics-is-only-bjp-to-blame/
2. Ibid.
3. https://www.aa.com.tr/en/asia-pacific/political-parties-avoid-wooing-muslim-voters-in-india-/1475630
4. http://twocircles.net/2010sep14/bharat-needs-colorful-political-canvas.html
5. Saloni Bhogale, 'Who Speaks for Muslims in Lok Sabha? The answer is quite tricky', *Hindustan Times*, New Delhi, 26 March 2019.
6. https://theprint.in/opinion/muslim-vote/muslim-mps-mlas-dont-always-work-for-muslims-see-akhilesh-govt-response-to-muzaffarnagar/234603/
7. Omar Khalidi (1995), *Indian Muslims Since Independence*, New Delhi: Vikas Publishing House.
8. http://twocircles.net/2018jun09/423650.html
9. http://www.ummid.com/news/2013/July/14.07.2013/asad-owaisi-in-jeddah.html
10. http://twocircles.net/2015apr26/1430024809.html
11. http://twocircles.net/2013apr17/muslim-parties-echo-minority-aspirations-secular-india.html
12. https://mail.google.com/mail/?shva=1#inbox/13c0f340ea0ed5a7
13. http://twocircles.net/2015aug29/1440824045.html
14. Rana Ayyub, 'The Vote That Counts', *Tehelka*, 24 December 2011 (Issue 51, vol. 8).
15. http://twocircles.net/2013aug26/new-variants-minority-politics.html
16. http://twocircles.net/2012jan09/congress-trying-capture-leadership-major-muslim-groups.html
17. *Lokmat* (Marathi), Pune, 24 February 2014.
18. Hilal Ahmed, 'Imagined Realities', *The Telegraph*, New Delhi, 30 October 2021.

19. https://theprint.in/opinion/fatwa-waving-ulema-had-power-to-swing-muslim-votes-until-coalition-politics-kicked-in/221389/
20. http://twocircles.net/2013apr23/ulema-center-stage-politics-elections-must-be-close.html
21. https://theprint.in/opinion/not-just-hindutva-indias-useless-ulema-leadership-has-silenced-muslims/321974/
22. http://twocircles.net/2014may28/beware-sympathisers-disguise.html
23. Rajeev Bhargava, 'On the Persistent Political Underrepresentation of Muslims in India', unpublished draft.
24. http://www.ummid.com/news/2018/February/19.02.2018/indian-muslims-in-2018.html
25. https://www.ummid.com/news/2014/March/09.03.2014/muslim-factor-in-ls-polls.html
26. Taken from an excerpt from 'Annihilation of Caste', drafted by Dr. B.R. Ambedkar in 1936.
27. An excerpt from the speech delivered by Dr. B.R. Ambedkar to the Constituent Assembly on 25 November 1949 (https://scroll.in/article/802495/why-br-ambedkars-three-warnings-in-his-last-speech-to-the-constituent-assembly-resonate-even-today).
28. Agarala Easwara Reddy and D. Sundar Ram (eds.), *Electoral Reforms in India*, New Delhi: Uppal Publishing House, 1992, pp. 2-3.

APPENDICES

Note: SC written in bracket against an assembly constituency indicates that the constituency is reserved for SCs.

ACs: Assembly Constituencies.

APPENDIX 1

Analysis of Assembly Constituencies of Andhra Pradesh

TABLE 1.1: ANALYSIS OF ACs AS PER PERCENTAGE OF MUSLIM VOTERS

S.No.	*Type of ACs*	*% of Muslim Voters*	*No. of ACs*
1.	Marginal	Upto 10	131
2.	Medium	From 10 to 20	34
3.	Sizeable	From 20 to 30	8
4.	Near Majority	From 30 to 40	2
5.	Majority	40 and above	0
TOTAL		All	175

TABLE 1.2: MEDIUM SIZE ACs (VOTER PERCENTAGE FROM 10 TO 19.9 PER CENT)

S.No.	*AC ID*	*AC Name*	*S.No.*	*AC ID*	*AC Name*
1.	78	Penamaluru	18.	129	Pulivendia
2.	83	Nandigama (SC)	19.	130	Kamalapuram
3.	85	Pedakurapadu	20.	133	Mydukur
4.	86	Tadikonda (SC)	21.	134	Allagadda
5.	88	Ponnur	22.	136	Nandikotkur (SC)
6.	91	Tenali	23.	138	Panyam
7.	94	Guntur West	24.	140	Banaganapalle
8.	95	Guntur East	25.	141	Dhone
9.	96	Chilakaluripet	26.	143	Kodumur (SC)
10.	97	Narasaraopet	27.	144	Yemmiganur
11.	98	Sattenapalle	28.	150	Guntakal
12.	100	Gurajala	29.	151	Tadpatri
13.	112	Giddalur	30.	162	Thamballapalle
14.	115	Atmakur	31.	163	Pileru
15.	117	Nellore City	32.	164	Madanapalle
16.	118	Nellore Rural	33.	165	Punganur
17.	125	Rajampet	34.	174	Palamaner

TABLE 1.3: SIZEABLE ACs (VOTER PERCENTAGE FROM 20 TO 29.9 PER CENT)

S.No.	*AC ID*	*AC Name*
1.	128	Rayachoti
2.	132	Proddatur
3.	135	Sirsailam
4.	139	Nandyal
5.	146	Adoni
6.	153	Anantapur Urban
7.	157	Hindupur
8.	161	Kadiri

TABLE 1.4: NEAR MAJORITY ACs (VOTER PERCENTAGE FROM 30 TO 39.9 PER CENT)

S.No.	*AC ID*	*AC Name*
1.	126	Kadapa
2.	137	Kurnool

APPENDIX 2

Analysis of Assembly Constituencies of Bihar

TABLE 2.1: ANALYSIS OF ACs AS PER PERCENTAGE OF MUSLIM VOTERS

S.No.	*Type of ACs*	*% of Muslim Voters*	*No. of ACs*
1.	Marginal	Upto 10	71
2.	Medium	From 10 to 20	118
3.	Sizeable	From 20 to 30	30
4.	Near Majority	From 30 to 40	11
5.	Majority	40 and above	13
TOTAL		All	243

TABLE 2.2: MEDIUM SIZE ACs (VOTER PERCENTAGE FROM 10 TO 19.9 PER CENT)

S.No.	*AC ID*	*AC Name*	*S.No.*	*AC ID*	*AC Name*
1.	1	Valmiki Nagar	17.	30	Belsand
2.	4	Bagaha	18.	31	Harlakhi
3.	6	Nautan	19.	32	Benipatti
4.	13	Harsidhi (SC)	20.	33	Khajauli
5.	14	Govindganj	21.	34	Babubarhi
6.	15	Kesaria	22.	37	Rajnagar (SC)
7.	16	Kalyanpur	23.	38	Jhanjharpur
8.	17	Pipra	24.	39	Phulparas
9.	18	Madhuban	25.	40	Laukaha
10.	19	Motihari	26.	41	Nirmali
11.	20	Chiraia	27.	42	Pipra
12.	22	Sheohar	28.	43	Supaul
13.	23	Riga	29.	44	Triveniganj (SC)
14.	24	Bathnaha (SC)	30.	59	Banmankhi (SC)
15.	28	Sitamarhi	31.	60	Rupauli
16.	29	Runisaidpur	32.	70	Alamnagar

Contd.

TABLE 2.2: *Contd.*

S.No.	*AC ID*	*AC Name*	*S.No.*	*AC ID*	*AC Name*
33.	71	Bihariganj	72.	131	Kalyanpur (SC)
34.	72	Singheshwar (SC)	73.	132	Warisnagar
35.	74	Sonbarsha (SC)	74.	133	Samastipur
36.	75	Saharsa	75.	135	Morwa
37.	76	Simri Bakhtiarpur	76.	140	Hasanpur
38.	77	Mahishi	77.	141	Cheria Bariarpur
39.	78	Kusheshwar Asthan (SC)	78.	143	Teghra
40.	80	Benipur	79.	144	Matihani
41.	84	Hayaghat	80.	145	Sahebpur Kamal
42.	85	Bahadurpur	81.	146	Begusarai
43.	88	Gaighat	82.	147	Bakhri (SC)
44.	89	Aurai	83.	149	Khagaria
45.	90	Minapur	84.	150	Beldaur
46.	91	Bochaha (SC)	85.	151	Parbatta
47.	92	Sakra (SC)	86.	152	Bihpur
48.	93	Kurhani	87.	154	Pirpainti (SC)
49.	94	Muzaffarpur	88.	155	Kahalgaon
50.	96	Baruraj	89.	157	Sultanganj
51.	97	Paroo	90.	159	Amarpur
52.	98	Sahebganj	91.	160	Dhuraiya (SC)
53.	99	Baikunthpur	92.	161	Banka
54.	102	Kuchaikote	93.	162	Katoria (ST)
55.	103	Bhorey (SC)	94.	165	Munger
56.	104	Hathua	95.	182	Bankipur
57.	106	Ziradei	96.	184	Patna Sahib
58.	109	Daraundha	97.	188	Phulwari (SC)
59.	111	Goriakothi	98.	194	Arrah
60.	112	Maharajganj	99.	196	Tarari
61.	113	Ekma	100.	206	Chainpur
62.	114	Manjhi	101.	208	Sasaram
63.	116	Taraiya	102.	211	Nokha
64.	117	Marhaura	103.	212	Dehri
65.	118	Chapra	104.	214	Arwal
66.	119	Garkha (SC)	105.	218	Makhdumpur (SC)
67.	120	Amnour	106.	223	Aurangabad
68.	121	Parsa	107.	224	Rafiganj
69.	125	Vaishali	108.	226	Sherghati
70.	126	Mahua	109.	227	Imamganj (SC)
71.	130	Patepur (SC)	110.	228	Barachatti (SC)

Contd.

TABLE 2.2: *Contd.*

S.No.	*AC ID*	*AC Name*	*S.No.*	*AC ID*	*AC Name*
111.	232	Belaganj	115.	240	Sikandra (SC)
112.	236	Hisua	116.	241	Jamui
113.	237	Nawada	117.	242	Jhajha
114.	238	Gobindpur	118.	243	Chakai

TABLE 2.3: SIZEABLE ACs (VOTER PERCENTAGE FROM 20 TO 29.9 PER CENT)

S.No.	*AC ID*	*AC Name*	*S.No.*	*AC ID*	*AC Name*
1.	2	Ramnagar (SC)	16.	62	Purnia
2.	3	Narkatiaganj	17.	63	Katihar
3.	5	Lauriya	18.	79	Gaura Bauram
4.	7	Chanpatia	19.	81	Alinagar
5.	8	Bettiah	20.	82	Darbhanga Rural
6.	10	Raxaul	21.	83	Darbhanga
7.	11	Sugauli	22.	95	Kanti
8.	12	Narkatia	23.	100	Barauli
9.	25	Parihar	24.	101	Gopalganj
10.	26	Sursand	25.	105	Siwan
11.	36	Madhubani	26.	108	Raghunathpur
12.	45	Chhatapur	27.	110	Barharia
13	46	Narpatganj	28.	158	Nathnagar
14	47	Raniganj (SC)	29.	172	Biharsharif
15	61	Dhamdaha	30.	230	Gaya Town

TABLE 2.4: NEAR MAJORITY ACs (VOTER PERCENTAGE FROM 30 TO 39.9 PER CENT)

S.No.	*AC ID*	*AC Name*	*S.No.*	*AC ID*	*AC Name*
1.	9	Sikta	7.	68	Barari
2.	21	Dhaka	8.	69	Korha (SC)
3.	27	Bajpatti	9.	86	Keoti
4.	35	Bisfi	10.	87	Jale
5.	48	Forbesganj	11.	156	Bhagalpur
6.	51	Sikti			

TABLE 2.5: MAJORITY ACs (VOTER PERCENTAGE FROM 40 PER CENT AND ABOVE)

S.No.	*AC ID*	*AC Name*	*S.No.*	*AC ID*	*AC Name*
1.	49	Araria	8.	57	Baisi
2.	50	Jokihat	9.	58	Kasba
3.	52	Bahadurganj	10.	64	Kadwa
4.	53	Thakurganj	11.	65	Balrampur
5.	54	Kishanganj	12.	66	Pranpur
6.	55	Kochadhaman	13.	67	Manihari (ST)
7.	56	Amour			

APPENDIX 3

Analysis of Assembly Constituencies of Gujarat

TABLE 3.1: ANALYSIS OF ACs AS PER PERCENTAGE OF MUSLIM VOTERS

S.No.	*Type of ACs*	*% of Muslim Voters*	*No. of ACs*
1.	Marginal	Upto 10	116
2.	Medium	From 10 to 20	54
3.	Sizeable	From 20 to 30	9
4.	Near Majority	From 30 to 40	3
5.	Majority	40 and above	0
TOTAL		All	182

TABLE 3.2: MEDIUM SIZE ACs (VOTER PERCENTAGE FROM 10 TO 19.9 PER CENT)

S.No.	*AC ID*	*AC Name*	*S.No.*	*AC ID*	*AC Name*
1.	12	Palanpur	16.	52	Jamalpur-Khadia
2.	16	Radhanpur	17.	53	Maninagar
3.	19	Sidhpur	18.	54	Danilimda (SC)
4.	24	Kadi (SC)	19.	56	Asarwa (SC)
5.	27	Himatnagar	20.	58	Dholka
6.	31	Modasa	21.	60	Dasada (SC)
7.	43	Vatva	22.	65	Morbi
8.	44	Ellisbridge	23.	75	Dhoraji
9.	45	Naranpura	24.	76	Kalavad (SC)
10.	46	Nikol	25.	77	Jamnagar Rural
11.	47	Naroda	26.	78	Jamnagar North
12.	48	Thakkarbapa Nagar	27.	81	Khambhalia
13.	49	Bapunagar	28.	86	Junagadh
14.	50	Amraiwadi	29.	89	Mangrol
15.	51	Dariapur	30.	93	Una

Contd.

TABLE 3.2: *Contd.*

S.No.	*AC ID*	*AC Name*	*S.No.*	*AC ID*	*AC Name*
31.	99	Mahuva	43.	126	Godhra
32.	104	Bhavnagar East	44.	141	Nirmali
33.	105	Bhavnagar West	45.	140	Dabhoi
34.	108	Khambhat	46.	141	Vadodara City (SC)
35.	109	Borsad	47.	142	Sayajigunj
36.	111	Umreth	48.	144	Raopura
37.	112	Anand	49.	147	Karjan
38.	113	Petlad	50.	154	Ankleshwar
39.	115	Matar	51.	156	Mangrol (ST)
40.	116	Nadiad	52.	159	Surat East
41.	118	Mahudha	53.	160	Surat North
42.	119	Thasra	54.	165	Majura

TABLE 3.3: SIZEABLE ACs (VOTER PERCENTAGE FROM 20 TO 29.9 PER CENT)

S.No.	*AC ID*	*AC Name*	*S.No.*	*AC ID*	*AC Name*
1.	1	Abdasa	6.	67	Wankaner
2.	2	Mandvi	7.	79	Jamnagar South
3.	3	Bhuj	8.	90	Somnath
4.	4	Anjar	9.	153	Bharuch
5.	11	Vadgam (SC)			

TABLE 3.4: NEAR MAJORITY ACs (VOTER PERCENTAGE FROM 30 TO 39.9 PER CENT)

S.No.	*AC ID*	*AC Name*
1.	150	Jambusar
2.	151	Vagra
3.	167	Surat West

APPENDIX 4

Analysis of Assembly Constituencies of Karnataka

TABLE 4.1: ANALYSIS OF ACs AS PER PERCENTAGE OF MUSLIM VOTERS

S.No.	*Type of ACs*	*% of Muslim Voters*	*No. of ACs*
1.	Marginal	Upto 10	142
2.	Medium	From 10 to 20	61
3.	Sizeable	From 20 to 30	18
4.	Near Majority	From 30 to 40	2
5.	Majority	40 and above	1
TOTAL		All	224

TABLE 4.2: MEDIUM SIZE ACs (VOTER PERCENTAGE FROM 10 TO 19.9 PER CENT)

S.No.	*AC ID*	*AC Name*	*S.No.*	*AC ID*	*AC Name*
1.	5	Kudachi (SC)	16.	43	Gulbarga Rural (SC)
2.	7	Hukkeri	17.	46	Aland
3.	9	Gokak	18.	48	Homnabad
4.	11	Belgaum Uttar	19.	51	Bhalki
5.	15	Kittur	20.	55	Manvi (ST)
6.	16	Bailhongal	21.	56	Devadurga (ST)
7.	21	Jamkhandi	22.	57	Lingsugur (SC)
8.	24	Bagalkot	23.	58	Sindhanur
9.	26	Muddebihal	24.	64	Koppal
10.	29	Babaleshwar	25.	65	Shirahatti (SC)
11.	33	Sindgi	26.	69	Navalgund
12.	35	Jevargi	27.	70	Kundgol
13.	36	Shorapur (ST)	28.	71	Dharwad
14.	39	Gurmitkal	29.	79	Bhatkal
15.	42	Chincholi (SC)	30.	81	Yellapur

Contd.

TABLE 4.2: *Contd.*

S.No.	*AC ID*	*AC Name*	*S.No.*	*AC ID*	*AC Name*
31.	84	Haveri (SC)	47.	145	Mulbagal (SC)
32.	86	Hirekerur	48.	152	Byatarayanapura
33.	87	Ranibennur	49.	154	Rajarajeshwari Nagar
34.	90	Vijayanagara	50.	156	Mahalakshmi Layout
35.	92	Siruguppa (ST)	51.	175	Bommanahalli
36.	94	Bellary City	52.	178	Hosakote
37.	95	Sandur (ST)	53.	183	Ramanagaram
38.	99	Chitradurga	54.	185	Channapatna
39.	104	Harapanahalli	55.	196	Hassan
40.	105	Harihar	56.	200	Belthangadi
41.	112	Bhadravati	57.	160	Mangalore City South
42.	115	Shikaripura	58.	204	Mangalore
43.	123	Sringeri	59.	206	Puttur
44.	136	Sira	60.	208	Madikeri
45.	139	Gauribidanur	61.	209	Virajpet
46.	143	Chintamani			

TABLE 4.3: SIZEABLE ACs (VOTER PERCENTAGE FROM 20 TO 29.9 PER CENT)

S.No.	*AC ID*	*AC Name*	*S.No.*	*AC ID*	*AC Name*
1.	12	Belgaum Dakshin	10.	74	Hubli-Dharwad West
2.	20	Terdal	11.	82	Hangal
3.	47	Basavakalyan	12.	83	Shiggaon
4.	50	Bidar	13.	93	Bellary (ST)
5.	54	Raichur	14.	106	Davanagere North
6.	61	Kanakagiri (SC)	15.	107	Davanagere South
7.	66	Gadag	16.	113	Shimoga
8.	72	Hubli-Dharwad East (SC)	17.	132	Tumkur City
9.	73	Hubli-Dharwad Central	18.	148	Kolar

TABLE 4.4: NEAR MAJORITY ACs (VOTER PERCENTAGE FROM 30 TO 39.9 PER CENT)

S.No.	*AC ID*	*AC Name*
1.	44	Gulbarga Dakshin
2.	45	Gulbarga Uttar

TABLE 4.5: MAJORITY ACs (VOTER PERCENTAGE FROM 40 PER CENT AND ABOVE)

S.No.	*AC ID*	*AC Name*
1.	30	Bijapur City

APPENDIX 5

Analysis of Assembly Constituencies of Rajasthan

TABLE 5.1: ANALYSIS OF ACs AS PER PERCENTAGE OF MUSLIM VOTERS

S.No.	*Type of ACs*	*% of Muslim Voters*	*No. of ACs*
1.	Marginal	Upto 10	156
2.	Medium	From 10 to 20	25
3.	Sizeable	From 20 to 30	15
4.	Near Majority	From 30 to 40	3
5.	Majority	40 and above	1
TOTAL		All	200

TABLE 5.2: MEDIUM SIZE ACs (VOTER PERCENTAGE FROM 10 TO 19.9 PER CENT)

S.No.	*AC ID*	*AC Name*	*S.No.*	*AC ID*	*AC Name*
1.	13	Bikaner West	14.	104	Masuda
2.	14	Bikaner East	15.	106	Ladnun
3.	20	Taranagar	16.	111	Merta
4.	24	Sujangarh	17.	118	Pali
5.	27	Jhunjhunu	18.	122	Phalodi
6.	33	Lachhmangarh	19.	123	Lohawat
7.	60	Kishangarh Bas	20.	137	Pachpadra
8.	79	Dholpur	21.	180	Bhilwara
9.	90	Gangapur	22.	189	Kota North
10.	92	Sawai Madhopur	23.	190	Kota South
11.	99	Pushkar	24.	191	Ladpura
12.	102	Nasirabad	25.	192	Ramganj Mandi
13.	103	Beawar			

TABLE 5.3: SIZEABLE ACs (VOTER PERCENTAGE FROM 20 TO 29.9 PER CENT)

S.No.	*AC ID*	*AC Name*	*S.No.*	*AC ID*	*AC Name*
1.	12	Khajuwala	9.	109	Nagaur
2.	22	Churu	10.	113	Makrana
3.	35	Sikar	11.	132	Jaisalmer
4.	65	Alwar Rural	12.	133	Pokaran
5.	68	Rajgarh Laxmangarh	13.	134	Sheo
6.	96	Tonk	14.	140	Chohtan
7.	97	Deoli Uniara	15.	153	Udaipur
8.	107	Deedwana			

TABLE 5.4: NEAR MAJORITY ACs (VOTER PERCENTAGE FROM 30 TO 39.9 PER CENT)

S.No.	*AC ID*	*AC Name*
1.	32	Fatehpur
2.	59	Tijara
3.	67	Ramgarh

TABLE 5.5: MAJORITY ACs (VOTER PERCENTAGE FROM 40 PER CENT AND ABOVE)

S.No.	*AC ID*	*AC Name*
1.	70	Kaman

APPENDIX 6

Analysis of Assembly Constituencies of Telangana

TABLE 6.1: ANALYSIS OF ACs AS PER PERCENTAGE OF MUSLIM VOTERS

S.No.	*Type of ACs*	*% of Muslim Voters*	*No. of ACs*
1.	Marginal	Upto 10	77
2.	Medium	From 10 to 20	23
3.	Sizeable	From 20 to 30	11
4.	Near Majority	From 30 to 40	5
5.	Majority	40 and above	3
TOTAL		All	119

TABLE 6.2: MEDIUM SIZE ACs (VOTER PERCENTAGE FROM 10 TO 19.9 PER CENT)

S.No.	*AC ID*	*AC Name*	*S.No.*	*AC ID*	*AC Name*
1.	9	Nirmal	13.	52	Serilingampally
2.	10	Mudhole	14.	55	Vicarabad (SC)
3.	13	Jukkal (SC)	15.	56	Tandur
4.	14	Banswada	16.	57	Musheerabad
5.	16	Kamareddy	17.	62	Sanathanagar
6.	20	Koratla	18.	69	Bahadurpura
7.	21	Jagtial	19.	75	Jadcheria
8.	26	Karimnagar	20.	92	Nalgonda
9.	36	Andole (SC)	21.	105	Warangal West
10.	43	Medchal	22.	106	Warangal East
11.	45	Quthbullapur	23.	112	Khammam
12.	46	Kukatpalle			

TABLE 6.3: SIZEABLE ACs (VOTER PERCENTAGE FROM 20 TO 29.9 PER CENT)

S.No.	AC ID	AC Name	S.No.	AC ID	AC Name
1.	7	Adilabad	7.	60	Khairatabad
2.	12	Bodhan	8.	64	Karwan
3.	38	Zahirabad (SC)	9.	67	Chandrayangutta
4.	39	Sangareddy	10.	68	Yakutpura
5.	51	Rajendranagar	11.	74	Mahbubnagar
6.	59	Amberpet			

TABLE 6.4: NEAR MAJORITY ACs (VOTER PERCENTAGE FROM 30 TO 39.9 PER CENT)

S.No.	AC ID	AC Name
1.	17	Nizamabad (Urban)
2.	58	Malakpet
3.	61	Jubilee Hills
4.	63	Nampally
5.	65	Goshamahal

TABLE 6.5: MAJORITY ACs (VOTER PERCENTAGE FROM 40 PER CENT AND ABOVE)

S.No.	AC ID	AC Name
1.	66	Charminar
2.	70	Secunderabad
3.	71	Secunderabad Cantt. (SC)

APPENDIX 7

Analysis of Assembly Constituencies of Uttar Pradesh

TABLE 7.1: ANALYSIS OF ACs AS PER PERCENTAGE OF MUSLIM VOTERS

S.No.	*Type of ACs*	*% of Muslim Voters*	*No. of ACs*
1.	Marginal	Upto 10	115
2.	Medium	From 10 to 20	142
3.	Sizeable	From 20 to 30	72
4.	Near Majority	From 30 to 40	44
5.	Majority	40 and above	30
TOTAL		All	403

TABLE 7.2: MEDIUM SIZE ACs (VOTER PERCENTAGE FROM 10 TO 19.9 PER CENT)

S.No.	*AC ID*	*AC Name*	*S.No.*	*AC ID*	*AC Name*
1.	31	Chandausi (SC)	17.	84	Mathura
2.	54	Moradnagar	18.	86	Etmadpur
3.	55	Sahibabad	19.	87	Agra Cantt. (SC)
4.	56	Ghaziabad	20.	89	Agra North
5.	57	Modi Nagar	21.	100	Kasganj
6.	61	Noida	22.	101	Amanpur
7.	62	Dadri	23.	106	Jalesar (SC)
8.	63	Jewar	24.	111	Gunnaur
9.	66	Syana	25.	112	Bisauli (SC)
10.	68	Debai	26.	117	Dataganj
11.	69	Shikarpur	27.	130	Bisalpur
12.	73	Atrauli	28.	133	Tilhar
13.	74	Chharra	29.	134	Powayan (SC)
14.	78	Hathras (SC)	30.	136	Dadraul
15.	79	Sadabad	31.	140	Sri Nagar (SC)
16.	81	Chhata	32.	141	Dhaurahra

Contd.

TABLE 7.2: *Contd.*

S.No.	*AC ID*	*AC Name*	*S.No.*	*AC ID*	*AC Name*
33.	143	Kasta (SC)	72.	244	Rampur Khas
34.	146	Sitapur	73.	245	Babaganj (SC)
35.	147	Hargaon (SC)	74.	246	Kunda
36.	152	Sidhauli (SC)	75.	247	Bishwavnathganj
37.	155	Shahabad	76.	249	Patti
38.	157	Gopamau (SC)	77.	251	Sirathu
39.	158	Sandi (SC)	78.	252	Manjhanpur (SC)
40.	159	Bilgram-Mallanwan	79.	253	Chail
41.	160	Balamau (SC)	80.	254	Phaphamau
42.	162	Bangermau	81.	255	Soraon (SC)
43.	163	Safipur (SC)	82.	256	Phulpur
44.	164	Mohan (SC)	83.	257	Pratappur
45.	165	Unnao	84.	258	Handia
46.	168	Malihabad (SC)	85.	262	Allahabad North
47.	169	Bakshi Ka Talab	86.	267	Ram Nagar
48.	170	Sarojini Nagar	87.	270	Dariyabad
49.	180	Rae Bareli	88.	273	Milkipur (SC)
50.	181	Salon (SC)	89.	275	Ayodhya
51.	185	Gauriganj	90.	276	Gosainganj
52.	189	Sadar	91.	277	Katehari
53.	190	Lambhua	92.	279	Alapur (SC)
54.	192	Kaimganj (SC)	93.	280	Jalalpur
55.	194	Farrukhabad	94.	281	Akbarpur
56.	195	Bhojpur	95.	182	Bankipur
57.	196	Chhibramau	96.	297	Katra Bazar
58.	198	Kannauj (SC)	97.	298	Colonelganj
59.	200	Etawah	98.	299	Tarabganj
60.	204	Auraiya (SC)	99.	300	Mankapur (SC)
61.	208	Bhognipur	100.	304	Bansi
62.	209	Bilhaur (SC)	101.	307	Harraiya
63.	212	Govindnagar	102.	309	Rudhauli
64.	215	Kidwai Nagar	103.	311	Mahadewa (SC)
65.	221	Orai (SC)	104.	314	Dhanghata (SC)
66.	223	Jhansi Nagar	105.	315	Pharenda
67.	235	Banda	106.	317	Siswa
68.	238	Jahanabad	107.	318	Maharajganj (SC)
69.	239	Bindki	108.	319	Paniara
70.	240	Fatehpur	109.	322	Gorakhpur Urban
71.	243	Khaga (SC)	110.	323	Gorakhpur Rural

Contd.

TABLE 7.2: *Contd.*

S.No.	*AC ID*	*AC Name*	*S.No.*	*AC ID*	*AC Name*
111.	330	Padrauna	127.	365	Shahganj
112.	331	Tamkuhi Raj	128.	366	Jaunpur
113.	334	Hata	129.	369	Machhlishahr (SC)
114.	337	Deoria	130.	371	Zafrabad
115.	338	Pathardeva	131.	373	Jakhanian (SC)
116.	339	Rampur Karkhana	132.	375	Ghazipur
117.	340	Bhatpar Rani	133.	378	Mohammadabad
118.	341	Salempur (SC)	134.	379	Zamania
119.	344	Gopalpur	135.	380	Mughalsarai
120.	345	Sagri	136.	382	Saiyadraja
121.	347	Azamgarh	137.	383	Chakia (SC)
122.	349	Phoolpur-Pawai	138.	387	Rohaniya
123.	350	Didarganj	139.	392	Bhadohi
124.	352	Mehnagar (SC)	140.	396	Mirzapur
125.	354	Ghosi	141.	193	Amritpur
126.	355	Muhammadabad-Gohna (SC)	142.	308	Kaptanganj

TABLE 7.3: SIZEABLE ACs (VOTER PERCENTAGE FROM 20 TO 29.9 PER CENT)

S.No.	*AC ID*	*AC Name*	*S.No.*	*AC ID*	*AC Name*
1.	6	Rampur Maniharan (SC)	17.	122	Faridpur (SC)
2.	21	Nehtaur (SC)	18.	123	Bithari Chainpur
3.	45	Hastinapur (SC)	19.	126	Aonla
4.	50	Chhaprauli	20.	127	Pilibhit
5.	51	Baraut	21.	128	Barkhera
6.	52	Baghpat	22.	129	Puranpur (SC)
7.	59	Hapur (SC)	23.	135	Shahjahanpur
8.	64	Sikandrabad	24.	138	Nighasan
9.	67	Anupshahr	25.	139	Gola Gokrannath
10.	70	Khurja (SC)	26.	142	Lakhimpur
11.	75	Koil	27.	144	Mohammdi
12.	102	Patiyali	28.	148	Laharpur
13.	113	Sahaswan	29.	149	Biswan
14.	114	Bilsi	30.	150	Sevata
15.	115	Badaun	31.	151	Mahmoodabad
16.	116	Shekhupur	32.	161	Sandila

Contd.

TABLE 7.3: *Contd.*

S.No.	*AC ID*	*AC Name*	*S.No.*	*AC ID*	*AC Name*
33.	171	Lucknow West	53.	284	Matera
34.	172	Lucknow North	54.	285	Mahasi
35.	173	Lucknow East	55.	290	Shrawasti
36.	175	Lucknow Cantt	56.	295	Mehnaun
37.	178	Tiloi	57.	296	Gonda
38.	184	Jagdishpur (SC)	58.	303	Kapilvastu (SC)
39.	187	Isauli	59.	306	Domariyaganj
40.	188	Sultanpur	60.	310	Basti Sadar
41.	211	Kalyanpur	61.	312	Menhdawal
42.	213	Sishamau	62.	313	Khalilabad
43.	214	Arya Nagar	63.	316	Nautanwa
44.	216	Kanpur Cantt	64.	329	Khadda
45.	248	Pratapgarh	65.	332	Fazilnagar
46.	261	Allahabad West	66.	333	Kushinagar
47.	263	Allahabad South	67.	346	Mubarkpur
48.	266	Kursi	68.	348	Nizamabad
49.	268	Barabanki	69.	356	Mau
50.	269	Zaidpur (SC)	70.	388	Varanasi North
51.	272	Haidergarh (SC)	71.	145	Maholi
52.	274	Bikapur	72.	176	Mohanlalganj (SC)

TABLE 7.4: NEAR MAJORITY ACs (VOTER PERCENTAGE FROM 30 TO 39.9 PER CENT)

S.No.	*AC ID*	*AC Name*	*S.No.*	*AC ID*	*AC Name*
1.	5	Deoband	14.	39	Dhanaura (SC)
2.	7	Gangoh	15.	42	Hasanpur
3.	9	Thana Bhawan	16.	43	Siwalkhas
4.	10	Shamli	17.	44	Sardhana
5.	11	Budhana	18.	46	Kithore
6.	12	Charthawal	19.	47	Meerut Cantt.
7.	14	Muzaffar Nagar	20.	48	Meerut
8.	15	Khatauli	21.	49	Meerut South
9.	16	Meerapur	22.	53	Loni
10.	22	Bijnor	23.	60	Garhmukteshwar
11.	24	Noorpur	24.	65	Bulandshahr
12.	36	Bilaspur	25.	97	Firozabad
13.	38	Milak (SC)	26.	118	Baheri

Contd.

TABLE 7.4: *Contd.*

S.No.	*AC ID*	*AC Name*	*S.No.*	*AC ID*	*AC Name*
27.	119	Meerganj	36.	288	Kaiserganj
28.	121	Nawabganj	37.	291	Tulsipur
29.	124	Bareilly	38.	292	Gainsari
30.	125	Bareilly Cantt	39.	294	Balrampur (SC)
31.	131	Katra	40.	301	Gaura
32.	174	Lucknow Central	41.	305	Itwa
33.	278	Tanda	42.	389	Varanasi South
34.	282	Balha (SC)	43.	390	Varanasi Cantt
35.	286	Bahraich	44.	58	Dhaulana

TABLE 7.5: MAJORITY ACs (VOTER PERCENTAGE FROM 40 PER CENT AND ABOVE)

S.No.	*AC ID*	*AC Name*	*S.No.*	*AC ID*	*AC Name*
1.	1	Behat	16.	29	Kundarki
2.	2	Nakur	17.	30	Bilari
3.	3	Saharanpur Nagar	18.	32	Asmoli
4.	4	Saharanpur	19.	33	Sambhal
5.	8	Kairana	20.	34	Suar
6.	13	Purqazi (SC)	21.	35	Chamraua
7.	17	Najibabad	22.	37	Rampur
8.	18	Nagina (SC)	23.	40	Naugawan Sadat
9.	19	Barhapur	24.	41	Amroha
10.	20	Dhampur	25.	76	Aligarh
11.	23	Chandpur	26.	120	Bhojipura
12.	25	Kanth	27.	283	Nanapara
13.	26	Thakurdwara	28.	289	Bhinga
14.	27	Moradabad Rural	29.	293	Utraula
15.	28	Moradabad Nagar	30.	302	Shohratgarh

APPENDIX 8

Analysis of Assembly Constituencies of West Bengal

TABLE 8.1: ANALYSIS OF ACs AS PER PERCENTAGE OF MUSLIM VOTERS

S.No.	*Type of ACs*	*% of Muslim Voters*	*No. of ACs*
1.	Marginal	Upto 10	80
2.	Medium	From 10 to 20	85
3.	Sizeable	From 20 to 30	39
4.	Near Majority	From 30 to 40	29
5.	Majority	40 and above	61
TOTAL		All	294

TABLE 8.2: MEDIUM SIZE ACs (VOTER PERCENTAGE FROM 10 TO 19.9 PER CENT)

S.No.	*AC ID*	*AC Name*	*S.No.*	*AC ID*	*AC Name*
1.	3	Coochbehar Uttar (SC)	17.	87	Ranaghat Uttar Paschim
2.	4	Coochbehar Dakshin	18.	89	Ranaghat Uttar Purba (SC)
3.	9	Tufanganj	19.	94	Bagda (SC)
4.	13	Falakata (SC)	20.	95	Bangaon Uttar (SC)
5.	15	Dhupguri (SC)	21.	96	Bangaon Dakshin (SC)
6.	17	Jalpaiguri (SC)	22.	97	Gaighata (SC)
7.	18	Rajganj (SC)	23.	99	Baduria
8.	20	Mal (St)	24.	100	Habra
9.	27	Phansidewa (ST)	25.	105	Bhatpara
10.	34	Kaliaganj (SC)	26.	106	Jagatdal
11.	35	Raiganj	27.	108	Barrackpur
12.	40	Tapan (ST)	28.	117	Rajarhat Gopalpur
13.	50	Maldaha (SC)	29.	119	Barasat
14.	78	Tehatta	30.	127	Gosaba (SC)
15.	84	Nabadwip	31.	131	Kakdwip
16.	86	Santipur	32.	132	Sagar

Contd.

TABLE 8.2: *Contd.*

S.No.	*AC ID*	*AC Name*	*S.No.*	*AC ID*	*AC Name*
33.	143	Diamond Harbour	60.	211	Chandipur
34.	147	Sonarpur Dakshin	61.	216	Kanthi Dakshin
35.	151	Sonarpur Uttar	62.	218	Egra
36.	164	Beleghata	63.	224	Kharagpur Sadar
37.	169	Bally	64.	227	Pingla
38.	171	Howrah Madhya	65.	228	Kharagpur
39.	173	Howrah Dakshin	66.	232	Chandrakona (SC)
40.	182	Udaynarayanpur	67.	233	Garbeta
41.	184	Domjur	68.	234	Salboni
42.	186	Sreerampur	69.	236	Medinipur
43.	187	Champdani	70.	256	Phulpur
44.	188	Singur	71.	245	Para (SC)
45.	189	Chandannagar	72.	255	Bishnupur
46.	191	Balagarh (SC)	73.	257	Indus (SC)
47.	193	Saptagram	74.	258	Sonamukhi (SC)
48.	194	Chanditala	75.	260	Bardhaman Dakshin
49.	196	Haripal	76.	262	Jamalpur (SC)
50.	197	Dhanekhali (SC)	77.	264	Kalna (SC)
51.	198	Tarakeswar	78.	265	Memari
52.	199	Pursurah	79.	266	Bardhaman Uttar (SC)
53.	201	Goghat (SC)	80.	270	Katwa
54.	202	Khanakul	81.	274	Galsi (SC)
55.	203	Tamluk	82.	275	Pandabeswar
56.	206	Moyna	83.	279	Jamuria
57.	207	Nandakumar	84.	280	Asansol Dakshin
58.	208	Mahisadal	85.	282	Kulti
59.	209	Haldia (SC)			

TABLE 8.3: SIZEABLE ACs (VOTER PERCENTAGE FROM 20 TO 29.9 PER CENT)

S.No.	*AC ID*	*AC Name*	*S.No.*	*AC ID*	*AC Name*
1.	6	Rampur Maniharan (SC)	7.	59	Hapur (SC)
2.	21	Nehtaur (SC)	8.	64	Sikandrabad
3.	45	Hastinapur (SC)	9.	67	Anupshahr
4.	50	Chhaprauli	10.	70	Khurja (SC)
5.	51	Baraut	11.	75	Koil
6.	52	Baghpat	12.	102	Patiyali

Contd.

TABLE 8.3: *Contd.*

S.No.	*AC ID*	*AC Name*	*S.No.*	*AC ID*	*AC Name*
13.	113	Sahaswan	27.	219	Dantan
14.	114	Bilsi	28.	235	Keshpur (SC)
15.	115	Badaun	29.	259	Khandaghosh (SC)
16.	116	Shekhupur	30.	261	Raina (SC)
17.	122	Faridpur (SC)	31.	267	Bhatar
18.	123	Bithari Chainpur	32.	268	Purbasthali Dakshin
19.	126	Aonla	33.	273	Ausgram (SC)
20.	181	Amta	34.	281	Asansol Uttar
21.	192	Pandua	35.	284	Dubrajpur (SC)
22.	195	Jangipara	36.	285	Suri
23.	200	Arambag (SC)	37.	288	Labpur
24.	204	Panskura Purba	38.	290	Mayureswar
25.	205	Panskura Paschim	39.	291	Rampurhat
26.	210	Nandigram			

TABLE 8.4: NEAR MAJORITY ACs (VOTER PERCENTAGE FROM 30 TO 39.9 PER CENT)

S.No.	*AC ID*	*AC Name*	*S.No.*	*AC ID*	*AC Name*
1.	6	Sitai (SC)	16.	145	Satgachhia
2.	7	Dinhata	17.	155	Maheshtala
3.	37	Kushmundi (SC)	18.	156	Budge Budge
4.	38	Kumarganj	19.	158	Kolkata Port
5.	42	Harirampur	20.	177	Uluberia Uttar (SC)
6.	51	English Bazar	21.	180	Bagnan
7.	67	Burwan (SC)	22.	183	Jagatballavpur
8.	71	Beldanga	23.	263	Monteswar
9.	118	Madhyamgram	24.	269	Purbasthali Uttar
10.	128	Basanti (SC)	25.	271	Ketugram
11.	129	Kultali (SC)	26.	272	Mangalkot
12.	133	Kulpi	27.	286	Bolpur
13.	135	Mandirbazar (SC)	28.	287	Nanoor (SC)
14.	138	Canning Paschim (SC)	29.	289	Sainthia (SC)
15.	144	Falta			

TABLE 8.5: MAJORITY ACs (VOTER PERCENTAGE FROM 40 PER CENT AND ABOVE)

S.No.	*AC ID*	*AC Name*	*S.No.*	*AC ID*	*AC Name*
1.	28	Chopra	32.	73	Hariharpara
2.	29	Islampur	33.	74	Naoda
3.	30	Goalpokhar	34.	75	Domkal
4.	31	Chakulia	35.	76	Jalangi
5.	32	Karandighi	36.	77	Karimpur
6.	33	Hemtabad (SC)	37.	79	Palashipara
7.	36	Itahar	38.	80	Kaliganj
8.	45	Chanchal	39.	81	Nakashipara
9.	46	Harish Chandrapur	40.	82	Chapra
10.	47	Malatipur	41.	98	Swarupnagar (SC)
11.	48	Ratua	42.	102	Amdanga
12.	49	Manikchak	43.	120	Deganga
13.	52	Mothabari	44.	121	Haroa
14.	53	Sujapur	45.	122	Minakhan (SC)
15.	54	Baishnab Nagar	46.	124	Basirhat Dakshin
16.	55	Farakka	47.	125	Basirhat Uttar
17.	56	Samserganj	48.	136	Jaynagar (SC)
18.	57	Suti	49.	137	Baruipur Purba (SC)
19.	58	Jangipur	50.	139	Canning Purba
20.	59	Raghunathganj	51.	141	Magrahat Purba (SC)
21.	60	Sagardighi	52.	142	Magrahat Paschim
22.	61	Lalgola	53.	148	Bhangar
23.	62	Bhagabangola	54.	157	Metiaburuz
24.	63	Raninagar	55.	161	Ballygunge
25.	64	Murshidabad	56.	174	Sankrail (SC)
26.	65	Nabagram (SC)	57.	175	Panchla
27.	66	Khargram (SC)	58.	176	Uluberia Purba
28.	68	Kandi	59.	292	Hansan
29.	69	Bharatpur	60.	293	Nalhati
30.	70	Rejinagar	61.	294	Murarai
31.	72	Baharampur			

Some Important Works Referred

Ahmed, Hilal, *Siyasi Muslims: A Story of Political Islams in India*, Penguin Random House India, Gurgaon, 2019.

Alam, Javeed, *Who Wants Democracy?*, Orient Black, Delhi, 2006.

Ambedkar, B.R., *Thoughts on Pakistan*, Nation Press, New Delhi, 2023.

Ambedkar, B.R., *Annihilation of Caste*, unpublished Draft.

Ansari, Iqbal A., *Political Representation of Muslims in India: 1952-2004*, Manak Publications, New Delhi.

Ashraf, K.M., *An Overview of Indian Muslim Politics (1920-1947)*, Manak Publications, New Delhi, 2001.

Beg, S.L., *Islam: Caste and Dalit-Muslim Relations*, Navyug Books International, Delhi, 2012.

Dinesh Goswami Committee on Electoral Reforms, 1990.

Ghai, Yash, *Public Participation and Minorities*, MRG International, London, 2001.

Granville, Austin, *The Constitution: Cornerstone of a Nation*, Oxford University Press, New Delhi, 2016.

Hasan, Zoya, E. Sridharan, and R. Sudarshans (eds.), *India's Living Constitution: Ideas, Practices and Controversies*, Permanent Black, New Delhi.

Jamil, Javed, *Muslim Vision of Secular India: Destination and Roadmap*, Mission Publications, New Delhi, 2016.

Jaffrelot, Christophe, Thomas Blom Hansen and Angana P. Chatterji (eds.), *Majoritasian State: How Hindu Nationalism is Changing India*, Harper Collins, New Delhi, 2019.

Khalidi, Omar, *Indian Muslims Since Independence*, Vikas Publishing House, New Delhi, 1995.

Lloyd and Susanne Rudolph, *In Pursuit of Laxmi: The Political Economy of the Indian State*, University of Chicago Press, Chicago, 1987.

National Commission to Review the Working of the Constitution (NCRWC) Report, 2002.

Rahman, Abdur, *Denial and Deprivation: Indian Muslims after the Sachar Committee and Ranganath Mishra Commission Reports*, Manohar, New Delhi, 2019.

——, *Sachar Ki Sifarishein* (Hindi), Kashyap Publication, Delhi, 2012.

Rao, B. Shiva, *The Framing of India's Constitution: Select Documents*, vol. II, Indian Institute of Public Administration, New Delhi, 1968.

Reddy, Agarala Easwara and D. Sundar Ram (eds.), *Electoral Reforms in India*, Uppal Publishing House, New Delhi, 1992.

Report of the National Commission for Religious and Linguistic Minorities (hereafter, the Ranganath Mishra Commission Report), Ministry of SJE, New Delhi, 2007.

Roy, Himanshu and Mahendra Prasad Singh, *Indian Political System*, Pearson, Noida, 2018.

Roy, Prannoy, and Drab R. Sopariwala, *The Verdict: Decoding India's Elections*, Penguin Random House, India, Gurgaon, 2019.

Singh, H.D. *543 Faces of India: Guide to 543 Parliamentary Constituencies*, Newsmen Publication, New Delhi, 1996.

Singh, L.P., *Electoral Reforms: Problems and Suggested Solutions*, Uppal, New Delhi, 1986.

Singh, V.B. and Shankar Bose, *State Elections in India: Data Handbook on Vidhan Sabha Elections 1952-85* (vols. 1 to 5), Sage, New Delhi, 1988.

Social, Economic and Educational Status of the Muslims of India: A Report (hereafter, Sachar Committee Report), PM's HLC, Cabinet Secretariat, GoI, New Delhi, 2006.

The Congress Scheme for a Communal Settlement, 28 October 1931, The Indian Round Table Conference (Second Edition), Proceedings of the Minorities Committees, Appendix 1.

Tiwari, R.K., *Political Parties, Party Manifestos and Elections in India, 1909-2014*, Routledge, New Delhi, 2019.

V.M. Tarkunde, *Towards Political Reforms*, 1975, Licchavi Lyceum (https://licchavilyceum.com).

Wahab, Ghazala, *Born a Muslim: Some Truths About Islam in India*, Aleph Book Company, Delhi, 2021.

Index

16th parliamentary elections (2014): Muslim elected members 50
1947 Partition, Indian Muslims, position of 24-6: PR system 25-6; Sardar Hukum Singh, in the CAD 25
1947 partition, repercussions of: Muslims, participation in democratic processes 17
1971: Muslim voting percentage within the community 16

Aam Aadmi Party (AAP) 233, 258: emerged from Anna Hazare's Movement India Against Corruption 258; party published a 'Vision Document' 258-9
Aam Aadmi Party (AAP), as a political alternative for Muslims 258-62: 2013, Delhi, Muslim-dominated areas 259; 2015, Muslims of Delhi, felt AAP was a major force 259; 2020, Delhi assembly elections 260; anti-CAA movement at its peak in Shaheen Bagh, Delhi 260-1; dual approach on issues related to Muslims and Hindus 261; February 2020, Delhi communal riots broke out 260; JIH and AIMMM issued letters in support of AAP 259
Adverse gerrymandering of constituencies 186-8
Ahmed, Hilal 234-5
Ajlaf (backward castes) Muslims 226, 228-9, 230, 239, 250
Alam, Aftab 239
Alam, Javeed 15-16
All India Muslim Personal Law Board (AIMPLB) 229
All India Majlis-e-Ittehadul Muslimeen (AIMIM) 55, 61-2, 65, 92, 107, 114, 117, 126, 138-9, 140, 148-50, 155, 158, 166, 169, 171, 201, 275, 280
All India Muslim Majlis-e-Mushawarat (AIMMM) 235, 259, 283: 1967, intervened in electoral politics as a Muslim representative body 284-5; 2019, decided not to issue any election statement 285; nine-point People's Manifesto 284
All India United Democratic Front (AIUDF) 59, 60, 61, 63, 92, 110-11, 169, 171, 205, 222, 280, 283
All-representative government 315
Andhra Pradesh Assembly, share of Muslims 106-8
Ansari, Khalid Anis 230, 251
Appeasement of minorities 174
Appeasement of the majority 174, 265
Arzal (degraded) Muslims 226, 228-9, 230, 239, 250
Ashraf and Pasmanda brand of politics, elements of 253-4: *Dalit-Pichda ek samaan, Hindu ho ya Musalman* 254; majoritarian and minoritarian fundamentalism, symbiotic nature of 254
Ashraf Muslims 490, 226, 228-30, 233, 239, 243, 250-7, 293

Assam Assembly, share of Muslims 108-11
Attempt to disenfranchise Muslims 220-4: BJP's anti-Muslim policies 221-2; Citizenship Amendment Act (CAA) 223; every caste/community is used as a vote bank by one or other party 221; Jim Crow system of mass disenfranchisement 220-1; NRC combined with CAA 222; right-wing elements, trying hard to disenfranchise Muslims 224
Austin, Granville 24, 45
Awami Vikas Party (Maharashtra) 280
Azad, Maulana Abul Kalam 14, 31, 286, 303: Composite Nationalism 303

Backward Classes (BC), proportion of 49
Baharampur: Revolutionary Socialist Party (RSP) 77
Bihar Assembly, share of Muslims 111-14
BJP's attitude towards Muslims 196-200: 1952 to 2004, BJP gave only 0.82 per cent nominations to Muslims 197; 2014 and 2019, not have a single Muslim MP 197; assembly elections, Muslim share in 197-8; BJP's rise results in limited political space for Muslims 198; cause split in Muslim votes 203; deep hatred for the religious minorities, against their political empowerment 197; ideological foundations, similar lines of the Nazi ideology advocated by Adolf Hitler 197; majoritarian politics, Congress and other secular parties shy away from giving tickets to Muslim candidates 199; minority-friendly parties have re-oriented themselves 199-200; nominated hardly any Muslims in the parliamentary and assembly elections 197; party's policy, ideology of 'Hindu nationalism' 196; politics of communalism and majoritarian nationalism to appeal Hindus 198-9
BJP's election campaign, Muslims' vote share in a constituency 170-1
BJP's exclusionary politics 94, 97-8, 308
Bunch of Thoughts 197

Captive Muslim votes 264
Casteism among Muslims 257
Chhattisgarh Assembly, share of Muslims 114-15
Christians, not allowed to contest LS seats reserved for SCs 94
Communal targeting 17
Communal Violence Bill 310
Community: mental and emotional churn within 264-5; political empowerment in states 171
Constituent Assembly Debates (CAD), rights of minorities 35-40: 27 and 28 August 1947, debate on the Report on Minority Rights 35; adoption of PR system by STV 38-9; B. Pocker Sahib Bahadur, view on 36; Dr. Ambedkar, demanded reservation for the SCs 39; extreme majoritarian view 35; G.B. Pant, extreme majoritarian view 35-6; idea of One Nation, Special Provision for Minorities 36-7; K.T. Shah favoured PR with STV 39; K.T.M. Ahmed Ibrahim, view on 37; Kazi Syed Karimuddin, view on 37;

Khaliquzzaman, view on 36; Mahavir Tyagi, extreme majoritarian view 35-6; moderate views 35; Pocker-Patel polarized perspective 37; Sardar Patel, extreme majoritarian view 35-6; Syed Kazi Karimuddin opposed the FPTP system 39; variant of the PR system with Single Transferable Vote (STV) or Non-Transferable Vote (SNTV) 38

Constituent Assembly Debates (CAD) 24, 35-40: rights of minorities 35-40

Constituent Assembly of India 24

Constitution (SC) Order, 1950 95, 182: Delimitation Commission 182; ST, category of 182

Constitution of India, minority representation 30-5: 16 May 1946, Cabinet Mission Plan 30; 27 and 28 August 1947, Report on Minority Rights discussed in Constituent Assembly 34; 27 July 1947, sub-committee report 33; 29 January 1947, Advisory Committee 30; 8 August 1947, Advisory Committee made recommendations in its report 34; Anglo-Indians, demanded a special treatment 32; Articles 292 and 294, 'Special Provisions Relating to Minorities' 34-5; H.C. Mookerjee (1877-1956), chairman of the sub-committee 31; Maulana Abul Kalam Azad, member of the Constituent Assembly 31; Muslims, strong support for reservation 32; reservation for the Scheduled Castes demanded 31; Sardar Patel, Chairman of the Advisory Committee 30-1; Sikh leaders, demanded reservation for the Sikh community 31; Sub-committee on Minorities 31; sub-committee, rejected reservation of seats for minorities in cabinets 33

CPI(M) 54-6, 58, 60-1, 65, 81-2, 84, 92, 129, 135, 143, 144, 161-4, 169, 205, 240

Current political condition 293-5: 17th Lok Sabha (2019-24), share of Muslim MPs 293; 1984 to 2009, Lok Sabha, share of Muslim MPs 294; 2013-15, assembly elections, comparison with previous elections 294; 2014, Lok Sabha, share of Muslim MPs 293-4; aggressive Hindutva politics of the BJP 294; BJP raking up anti-Muslim issues 295; electoral marginalization due to political deprivation and political exclusion 294

Dalit-Muslim unity 224-31: 2014 onwards, vigilante mobs lynched Muslims and killed Dalits 226; Asaduddin Owaisi, trying to bring them together 227; Ashraf Muslims seem to be ready to forge an alliance with Dalits 226; building a prosperous, egalitarian and casteist-free India 229; Dalit Muslim Ekta Manch 227; Dalits, never considered part of the *Sanatan Dharma* 228; efforts to bring them together on common platforms 226; hardly advanced beyond mere sloganeering or at best strategic political alliances 227; Jamaat-e-Islami, political wing of 227; militant Hindutva, often goes against the interests of the marginalized castes 224;

Namashudra (Dalit) and Muslims, political alliance formed between 227; need for a broad-based unity 227; poor representation of Muslims and weak leadership in Dalits 224-5; *Thoughts on Pakistan* 226-7
Delhi Assembly, share of Muslims 115-17
Delimitation Commission 94, 96, 166, 168, 181, 182, 183, 185, 186, 187, 291, 309: biased officials of 309
Democracy 13-17, 24, 35, 37-8, 59, 84, 97, 98, 100, 129, 174-6, 180, 190-1, 207, 209, 212, 214, 238, 242, 247, 250, 258, 269, 272, 274, 275, 276, 291, 292, 292-3, 296, 298, 304-7, 310-14: legal and constitutional characteristics of 313: Gandhi's views 14
Democratic India 14, 45, 242: Nehru's views 14
Democratic institutions 14, 17, 96, 176, 184, 250, 312, 313
Dr. Ambedkar 31, 32, 39, 226-7, 297, 305-7: 25 November 1949, speech in the Constituent Assembly 305; views on democracy 305
Draft Constitution, legislative provisions, 40-1: 11 May 1949, Advisory Committee met to take up H.C. Mookerjee's resolution 41; abolition of reservation 44; Anglo-Indians under Frank Anthony 45; Communist Party's organ *People's Age* on the PR system 43; Homi Mody, dissuaded from demanding reservation for the Parsi community 45; Hukum Singh's view 44; Mazhabi Sikhs (Sikh Scheduled Castes) 45; population based quota of seats under joint electorate for minorities 45; PR was a great system to ensure fair representation of each group 43-4; presence of minority groups in Parliament 41; provision of reserved seats, considered as a temporary compromise 44; Sikh Scheduled Castes 41-2; Tajamul Hussain, opposed the insertion of word 'minority' in the Constitution 43

Economic democracy 14
Election Commission of India (ECI) 15, 98, 174, 176-9, 181, 216-17, 290-1, 314
Election results, review of 192-3: UCHs, disproportionally represented at the cost of the OBCs, Muslims and other minorities 192
Electoral democracy, affirmative action in 193: adopted system, chances of 193; fixed quota 193; fixed quota of seats, provision of 193
Electoral reforms, reports on 176-80 Mehmoodur Rahman Committee (MRC) report 179; NCRWC's Consultation paper on 'Review of Election Law', Processes and Reform Options 177-8; post Sachar Evaluation Committee 179; socio-economic conditions of Muslims in various states 179
Elite class 15

Fatwa 235, 236, 242, 284, 286-7
First General Elections (1952): Muslim elected members 50
Functioned democracy 13

Gandhi, Mahatma 14, 25, 26, 28, 29, 46, 55, 154, 185, 186, 188, 210-11, 261, 287
Golwalkar, M.S. 196
Government of India Act, 1935 29, 34
Gujarat Assembly, share of Muslims 117-21

Haryana Assembly, share of Muslims 121-3
Hashmi, Shabnam 262
Hawari, Waqar 254
High castes 15
Hindu khatre mein hain (Hindus are in danger!) 97
Homogeneous group 239
Hussain, Tajamul 38, 40, 43, 54, 59, 61, 309

India, need for inclusive democracy 292-3: Preamble of the Constitution 292; secular democracy 292
Indian democracy 14-15, 17, 24, 84, 175, 176, 197, 199, 292
Indian democracy, non-inclusive functioning of 175-6: International Covenant on Civil and Political Rights (ICCPR) 175; minorities and OBCs, deprived of the political right to be represented proportionately 175; Muslim candidates, difficult to get elected from mixed constituencies 175-6
Indian National Congress during the 1920s and 1930s 24
Indian political scenario: variants of PR, or mixed PR system 191
Indian Secular Front (West Bengal) 280
Indian Union Muslim League (IUML) 59, 60, 61, 65, 92, 125, 130, 131, 144, 145, 147, 166, 169, 171, 280
Institutions of democracy 15: checks and balances 15; Comptroller and Auditor General (CAG) 15; Election Commission of India (ECI) 15; free press 15; legislative wings 15; public education 15; Supreme Court (SC) 15; universal adult suffrage 15
International Covenant on Civil and Political Rights (ICCPR) 19-20, 175
Ittehad-e-Millat Council (IMC) 280

Jaffrelot, Christophe 99, 174, 199, 244, 249, 267
Jamaat-e-Islami Hind (JIH) 229, 259, 285
Jamiat Ulema-e-Hind (JUH) 229, 253, 283, 285, 286
Janta Party 54, 84, 112, 125, 133, 152, 285, 287
Janata Party (Secular) (JNPS) 54-5
Jharkhand Assembly, share of Muslims 123-4
Joint electorates 25, 28, 33, 34, 37, 38, 45

Kaka Kalelkar Commission 257
Karnataka Assembly, share of Muslims 124-8
Kerala Assembly, share of Muslims 128-31
Khalidi, Omar: advice to Muslims on overcoming political deprivation 272

Lok Sabha: average Muslim representation in 49; seats, Muslim influence in 81-2
Lok Sabha elections 51-62: 15th General Elections of 2009, Muslim elected members 58-60;

16th General Elections (2014), Muslim elected members 60-1; 17th General Elections (2019), Muslim elected members 61-2; 1957 General Elections, Muslim elected members 53-4; BJP under Atal Behari Vajpayee, Muslim candidates nominated 57-8; first General Elections, Muslim elected members 51-2; seventh General Elections (1980), Muslim elected members 54-5; eighth General Elections (1984), Muslim elected members 55-6

Love Jihad 97, 249, 295

Low representation in state assemblies, reasons for 165-9: demographic distribution of voters 165-6; fielding non-Muslim candidates from Muslim-dominated constituencies 168-9; low nomination by mainstream parties 166-7; Muslim votes, division of 168; Muslim-dominated constituencies for SCs, reservation of 167-8

Madhya Pradesh Assembly, share of Muslims 132-4

Madhya Pradesh, Muslim-dominated constituencies 136-7

Maharashtra Assembly, share of Muslims 137-40: 2019, Muslim MLAs share 139; AIMIM 138-40; low political representation, reasons for 140; Muslim-dominated constituencies 140-1; Vanchit Bahujan Aghadi (VBA) 139

Maitra, L.K. 40

Majoritarian State: How Hindu Nationalism is Changing India 99, 199, 267

Mandal Commission 244, 245, 257, 296

Mehmoodur Rahman Committee (MRC) report 101, 179: condition of the Muslim community in the state 101

Micro-level training 312

Millat Party 280

Minority political representation, United Nation's concern 19-22: Article 27 of the ICCPR 20; effective participation of minorities, mechanism for 20; European Centre for minorities issues, mechanisms of effective participation 21; European countries facilitates minority representation 21; International Covenant on Civil and Political Rights (ICCPR) 19-20; Liberal Declaration on the Rights of Minorities (2000) 21; national minorities, effective participation, European concern 21; pluralistic and genuinely democratic society, need for 19; Proportional Representation, electoral system of 21-2; provisions to ensure a proper political participation 19; UN Declaration on the Right of Persons Belonging to National or Ethnic, Religious and Linguistic Minorities 20

Missing Muslim names from voter lists 214-20: All India Milli Council (Mumbai), deleted from voter lists in Muslim-dominated pockets 217; Centre for Research and Debates in Development Policy (CRDDP) 215; citizen facility centres, documents, eligibility and useful forms, etc. 219-20; deleting names in bulk, reduces the strength of Muslim voters 214; district election offices across India, inadequate manpower 218; ECI violated its own SOP 216-27; H.D. Deve Gowda, petition alleging about Muslim voters' name being dropped 216; Hebbal AC in Bangalore, names deleted from the draft list 216; illiteracy among the Muslims and Dalits 218-19; Khalid Saifullah, worked for the enrolment of the missing voters 214-15; Mission 2019, no voter Left Behind 215; misuse of Form 7 219; Mumbra-Kalwa (149) AC, Maharashtra, voter names deleted from electoral rolls 218; Standard Operating Procedure (SOP) of the ECI 216; Systematic Voters' Education and Electoral Participations (SVEEP) programme 220

Mixed-Member PR (MMP) 190: compensatory regional or national party-list PR election 190; FPTP/majoritarian election 190

Mookerjee, H.C. 40

Mujtaba, Syed Ali 81-2

Muslim community 13, 16, 18, 24, 42, 81, 100, 101, 120, 121, 147, 167, 179, 182-3, 185, 195-6, 206, 211, 213-14, 226, 228, 230, 233, 236, 241-2, 250, 251, 253, 256, 258, 264, 273, 290, 307, 309

Muslim legislators, performance of 269-72: 2 per cent questions raised in Lok Sabha about Muslim issues 270; education, safety, security and issues of ensuring justice, don't get much importance 270; failed in their basic duty to protect the interest of Muslims 269; many crucial occasions, Muslim MPs have remained silent 270-1; parliamentary debate on the Triple Talaq Bill, Muslim MPs remained silent 270-1; questions about Hajj, biggest share 270; number of questions they ask in legislative bodies 269; questions regarding Muslim education 270; September 2013, Muzaffarnagar riots, Muslim MPs remained silent 271

Muslim masses 25, 208, 210, 213, 241, 275, 310: greater faith in democracy and bigger participation in democratic process 311; strengths 310; weaknesses 311

Muslim MLAs, mostly from regional parties 169-70

Muslim Munnetra Kazhagam (MMK) 276, 280

Muslim religious leaders (*ulema/ maulvis*) 207

Muslim representation, current condition of 265-9: 2019 Lok Sabha elections, Muslims MPs share 265; aggressive Hindutva politics of the BJP 266-7; anti-Muslim sentiment stoked by the BJP leaders 266; BJP's entire political agenda, directed against Muslims 268; communal consolidation, secular parties do not give tickets to Muslims in respectable proportion 267; communal politics and appeasement of majority community 265; deprived in state assemblies 266; FPTP system, many flaws, disadvantageous for religious minorities 267-8;

Majoritarian State: How Hindu Nationalism is Changing India 267; no Muslim CM in any state 265; reasons for this dismal condition 266; rise of the BJP 267; *The Verdict* 267-8; Wajdi, Maulana Nadeemul 268

Muslim STs, discrimination against 182-3: Muslim tribal groups 182

Muslim vote bank 233, 234

Muslim vote bank, myth or reality 234-40: 1967, Muslim votes started to deviate from the Congress 235; 2017 Gujarat elections, Muslim voting pattern in 237-8; eve of every election, the clergy issued *fatwas* to direct Muslim voters 236; *Fatwas* issued by Abdullah Bukhari of Delhi's Jama Masjid 235-6; Indian Muslims are as diverse as the Hindu community 239; Muslim population vote for secular regional parties 240; Muslims, not averse to voting for the BJP 238-9; secular parties, address only the identity and religious issues 236; secular parties, focus on religious tokenism 236; *Siyasi Muslims: A Story of Political Islam in India* 238; strong assumption, Muslims form a single monolithic homogeneous group 239; UP, Muslim voting pattern in 237

Muslim vote *en masse* 234

Muslim voters 18, 51, 53-4, 56-9, 69, 71-4, 77, 81, 83-4, 87, 95-6, 115-17, 119-20, 124, 127-8, 131, 137, 141-3, 149-53, 156, 159, 165-7, 169, 178, 186, 195, 200, 202-6, 214-17, 234, 236-9, 277, 280-1, 284-7, 289, 291, 298, 310, 311, 315: BSP, monopoly over Muslim voters 158; Congress, monopoly over Muslim voters 111, 112, 139, 151, 158, 161; uniform spread as a strength if they work unitedly 311

Muslim-dominated assembly constituencies 131-2

Muslim-dominated constituencies for SCs, reservation of 183-6: SCR recommended rational delimitation procedure 185; Section 9(1)(c) of the Delimitation Act, 2002 185

Muslim-majority constituencies 71-82: 24 PCs, majority and absolute majority position 72, 76-7; 42 sizeable Muslim constituencies 71-2; Baharampur 77; divided and not in dominant position 309

Muslim-majority constituencies, several Muslim candidates in 200-4: divides Muslim votes 200; Hindu vote consolidation 202-4; non-Muslim candidates (mostly fielded by the BJP) win 200; plenitudes of Muslim candidates, promoted by BJP to split Muslim votes 203; secular parties give tickets to Muslims only 203; spoiler candidates take away big chunk of votes 201; UP's Rampur PC in 2014 200; vote-splitting 201-2

Muslims: as the new untouchables in Indian politics 308-9; as vulnerable section 16; must adopt the principle of mutual co-existence 311-12; percentage of population 49; traditionally backed the Congress-NCP combine 81

Muslims and other underrepresented segments fair share in politics, minimum measures 290-2:

affirmative gerrymandering may be done by the Delimitation Commission 291; Communal polarization during elections, ECI must implement the code of conduct strictly 291; cumulative voting or adopting Single Non-Transferrable Vote (SNTV) system 291; doing away with the FPTP system 291; new Delimitation Commission must be appointed 291; Presidential Order of 1950 must be amended 291; Representation of the People Act, 1951 291

Muslims as politically awakened community 296-8: BJP's or Hindutva's political growth, antithetical to the empowerment of OBCs 297-8; no real Dalit leaders being elected 297; political representation 296

Muslims in state assemblies 102-5

Muslims representational deficit, reasons for 92-9: BJP's communal and exclusionary politics 97-8; FPTP system, impact upon the representation of Indian Muslims 98; legal/constitutional or government safeguards, absence of 98; non-Muslim voters do not support Muslim candidates 96-7; PR system or the preferential voting system/ranked choice voting system 98; Reserved Constituencies, notification of 95-6; The Constitution (Scheduled Castes) Order, 1950 94; under-nomination or less nomination as candidate 94; Zakat Foundation of India 96

Muslims, constituency-wise representation 69-71: marginal Muslim constituencies 69-71; sizeable and near-majority Muslim constituencies 71

Muslims, lack of leadership among 207-14: All India Momin Conference 213; deprived sections amongst the Muslims, no say in politics 213-14; *Indian Muslims: The Way Forward* 212; inefficient leaders 209-10; majority of Muslim leaders, hailed from elite groups and upper-castes 212-13; majority of Muslim leaders, no mass base 213; Muslim base parties, must adopt approach to create leaders from the deprived sections 214; Muslim leader, qualifications of 212; Muslim leadership, moral bankruptcy of 209-10; Muslims, political backwardness of 207; non-Muslim leaders in the party, take up the issues of the Muslim masses 210; traditional belief in the Congress, 'only a Hindu can be a Muslim leader' 211; *ulema*, must understand the dynamics of politics and reorient themselves 209; *ulema,* practiced politics of 'religious difference' 208; *ulemas* 207-8; *ulemas* in various regional and OBC based parties 208

Muslims, need for their own political party 272-84: Abdul Raheem Qureshi, views on 276; AIMIM, political journey to expand in different parts of the country 275; as pressure groups with non-partisan stance 272; Dalit scholars, feel Muslims must have a separate political identity 275; forming social alliance with regional parties 274; growing consciousness for forming a separate political entity 273-4;

identity-based negative politics 279-80; issues that the community must put on electoral agenda 273; Muslims, no longer willing to play second fiddle 277; no feasibility of Muslims forming a religion-based political identity 277; objectives when forming a political party 281-2; Owaisi, views on 275; Rasool Abdul of Muttahida Muslim Mahaz, views on 276; religion-based shrill Muslim politics, net result of 279; strategies to adopt 282

Muslims, nomination by national parties 135-6

Muslims, nomination of 82-92: 1977 till 2004, by the Janata Party formations (JP, JNP, BLD, etc.) 84; 1989 to 2019, BSP nominations 87; 1998 till 2019, by the JD formations (RJD, JDU, JDS, LJP and RLD) 84, 87; BJP's ideology of Muslim exclusion 83-4; by AIMIM, AIUDF and IUML, the Muslim base parties 92; by Biju Janata Dal (BJD) 87; by NCP and TMC 87; by the regional parties 87; Congress, low number of nominations to Muslims 83; CPI and CPI(M), Muslim share of representatives 84; NCP, TMC, DMK, and AIADMK, winning Muslim candidates 87; nominations by the PSP 84; representation deficit of Muslims 82

Muslims, political representation of 17-19: contributory conditions 18-19; massive marginalization 19; Muslim MPs, elected to Lok Sabha from 10 states only 18; no Muslim MPs in Rajya Sabha 18; political underrepresentation at all levels 17-18

Muslims, political strength of 298-9: Muslim-dominated PCs and ACs 298

Muslims, state-wise representation 62-8: J&K, regularly returning Muslim members 64; mainly from UP, WB, Bihar, Assam and J&K 62; UP, Muslim members 65, 67; West Bengal, Muslim members 67

Muslims, suitable options for 299-300: composite nationalism, need to follow 304-5; creation of good leaders in the community 303-4; dilution of SC/ST Prevention of Atrocities Act, agitations against 301; ground level planning and training 302-3; Muslim leaders and candidates, need to maintain secular outlook and show broad mindedness 302; *Muslim Vision for Secular India* 300; Muslims leaders must train the masses for 'mutual co-existence' 305; must communicate with Hindu OBCs 301; must design training courses for general voters 302-3; must support the tribal rights groups 301; national and general issues 304-5; need for forward-looking secular leadership 304; political space needs to be secular and seen to be secular 301-2; should be part of the deprived majority 300; should expand their support base 300-1; ways in which could be used 299

Muzaffarnagar riots of 2013: anti-Muslim rhetoric and communal polarization 60-1

National Commission to Review the Working of the Constitution (NCRWC) 49
National Democratic Alliance (NDA) government (1999-2004) 58: massacre of Muslims in Gujarat in 2002 58; Parliamentary Constituencies (PC) 58
NCRWC's Consultation paper on 'Review of Election Law, Processes and Reform Options' 177-8: FPTP system, representative character of our elected legislatures 177; SCR underlines the political deprivation of Muslims 178; underrepresentation of minorities, especially the Muslims 178
NDA's 78-member union cabinet 264
Nehru Committee: no separate electorates recommended for minorities 27; Report, 10 August 1928 26-7, reservation of seats 26-7
Non-Muslim voters 18, 71, 95, 96-7, 182

OBCs, political deprivation of 243-7: BJP, started nominating non-Yadav OBC candidates 246; BSP-SP alliance in UP 246; Janata Dal, OBCs began to organize politically 244; Mandal Commission (Mandal I), implementation of 245; Mandal enabled OBCs to gain political strength 245; Mandal III 247; no reservation of seats 243-4; OBC category, Rohini Commission suggested bifurcation of 246-7; OBC politics, revival of 246; OBC representation, decline of 245-6; politics of quota does not appeal to the OBCs 246; UCHs or *savarnas*, cornering disproportionate number of seats 244; V.P. Singh government, implemented the Mandal Commission report 244
Omvedt, Gail 229
Owaisi, Akbaruddin 148, 149
Owaisi, Asaduddin 62, 227, 234, 240, 241, 243, 269, 275
Owaisi, Sultan Salahuddin 55, 62

Pace of Socio-Economic Change and Development 49
Parcham Party 280
Parliament, constitutional provisions 15: Parliament and state assemblies, seats reserved for SCs and STs 15
Parliamentary Constituencies (PC) 58
Party-list PR system 190: Closed lists 190; Open lists 190
Pasmanda activists 254
Pasmanda groups 253
Pasmanda movement 257
Pasmanda Muslims (both *ajlaf* and *arzals*) 230, 233, 250-3, 256, 300, 301: *ajlaf* (OBC Muslims) 250; All India Pasmanda Muslim Mahaz (AIPMM) 250; *arzal* (Dalit Muslims) 250; Muslimness with the Ashraf Muslims 230; *pasmanda* discourse 250; political representation of 251-2; politics of 250-8
Pasmanda Muslims, reasons for political deprivation 252-3: *ashraf* community 252-3; Ashrafs are socio-economically empowered 253; lack of leadership among them 253; *Mahagathbandhan's* Muslim

candidates in Bihar 252; secular regional/OBC base parties 252
Pasmanda politics 253: will demolish the inter-community hatred 258
Pasmanda politics, challenges before 255-7: all parties consider Muslims as a monolithic whole 256; Ashrafs do not support the idea of Pasmanda Muslims 256; communal politics 257; location and limited expansion 256; minority/majority, or Hindu/ Muslim politics, feasibility of Pasmanda discourse 256
Pasmanda politics, demands of 254-5: AIPMM, 14-point demand charter 254; Ashraf Muslims, winnability and political strength 254-5; economic security and government policy to help artisanal groups 255; *jiski jitni sankhya bhari, uski utni hissedari* 255
Peace Party of India 280
Pillai, Muniswami 41
Political democracy 14, 306-7
Political deprivation of Hindu OBCs and Muslims 295-6
Political empowerment 312
Political parties: exploited the influence of *ulema* 284
Political representation 17, 19, 22, 24-5, 28, 38-9, 56, 147, 171, 192, 193, 195, 203, 208, 250, 251, 272: empowerment of women 188; of Pasmanda Muslims 251; of minority communities 49, 178; of Muslims in Maharashtra 140; values to whom must remain faithful, Rajeev Bhargava's view 290; of Muslims 17, 19, 179-80, 183, 186, 196, 265
Praja Socialist Party (PSP) 53-4
President (Scheduled Castes) Order, 1950 181-2: 1956 and 1990, order modified, Sikh Dalits (Mazhabi Sikhs) and Buddhist (neo-Buddhist) religions included 181; Dalit Christians and Muslims, fighting legal and political battles to get SC status 182
Proportional representation system (PR system) 22, 25-7, 32, 38-9, 43-4, 98, 189-92: geographical PR 189; political PR 189; widely used variants 190

Qaumi Ekta Dal of Mukhtar Ansari 280

Rajasthan Assembly, share of Muslims 141-3: Muslim-dominated assembly constituencies 143
Ram, Kanshi 229, 255, 281, 297, 303
Rampur constituency, Muslim candidates 77, 79
Ranganath Mishra Commission 310
Rashtriya Inquilab Party 280
Rashtriya Janata Dal (RJD) 56, 60, 61, 64, 84, 88, 92, 99, 113-4, 115-6, 123, 162, 166, 169, 199, 201, 244, 246, 248
Rashtriya Lok Samata Party (RLSP) 246
Rashtriya Swayamsevak Sangh (RSS) 58, 196, 250, 258, 279
Rashtriya Ulema Council 280
Rastriya Majlis Party (Bihar) 280
Religious identity of minorities 17
Roots of Totalitarianism: The Ideological Sources of Fascism, National Socialism, and Communism 313

Saamna 221, 234
SC and ST (Prevention of Atrocities) Act 310

SC status to Muslims, denial of 181-2: Articles 330 and 332 of the Constitution 181; President (Scheduled Castes) Order, 1950 181-2
Second General Elections (1957: Muslim elected members 50
Second Round Table Conference, October 1931: Congress scheme for communal settlement 28
Secular parties, use of Muslims 240-3: appeasement of Muslim religious leadership 241; Congress and other secular parties, only Muslims need secularism 241; Congress turned to the *ulema* to get Muslim votes 241; India's political lexicon, 'secularism' became synonymous with 'Muslim vote bank' 240-1; Muslim community, diversity of 241; Muslims, have become untouchables for the secular camp 243; Owaisi, targets political parties for using Muslims as a vote bank 240; programmes to save secularism, organized by secular parties in Muslim-dominated areas 242; Sangh Parivar parties, 'appeasement of Muslims' 240-1
Secular votes, division of 204-6: 2014 general elections, division of votes between the SP, BSP, and Congress 205; 2017 assembly elections, division of votes between SP and BSP 205; 2019 Maharashtra assembly elections, VBA wrecked prospects of candidates of the Congress-NCP alliance 206; community leaders and organizations, need to spend no time to unite the community 206; Kairana AC 205; Moradabad's Thakurwara 205; Rudauli 206
Shia Muslims, *ashraf* category (upper castes) 40
Simon Commission 26
Sardar Hukum Singh 25, 39, 44, 46, 176, 309
Single Transferable Vote (STV) 38, 39, 190
Social democracy, goal to achieve 305-7: contradictions in Indian society, Dr. Ambedkar's views 306-7; Dr. Ambedkar, warnings for survival of democracy 305-6; fraternity, Dr. Ambedkar's views 307; liberty, equality and fraternity, Dr. Ambedkar's views 306
Social Democratic Party of India (SDPI) 126, 280
Social diversity 24, 37, 180, 181, 314
Socio-economic inequality 314
Sardar Patel 30-1, 35-6, 38, 41, 43, 45, 309: major role in abolishing the reservation of seats for minorities 46
Shia Muslims 40
Srinivas, M.N. 235: used the term 'vote bank' 235
State level committees 174: backward socio-economic situation of the Muslims 174-5
Sunni Muslims 40

Tamil Nadu Assembly, share of Muslims 143-7: AIADMK 144-5; Manithaneya Makkal Katchi (MAMAK) 144-5; Muslim-dominated assembly constituencies 146-7; Viduthalai Chiruthaigal Katchi (VCK) 144
Telangana Assembly, share of Muslims 147-50: AIMIM MLAs 148; main parties in the state 148-9; Muslim-dominated assembly

constituencies 149-50; TRS (now, the BRS) 148-9
The Constitution (Scheduled Castes) Order, 1950 94-5: Dalit castes of Muslims (along with Christians), not allowed to contest LS seats reserved for SCs 94; recent Delimitation Commission 94; passed under Article 342 of the Constitution 95

Ulema 207-10, 213, 241, 280, 284-9
Ulema, influence on Muslims, in matters of politics 284-90: Abdullah Bukhari, 1980s, 'election *fatwa*' 287; AIMMM, published a nine-point People's Manifesto 286; Bukhari, Abdullah, issued election statements 285; Bukhari, Ahmed, Shahi Imam, issued election statements 285; clear distinction between political and religious leaders 288; *Imam-e-Hind* 287; in past, *ulema* gauged mood of common Muslim voters 287; Muslim expectation of their leaders 288; Muslim othering project 289; Muslims, don't look to *ulema* for political guidance 289; political *fatwas* issued by the Bukharis or the Shahi Imam of Jama Masjid of Delhi 287; secular parties, use *ulema* to influence Muslim voters 289; *ulema* of Mumbai, more vocal 285; *ulema,* actively participating in politics in variety of ways 286; *ulema*, influential in political matters 286
Under-nomination of Muslims by political parties 180-1: affairs of political parties, hegemonic control over 180; anti-Muslim sentiments 180; BJP, thrives on a 'hate Muslim' agenda 180; inclusive democracy, idea of 180; People's Representation Act (PRA) 180
Undivided India: Muslims, significant share to the country's population 25
United Nations (UN) 19: Framework Convention for Protection of National Minorities (FCNM) 19
Universal adult franchise 15
Upper-Caste Hindus (UCH) 15, 97, 159, 174, 175, 192, 207, 211, 224, 244, 245, 247-9, 293, 295-7, 301: BJP, aggressively protects the UCH interests 245; disproportionally represented at the cost of the OBCs, Muslims and other minorities 192, 207; domination in politics 159; enjoying disproportionate political benefits 175; leaders, try to disenfranchise OBCs and Dalits 224; monopoly over politics and institutions of democracy 247; or *savarnas* cornering disproportionate number of seats 244; political domination, consequences of 249; reaping the benefits of communalism 301; share in Lok Sabha 247-8
Upper-caste politics, return of 247-50: 1984, share of UCH MPs 247; political domination 248; Sangh Parivar attempted enforcing the value system 249; UCHs, political domination of 249; UPA-I government, reservation of seats for educational institutions 248